D1285350

SLAVE REBELLION
IN BRAZIL

SLAVE REBELLION IN BRAZIL

The Muslim Uprising of 1835 in Bahia

· João José Reis ·

TRANSLATED BY ARTHUR BRAKEL

The Johns Hopkins University Press
BALTIMORE AND LONDON

Originally published as *Rebelião escrava no Brasil: A história do levante dos malês, 1835* (São Paulo: Editora Brasiliense, 1986). Translation published by permission of the author. English-language edition revised and expanded by the author.

Johns Hopkins Paperbacks edition, 1995
04 03 02 01 00 99 98 97 96 95   5 4 3 2 1

The Johns Hopkins University Press
2715 North Charles Street
Baltimore, Maryland 21218-4319
The Johns Hopkins Press Ltd., London

Library of Congress Cataloging-in-Publication Data
Reis, João José.
[Rebelião escrava no Brasil. English]
Slave rebellion in Brazil : the Muslim
uprising of 1835 in Bahia / by João José Reis ;
translated by Arthur Brakel.
p.   cm. — (Johns Hopkins studies in
Atlantic history and culture)
Includes bibliographical references and index.
ISBN 0-8018-4462-2 (alk. paper)
ISBN 0-8018-5250-1 (pbk.: alk. paper)
1. Slavery—Brazil—Salvador—Insurrections, etc.
I. Title.   II. Series.
HT1129.S24R4513   1993
326´.097284—dc20   92-27067

A catalog record for this book is available
from the British Library.

For Musa, Elias, and for Cicinha

Contents

List of Illustrations   ix
Preface to the English-Language Edition   xi
Preface to the Brazilian Edition   xiii

PART I   Bahian Society, Economy, and Rebellion
         during the Time of the Muslims
1 Hard Times   3
2 Revolts of the Free People   21
3 The Rebellious Tradition: Slave Revolts prior to 1835   40

PART II   The Muslims and the Rebellion of 1835
4 The Battle for Bahia   73
5 The Sons of Allah in Bahia   93
6 A Bahian Caliphate? The Malês and Their Rebellion   112
7 Malê Profiles   129

PART III   The African Community in Revolt
8 Roots: Ethnic Motivation in 1835   139
9 Workers, Slave and Freed: Occupational Profile
   of the Accused   160
10 Making Do: Africans away from Work   175

PART IV   The Anti-African Backlash
11 The Repression after the Uprising   189
12 The Punishment   205

Epilogue   231
Notes   233
Works Cited   261
Index   271

Illustrations

Figures

1. A view of Salvador, ca. 1840 — 4
2. Piedade Square — 9
3. Cachoeira, as seen from across the Paraguaçu River — 33
4. The count of Arcos, governor of Bahia, 1810–1818 — 46
5. Plantation slave hut — 56
6. Pedro Rodrigues Bandeira — 60
7. Ladeira da Praça — 78
8. The Municipal Council House — 81
9. The Provincial Government Palace — 82
10. Two views of Água de Meninos — 86
11. Malês' spiritual arsenal — 101
12. Coronation of black kings and queens — 150
13. Chair porters bearing a woman of ill-repute — 162
14. A woman buying fish on the beach to resell — 168
15. Francisco Gonçalves Martins, viscount of São Lourenço — 193

Maps

1. The Bahian Recôncavo — 2
2. The City of Salvador — 76
3. Downtown Salvador — 80

Preface

TO THE ENGLISH-LANGUAGE EDITION

Slave Rebellion in Brazil is a considerably revised and expanded version of my book *Rebelião escrava no Brasil,* first published in 1986 in Brazil. Vivaldo da Costa Lima, Eugene Genovese, and Paulo F. de Moraes Farias offered me comments that have been essential to the improvement of the original. I also thank Patricia Aufderheide, who put her research notes at my disposal. Arthur Brakel incorporated last-minute revisions into his translation of the original and allowed me to work with him on the translation itself. The text was further improved by Joanne Allen's meticulous copy-editing and the suggestions (regarding both content and style) by an outside reader, who, though unknown to me, should be made aware of my appreciation. Jacqueline Wehmueller was an early supporter of the publication of this version of my book. However, it would not have been possible without Rebecca Scott's generosity and enthusiasm. Much of the work for the revised edition was done during my stay in London, from 1987 to 1989. I am grateful to Leslie Bethell for his friendly support while I was a fellow at the University of London's Institute of Latin American Studies. I also thank the directors and employees of the following institutions: the Arquivo do Estado, Arquivo Municipal, Arquivo da Santa Casa de Misericórdia, Museu de Arte, and Instituto Geográfico e Histórico, in Salvador; the Torre do Tombo, in Lisbon; the Public Record Office, the British Library, and the library of the School of Oriental and African Studies, all in London; and the Archives du Ministère des Relations Exterieures, in Paris. The research for this new edition was supported by the Conselho Nacional de Pesquisas—CNPq, the Brazilian Research Council.

Preface

TO THE BRAZILIAN EDITION

Beginning the night of January 24, 1835, and continuing the following morning, a group of African-born slaves occupied the streets of Salvador, the capital of the Brazilian state (then province) of Bahia. For more than three hours they confronted soldiers and armed civilians. The rebellion's organizers were identified as Malês, as Muslim Africans were called in nineteenth-century Bahia.

Even though it was short-lived, this was the most effective urban slave rebellion ever to occur on the American continent. Hundreds of Africans took part. Nearly seventy were killed. And more than five hundred, according to a conservative estimate, were sentenced to death, prison, whipping, or deportation. If an uprising of equal proportions were to happen today, in a Salvador with over 1.5 million inhabitants, it would entail the sentencing of over twelve thousand people.

The rebellion had nationwide repercussions. In Rio de Janeiro the news most likely reached the public in newspapers that published the report by Salvador's chief of police. Fearing that the Bahian example might be followed, the authorities in Rio began to watch blacks very carefully. The Bahian rebels rekindled debate on slavery and slave trade in the Brazilian Parliament.

The seriousness with which the ruling elites addressed the uprising can be seen in the extensive inquiry they carried out, which produced a wealth of documents on the rebellion and on Africans living in Salvador. Once again, the history of the oppressed comes to light through the quills of police and court scribes. The quality and the quantity of these papers make them priceless testimony on urban slavery and African culture in the Americas. There were, for example, more than two hundred hearings, in which, despite obvious intimidation, Africans spoke about their rebellion as well as about their cultural, social, economic, religious, domestic, and even intimate lives.

This book is based on the declarations of African prisoners and on other documents in the inquiry. It tells the rebels' story and the story of the 1835 rebellion. Part 1 outlines the social, economic, and political scene of Salvador in the early nineteenth century. The reader who wants to go directly to the main event will find it in part 2, chapter 4, "The Battle for Bahia." The following two chapters describe the formation of the Islamic community in Salvador and analyze this community's role in the insurrection. Then, the brief chapter called "Malê Profiles" introduces the salient characters in the revolt. Part 3 discusses the formation of an African culture based on ethnic identity and expressed in the organization of labor and of everyday life in the community. It also suggests ways in which ethnic identity, urban slavery, and the economic and domestic lives of local Africans may have influenced the rebellion. Finally, part 4 examines the repression of the rebels and punishment meted out to them.

Many people have contributed to this book. Maria do Carmo Barreto and Aída Valadares helped me collect the data. The employees at the Arquivo Nacional in Rio de Janeiro and at the Arquivo do Estado da Bahia facilitated my access to documents.

An early version, which I defended as a doctoral dissertation at the University of Minnesota, and other studies of mine on this subject have been discussed and criticized by Kátia Mattoso, Stuart B. Schwartz, Emília Viotti da Costa, Eugene Genovese, Dale Tomich, and Renato da Silveira. Many of their observations have been incorporated.

The support of Cicinha and Demian was absolutely essential, and I thank them both, affectionately. She oversaw and criticized various sections of my dissertation. He wanted me to be done with it, and gave me extra incentive to finish.

In its present version the text has been improved thanks to the suggestions of my friends João Santana Filho, Luciano Diniz, and Paulo César Souza. Paulo was involved with this book right from the start and stayed with it to the end.

Maria Amélia added her valuable opinions and affectionate stimulus, especially in the last few critical months of writing. It is with great feeling that I mention my debt to her.

Parts of the book have been discussed by colleagues and students at the Universidade Federal da Bahia. I thank Professor Luís Henrique for his support.

The photographic reproductions were kindly furnished by Sofia Olszewski, and the final typing was done by Anatálio da Cruz.

I thank both the Ford and Rockefeller foundations for their financial assistance during the years 1979 and 1981–82, which helped me carry out the research for this book. I did more research and wrote the final version under the auspices of the Conselho Nacional de Pesquisas–CNPq during the years 1984 and 1985. The master's program in social sciences at the Universidade Federal da Bahia paid for the final typing.

PART I

Bahian Society, Economy, and Rebellion during the Time of the Muslims

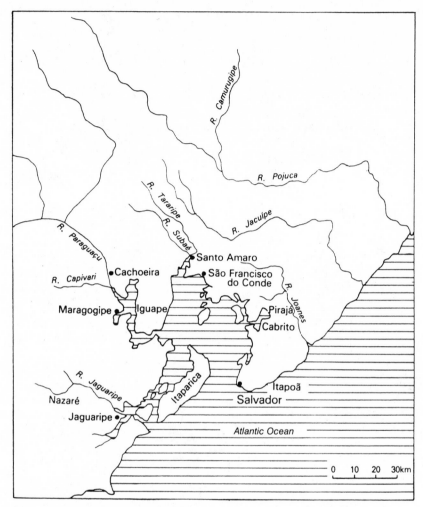

MAP I. The Bahian Recôncavo

· I ·

Hard Times

The province (now state) of Bahia was one of the most prosperous sugar-producing regions of the New World. Sugar plantations, or *engen-hos,* [1] worked mainly by slaves, were situated in the Recôncavo, a fertile, well-drained wetlands area surrounding the Bay of All Saints. The provincial capital and port city of Salvador was located on the southeasternmost point of the bay, in a splendid mountainous spot, which caused the city to be divided into upper and lower halves. In 1805, the British navy commander Sir Robert Wilson, who had traveled extensively, claimed that "the view of this Bay . . . is perhaps the most magnificent in the world." [2]

Hidden in the "magnificent view" was a complex social hierarchy based on slavery. Sugar planters controlled both the land and the principal means of production. Not only for that reason but also because of their tremendous social, political, and symbolic power, they were the ruling class par excellence. Even discounting all the hyperbolic seigniorial mythology produced to exaggerate the planters' omnipotence, they had immense power. Slaves made up the great bulk of the laboring class and were political, social, and economic subordinates of the planters. Any analysis of the situation must recognize the relationship between master and slave as the structural matrix of that society and economy. This elementary paradigm, however, appears in different forms and with different meanings. In the case in point, slaves were not owned just by people one could rightly call "the ruling class," namely, wealthy planters and urban merchants. People in very different social and economic circumstances owned slaves. There were even cases of slaves owning slaves.

Beyond (but by no means outside) the matrix of slave and master, other groups fulfilled important social, economic, cultural, and political functions in nineteenth-century Bahian society, especially (but not exclusively) in its urban sector. The poor, especially those of African descent, grew more and more numerous after the middle of the eighteenth cen-

Fig. 1. A view of Salvador, ca. 1840. Reprinted from Wildberger, *Os presidentes da província da Bahia* (Salvador: Typographia Beneditina, 1949).

tury. They, along with the slaves, constituted the vast majority of the population.

The Population of Bahia

Around 1798 Luís dos Santos Vilhena estimated the inhabitants of Salvador and the Bahian Recôncavo, which together had the greatest density of population in the region, to number around 110,000. Concerning these people, he said: "One third . . . might be whites and Indians, with the rest being blacks and mulattos." Although Vilhena's proportions might give us an idea of the racial and ethnic makeup of the time, his numbers seem out of date. In 1808 a census was taken in Salvador and the thirteen rural parishes in the district of Bahia. (This excluded Cachoeira, Santo Amaro, and the southern part of the colonial province of Bahia.) The census produced the following data: 50,451 whites, 1,463 Indians, 104,285 free or manumitted blacks and mulattos, and 93,115 slaves, both black and mulatto. In a population of 249,314, 37 percent (93,115) were slaves, and 63 percent (156,199) were free. Whites constituted 20.2 percent, whereas free and manumitted blacks and mulattos added up to 41.8 percent.[3]

The makeup of Salvador itself was different. A census in 1775 counted 12,720 whites (36 percent), 4,207 free mulattos (12 percent), 3,630 free blacks (10.4 percent), and 14,696 slaves, both black and mulatto (41.7 percent)—35,253 people in all. A census in 1807, which unfortunately did not distinguish between slaves and free people, counted 25,502 blacks (50 percent), 11,350 mulattos (22 percent), and 14,260 whites—a total of 51,112.[4]

In the thirty-two years between 1775 and 1807, Salvador grew by 31 percent. The African and Afro-Bahian population, both slave and free, rose by 39 percent, and its relative proportion vis-à-vis the entire population jumped from 64 percent to 72 percent. These data support all the assertions made up to now concerning demographic trends in Brazil at that time. The population "of color" was, in the words of one author, "the class in nineteenth-century Brazilian society which grew most rapidly."[5]

There are, unfortunately, no data of any type concerning changes in Salvador's population between 1807 and 1835, the year of the Malê rebellion. One can only speculate. If the city's growth remained constant, if it grew at about 1 percent per year, in 1835 the population would have grown to 65,500, which is the working hypothesis of this study. Table 1 extrapolates from the data for the years 1775 and 1807 to show how the 65,500 people living in Salvador in 1835 were divided according to their color, birthplace, and legal (free, slave, and freed or ex-slave) status.

The population was divided according to place of birth into Brazilians, Europeans, and Africans. As will be seen throughout this book, the diverse origins of these segments of the Bahian population are related to different patterns of political, social, and cultural views and behavior. But there were color differences among native-born Brazilians as well. There were blacks, who were always referred to as *crioulos*. There was the *cabra*, whose color was somewhere between that of a black and a mulatto, and the mulatto, also known as *pardo*, or "tan." And there were whites. Native blacks were distinguished from African blacks, and the African was always referred to as a *preto* ("black"). There were Brazilian whites and European whites, the latter almost always Portuguese. There was no doubt concerning the mulattos' nationality. Like the Brazilians, the Africans were also distinguished, not by color but by ethnicities or nations. On top of this, Africans and Afro-Bahians could be free, slave, or freed, the latter ex-slaves for whom freedom did not mean absolute legal equality with the free. Whites were never enslaved. This complicated set of statuses and relationships sharply partitioned the society of the time and shaped the behavior of all its members.

Table 1

POPULATION ESTIMATES FOR SALVADOR IN 1835

Origin	Absolute Number	Percentage
Africans		
Slaves	17,325	26.5
Freed	4,615	7.1
Brazilians/Europeans		
Free whites	18,500	28.2
Free and freed "of color"[a]	14,885	22.7
Slaves	10,175	15.5
Total	65,500	100

[a]This figure includes crioulos, cabras, and mulattos.

Note: This table assumes: (1) a 1 percent annual growth in population between the years 1808 and 1835; (2) the same proportions between slaves and nonslaves (white, black, and mulatto) as in the 1775 census; (3) the same proportion of African to Brazilian slaves as in table 2; (4) that freed (i.e., manumitted) Africans represented a little less than 25 percent of free or manumitted blacks and *mestiços* (i.e., people of mixed European and African ancestry).

All the population estimates for Salvador have indicated that the number of slaves was less than the combined number of free and freed people. In 1835 there were 27,500 slaves (42 percent of the population) and 38,800 free and manumitted (58 percent). As I said, this is an extrapolation from the 1775 census proportion, which, considering the growth of the slave trade to Bahia in the first three decades of the nineteenth century, may seem a conservative estimate. Perhaps it is. My numbers, however, consider, first, that most of these slaves (ca. 7,000 on average per year) were sent to the plantations or reexported to other Brazilian provinces; and second, that if the slave population increased as a result of importation, the free population of color was also growing fast as a result of natural reproduction and, less significantly, of manumission. The Brazilians of color, free or manumitted, and the freed Africans were 29.8 percent of the population, or 19,500 people, which means that even if slaves made up less than half the population, the sum total of all blacks and mulattos, be they slaves or not, was a significant majority of the population: 71.8 percent. The 18,500 whites constituted the racial minority in Salvador, or 28.8 percent of the population. The provincial president, Francisco de Souza Martins, wrote in 1835: "The blacks significantly outnumber whites."[6]

The central characters in this book, the Africans, were, in the majority, slaves. Only 21 percent of the 21,940 Africans had been manumitted. The 17,325 Africans who remained enslaved were the majority of all slaves in Salvador at the time of the rebellion. In other words, most slaves were foreigners.

During the almost four hundred years of its existence, Brazilian slavery consumed many generations of Africans. The slave population had a characteristically high rate of infant mortality and an extremely short life expectancy owing to the dire conditions under which slaves lived and worked, as well as to the treatment they received from their masters. Contrary to the situation in the United States, in Brazil the slave population was systematically reinforced by African imports, since the ones who arrived did not create sufficient progeny to allow the economy to expand or even maintain an equilibrium. Beyond the high mortality rates, a more important factor may have inhibited the nationalization of the slave labor force: few of the slaves were women, and these few, as well as their children, were manumitted more often than men. In 1778 José da Silva Lisboa was to write, "Because of the obvious benefits accruing from male labor over female, there are always three times as many males as females among the slave population, which perpetuates the pattern of their failure to propagate as well as their failure to increase in number from generation to generation."[7]

Silva Lisboa calculated that there were three men for each woman, or, to put it more technically, 300 men for every 100 women. In a recent study Stuart Schwartz reported finding a ratio of 275 men to 100 women in a sample from six plantations in the year 1816. I found the slave population in mainly rural areas between 1813 and 1827 to show a less drastic disproportion: 158 men to 100 women. The situation in Salvador was much more balanced, as can be seen in table 2. In the capital there were 128 men to every 100 women. That is, 56 percent of the urban slaves were men.[8]

These numbers show that the high percentage of Africans in the slave population created the numerical imbalance between the sexes. In fact, if we separate the native-born slaves from the Africans, the native-born population had a slightly higher percentage of women over men: 92 men to every 100 women, contrasting with 156 men to every 100 women among the Africans. Based on these figures, the number of female slaves in Salva-

Table 2

SEX AND BIRTHPLACE OF THE 1835 SLAVE POPULATION
IN SALVADOR, 1811–1860

Birthplace	Men	Women	Total	% Male	Proportion M/F × 100	% Birthplace
			(sample)			
Brazil	1,237	1,339	2,576	48	92	37
Africa	2,657	1,699	4,356	61	156	63
Total	3,894	3,038	6,932	56	128	100

Source: Adapted from Andrade, "A mão de obra escrava," appen. tables 3 and 3.1 (based on probate records).

dor must have been around 14,170 during 1835, and only 6,750 of these women were born in Africa. Some 10,575 African men vied for these African women. Chapter 10 shows how this disparity between men and women seriously limited the formation of African families, even among the freed population. This was an important source of dissatisfaction among the almost 22,000 Africans constituting 33 percent of Salvador's population.

Social Hierarchy, Wealth, and Poverty

Beyond their differences in color, national and ethnic background, and legal status, the 65,500 inhabitants of Salvador belonged to different social and occupational groups. The few existing analyses of Bahian social strata during this period generally agree in dividing that society into three or four levels, each of which was internally divided. Kátia Mattoso, who has proposed the most elaborate model for the social structure of nineteenth-century Bahia, distinguishes four basic categories. At the summit were the planters, large-scale merchants, high-ranking state and church officials, and finally, military officers above the rank of sergeant major. These people had power and wealth. They aspired, often successfully, to titles of nobility, which the Brazilian imperial government awarded beginning in 1822. The next category was made up of middle-level government and church officials, professionals, officers in the military, merchants, wealthy master artisans, and a sizable contingent of Bahians who lived off income generated from renting buildings or slaves or from moneylending. The third rank was made up of lower-level civil servants, soldiers, less prestigious professional groups, innkeepers, artisans, and street vendors. Finally, at the bottom of the social pyramid came the slaves, beggars, and vagabonds—the "dangerous classes" of the time.

In constructing her model, Mattoso uses various criteria and gives special emphasis, á la Weber, to social prestige, income, and political power. She distinguishes the top group from the next one principally in terms of income and secondarily by individuals' occupations and their positions within the state apparatus. For Mattoso, prestige is an important factor; even though there were enormous differences in income from planter to planter, she put all of them on the same step of the social ladder. On the other hand, she put large-scale merchants there more because of their financial power than because of their prestige. If Vilhena's observation for the beginning of the nineteenth century was correct, some people used intermediaries to do their business because "it would be less than proper to let it be known they were involved in trade." Still, Mattoso points out differences within each category, differences in political power, prestige, income, and legal status. A lower status on one of these levels

FIG. 2. Piedade Square, a cross section of life in Salvador, with chair porters, beggars, street vendors, priests, churchgoers, slaves, masters, and mistresses. Drawing by Johan Moritz Rugendas, reprinted from his *Malerische reise in Brasilien* (Paris: Englemann & Cie, 1835).

could be compensated with advantages at another level. She suggests that at least as far as material well-being was concerned, slaves, or at least urban slaves, should not be considered as being at the bottom of the Bahian social hierarchy. Economically speaking, beggars and vagabonds were probably in more dire straits than slaves. One wonders which would be more socially edifying in that society: to be free and starving or enslaved and fat.[9]

F. W. O. Morton also discusses Salvador's social structure of this period. His scheme is simpler than Mattoso's, even though he identifies the same groups she does. He uses the expression "individuals able to claim noble status" to define the Bahian elite, which for him comprised "the leading landowners, officials, and merchants." He used both economic and political criteria in his classification. Next come the professionals, bureaucrats, noncommissioned military officers, retail merchants, and cane farmers. In third place comes what Morton calls the "free lower class," made up of small-time retailers, street vendors, artisans, salaried workers, and soldiers.

Morton's analysis gives special emphasis to skin color and place of birth. The "upper class" was totally white and divided between Portuguese and Brazilians, the latter being more numerous. The "middle class" was divided into mulattos, whites, and a very few *crioulos,* or native-born blacks. Most of the Portuguese and Brazilian whites were in this category. Most of the mulattos were in the "lower class," but there were a few whites in this category as well. Finally, at the very bottom were the slaves, divided into Africans, crioulos, and mulattos. Morton's concentration on skin color is well-taken, but his analysis basically reproduces the modern notion of the existence of three classes: high, middle, and low. Moreover, slaves seem to be mere appendages in his model.[10]

Both Mattoso and Morton agree that Bahia in general, and Salvador in particular, did not have a completely rigid social structure. In other words, social mobility within and among the groups existed, in spite of the economic rigidity and legal or racial and ethnic barriers restricting upward mobility. Good connections, family ties, a degree from a European university, money—all these helped in the quest for higher social status, that is, as far as free, and almost exclusively, white people were concerned. One could find lawyers or physicians who were mulattos, but never blacks. On the other hand, slaves, especially those in the city, could, through great personal effort, buy their freedom, and a (very) few even became prosperous business men and women.

But this flexibility of the social structure should not make one forget that Bahia was still a slaveholding society; that thousands of people went on being other men and women's chattel; and that racism and ethnic intolerance played an important role in defining who should obey and who should give orders. Africans, for example, might well enjoy some success in the material world, but at the price of social alliances that usually compromised much of their independence, dignity, and identity. Whites, regardless of social standing, demanded that freed African slaves accept Brazilians' ways of doing things. Beyond this, economic prosperity came to very few people.

In the nineteenth century the great majority of Salvador's free population lived "on the brink of poverty."[11] This is no exaggeration. The police archives of the time are full of reports from justices of the peace and other authorities complaining daily about the growing number of beggars and jobless people wandering through their jurisdictions. These people had gone over the brink of poverty into destitution. Scores of complaints tell of apprehending children abandoned by their parents or, in the case of orphans, by poor relatives. The justices of the peace would send them to the São Joaquim Orphanage, which was the only educational facility re-

Table 3

ESTIMATE OF THE DISTRIBUTION OF WEALTH
IN SALVADOR, 1800–1850

Groups	% of Wealth	Mean Value of Wealth (*réis*)[a]	Number of People
Richest 10%	66.9	64,086,500	41
Next 30%	26.4	8,571,847	118
Next 30%	5.6	1,832,127	118
Poorest 30%	1.1	357,220	118
Total	100	9,727,352	395

Source: AEBa, *Inventários e testamentos.*
[a] In 1835 1,000 *réis* (sing. *real*) were worth approximately 40 English pence.

served for the poor. There, and under severe discipline, they learned to work with their hands. If they somehow failed to run away, these children became artisans, without much chance of finding work in a predominantly slave-labor society undergoing an acute economic crisis.

There was much poverty, and what little wealth there was could be found in the hands of a small minority. Table 3, which is based on data from the probate records of 395 people who died in Salvador between 1800 and 1850, gives an idea of the distribution of wealth in the first half of the nineteenth century. This sample represents people who left something to their descendants, but their having wills does not mean they were all wealthy. Both rich planters and poor African artisans are included in the sample. But while the planters are typical of their class, the Africans were probably some of the "fortunate few" in their community. In other words, the profile presented here is, in all truth, optimistically skewed, yet it evinces a society characterized by profound economic disparity.[12]

The richest 10 percent controlled 67 percent of the wealth. The top 5 percent possessed 53 percent of the wealth. The ten wealthiest individuals in the sample stand out as owners of 37 percent of the entire inventory. Those ten people—planters and large-scale merchants—represent only 2.3 percent of the total.

On the other hand, the poorest 60 percent laid claim to only 6.7 percent of the wealth. They were, beyond doubt, members of the free Bahian lower class, which was also internally stratified. The poorest 30 percent reveal themselves to be owners of a paltry 1.1 percent of the property under consideration. They probably represent those described as living "on the brink of destitution." Wealth was more evenly distributed among the 30 percent coming after the richest 10 percent. This group laid claim to 26.4 percent of the entire inventory. Using modern terminology, they could be called the middle class of the time.

Another way to consider the socioeconomic disparities would be to compare the average wealth of the people situated in each group. The average value of the holdings of the top 10 percent was 64,860,500 réis, which was more than the price of a huge, profitable sugar plantation in the year 1800. The planters in particular possessed an even higher average, 82,980,000 réis. In slaves alone they had investments averaging 12,360,000 réis. They were without a doubt the greatest economic force in Bahia.

On the other hand, the average worth of the poorest 30 percent was 357,220 réis, the approximate equivalent of the price of a slave during the 1820s, or the yearly salary of a second-class clerk in the ministry of finance in 1824. It was barely enough to feed a family of three (4 kilos of beef jerky, 6 kilos of beans, and 2 kilos of manioc flour per week) and to pay the rent on a hovel, based on prices during the middle of the 1830s.

One more exercise in comparative wealth shows that the richest 10 percent left an average of 7.5 times as much as the next richest group and 180 times as much as the poorest 30 percent.

In spite of the dense concentration of wealth, slaveholding interests were spread throughout Bahian society. One need not have been rich to own a slave. Only the very poorest people had no slave. José da Silva Lisboa commented in 1781, "It is considered a sign of extreme mendacity not to have slaves. One might endure all sorts of domestic hardships, but slaves are a must. One must have at least two negroes to carry the richly decorated sedan chair, and a servant to accompany this procession. Whoever was seen on the street without his cortege of Africans was sure to be taken for a man in dire economic straits." [13]

The estates of the 395 people in this sample show that only 13 percent of them had no slaves whatsoever (see table 4). They were probably what Silva Lisboa would consider people in "dire economic straits." The majority, or 65 percent of the people in the sample, owned no more than ten slaves. All the artisans, without exception, had at least one. Two of the wealthiest had more than eleven. Priests, military men, bureaucrats, druggists, innkeepers, and farmers, in addition to the planters, large-scale merchants, and slave-renters, all invested in slaves. Even ex-slaves from Africa followed this pattern: of the twenty-five in this sample, only four had no slaves. It is likely that most of Salvador's slaves were the property of small-time slaveholders, people with no more than ten slaves.

Contrary to what Silva Lisboa wrote, however, it was not for the sake of ostentation that those people kept slaves. Many Bahians were sustained by the one, two, or three slaves they owned. (Urban slavery is discussed in chapter 9.) Writing during the 1840s, the English merchant James Wetherell made the following observation about the small-time slaveholder: "In many cases, the possession and use of slaves is their only livelihood." [14] However, anyone depending on only one slave lived very poorly, since the

Table 4
PROPERTY DISTRIBUTION IN SLAVES, BY OCCUPATION AND
PLACE OF BIRTH OF OWNER,
IN SALVADOR, 1800–1850

	Number of Slaves							
	0	1–10	11–20	21–30	31–40	41–50	51+	Total
Occupation								
Planters	0	1	0	1	0	2	5	9
Merchants	5	39	10	5	1	1	0	61
"Living off 'incomes'"	5	14	6	0	0	0	0	25
Landlords	3	10	1	1	0	0	0	15
Ranchers	0	7	3	2	0	0	1	13
Civil servants/professionals	0	5	1	0	0	0	0	6
Slave renters	0	32	16	2	2	0	2	54
Farmers	1	18	5	1	1	0	1	27
Clerics	1	7	1	0	0	0	0	9
Military officers	3	9	0	0	0	0	0	12
Small-time merchants	1	7	0	0	0	0	0	8
Artisans	0	12	1	0	1	0	0	14
Others	3	6	1	1	0	0	0	11
Unknown	30	89	8	2	0	2	0	131
Birthplace								
Brazil	19	103	23	3	3	1	5	157
Europe	13	61	15	3	2	1	2	97
Africa	4	20	1	0	0	0	0	25
Unknown	16	72	14	9	0	3	2	116
Total	52	256	53	15	5	5	9	395

Source: AEBa, *Inventários e testamentos.*

most one slave could earn in 1835 was 120 milréis a year. It is quite likely that at least 40 percent of the free population, many of whom were poor as well, owned slaves. It was so common that all free persons probably aspired to own at least one. And this was true not only for the people of Salvador but for people throughout the Recôncavo.[15] There was, then, a widespread commitment to slavery among the free classes. Maintaining slavery was not just the aim of a handful of wealthy individuals, even during a time of great economic hardship, such as the years 1820–40, when the institution's shortcomings became obvious.

Economic Fluctuations

After many years of stagnation, the Bahian economy once again began to prosper in the late 1780s. The change led one chronicler to call the period the "happy time." The price of sugar on the international market had gone up, more and more plantations were growing sugarcane as well as cotton and tobacco, and the importation of African slaves was on the rise. People invested exclusively in export products, which is why no increase in the cultivation of foodstuffs occurred amidst the "happy time." Economic growth continued up to the beginning of the 1820s, when the war of independence in Bahia (1822–23) marked the end of the upward trajectory. It was followed by an acute depression.

The depression of the twenties and thirties revealed the local economy's dependence on external markets. During this period Cuban sugar production increased and began to supply a considerable part of the international market. Cuban sugar, along with European beet sugar, crowded out the lead chariot of the Bahian export economy. Cotton was planted far inland, and the lack of decent highways made transportation costs very high, turning Bahian cotton into a weak competitor of its American counterpart in the European market. At the same time tobacco growers, whose crops were mainly traded for slaves in Africa, saw their market shrink as the result of certain laws (the 1831 law being the most important) that slowly squelched the slave trade. Simultaneously, conflicts arose with the Portuguese tobacco trade once Brazil became independent, in 1822.[16]

The war of independence and the anti-Portuguese atmosphere that followed it aggravated the province's economic woes. With Portuguese forces occupying the capital during the conflict, export commerce from the port of Salvador came to a virtual halt. Moreover, the sugar barons directed their resources toward fighting the Portuguese. In the course of the war, many plantations were ruined. When the Bahian side had won the dispute, one more stroke of bad luck befell local commerce: the flight of Portuguese merchants from the province. They were a key element in both the production and the movement of export goods. They financed the engenhos and their owners; they bought sugar and marketed it in Europe; they were deeply involved in the slave trade; and they brought back European goods, including replacement parts for the sugar mills.

In the years prior to independence, Portuguese merchants were already in competition with English adversaries, but there is no doubt that they went on being a vital part of the dependent, sugar-exporting economy of Bahia. They owned most of the commercial capital. *Merchant* and *Portuguese* were synonyms. Huge numbers of these people decamped after the war and stayed away during the years that followed, a period of widespread anti-Portuguese sentiment. It is impossible to determine with any accuracy the effects the Portuguese flight had on sugar dealings in Salvador, but they appear to have been considerable, especially since it happened at a point when prices had fallen on the international market.

Moreover, the planter class felt honor-bound to maintain the commercial partnerships established during colonial times.

The slave-based economy also underwent reverses of another sort. As a result of the English prohibition and persecution of the South Atlantic slave trade, plantations began to suffer from a scarcity of laborers. This situation was aggravated by the development of coffee plantations in southern Brazil, which, beginning in the 1830s, turned that region into an eager market for black slaves. By the middle of that decade, Bahia and other northeastern provinces became slave-exporting areas for the southern market. The price of slaves rose tremendously in Bahia. Their average price was 175,000 réis in 1810, 200,000 in 1820, 250,000 in 1830, and 450,000 in 1840. While the price had risen 30 percent in the twenty years between 1810 and 1830, during the next ten years it rose 45 percent. Sugar production was also compromised during this period by a plague that infected the local cattle in the beginning of the 1830s.[17]

In spite of hardship in the export economy, sugar remained on its throne. The number of plantations had greatly increased during the prosperous years, and it continued to grow afterwards. Between 1827 and 1840, on the average, 23 plantations were founded every year, and sugar exports, after an abrupt fall in the early twenties, recovered and even exceeded amounts exported in the previous decade. This meant that the cane fields did not give way to land for the growth of foodstuffs.[18] It also meant that given the scarcity of hands during a time when production levels were maintained and even increased, the slave's lot entailed more and more work, which must have contributed to the increase in individual flight as well as to the increase in collective uprisings during that period.

Some problems hit both the export sector and the foodstuff sector equally hard. The cattle plague, for example, reduced the number of pack animals on the plantations as well as the availability of meat for a rapidly growing population. Other factors affected food production more than export crops. Droughts were (and still are) especially severe beyond the Recôncavo, where much of what was eaten in the capital and surrounding area was grown. There were devastating droughts in the northeast in 1824–25 and for four years in a row beginning in 1830. Throngs moved into the towns·of the Recôncavo and into Salvador. At the close of 1833, the president of Bahia was begging the imperial court in Rio de Janeiro for emergency aid in the form of food.[19]

The prices of manioc flour and other staples broke all records in the towns and cities of Bahia, especially those in the Recôncavo. In Salvador local authorities kept tighter control on speculators. In March 1834 the Cachoeira city council, which presided over the second largest district of the province, with six thousand people in the city proper and sixty thousand in the municipality, sent a letter to the provincial president claiming that "the price of manioc flour had become so excessive . . . that the least fortunate class of people could not help but suffer famine, which has brought about the death of several people." The councilmen asked the provincial authorities to send "a boat with a great amount of manioc flour, which they could sell for the price at which it was retailed in Salvador." Some months before, the same city council had promulgated a law against black-marketeers. They set up a fine of 30,000 réis and a week's imprisonment for "scalping" staple foodstuffs: manioc flour, corn, and beans.[20]

Because of popular pressure, the local authorities also punished speculators by confiscating their merchandise. In 1834 a merchant filed a complaint in the Tribunal da Relação, the highest court of appeal in the province, against an inspector in the Santana do Catu Parish. He claimed that the inspector had illegally confiscated one of his shipments. In his defense the accused described black-market operations and the people's reaction to them. According to him, these merchants often pretended they were "paying debts with manioc flour . . . surreptitiously marketing it on wagon trails off the main road." It was a time "of extreme famine and great outcry from the local people." Under pressure from that "outcry," the inspector seems to have forced the merchant to sell 756 liters of his ground manioc to the public at a reasonable price.[21]

The establishment of "fair prices" was a form of direct, popular justice similar to ransacking, albeit somewhat less violent. Consumers forced the authorities to restrain speculators. It was market control similar to what Edward Thompson has called "the moral economy of the crowd," a concept he uses to describe the phenomenon in eighteenth-century England.[22] The Brazilian black-marketeer, like his English counterpart, was the local embodiment of the usurious spirit in a growing world market economy. Such practices were in direct conflict with the still paternalistic character of the local society, notwithstanding the entirely commercial nature of the export economy. Pressured by the populace, the authorities tried to restrain the savagery inherent in speculators' profit-oriented morality and thus maintain the precarious social equilibrium in the province.

Bahian rulers were genuinely troubled by the explosive potential contained in the events of the time. The provincial president warned the national government about the "discontent among the people concerning excessively priced commodities, especially staple foodstuffs."[23] In the eyes of those responsible for law and order in the province, it was clear that city dwellers' tendency to rebel was closely linked to high costs of living. The popular uprisings of that time—the subject of the next chapter—were, at least in part, food riots.

The rise in prices was further stimulated by the flood of counterfeit money into the local market. This extra inflationary impetus was first brought on by an enormous quantity of coins made from a copper of extremely poor quality and easily imitated. These coins had initially been put into circulation by the provisional government during the war of independence. With the end of the war, no one tried to remove the bad money from the marketplace. Quite the contrary: Bahia became a paradise for counterfeiters who had no difficulty producing coins. Copper plates were readily available on the open market, since they were used both in shipbuilding and at the sugar mills. Only at the end of the 1820s did the government decide to redeem the forged coins. And on this occasion the Bahian president concluded that the high prices brought about by the currency crisis in the province, "besides menacing the well-being of all its inhabitants, . . . offers the somber prospect of a collapse of public peace if the evil is not promptly eradicated." He saw currency redemption as the only means for preventing "total anarchy."[24]

The redemption of counterfeit coins was begun, as planned, in the beginning of 1828. However, one more snag appeared: merchants refused to accept the new coins, claiming they were also bogus. In December 1832 the Cachoeira city council complained once more to the authorities in Salvador. Merchants, innkeepers, and farmers in the Recôncavo would not accept the new money from their customers. Many of those merchants and innkeepers were Portuguese, which further strained the locals' patience. The councilmen warned that the situation could end up "disturbing public tranquility" at any time, since impoverished consumers were not about to stand for the absurd situation in which they could not spend the little "official" money they had on hand. The state guaranteed that the money was good, but it had no power to guarantee its acceptance in the marketplace.

As 1832 drew to an end, local complaints were sent in vehement letters from the provincial Government Council (Conselho Geral) to the national government in Rio de Janeiro: "Revolutionary measures have been mentioned by the local populace as the only guarantee against the scorn and indifference with which their greatest hardship is considered." In July 1833 the provincial president, conveying the warnings of the local magistrates, would reiterate that "the outcry had spread among all the people." He also maintained that "it was not possible to quell the despair of the breadless." Two months later the president would complain that the poor were trying to intimidate the government "through violence" into adopting definitive measures against inflation. He also asked for federal intervention in the local currency crisis. Finally, in 1834, the imperial government would sponsor one more redemption of counterfeit money. This attempt was more successful than the first, but it did not solve the problem completely. A report from the British consulate in Salvador indicated that half of the copper coins in circulation in 1836 were still bogus.[25]

Drought, scarcity, reduction of land available for growing food, counterfeit money—all of these worked together to raise the prices of basic commodities. One *arroba*, or approximately fifteen kilos, of beef jerky jumped from 1,930 réis in 1824 to 2,600 réis in 1831 and to 3,245 réis in 1834—a rise of 68 percent in ten years. The wholesale price of beans rose 25 percent between 1824 and 1831, from 1,680 to 2,240 réis per *alqueire* (18.135 liters). The same quantity of manioc flour, which cost 630 réis in 1824, would rise 25 percent in price by 1831.[26] These are comparatively mild rises in price compared with Brazil's and other Latin American countries' recent annual four-digit inflation. Present-day Bahian poverty may be even worse than that of nineteenth-century Bahian slave society. One must remember, however, that there was no regular readjustment of wages during those times. And because of this, small jumps in prices had profound effects on impoverished consumers, both free and slave, with incomes (in the event they had incomes) that were absolutely static. In addition, the prices quoted above were wholesale prices, paid by the Naval Arsenal, a state institution. Clearly, people buying these goods on the retail market contended with much higher prices and had no way of avoiding the speculators' webs.

The situation of Salvador's underprivileged becomes clearer once price fluctuation is compared with that of wages. Mattoso has shown that wage workers saw their real incomes diminish between the years 1751 and 1830. She concludes that at the time of independence, in 1823, the predominant climate of Bahia was one of "intense economic oppression."[27] Unfortunately, there are no studies on wages and prices during the 1830s, when the recession was at its lowest ebb. It was a most difficult decade.

Besides ransacking Portuguese establishments, which Bahians invariably did in the heat of anti-Portuguese rallies, they also used peaceful and relatively organized means for demanding better treatment. Frequent petitions for better wages were sent to the authorities. In 1829, for example, on a petition with sixty-two signatures, customs agents protested the "scanty payment drawn to help with life's necessities." They were demanding a raise of 56 percent over their daily wage of 640 réis. They hinted that they would start taking bribes and ignoring contraband in the event their petition went unheeded. In 1830 officers in the military also asked for a raise. Indeed many of the military revolts of that period had placed salary improvements on their lists of demands. In the face of military unrest, the Provincial Council of 1834 pressured the president to raise soldiers' daily ration in view of the "excessive and unforeseen rise in the cost of living."[28]

The fall in wages was accompanied by one more phenomenon typical of economic crises: unemployment. Free workers had always had a minor role in the Bahian slave economy, but as time went by the number of people on the street and unemployed grew tremendously. Vilhena wrote about this matter at the end of the eighteenth century, during the period of economic growth. However, viewing matters, as he did, through a European moralistic lens, he was to attribute the phenomenon to the freeman's "tropical sloth." The situation seems to have gotten considerably worse with the mushrooming free population and the recession.

The war of independence ended, leaving Bahia in the depths of a depression. The many vagabonds, beggars, aged and abandoned slaves, the chronically infirm, the blind, and the highwaymen had their ranks enlarged by the artisans dismissed from the military arsenals, the soldiers mustered out of the army, and peasants fleeing the droughts in the interior and heading for the city. The public sector, which employed a good part of the free, urban labor force, was weakened by the state financial crisis felt throughout the nation. In Salvador budget cutbacks cost many artisans their jobs. These were carpenters, masons, blacksmiths, and so on, who worked in naval and military construction. The local government also saw its resources dwindle and, as a consequence, had to lay off many workers.

The heat was on, and it surfaced in Bahia, sometimes in the form of inarticulate pressures and peaceful protests, sometimes in violent eruptions. In November 1830 the craftsmen at the local mint (the Casa da Moeda) were let go from jobs they considered guaranteed for life. In the beginning of 1831 they petitioned the imperial government "because they felt their rights had been abrogated." They believed that not only had "national laws" been disobeyed "but also universal, general rights of man established among all Nations" had been neglected. They demanded their jobs back and threatened not to accept the outrage passively:

> In the light of such considerations it seems incredible that the aforementioned Provision [of the National Treasury] had the aim of expelling the petitioners from their posts, barbarously depriving them of their wages, and punishing them for no crime. Indeed said Provision deprived them of their necessary and indispensable sustenance, throwing them into the dangerous sea of poverty and disgrace, and even into despair and crime. Hunger gives bad counsel.[29]

There is no record of an imperial response to this petition. During that same year there were several popular revolts.

In 1832 the first organization of free workers was founded in Bahia. It was the Craftsmen's Society (Sociedade dos Artífices). Organized by carpenters of the Naval Arsenal, the association, a secular version of traditional Catholic lay brotherhoods, "principally proposed to develop a program of mutual aid to its members."[30] It was free workers' attempt at coping collectively, but on their own, with the hardships of the time, foremost among them unemployment.

The authorities sensed danger in the wake of these firings. In August 1835 the president of Bahia informed the imperial government that the artisans were out looking for jobs every day and that, not finding any work, they were prone to "disorder and public commotion." Three months later he appealed to the government in Rio de Janeiro: "What I need to obtain from His Imperial Majesty, and what would greatly help in reinstating public peace, is the power to employ people in the War and Naval arsenals, from where they have been dismissed pursuant to the reductions demanded by the respective ministries." He added: "His Majesty knows right well the danger of such measures, principally in times like these." The president also passed on to the central government what the naval quartermaster had told him: that every day at the arsenal there were long lines of artisans looking for work. Seven years earlier, in 1828, when the arsenal was fully staffed, the president, the viscount of Camamu, already worried about the growing number of unemployed free and freed workers, had asked the quartermaster why he employed rental slaves rather than these workers. The quartermaster responded: "Freed slaves and free people will not deign to work in the arsenal."[31] By 1835 free workers were begging for the jobs they had not deigned to work at in 1828. The times had changed.

This chapter sheds some light on the society in which the Malê rebellion would take place. Bahia was marked by profound social inequity, which was aggravated by the rapid growth of both the free and the slave population. The economic slowdown of the twenties and thirties, as well as the turbulent process of decolonization and the formation of a nation state, would converge to undo the political apathy more or less typical of Bahian colonial society. There were, at regular intervals, violent moments.

The 1835 rebellion was a particularly dramatic moment in this series of popular protests. Africans, be they slave or freed, made up a numerically significant part of Salvador's population but found themselves on the lowest rungs of the Bahian social ladder. Even though some possibilities of social mobility seem to have existed, these were limited and should not be blown out of proportion. Some Africans did relatively well, even better than some poor whites, but not even these fortunate few were totally integrated into the social system. Even if the adversities stemming from domination and exploitation could be partially alleviated by letters of manumission and a modicum of material wealth, daily ethnic discrimination continued as usual.

· 2 ·

Revolts of the Free People

*You see . . . what all has happened in this province to bring
about . . . a widespread apparent lack of confidence
in the stability of the situation.*
—Luís dos Santos Lima, president of Bahia (1831)

The 1835 rebellion occurred in a tumultuous political and social at-
mosphere, tumultuous both in the province and throughout Brazil. Once
the country achieved independence, in 1822, Brazilian society had to face
problems typical of incipient nation-states throughout Latin America: rivalry and competition among different regions of the same country; divisions within the ruling classes; conflicts between federalists and centralists,
liberals and conservatives, republicans and monarchists. In many areas of
Brazil these divergent interests turned into popular revolts against the mo-
narchical system adopted by the architects of independence and against
the crowned head of state himself, Dom Pedro I.[1]

The rebels' struggle for local autonomy constituted a serious threat to
the political unity of the ex-colony. What was perhaps even more important, local movements had the support and participation of groups who
up to then had been on the fringe of the political process: landless peasants, urban poor, freed slaves, soldiers, and in some cases even slaves. Rebellions such as the Confederação do Equador (Equatorial Confederation)
in the province of Pernambuco, the Balaiada in Maranhão, the Cabanagem
in Pará, and the War of the Farrapos (Ragamuffins) in Rio Grande do Sul
were, in part, organized expressions of fear that independence might not
offer local groups any possibility of improving their lot.

The province of Bahia was one of the most restive areas of the country.
Between 1820 and 1840 it was the stage of an anticolonial war, military
revolts, anti-Portuguese manifestations, street riots, sackings, liberal and

federalist rebellions, and slave uprisings. This atmosphere of widespread conflict explains in part the 1835 rebellion. The African rebels appear to have understood that the institutional breakdowns and divisions among Brazilians could contribute to the success of their revolution.

In this chapter I examine the revolts made by free people in Bahia prior to the Malê rebellion. This examination helps to complete the portrait of Bahian society outlined in chapter 1. It adds vitality and color to the picture and puts the 1835 rebellion—its tactics, objectives, and limitations—in perspective.

In July 1823, Brazilian troops entered Salvador after winning the war against the Portuguese. However the war's end would not exactly usher in a time of peace in the province. On the contrary, pent-up social tension from the colonial era began to surface. Between 1823 and the final years of the 1830s, there was one uprising after another in Bahia. Those carried out by free people can be divided conveniently into three main categories: (1) anti-Portuguese disturbances, known as *mata-marotos,* or "kill the rascals"; (2) military revolts; and (3) liberal or federalist movements, quite often heavily tinged with republican tones.

This typology should not be considered complete, rigid, or exclusive. In the backlands land disputes also turned into social revolts, as happened when Kiriri Indians rose up against local farmers in 1834. Besides, grievances and participants in the various types of revolts were often intertwined. Military revolts were seldom just protests concerning life in the barracks. They derived more often from racial tension, economic hardship, and dissatisfaction with civilian and military authorities. They included civilians who had similar gripes with the system. Federalist fever rampaged through the military posts and turned many officers into revolutionary figures. And federalist movements, along with the sweeping reforms they proposed, also included proposals for very specific changes in military protocol. Finally, all nonslave revolts of the time were anti-Portuguese, and when it was time to "kill the rascals," civilians, military, and liberal partisans all took part.

Mata-marotos were largely movements of the Bahian free people, known as the *plebe* in the capital and the towns of the Recôncavo. In Bahia the term *plebe* ("pleb") was current in the vocabulary of the times, along with pejorative terms such as *canalha* ("scum"), *classe baixa do povo* ("low-class folk"), *populaça* ("riffraff"), and so on. These terms refer basically to the free poor: artisans, street vendors, washerwomen, day laborers, vagabonds, prostitutes, men and women in the majority of cases with some African forebears, as well as a relative minority of poor whites.

Whenever this group mobilized, one could momentarily find slaves, especially native-born slaves, in its midst. Streetwise slaves closed ranks and joined the riots, whose timing and structure allowed all participants a modicum of anonymity.

People from the middle sectors of Bahian society also participated in these movements. They were small-time merchants, master craftsmen, bureaucrats, professionals, students, military officers, clerics. These professions were, to varying degrees, fraught with competition between Europeans and Brazilians. Many leaders of mutinies, liberal revolts, and anti-Portuguese demonstrations came from the middle sector. Young people became involved in street movements and participated shoulder to shoulder with the truly plebeian mobs. Nonetheless, one must never forget that as far as political action is concerned, these middle sectors of the population formed a divided contingent of Bahian society. Many of its members joined reactionary forces in times of real conflagration.

The rebellious colloid will settle once it is examined part by part, beginning with the mata-marotos, or anti-Portuguese, manifestations.

Anti-Portuguese Disturbances

Although it differed in perspective and intensity from group to group, anti-Portuguese sentiment permeated Bahia. Wealthy Brazilians had led an armed movement against the colonizers. They were especially resentful of the privilege and success Portuguese merchants had enjoyed in the colony. To a certain extent Bahia's war of independence had been a struggle between debtors and creditors. But the most important plantation owners concluded, once they won the war, that the Portuguese were indispensable business partners. However, even if planters accepted the Portuguese as business partners, they wanted to keep the country's political reins to themselves, which proved difficult given the monarch's thirst for power and his retention of many fellow Portuguese in governmental posts. This state of affairs weakened local elites' autonomy throughout the country. The Constitutional Assembly, which the planters dominated, was their only means of keeping the emperor in check. When Dom Pedro dissolved the assembly in November 1823, the relationship between the Bahian elite and the government in Rio de Janeiro cooled considerably.

The anti-Portuguese sentiment of the common folk was not focused on the distant emperor. The poor considered Portuguese merchants and innkeepers to be more important enemies. The local Portuguese were their social and even personal adversaries, and people accused them of speculating with the price of basic commodities at a time when inflation and scarcity prevailed. For these people, anti-Portuguese talk was not just political rhetoric: it offered a seemingly genuine means of bringing about direct social justice. On a practical level, demonstrations and protests gave them the chance to ransack European stores and warehouses and to enjoy the taste of good food and wine for a day or two.

Even though it was not explicitly stated in the anti-Portuguese rhetoric of the time, one should not forget that racial revenge was a motivating force that contributed to the personal, physical violence perpetrated against the Portuguese. Both Europeans and native-born whites were racially prejudiced, making it natural for both Africans and Afro-Bahians to resent whites in general. During the period under examination, Europeans were the most vulnerable white target. They were not innocent scapegoats; rather, they were the weak link in Bahia's white community.

In 1823 Salvador was the stage of constant anti-Portuguese agitation. The black and mulatto underclass was predominant in the scenery. In September, French consul Jacques Guinebaud was to write: "Black soldiers and entire battalions of mulattos roam the streets, robbing and beating up Portuguese and other foreigners, insulting the government in Rio de Janeiro and shouting: 'Death to the Emperor! Death to the Portuguese! Death to the *janeiristas* [supporters of the government in Rio]! Long live Independence and the Republic.'"[2] In Salvador the break with the new government seemed complete. Republican sentiment was linked to the patriotic, anti-European campaign. The Afro-Bahian masses ruled the streets, and the affluent white minority became fearful.

Perhaps no one has left a better description of the situation than Maria Bárbara Garcez Pinto de Madureira, a planter's wife. In September she wrote a letter to her husband, who was in Europe: "I have nothing to tell you about this city—except that it will soon be depopulated as far as European families are concerned. Even those families who would love to stay on as Brazilians are attacked nightly, and are beaten regularly." This was the "nothing" she had to tell. Later on in the same month, the patrician lady of the Aramaré Plantation registered the travails of persons from her class:

> I am still in town and only at the end of the month will I leave. It is hard to be here, seeing that the city has become a sanctuary for blacks. Everything one sees and hears causes smaller and weaker souls to wither. . . . The sensible people here feel as I do, but there are more bad ones, since blacks and mulattos outnumber whites. Every day more people leave town. Business has come to a halt, so to speak. I do not know. I do not know what will become of us. Such rabid language coming out of the mouths of blacks. May heaven ward off the bolts of lightning their rage hurls our way.[3]

This woman provides the proper perspective: her city was in the hands of blacks; whites were leaving in droves; "sensible people" feared black rage; and her hope of salvation rested on divine intervention. A devastating turn of events for the privileged classes.

The anti-Portuguese street riots intensified when news of the emperor's dissolving the Constitutional Assembly and his incarceration (12 November 1823) of delegates reached Bahia. The urban underclass and its radical leaders, "anarchists" according to the authorities, took to the streets once more. Provincial authorities felt they could not maintain order. "There is not a little fervent unrest, which the government tries to control as much as possible," was what the provisional Bahian government relayed to Minister Maciel da Costa on 15 December. Five days later Rio de Janeiro was to learn that Salvador had been "on the brink of anarchy for three days, thanks to continuous mutinies and a total paralysis of commerce." In order to dampen some of the ardor, government officials called a meeting of "A Council composed of the present Government, Town Councils, Church Officials, Civilians, Military Officers and concerned, illustrious Citizens," which finally composed a letter protesting the assembly's dissolution. The text of this letter, addressed to Dom Pedro, timidly expressed the council's disappointment concerning the events in the country's capital. It recommended that severe measures be taken against all Portuguese known to defend their nation's cause. It promised to expel all Lusophiles. What had been mere "public opinion" became respectable platforms. Politicians in Bahia acknowledged that the "prospect of anarchy had obliged them" to adopt anti-Portuguese measures, freely admitting, nonetheless, that there was no law authorizing them to proceed in such a fashion. However, while they attempted to placate the townsfolk with anti-Portuguese promises, they also tried to protect themselves from dissident politicians and intellectuals by establishing press censorship "so as to restrain writers' leeway, since at every turn these people had run roughshod over both the government and private citizens."[4]

The city calmed down. In February 1824 the constitution Dom Pedro granted was ratified, and the recently empowered first president of the province, Francisco Vicente Vianna, was to write, bedazzled: "It is amazing . . . the enthusiasm with which upright and honest citizens appeared at the Municipal Chamber and mixed in with the authorities . . . with the Cabildo [Town Council], clerics, military commissioned and noncommissioned officers, as well as with the common folk in perfect harmony, tranquility, and peace."[5] This political pact would be quickly broken. On 31 March 1824 a group of officers in the military occupied the Town Council and demanded that the president carry out the promise he had made in December to expel all Portuguese. He gave in, partially, and actually expelled many of them.[6] Only thus was peace reinstated—for the time being. The next big anti-Portuguese explosion would occur seven years later.

The protests of 1831 were brought on, once again, by events in Rio de Janeiro, where opposition to the emperor in the Parliament, in the press, and in the streets was growing. With his father's death in 1826, Dom Pedro became involved in succession disputes in Portugal and let matters slide in Brazil, furnishing his critics with ammunition to challenge his leadership. At the same time, the old question of executive privilege continued to motivate serious opposition in Parliament. Plantation owners as well as other sectors of the privileged classes were not comfortable with the immense power, ironically called "moderating power," that the emperor retained in the 1824 Constitution. Brazil was in political turmoil, and the people read and heard the nasty words of a militantly federalist and liberal press. In 1831 it came to a head. On 13 May Dom Pedro returned to Rio de Janeiro from the province of Minas Gerais, where he had made a proclamation challenging his political enemies. A welcome rally organized by his compatriots turned into a street brawl between Portuguese and Brazilians. The former blindly supported him and used the reception to express in both words and deeds their differences with the locals. This led to the famous "Night of Bottle Blows" (Noite das Garrafadas).

When the news of this incident reached Salvador, agitation began. On 4 April armed civilians as well as almost all the soldiers in Bahia occupied Fort Barbalho and demanded the resignation of the provincial commander in chief, the Portuguese João Crisóstomo Callado. Along with him, all officers born in Portugal were to be dismissed. Three days later there were eight thousand people at the fort. The movement appeared so strong that the provincial president, Luís Paulo de Araújo Basto, gave in to the demands and, in a final act of weakness, resigned immediately afterwards. There was a momentary truce until 13 April, when a rumor that an eminent Bahian businessman had been murdered by a Portuguese spread through the streets of Salvador. Mayhem followed. Many Portuguese were badly beaten, and others were killed. Their houses, inns, and stores were sacked.[7]

Thirty-seven years later, Viridiana Barata, the daughter of the legendary liberal politician Cipriano Barata, described what she had seen:

> On the 13th of April of 1831 at eleven in the morning, more or less, we heard a great hubbub in the street. We ran to the window and saw a man, covered with blood and apparently dead. He was on a divan carried by blacks and surrounded by a huge throng yelling: "The Rascals killed a Brazilian. Death to the Rascals!" And while most of the people marched on with the corpse, the violence, beatings, and break-ins, etc., etc., commenced.

A little later:

> We found the lower city in a state of total anarchy. Every Portuguese home was broken into and every family the victim of their furor. All shops and stores were likewise broken into; faucets yanked from all barrels of any liquid whatsoever, shelves broken, fabric ripped and tossed into the street, and the owners or employees found therein killed.

The protesters chanted:

> Beat it, rascals, beat it
> You can leave at will
> We no longer want
> You rascals in Brazil[8]

The Portuguese consul lived to tell his version:

> [It can be] supposed that earlier fracases involving the lowlife and slaves foreshadowed that rebellion, especially because of the way they stoned the Portuguese both in their houses and on the streets. They exceeded the expression of ire, rage, and barbarity with which these same people acted on the said fourth of April when they were given access to arms and ammunition at the arsenals.[9]

The consul clearly describes slaves participating in demonstrations and firearms in the hands of the common people once Fort Barbalho was occupied—a quasi revolution in Salvador.

The 1831 uprising quickly spread throughout the Recôncavo. In Cachoeira on 15 April, the people took over the town and harassed the Portuguese, jailing some of them. They occupied the Town Council and, under the influence of radical aldermen, set up a committee to investigate the local Portuguese and make a list of those who should be expelled from the province. Things were a bit rougher in Santo Amaro. In an unpublished "Memoir," the secretary of the Town Council, the conservative João Lourenço de Attaide Seixas, tells us that in the worst incident, on 17 April, he found "the streets occupied by the armed rabble and soldiers of the Militia. They were breaking into houses, beating the Portuguese and taking them prisoner, ransacking their houses and stores. . . . Soldiers shouted that they did not care about laws or authorities, and these declarations were repeated by blacks and even slaves."[10] As in Salvador, slaves and free blacks in the Recôncavo were conspicuous in these fracases.

Also according to Seixas's account, the people who took over the Town Council in Santo Amaro compiled and approved by acclamation a list of Portuguese enemies. Some gave personal reasons for blacklisting specific individuals. It is revealing that one man declared to the assembly that a particular Portuguese innkeeper should be expelled from the province because the man had refused to sell him merchandise on credit. The issue of Portuguese monopolies, tinged with personal resentment, surfaced in the radical patriotic eddy.

The 1831 protests attenuated when the province learned of Dom Pedro's abdication on April 7. Reactionary forces seized the day. On 18 May planters in the Recôncavo sent a long manifesto to the provincial government. In this manifesto they had harsh words for the "anarchy" that had swept through Bahia in April. They were energetically opposed to the deportation of any Portuguese and argued that deportation would ruin the sugar business. They wrote that "as trade is persecuted and attacked with no protection whatsoever, it flees, taking with it many millions of réis in real wealth . . . and leaves the Province devoid of Capital and its share of the market."[11]

Large landowners in Bahia were more concerned about their ledgers than about a political analysis of the situation. For them, politically speaking, the abdication and return of the emperor to Portugal were tantamount to Brazilians' having at last taken over the state. Once Dom Pedro was out of the fray, they wanted business as usual. To contain the "continuous revolutions" they recommended that the government get tough: "Perhaps the Authorities lack the proper strength." But the Bahian patricians' desire for social peace was not to be respected by the plebeians. There were to be three more military revolts in 1831.

Military Revolts

By now it should be obvious that the military was always present in the Bahian movements of the period. The barracks housed endless discontent. At the highest levels of the military hierarchy there was hostility between career officers, who usually came from military or "middle-class" families, and former cadets, usually men from "aristocratic" families. Each group tried to make its mark on the newly independent government's armed forces. After the war, the chain of command was so entangled that the soldiers did not always know whom to obey. This, of course, caused discipline to slacken and nurtured dissatisfaction among the troops, most of whom were ragged privates coming from the poorest and most oppressed classes of the free populace. The political behavior of mulatto battalions always suggested race and class protest.

Another source of unrest during this period was the presence of troops from other provinces. These soldiers, already upset at being far from home and plunged into destitution with no support from their families, were often at odds with the locals—or they joined them in the revolts. The northeastern battalions were particularly rebellious. The Minas Gerais battalion usually sided with order, and on a daily basis its soldiers found themselves at loggerheads with the Bahians and northeasterners. Added to their humble origins was their bad luck at having been drafted; they were called to service only to be poorly fed, physically abused, and absurdly paid. They were victims of a nation mired in a financial crisis and unable to sustain them with minimal dignity. The military was riddled with dissatisfaction and permeable to influence from widespread social unrest.

The first important military revolt of this period occurred on 25 October 1824, when the commandant of the army's Third Battalion, made up mainly of soldiers of color, was called to Rio de Janeiro. Major José Antônio da Silva Castro's dismissal presaged the disbanding of his battalion, which would leave unemployed men who had contributed to the victory against the Portuguese. Life in the barracks could be tough, the food terrible, pay unreal, but at least it was something. The battalion's reaction, which came about without Major Castro's approval, but with the participation of junior officers, was radical. They occupied the headquarters and executed Bahia's military commander in chief, General Felisberto Gomes Caldeira.

On the following day two more battalions (including the greater part of the artillery forces) joined the rebels. The forces loyal to the government lost no time in abandoning the city and headed for Abrantes, the domain of the powerful Albuquerque family. In Salvador, our principal witness described the scene as follows: "Stores and saloons are all closed. Gangs roam the streets killing and robbing. Part of the population is in the harbor aboard ships or has fled into the countryside." [12] But the rebels did not know exactly what to do with the city once they had taken it. They wanted to stay, but they had no plan for governing. They felt cornered, and in several almost repentant proclamations, they attempted to justify having executed the commandant.

The impasse lasted an entire month. Salvador, ungoverned and unbalanced as it was, became chaotic. On 24 November Guinebaud reported: "It is practically unnecessary to add that total anarchy reigns throughout the city. Lootings and murders happen every day, with no one particularly upset about it. All commerce has been suspended, and the shops only open so as to be precipitously closed at the first rumor." [13] The Frenchman suggested that the people of Salvador and the military took advantage of the situation and looted, but not even this happened. They remained remarkably passive while troops loyal to the government requested and received reinforcements from the planters in the Recôncavo, who knew exactly what they wanted. Unorganized, without definite leadership, with no clear objectives, rebel forces gave up without a shot. They had been convinced by their former commanding officer to leave Salvador and go to Pernambuco, ostensibly to help the government keep the peace in that province. There a recent federalist movement known as the Equatorial Confederation had tried to separate the northeastern provinces from the rest of the empire.

When the episode was over, the consul remarked:

One supposes that the Emperor will finally open his eyes about the extreme danger of admitting Negroes into his armed forces. The black caste, be it freed or native-born, is still more or less the object of scorn on the part of whites. Their social circumstances make them hate their masters and force them to oppose the status quo. Thus Blacks join any effort to topple the State. Any change can only help them.[14]

Guinebaud was basically right. Nonetheless, what Afro-Bahians really wanted was greater participation in what the consul called the whites' "system of civilization" *(sistema de civilização)*. Social stability could be fostered, not by expelling blacks from the armed services, but by eliminating racism. The military divided soldiers into whites, blacks, and mulattos. Racial discrimination was transparent in the military classifications, which reflected society at large. In these circumstances peace would always be a lie waiting to be uncovered sooner or later.

If Guinebaud was right and there were blacks among the ranks of the rebels, there were also loyalist blacks. Such was the case of the famous Batalhão dos Henriques (a battalion named after Henrique Dias, a hero in the war to expel the Dutch from Brazil in the seventeenth century), a militia unit, now known simply as the Primeiro Batalhão de Milícias, the "First Militia Battalion." During the 1824 uprising it remained in Salvador and protected the bank and other public buildings. By doing this, the Henriques maintained their colonial tradition of siding with power. They were an exception, it is true, but their stance shows that Afro-Bahian troops were divided.[15]

The rebellion of 25 October 1824, also known as the Periquitos (Parakeets) rebellion because of the soldiers' green uniforms, did not go unpunished. In 1825 two rebel leaders, Major Joaquim Sátiro da Cunha and Lieutenant Gaspar Luís Lopes Villas Boas, were tried and sentenced to death by a special military commission headed by the new commander, José Gordilho de Barbuda, a hard-liner who was later to become the viscount of Camamu and provincial president. For the next six years a relative peace settled into the barracks, thanks in part to the new, authoritarian commander, who went so far as to engage in a vigorous duel of words with President Vianna, a liberal, who had recommended a more moderate sentence for the 1824 rebels.[16]

Nonetheless, unrest continued in the military. Soldiers were extremely unhappy with the constant delays in their pay. In July 1825, after the well-heeled Minas Gerais battalion had left, pamphlets circulated throughout the city denouncing the soldiers' hardships. In 1828 a plot was discovered, and several officers were jailed. Two years later, in February 1830, Gordilho de Barbuda, provincial president since 1827, was gunned down in broad daylight by a horseman on the busy Largo do Teatro, the present-day Castro Alves Square. With some plausibility, Morton has credited the counterfeit-coin mafia with this assassination, persecuted as it was by the president, but the Bahian historian Braz do Amaral argues that the victim, in his rapid transit through Bahia, had acquired many enemies, both political and personal. Any one of them, including his military rivals, could have killed him.[17]

Between March and May 1831, soldiers took part in the anti-Portuguese riots. Before this, on 31 January, sailors on the warship *Carioca* rose in mutiny against their officers, whom they reviled as despots. On 12 May the Piauí battalion seized Fort São Pedro and demanded freedom for political prisoners incarcerated during the previous months. They also demanded the ouster of the provincial president, a merchant named João Alves Cezimbra, as well as that of the interim commander, a sugar planter and the archreactionary chief of the Albuquerque clan, the viscount of Pirajá. In addition, they called for the expulsion of all Portuguese. The revolt did not extend to other divisions, but several members of the Bahian underclass joined the rebels at São Pedro. Both President Cezimbra and Commander Pirajá resigned, but the expulsion of the Portuguese was postponed once again.[18] Being under the thumb of the Portuguese and their capital, the Bahian elite opted to restrict some of its members' power. Be that as it may, the fall of two of the most important figures in the province represented quite a victory for the movement.

After the May rebellion, the new Bahian leaders took measures to neutralize military opposition. In July they created a new Municipal Guard, which would recruit among the increasingly conservative middle-class urbanites. This organization would be the political and military antidote to the ragged regular troops and would replace army soldiers guarding the city in shifts. Beginning in September, many of these troops were dismissed, only to swell the ranks of idle bodies filling the streets—living proof of the province's economic straits. Lastly, severe military discipline was reintroduced in the barracks by the new commander, Antero Brito.[19]

These changes did not head off another rebellion on 31 August, once again at Fort São Pedro, this time led by the Artillery Corps. This uprising was unique insofar as only enlisted men revolted, and their grievances were of a strictly military nature, specifically: frequent reviews, bad food, the wearing of an uncomfortable leather collar as part of their dress, and delays in being paid. As always in military demonstrations of this type, protesters demanded the resignation of their commanding officer. In spite of the adherence of "some lower-class civilians" (according to the deposition of one sergeant), the rebellion lasted only one night. On this occasion their grievances were not addressed, which suggests that officers' support or participation in these movements was a key factor in their success.[20]

Two months later one more revolt, this time clearly organized by federalist officers, occurred at São Pedro, which had become the point of origin for military subversion in Salvador. The mutineers rose in the name of federalism, demanding the ouster of Commander Antero de Brito and of all Portuguese who had been recruited for the recently created Municipal Guard. Again civilians joined, swelling the rebels' ranks. But no other military unit joined, and the revolt failed. President Barros Paim declared that "some desperate men who thought that with the help of certain unsavory individuals they could carry out their evil deeds" were held back by the loyalty of the majority of the soldiers and the rapid deployment of the Municipal Guard, which on this occasion did what it was created to do.[21] The October revolt was the first explicit manifestation of federalist sentiment in the province of Bahia. For the next two years federalist movements dominated the Bahian political arena.

Federalist Rebellions

The federalist platform had many supporters among Bahian political leaders, intellectuals, and the military. Regional autonomy seemed to be an attractive alternative to the centralized nation-state begun in 1822 and legitimized in the 1824 Constitution. A confederation suggested the possibility of greater political space for radical liberals and even the viability of a republic.

The federalist movement in Bahia grew little by little. It was in many ways a pluralistic movement. It had no definite program or ideology. It included republicans and constitutional monarchists. Sometimes it advocated a radical break from the central government, at other times a partial and temporary breaking away. It constantly struggled to reconcile radicals and moderates. Perhaps this is why Bahian federalism had to wait an entire decade before it launched its own rebellions. Until that time Bahian federalists, and then only the most fervent ones, participated in sudden uprisings (popular, almost spontaneous outbursts such as the mata-marotos) or in military revolts. They were without a doubt effective agitators. Beginning in 1831 their study and debating "clubs," as political groups were called at the time, acquired an organizing and directing role capable of proposing and trying to effect change in Bahian society. Their movement culminated with the occupation of Salvador for several months during the federalist revolt of 1837–38.

Between the end of 1831 and the beginning of 1832, federalist and republican sympathizers, including the soldiers and officers involved in the São Pedro revolt, sought refuge in the Recôncavo. They gathered in Cachoeira, a city with a radical tradition. On 16 February they joined a rebellion in the neighboring town of São Félix, on the other side of the Paraguaçu River. The leader of the movement was Bernardo Miguel Guanaes Mineiro, a captain of the militia, the recently elected justice of the peace in São Félix, and also a municipal councilman in Cachoeira. Three days later, on 19 February, the rebels crossed the river once more and occupied

FIG. 3. Cachoeira, as seen from across the Paraguaçu River, site of the 1832 federalist rebellion. Many slave rebellions also took place on nearby sugar plantations. Drawing from Johann Baptist von Spix and Karl F. von Martius, *Viagem pelo Brasil, 1817–1820: excertos e ilustrações* (São Paulo: Melhoramentos, 1968).

the Cachoeira city council. Following tradition, they called a special meeting, but even counting Guanaes Mineiro, only three councilmen were present, since the others had fled because they did not support the rebellion. At this meeting a liberal-federalist manifesto with twenty-four items was presented—the first document of that nature to appear in ten years of social struggles in Bahia.

The Cachoeira manifesto was a strongly worded liberal document criticizing the "oppression" Bahians endured "under the present provincial government, under the Portuguese and their followers, and under the ruinous government in Rio de Janeiro." The federalists were speaking for the people at large. They adopted the revolutionary principle, stylish at the time, that the people, in their sovereignty, had the "natural right" to bear arms against "intrigues and schemes of Aristocrats and self-servers"—a daring message to the sugar barons of the Recôncavo. Their platform did not address the issue of a republic. It did declare Bahia a federated state, with its own laws, armed forces, and finances. Its connection with the rest of the country and the national government was to be limited to international relations and Bahia's share of the national debt, which would be honored.

The new order would begin by forming a provisional revolutionary government; then a provincial constituent assembly would write a constitution. The assembly would establish the rules for calling up an electoral college, which in turn would elect the president. The central government would no longer appoint provincial presidents. But there would still not be universal suffrage.

The release of all political prisoners, the abolition of laws of exception against dissidents, and the end of political censorship of the press were some of the immediate liberalizing measures they proposed. The federalists also promised to improve the lot of the common criminal. The criminal code was to be reformed and its sentences made less severe. The inhuman imprisonment of people in the holds of ships would come to an end. A *presinganga* (from the infamous English "press gangs"), or prison ship, would be symbolically "burned in a place where the People could watch and enjoy the fire." The federalists knew the value of political spectacle of this kind.

As was to be expected, the Portuguese received special attention in the manifesto and appeared in many of its articles. All those born in Portugal and not married to Brazilian women, or without an established business, should be deported, unless they agreed to become farmers. All Portuguese working in the public sector, including the military, would be dismissed. In addition, Article 18 determined: "The People also will deport all those Portuguese who, even though they may be married to Brazilian women, have been identified as enemies of Brazil." One Portuguese in particular was singled out by the federalists and bore the entire brunt of Article 23, which stated: "The tyrannical ex-Emperor of Brazil will face a firing squad in any part of this province, should he dare to show his face."

Nonetheless, at the same time that it threatened to expel the Portuguese, the manifesto favored any rich ones who might want to immigrate. It sought to control the Portuguese involved in small and middle-sized businesses, but Portuguese "bringing with them important businesses" were welcome. "Learned" Portuguese were also welcome, but both they and the wealthy merchants would need to have reputations of being "very liberal." Ideological purity would not be set aside owing to any economic or "scientific" need the Bahians might have. Little was said about economic issues in Bahia. Besides the measures intended for the Portuguese, the federalists promised to improve the lines of food supply into Salvador and to eliminate the counterfeit money in circulation.

The rebels deemed their "Revolution" (their term, capital letter and all) "entirely just and holy" and their leaders "worthy saviors of the Fatherland." The manifesto was signed "The Sovereign People."[22]

The São Félix rebellion lasted less than two weeks. Plantation owners were quick to form a counterrevolutionary movement. Rebels, however, were unable to enlist help from beyond the borders of São Félix and Cachoeira. Even there the people may have cheered the movement's defeat, at least in the interpretation of the victors. It is, however, true that there was scant mobilization of rebel forces. It seems that the leaders believed the people would quickly and happily support their plans for change. Only in Feira de Santana did the federalist "party" have a timid backing from the people, but loyalist troops quelled the uprising almost before it began.

The official forces, called "The Harmonizing Army" (Exército Armonizador), were once more under the command of that pillar of law and order, the viscount of Pirajá. On 24 February the viscount's signature headed an open letter to the provincial president. In this letter members of the richest and most important families of the Recôncavo, and their political clients, all meeting at the Nazaré Plantation, expressed their total disapproval of the "anarchical movement" at São Félix. They promised to marshal all their resources against the rebels.

Meanwhile the rebellion was almost over. On 23 February Colonel Rodrigo Antônio Falcão Brandão, another son of an important "aristocratic" family, had occupied São Félix and routed the dissidents in refuge there. Guanaes Mineiro, Custódio Bento, Lieutenant Luís Onofre, and other leaders were captured, but many managed to escape. There was little gunfire in this rebellion. Only one loyalist soldier was seriously wounded. The government's main tactic was to seal off Cachoeira and São Félix so that neither sympathizers nor supplies of any kind could enter.[23]

The rest of 1832 passed in a state of relative calm, except for frequent rumors of conspiracies, which Bahians were used to by then. In 1833 the federalists were on the move once more, this time in Salvador itself. Five people were arrested in January for trying to incite the artillery soldiers into action. During the same month there was an attempt to break into the hospital prison, most certainly to set political prisoners free. At the same time, Salvador was bombarded daily with federalist pamphlets. Finally, in the predawn hours of 9 March, a group of armed men ("the vile underclass," in the words of the president) attacked the cavalry barracks in Água de Meninos but was immediately repelled. A cavalryman was seriously wounded in the skirmish, and on the rebel side, a black and a mulatto were taken prisoner.[24]

The year's most serious episode began on 26 April. The political prisoners at Forte do Mar (a fortress surrounded by water, today Fort São Marcelo) rebelled. The rebellion was headed by Guanaes Mineiro, Lieutenant Daniel Gomes de Freitas, and Alexandre Ferreira Sucupira (an exlieutenant in a mulatto battalion the government had disbanded). Sucupira had been active in the São Félix rebellion but was in prison because of his involvement in the attack on the cavalry barracks in March. Among the "guests" at this prison was the famous Cipriano José Barata, who had been in prison since the disturbances of 1831. He did not join the federalists rebels, perhaps because of his age—he was in his seventies.

After taking the island fort, the insurgents raised the white and blue federalist flag and attempted to negotiate with the provincial authorities. They expected the authorities to resign and respect the new federalist order. Of course, these demands did not stimulate dialogue. President Joaquim José Pinheiro de Vasconcellos was not caught unaware. He had already ordered a general alert for the city and had sent a warship to block communication with the fort.

For the next three days shots were fired between rebel and loyalist artilleries. The federalist canons hit several government buildings, but they were finally silenced, either because of a lack of ammunition or by loyalist bombardment. On the fourth day the rebels surrendered in spite of secret intelligence they had received that the rebellion would break out in the city at any time during the next two days. This intelligence must have been false, as Salvador was immobilized and under strict military control. Its streets were occupied by municipal and regular troops, as well as by the recently inaugurated (1831) National Guard, which rounded up all the city's law-abiding inhabitants. This allowed the local government to stop the revolt from reaching the shore.[25]

When Forte do Mar was retaken, on 29 April, the police found a new federalist manifesto. A good part of this document reiterated the 1832 program described above. But the text had been edited. It was better organized, with a clearer exposition of principles and objectives. The dissidents were obviously studious political prisoners. They had studied and discussed the reforms they planned to introduce into Bahian society.

The new program paid more attention to social and economic problems in the province. It proposed what were then modern, grass-roots solutions. The anti-Portuguese spirit was still present but diluted in a wide-reaching slate of nationalistic reforms. Portuguese, for that matter all foreigners, would be prohibited from owning retail businesses. This sector of the economy would henceforth be under Brazilian control, except for peddling, which was blacks' work and not even mentioned. They were defending the interests of Bahian merchants and innkeepers. To protect local tradesmen, all imported manufactured goods would be subject to heavy tariffs "so as not to weaken factories and workshops belonging to carpenters, tailors, cobblers, and to all who may have established whatever branch of industry in this Province, even foreigners." It was only from marketing, not from production, that Europeans should be barred, which shows how important commercial capital was at that time.

Federalists promised not only to "oblige farmers to plant vegetables so that there would be enough to eat" but also to cut the tax on food in half. Black-marketeers would be rigorously punished. The war against inflation would become more spirited, with harsh punishment for counterfeiters who worked "to benefit the rich and against the poor." They also promised "to diminish and destroy all taxes that weighed on the People." One of those to be abolished was the tax on urban buildings in which owners resided. They would continue to tax rental property. To fight unemployment in the public sector, they guaranteed "honest work for a large number of individuals whom the tyrannical budget Law cast from the Stations where they made their living."

The rebels' social concerns included "beggars and young people wandering rudely and crudely about." Justices of the peace would be required to provide care and vigilance for these people on the fringe of society—"some because of extreme poverty, others because of neglectful parents and guardians."

The poor would also be helped by a reform of the judicial system involving the creation of a Universal Jurors' Court (Tribunal de Júri Universal) and by combating favoritism and corruption. In this court "all citizens accused of whatever crime" would be "equally tried." "All [special] influence" favoring the privileged would be expressly prohibited. The number of appellate judges *(desembargadores)* would be reduced, and all employees of the judicial system would only receive the salaries and bonuses paid by the state. All fees paid to state judicial staff directly by plaintiffs or defendants would be eliminated.

Two proposals in the program were aimed directly at the Bahian landed gentry: an end to primogeniture rights *(morgado)* and the confiscation of idle land. To put an end to primogeniture (which was not widespread in Bahia) was to break up inheritances and widen claims on estates. Expropriation of idle property attempted to weaken owners' strangleholds on land or at least to motivate them to cultivate it. The rebels planned to create an affluent, productive rural class committed to the new government. Properties that had no legitimate heirs would be given to "Brazilians who had distinguished themselves serving and defending the Fatherland"—as long as they promised to put the property to productive use. The new state would both redistribute idle land and finance the new landholders. These measures demonstrate the federalists' desire to introduce modern, bourgeois patterns of ownership into Brazil and to do away with the colonial model still in force.[26]

In their programs and struggles Bahian political reformers never addressed a fundamental part of their society: the system of slavery and racial discrimination. In general the political objectives of free Bahians lay elsewhere. The short-lived federalist rebellions sought to establish a new type of political order as well as a modicum of social justice among those already free. They sought to mobilize city dwellers and farmers, a great number of whom, including many of the rebels, owned slaves. Federalists were defeated in 1831, 1832, and 1833. Later on, the Sabinada—a longer and initially victorious rebellion (1837–38)—tried to carry out the federalist program, but only timidly did it attempt to tamper with slavery. In one decree the rebels proposed freeing native-born slaves if they had taken up arms on the side of the revolution; however, they would keep Africans as slaves.[27] (As we shall see in later chapters, the distinction between native and foreign slaves was fundamental to the politics and social fabric of slavery in Bahia.)

The anti-Portuguese movements and the majority of military revolts had no program for social or political reform. They were, one might say, movements of the moment. The people of Salvador and those in rural settlements took justice and authority into their own hands when they saw that their rulers were reluctant to punish anti-Brazilian Portuguese and speculators in commodities. These movements were also full of poor people merely trying to line their bellies during times of want. Many Portuguese fell victim to the poor's fury—they were beaten, killed, and robbed. It is hard to say that justice was done, but it is equally hard to pass judgment on the violence of the oppressed. If the purpose of anti-Portuguese riots was to punish the Portuguese and drive them from Bahia, they were partially successful. The Portuguese were punished, and many fled the province, but a large number of them stayed on.

Popular movements and military uprisings scored other victories. They were able to topple military commanders and more than one government, a feat that has never been repeated in Bahia. They made the provincial rulers respect, albeit not agree with, what they called "public opinion." This is clearly a time in Bahian history when the privileged classes lost some of their mandate. The economic crisis fused with the leadership crisis and produced rebellions of or in the name of the underdog. There was never a true revolution in the province because practically no one among the free—with the possible exception of the freed Africans—wanted to be on the same social footing with the slaves. Against the slaves all free Bahians joined forces, regardless of class or color.

While they were absent from the reformists' programs, slaves were not totally missing in the plans of radical politicians nor in lower-class movements. In 1832, in the face of defeat, the São Félix rebels threatened to incite slaves throughout the Recôncavo into revolt. This gesture was the fruit more of despair than of early abolitionist idealism. It was an act of men "who had lost," to use the words of the provincial president.[28] Earlier, in 1831, Antônio Joaquim Pires de Albuquerque, the militia chief of Santo Amaro, had accused liberal agitators of fomenting unrest among the slaves and of promising them freedom and land.[29] While there may have been rebels with Haitian inclinations, radicals of that nature must have been few. Even so, their speeches did not go unheeded by a member of the Albuquerque clan who happened to be the owner of great tracts of land and of many slaves. The owners of Bahia had their ears to the ground.

Many slaves seem to have joined these movements spontaneously. In the heated anti-Portuguese riots of 1831 in Santo Amaro, slaves, soldiers, and free civilians joined the fracas. There is a precious item to be added to this fact: some slaves went so far as to occupy chairs and participate in council debates! One such case was described by the council secretary, Seixas: "And then I saw a Black, José Ignácio, a slave of Félix da Silva Monteiro. The slave was seated at one of the council chairs. I asked him who he was, and he answered that he was a Citizen, just like me, and he pulled out a pointed knife and slammed it on the table."[30]

If a slave could talk like that to a white man, to a councilman, to a "legitimate" citizen, then the slaveholding social order was in trouble. Even more interesting is that Seixas knuckled under and did nothing to reprove the new black citizen. This episode in Santo Amaro is the most daring one found coming from a slave. But slaves in Salvador, in 1831 and on other occasions, also became involved in disturbances recorded in the depositions of Dona Viridiana Barata, the Portuguese and French consuls, and others. The outlook was disturbing, beyond doubt.

Even political dissidents showed their uneasiness in the face of slave agitation, especially during the Recôncavo's chaotic days of 1831. On 18 April Cachoeira's radical council resolved to buttress the city's defenses against possible attacks from slaves; at the same time it was planning its attack on the Portuguese. The following week councilmen attributed rumors of an imminent slave revolt to a Portuguese plot. They requested that the provincial government send troops to defend them from two foreign enemies: Africans and Europeans.[31] The councilmen in Cachoeira most certainly owned slaves, and they did not want to lose them, much less have their heads cut off by their own slaves. These heads neither planned nor dreamed of a new, slaveless order in Bahia.

Beyond all this, the movements of the free underclass were not impermeable to slave participation. It must not have been difficult, particularly for native-born black (crioulo) and mulatto slaves, to join the collective outbursts of people with the same skin color and accent. The underclass was, after all, Afro-Bahian, and in the heat of the skirmishes it often included even people born in Africa. The Africans, however, generally used the confusion reigning in the province to fight their own battles—against all free Bahians, be they patrician or plebeian; mainly against whites but against nonwhites too.

· 3 ·

The Rebellious Tradition

SLAVE REVOLTS PRIOR TO 1835

Death to Whites! Long live Blacks!
—Call to arms, Urubu Quilombo uprising (1826)

Well before the free underclass and the federalist rebels were to begin their movements, slaves in Bahia had begun to rebel. *Quilombos,* or runaway slave (maroon) communities, had existed since the beginning of Bahian slavery, and slave rebellions became more frequent in the early nineteenth century. Some of the reasons for these rebellions have already been mentioned: the growth of the sugar economy, the growing number of slaves imported from Africa, the greater burdens of work demanded from slaves, the crisis in foodstuffs, as well as rifts among the free populace. Other factors, to be discussed in this chapter and in future chapters, include geographic elements favoring the establishment of quilombos, inefficient law enforcement, and the organizational and ideological importance of slaves' religion and their cultural or ethnic identity.

With their sudden or planned uprisings, both in the capital and in the towns of the Recôncavo and on the plantations and in fishing marinas, African slaves kept their owners permanently on edge. On several occasions rebels' plans were nipped in the bud. Some uprisings had a large number of participants, whereas in others only a few dozen people took part. Some never went beyond the boundaries of a specific plantation. This type of uprising usually culminated in the punishment of an especially cruel overseer or master. In other cases slaves from several plantations joined forces and killed free men and fellow slaves who had failed to support them. They also burned cane fields and houses in rehearsals for sending the entire slaveholding edifice up in smoke. Without exception the rebels were defeated, sometimes brutally, but their constant defiance caused slavery and ethnic relations in Bahia to be especially charged during those years. When the Malês organized their 1835 rebellion, they were acting as heirs to a rebellious tradition.

War on Whites

The first attempts at slave rebellion in nineteenth-century Bahia occurred in or around Salvador. A large part of African community life was reconstituted or reinvented in the capital and especially in its suburbs. At the end of the eighteenth century, Luís dos Santos Vilhena, a teacher of Greek concerned about where civilization in the Bahian tropics seemed to be headed, was to write: "It does not seem politically wise to permit throngs of negroes, of both sexes, to have their barbarous war drum dances in the streets and squares of this city. They dance in a lascivious fashion, sing heathen songs, speak in strange tongues, all the time screaming horrendously and in a dissonant manner which arouses both fear and suspicion."[1] Had Professor Vilhena ventured into Salvador's outskirts, the state of affairs there would most likely have seemed even more suspicious and fearsome.

The hills, woods, lagoons, and rivers of the countryside provided ecological support for the development of an independent, quasi-clandestine African collective spirit. The city was surrounded by mobile quilombos and religious meeting places; if destroyed in one place, they reappeared elsewhere, nourished as they were by the uninterrupted stream of slaves capitalizing on the relative freedom of urban slavery.

These suburban quilombos were very special. They must have had very few permanent residents. Indeed they probably functioned mainly as "resorts" for slaves who sought a few days' respite from their masters, as well as for freed Africans longing for something closer to African ways of life. If some individuals decided to stay, they never stayed very long. They soon fell prey to slave hunters *(capitães do mato)* eager for rewards, or they ended up being captured in the frequent police raids. However, the majority of residents probably returned calmly to the city and to their masters after enjoying a rest, since life on a quilombo could be hard. These communities were unstable, and their proximity to Salvador made both their creation and their destruction very easy, except when the slaves resolved to flee into the bush, as many did. In those "free territories" the war drums boomed in worldly celebrations, in homage to African deities, and to call warriors to battle when inhabitants chose to fight the militia. Joy and fear, struggle and death, were the quilombos' daily bread.

João Saldanha da Gama, count of Ponte, was one of the most ardent enemies of suburban quilombos and slave indiscipline generally. In April

1807, less than two years after becoming governor of Bahia, he wrote to the Portuguese Overseas Council:

> Seeing that slaves frequently and repeatedly escaped from masters in whose service they had been engaged for years . . . I became curious (an important trait in this land) about where it was they went. I soon learned that in the outskirts of this capital and in the thickets that surround it, there were innumerable assemblages of these people, who, led by the hand of some industrious charlatans, enticed the credulous, the lazy, the superstitious, those given to thievery, criminals, and the sickly to join them. They lived in absolute liberty, dancing, wearing extravagant dress, phoney amulets, uttering fanatical prayers and blessings. They lay around eating and indulging themselves, violating all privilege, law, order, public demeanor.[2]

These quilombos were busy religious centers where members of Salvador's black population, both slave and free, sought cures for illnesses, guidance from African priests, and meetings with ancestral deities. The count's spies found two of the principal locations for these "assemblages": the present-day neighborhoods of Nossa Senhora dos Mares and Cabula.

The slave hunter Captain Severino da Silva Lessa, with his own assistants and police corporals, was put in charge of bringing the inhabitants of these quilombos in. With eighty well-armed regular troops they attacked, meeting resistance and inflicting casualties, but doing "nothing worthy of remark" according to the count, who may have wanted to hide any of his men's excesses. Seventy-eight people, both slave and free, were taken prisoner. The men were sentenced to forced labor at the military arsenals, whereas the women went to jail.

The hard-line governor gloated at having made up for the "masters' indulgences." According to him, black independence was brought into line through his efficient police work: "Slaves are now very different in the proper way they obey their masters, and the freedmen show much more deference to whites than before."[3] A month later, the discovery of an elaborate conspiratorial network would quell the governor's jubilation. It seemed that his tactics had caused blacks to react in kind.

The 1807 plotters had planned an uprising for 28 May, during the Corpus Christi celebrations, but on the twenty-second they were betrayed by a slave loyal to his master, who brought the news to the count (Saldanha da Gama). The governor was skeptical; however, his characteristic efficiency in these matters obliged him to put his spies to work. He learned that the subversive plan was real. On the twenty-seventh, the count used his own brand of cunning against the rebels:

> I attended and participated in the Corpus Christi procession, giving no hint of what I had in mind. Once it was over, I sent both the Infantry and the Artillery Chief orders I had written telling them to mount specific patrols. Then, in the afternoon, with no drum roll and with no no-

tice in the city, with its exits and entrances under surveillance, and rural officers on the roads, the indicated house was surrounded and searched. . . . Then and there the alleged leaders and captains [of the revolt] were taken prisoner. There were seven in all in the hovel, as well as four hundred arrows, a bundle of rods to be used as bows, piles of rope, knives, pistols, one shotgun, and a drum. The rural officers caught three of the ringleaders, who had fled earlier that afternoon, and military patrols on rounds caught a few more identified as agents or enticers.[4]

As a diversionary tactic, would-be rebels planned to set fire to the Customs House in the lower city and to a chapel in the Nazaré neighborhood. Urban and rural slaves would join forces to "make war on whites," according to the count. The goal of the uprising is believed to have been to capture ships in the harbor and make a massive flight back to Africa—an extravagant plan, and probably the figment of certain police officers' imagination or of some very imaginative informant. However, an elaborate clandestine organization appears to have existed, with a "captain" in each parish of the city and a commander, known as the "ambassador" (an ironic title, since diplomacy had no role in this struggle). Supposedly, Hausas, both slave and freed, played the major roles in the plot. The Hausas were an African people among whom Islam was widespread and who were well represented in Bahia at the time. They were quite likely responsible for the first slave revolts of the nineteenth century. In fact, both of the leaders executed later on were Hausas. One was a slave, the other an ex-slave. The other eleven involved in the plot were punished publicly, each with 150 lashes, to set an example for sympathizers and potential rebels. On top of the floggings, which were quite severe punishment for a revolt that never took place, the governor strictly prohibited all meetings and celebrations involving Africans. He also interdicted the movement of freed Africans in Salvador and the Recôncavo.

The repressive measures of 1807 were, however, to no avail. Two years later the scenario for rebellion shifted to the Recôncavo, or more precisely, to the area around the town of Nazaré das Farinhas, a center for the production of foodstuffs. The rebel contingent there consisted mainly, though not entirely, of Hausa slaves who had fled Salvador and various plantations in the Recôncavo and had formed a quilombo along the Prata River. On 5 January around three hundred inhabitants of the quilombo attacked Nazaré, apparently in search of arms, ammunition, and food. The attack was unsuccessful. The rebels were pushed back into the bush, leaving their casualties behind. Two days later troops from Salvador and the local civilian militia set off after the insurgents and defeated them in a bloody battle. Many surrendered to save their lives; others managed to escape. No one knows what became of the eighty-three men and twelve women taken prisoner. The fugitives dispersed into bands of four or five people and roamed over the Recôncavo. Police in the town of Feira de Santana, which lies on the border between the humid Recôncavo and the arid *sertão,* or backlands, reported having spent the early part of March hunting rebels recently arrived in those parts and going around "killing, stealing, and setting fire to the places they visited." Some of the rebels may have reached Sergipe, across the northern border of Bahia Province, where local authorities accused them of inciting a rebellion.[5]

In many ways the 1809 rebellion became a dangerous precedent for Bahian slave society. Notwithstanding the large number of participants, there were no betrayals, no leaks of information. It was more difficult to be a spy or informer in a rural environment; spies and informers work better in densely populated areas. Another unsettling aspect of this revolt was that this time Jeje (Aja-Fon) and Nagô (Yoruba) slaves joined the Hausas, indicating that ethnic differences were not insurmountable obstacles to coordinating slave mobilizations. Raymundo Nina Rodrigues suggests that the Nagôs, through a secret society known as *Ogboni,* took command of the movement, but his interpretation, lacking as it does any documentation, is improbable. What would an Ogboni (which is dedicated to earth worship and is peculiar to the Yoruba kingdom of Oyo, where it monitors the power of the *alafin,* or "king," of Oyo) be doing in Bahia? Also, how can one explain a Yoruba political structure in command of a predominantly Hausa revolt?[6]

Naturally, the reins on the slave population were tightened after this uprising. Colonial administrators adopted a series of measures to counter what they considered excessive liberality on the part of the masters. A magistrate in the Recôncavo town of Maragogipe took the following precautions: On 31 January, Judge Joaquim Ignácio da Costa ordered all slaves hired out and living away from their masters to return to their masters' dwellings within twenty-four hours; if they did not, they would be imprisoned and flogged. Owners of houses and inns renting rooms to slaves would be liable for a fine of six milréis (approximately 4.44 pounds sterling) for each illegal lodger. An earlier curfew was established for slaves without signed passes from their masters. All dances, with or without drums, during the day or at night, were expressly forbidden. The judge also asked the government for permission to shoot to kill any suspected slave resisting arrest.[7] These measures were typical of the count of Ponte's era. Fortunately for the slaves, his administration was coming to an end.

Slave Rebellion and Enlightened Slave Control

The iron hand of the count of Ponte was replaced by the lighter hand and more intelligent head of the count of Arcos, who governed Bahia from 1810 to 1818. His administration was conspicuous for its economic prosperity and the completion of important public works: the Public Garden (Passeio Público), the São João Theater, the Chamber of Commerce Building (Casa do Comércio), and the Public Library. Arcos was an enlightened despot. In contrast with his predecessor, he considered slave-owners to be excessively severe and niggardly. They punished their slaves too harshly, made them work like animals, fed them poorly, and deprived them of any leisure time. As far as he was concerned, these were the reasons for slave unrest in the region. In some of his letters the count showed that he (a man of the Enlightenment) actually believed that *slavery itself* caused rebellions. He refused to add state terror to seigniorial terror; on the contrary, he would act to attenuate seigniorial excess.

Arcos was not unmindful in matters of security, however. He had, after all, a professional military background. He was the one responsible for the restructuring and strengthening of Bahian forces, but his aim was to defend the Portuguese empire from external enemies and from nationalist rebellions that had shown signs of life in other Iberian possessions in the Americas. Of course, since he was the supreme officer of the law, his job included controlling black rebelliousness, but the weapon he chose to use was dissuasion rather than repression. He believed Africans should be permitted to practice their religions, play their music, and dance traditional dances, since the free expression of African traditions would exacerbate ethnic differences. To unite Africans, even by forcing white civilization on them through Christianity, would be dangerous. He preferred to place his bets on the old tactic of dividing and conquering. In addition, he argued, some worldly leisure and religious rituals would help slaves "enjoy themselves and forget their woes for a few hours." He seems to have believed that slavery was a necessary evil, but one that could be attenuated and made bearable for its victims.[8]

Nonetheless, like his predecessor, Arcos missed the mark. During his administration, at least three important revolts took place in Bahia. For several days at the beginning of 1814 a large number of slaves abandoned Salvador and converged at a nearby quilombo. On 28 February a force estimated at 250 attacked fishing marinas where they had allies. At a marina belonging to Manuel Ignácio da Cunha, a prominent figure among the Bahian economic elite, slaves killed the overseer and members of his family. They burned fishing nets, their instrument of work, then joined others coming from the quilombo and attacked other marinas and the village of Itapuã. They killed many people, including male and female slaves who refused to support them. Among the whites the merchant Luis Antônio dos Reis was killed in the presence of his wife, who was beaten but escaped with her life. The insurgents cried out for freedom and cheered blacks and their "king" while urging death for whites and mulattos. With this in mind, they marched off toward the Recôncavo, setting

FIG. 4. The count of Arcos, governor of Bahia, 1810–1818. Portrait courtesy of the Museu de Arte da Bahia.

fire to many houses (more than 150 in one account) as well as to plantations along the way. They never reached the heart of the cane fields, however.

On the bank of the Joanes River, near Santo Amaro de Ipitanga, they were halted by cavalry troops rapidly dispatched by the government. The slaves fought fiercely, shouting "Death to whites and mulattos," the latter constituting the backbone of Bahian regulars and its militia. Against the soldiers' bullets they used bows and arrows, hatchets and sickles, and a few rode horses. The battle lasted only an hour, and the rebels were defeated, losing fifty-eight men and killing only fourteen soldiers.

Four slaves were later sentenced to death, many were sentenced to public floggings, and twenty-three men, quite likely freedmen, were deported to the Portuguese port of Benguela, in southern Angola. In addition, over two dozen died of abuses while in prison. Arcos could be cruel when he thought he needed to be. Included among the victims were many who, according to one police report, appear to have committed suicide—by drowning in the river or by hanging. Other insurgents broke through the lines and appear to have gone on fighting beyond the Bahian frontier, in Alagoas, where in December 1815 they reputedly planned an uprising that never materialized. Others probably retreated into the quilombos in the thickets and hills surrounding the capital.

This uprising obviously shared some common traits with its predecessors. As in the plot of 1807, the 1814 rebels seem to have been carefully organized. Like those in 1809, they attacked a town and, when defeated, disappeared into the bush. Unfortunately the police reports are incomplete, but they still provide many paths toward understanding the organizational structure of the uprising. They mention, for example, that Nagôs as well as other ethnic groups joined forces apparently under the command of Muslim Hausas. The leader may have been someone known as João, reputed to be a *malomi,* or priest, in the words of the Police scribe. The word *malomi* means the same as *malām,* which is a Hausa term denoting the *mu'allim,* an Arabic word for a Muslim preacher. (In later years the Yoruba term *alufá* would prevail in Bahia.) This is the first bit of uncontroversial evidence of Muslim presence and organizational role in a Bahian slave rebellion. It is much better evidence than the amulets taken from the Hausa rebels in 1807.

Malomi João led the revolt from his base in a quilombo. His principal agent in Salvador was a slave known as Francisco Cidade, who, taking advantage of the relative freedom urban slaves enjoyed under the count of Arcos, maintained contacts with Africans throughout the Recôncavo and on the islands in the bay. He collected money and sent it and food to the quilombo regularly. On one of his trips to Itaparica Island, he is reputed to have conferred the title "Duke of the Island" upon someone known as David. This suggests that the rebels were trying to contrive their own power hierarchies using the European nomenclature that had become familiar to them for identifying individuals with political and social power. This is how African terms such as *malomi* got mixed together with Luso-

Brazilian terms such as *duque* (or *embaixador,* "ambassador," back in the 1807 slave conspiracy). A similar phenomenon occurred in postrevolutionary Haiti. There is good evidence suggesting that Brazilian slaves knew about Haiti and considered it an almost mythical touchstone of black statehood in the West. Luiz Mott has published an 1805 document maintaining that blacks in Rio de Janeiro wore necklaces bearing the image of Dessalines within a year of his declaring Saint Domingue's independence. These are signs of elasticity, adaptability, and the extended information networks that characterized, in war and in peace, slave cultures of the New World. Just like Duke David of Itaparica, others were probably named dignitaries in a new and clandestine power structure and were made local leaders in the rebellion to come.[9]

The name Francisco Cidade appears on the police blotter as the "president of his Nation's dances, its protector and agent." This is remarkable because such a description is more suited to a Sarkin Bori, the title of the male leader of the Hausa Bori possession cult, which is usually run by women. This is true even if one posits considerable sincretism in Hausa Islam. Perhaps Islam in Bahia, which was far more free from orthodox vigilance than in Africa, absorbed aspects of African rituals more readily. It may even have adopted the dances of the traditional ethnic religious. Or perhaps Cidade was the leader of pagan Hausas who in 1814 may have joined the Muslims against the Bahian slaveholders. One more possibility that should not be discarded is that he may have been in charge of the African dancers and musicians who took part in the yearly celebrations of black Catholic lay brotherhoods *(irmandades)*. These celebrations were a creative melange of the sacred and the profane in which fictive kings and queens were enthroned and surrounded by their nobles, which may have included the dukes. The kings and queens presided over celebrations that symbolically inverted the prevailing order. If this was the case, it would be an especially interesting alliance between Islam and Afro-Catholicism in 1814. The fact that there were Muslim members in one of Salvador's black brotherhoods dedicated to Our Lady of the Rosary has been mentioned by Pierre Verger.[10]

While some may still doubt that slaves of different religious persuasions joined forces, there is no doubt that Bahian slaveowners closed ranks and criticized the count of Arcos's policies. Salvador's merchants remonstrated that rebels had succeeded in joining forces across ethnic boundaries, which could have been their way of criticizing the governor's policy of promoting ethnic diversity by permitting African drum dances *(batuques)*. They also pointed out that the uprisings were growing more violent by the day and as proof cited the more than 150 houses burned and the more than fifty people who lost their lives at the rebels' hands. They argued that slaves were not to be "indulged," that "fear and severe punishment is the only way to make them behave." They also attacked the governor head-on, maintaining that he was lazy, indulgent, and useless. They denounced his order that even after the February uprising permitted slaves to gather during the day at the Graça and Barbalho meadows—neither Arcos's prohibition of slave gatherings in any other part of the city nor his prohibition of all gatherings after 6:00 P.M. carried any weight among Salvador's proprietors.[11]

Hausas attacked again in 1814, this time in Iguape, where Bahia's largest sugar plantations were located. On 23 March the magistrate in Maragogipe received a short and alarming message from Major João Francisco Chobi, the chief of the town's military detachment: "I communicate to Your Lordship that Iguape is in flames and under attack from blacks. For this reason I have given the necessary commands to my soldiers so as to curtail the expected consequences." The magistrate got more news from other sources.

The uprising appears to have begun between 4:00 P.M. and 5:00 P.M., midway through the workday in the cane fields. March was a month of intense toil—both harvest time and planting time. This was not a desperate uprising; it had an "aim," according to the magistrate. The slaves would gather at the Ponta Plantation, one of the region's largest, and from there they would take the town of Maragogipe. All roads leading to Maragogipe were occupied by regular troops and the militia. Three freed Hausas in regular contact with the slaves at the Ponta Plantation were arrested. Unfortunately, that is all we know about this uprising. Apparently, once the revolt was quelled, many slaves went back to their hideouts, following the pattern set in previous revolts.[12]

Arcos, as before, did not assign much importance to this episode. According to information he claimed to have, the rebels consisted of only "slaves from a few Iguape plantations." It followed that "to punish all slaves severely," as planters and local officials wanted, would be "brutally stupid" and prejudicial to local agriculture and commerce. Moreover, such repression would show slaves how much free people feared them, which in itself could be dangerous, in the subtle mind of the count. A few days earlier he had informed a military chief in Cachoeira that he could not "keep the militia in a state of alert on the basis of a fear deriving, perhaps, from planters' feelings of guilt for the offenses and abuses inflicted daily on their Slaves."[13] With thoughts like that, the count entered onto a collision course with the Recôncavo planters that would end in a conflagration following the last important uprising under his administration.

On 12 February 1816, after a religious celebration, slaves in the towns of Santo Amaro and São Francisco do Conde went on a rampage. They burned several plantations, including Cassarangongo and Quibaca. They attacked houses and people in Santo Amaro, killing several whites as well as slaves who refused to join the rebellion. The uprising, which seemed to have been a spontaneous extension of the celebration, lasted four days, spreading terror through the entire area. It was put down by militias and, remarkably, by loyal slaves under the command of militia colonel Jerônimo Fiúza Barreto, the owner of the Quibaca Plantation. Barreto's accomplishment later gained him the worthy title "Savior of the Recôncavo." At least thirty slaves were caught and sent to Salvador.[14]

A movement of such magnitude could scarcely have been entirely spontaneous. In addition to the cheap rum *(cachaça)*, the celebrants probably soaked up the words of some agitators who had planned the movement in advance. It also appears they had coordinated their movement with slaves in Salvador, or at least in the outskirts, leagues away from Santo Amaro and São Francisco. In a communiqué dated 11 February 1816, Judge Henrique Vilhena told the governor that a police corporal from Cabula, an area riddled with quilombos since the count of Ponte's administration, had sought him out, accompanied by a man who

> brought in tow a slave of his so that I could hear it from his own mouth. And as I listened, the aforementioned slave told me that when he passed a black on the road next to a field belonging to his master, the black asked him whether he had not also been invited and wanted to take part in the uprising planned for Monday, the twelfth, of the current month. The black had also said that the night before, there would be a big banquet, where they would get together, and for that event he was gathering a basket of mangoes.[15]

As the judge was ill, he could not follow up on the case and sent it on to the governor, who quite likely considered it another false alarm. The plot, whose description (its date, the banquet before the uprising) makes it seem very similar to the one in the Recôncavo, never came off—either in Salvador or in the surrounding area. Why not? I offer three hypotheses: (1) the plotters in Salvador may have set out for the Recôncavo, probably by boat, to take part in the uprising there; (2) there may have been an incredible coincidence of dates and features in the Cabula and Recôncavo revolts; and (3) the slaves in Cabula may not have been able to coordinate their uprising with the one in the Recôncavo. The third hypothesis is the most plausible.

The 1816 uprising was, up to that point, perhaps the most dangerous of all uprisings in the Recôncavo. For several days after the rebels' defeat, local landowners, both rich and poor, were in a state of panic. This state of affairs led to the formation of vigilante groups, who on several occasions beat and murdered blacks (both slave and free) suspected of rebelliousness or acting more brazen than normal. Besides taking violent and illegal measures, which ran counter to Arcos's directives, landowners in the Recôncavo banded together in search of more durable political solutions.

As far as the planters were concerned, the 1816 rebellion, preceded as it was by a religious celebration, undermined once and for all Arcos's argument that religious celebrations and rebellions were incompatible. The planters organized a packed meeting in São Francisco do Conde on 27 February to deal with the matter. During that assembly of notables, people suggested some drastic measures, such as the deportation of any free or freed black under suspicion and the hanging without trial of any rebel slave. However, measures such as these were not received sympathetically by the majority, because in addition to their being unacceptable to the governor, the execution of slaves would also be prejudicial to their owners, who knew full well that today's rebel slave, after a flogging, would be tomorrow's cane cutter. They decided instead to send a petition to the count proposing less drastic remedies. They proposed that no black, regardless of status, should be allowed to sit in the presence of a white. Since they felt the state was remiss, another item on their list obliged masters to administer 150 lashes to any slaves caught off their owner's property without written authorization from the master. To drive the lesson home, such a sentence would be executed in the presence of the slaves' families, in the event they had any. In addition to these measures, the plantation owners suggested that the government sponsor the immediate settlement in the Recôncavo of European families, one hundred to begin with, so as to diminish the demographic imbalance in an area where blacks vastly outnumbered whites.

Before their encounter with Arcos, the members of the planter class had never found themselves so at odds with the colonial administration in matters of slave control. The plantation owners, used to having the count of Ponte call them paternalistic, were now defending that leader's harsh legacy. At the meeting on 24 February, someone ventured that only with the removal of the governor would peace reign in the slave quarters, or rather, would it reign in the big houses. This opinion was heartily applauded by those present. But the lords of the Recôncavo were not prepared to undertake a coup d'état, notwithstanding the leadership provided by the military commander of Bahia, Brigadier Felisberto Caldeira Brant Pontes, the future marquis of Barbacena, who was also a large landowner whose slaves had revolted. The Ponta Plantation, where the rebels of 1814 had concentrated, belonged to him, as did the Santana Plantation in Ilhéus, in southern Bahia. The slaves at Santana also were not passive at all.

Brant Pontes became a tenacious adversary of Arcos's. He wrote to the court in Rio de Janeiro complaining that after so many rebellions, it was high time the governor acknowledged his deficient means of slave control and prohibited their festive and religious gatherings. The count seemed impermeable to all arguments. Arcos was incapable of "writing or pronouncing as much as a syllable against the slaves," wrote the brigadier, seeking ammunition for his argument in modern history and in ancient myth.

> Las Casas kneeling at the Throne of Spain begging for Royal mercy for the Indians, Wilberforce and others arguing in the English Parliament for the abolition of slavery, are, without doubt, benefactors of humanity. But those very words from the mouth of a Mexican Viceroy or a Jamaican Governor would bring about the murder of all Spaniards and Englishmen, and evoke Universal Wrath. This is, without exaggeration, our situation!
>
> In this place, blacks are the favorite sons of His Majesty's Representative. Their brazenness is, for that reason, hardly remarkable, nor are the whites' fright and confusion, finding themselves, as they do, between Scylla and Charybdis.

In July Brant Pontes went in person to Rio de Janeiro to protest in the name of the Bahian planter class. There he wrested an order from the royal government that would put the measures approved in the meeting at São Francisco do Conde into practice. On his return to Bahia, Arcos arrested him for insubordination but held him only a few days, explaining to the court that Commander Brant Pontes had attacked him verbally. The government in Rio backed Arcos and sent a warning to the brigadier expressing a desire to see them reconciled with one another in the better service of their king. Quite soon, in 1817, the two adversaries would be united in putting down a revolt of free men against Portuguese colonialism. It originated in Pernambuco but spread to other parts of the northeast. As far as Arcos was concerned, this, and not slave riots, was a truly dangerous insurrection. His greatest obligation was not to slavery and the interests of slaveowners but to the Portuguese colonial state and to his king.[16]

The Bahian gentry, let it be said, were often inimical both to slaves and to the king. Many probably sympathized with the Pernambucans' cause but held back in view of Arcos's efficient and harsh retaliation. Both out of fear and owing to Arcos's threats, landowners in Bahia were obliged to finance a good part of the count's campaign against the Pernambucan rebels. Some suspect, perhaps groundlessly, that the governor, himself in personal financial difficulties, may have accepted a bribe or two in exchange for overlooking the rebellious inclinations of certain rich Bahian subjects. Be that as it may, at the end of his administration, Arcos seemed at peace with the planters, who bade him farewell with a gala dinner dance at the Casa do Comércio, which he had built.

Their reconciliation could have been aided by the fact that the 1816 revolt was the last important one under Arcos. While quilombos kept springing up all over Bahia, this was, in fact, the last slave rebellion reported before the Luso-Bahian conflict of 1822–23.

Slave Rebels and the War of Independence

During the war of independence, at least three revolts took place on Bahian territory. In May 1822, before the actual war, the 280 slaves on the Boa Vista Plantation on Itaparica Island refused to accept the new overseer appointed by their master, José Ignácio Acciavoli Brandão e Vasconcelos, a powerful merchant. Their master overruled their protest, and four days later the overseer was dead and the slaves had declared war. The military commander of Salvador, the Portuguese Brigadier Ignácio Madeira de Melo, whose authority was being contested locally and who was afraid to lose more ground in Salvador, refused to send troops to quell the movement. But the local civilian militia took charge: 32 rebels were killed and 80 were wounded, according to an officer in the French navy stationed in Bahia. He wrote: "You have here the beginnings of a slave war, with its incalculable results."[17]

The planter Dona Maria Bárbara Garcez, a friend of Acciavoli's, noted only twenty-five deaths among the slaves and eighteen prisoners, but she did count the death of the plantation administrator among the casualties on the master's side. It is also interesting to note that, accustomed as she was to dealing with slaves, Dona Maria did not agree with the French officer, although a Portuguese officer by the name of Gouveia Osório did. She criticized Gouveia Osório in a letter to her husband: "And that 'nobody' Osório wants to make something big out of this, saying: 'Here it comes!' No matter how often we tell him that 'things like this happen all the time,' he wants to make the most of it." These foreigners feared that the animosity between white Brazilians and the Portuguese would make space for a massive insurrection along the lines of the Haitian model, and they believed that the revolt on the Boa Vista Plantation was a dress rehearsal. In March, Madeira de Melo himself had a proclamation printed and circulated. He accused "some enemies of Order" of spreading "heinous ideas of insurrection" among the slaves. Among those ideas was the notion that the king had already freed them but the masters had refused to go along. (Similar rumors had preceded a large insurrection in Jamaica in 1831.) Word of disorderly conduct and plots among the slaves, which, according to Madeira would lead to a new Saint Domingue, caused him to instruct local authorities to investigate and suppress all instigators. Still the Itaparica incident did not seem to have had any repercussions beyond the island's slave community. It was a local incident, with specific motives and a limited objective. Dona Bárbara was right.[18]

The same cannot be said about a rebellion in São Mateus, during

September, about which very little is known, unfortunately. In São Mateus, according to a police report, African-born freedmen and slaves "rose up against whites and *mestiços*." On many occasions slaves and freed Africans united against the native-born, but at São Mateus *crioulos* were spared, and this was unusual. The movement was squelched, however, and two Africans were arrested, one of whom the other rebels called their king.[19]

As tensions grew, Brazilians began to accuse the Portuguese of inciting the slaves to revolt. Several such accusations were received by the provisional government in Bahia, which was headquartered outside Salvador. To counter this, at the end of November 1822 the provisional government ordered severe measures of control over the region's slaves: all slave get-togethers, regardless of purpose, were prohibited, and this included religious and secular celebrations with drum beats in the background. Slave-owners were admonished to forbid slaves from keeping any firearm or weapon, as well as implements capable of cutting—sickles, machetes, or knives—in their quarters. Masters should make sure slaves did not leave their property without written permission nor go anywhere bearing arms, even with written permission. Slaves who disobeyed the first measure would be sent to their masters for punishment; in the second case they would be taken to town and given 150 lashes, then sent back. The government only allowed slaves driving carts and pack animals and slaves carrying foodstuffs to fairs to go abroad without written permission. Finally, if found within town limits, all *black* slaves (but no mulattos) would be arrested if they were found out-of-doors after 9:00 P.M. without written authorization from their master. They would receive 50 lashes or, in the event they were armed, 200.[20]

The Bahian leaders apparently knew what they were doing, since on the following 19 December, in the middle of the war, a group of nearly two hundred slaves attacked Brazilian troops stationed close to Salvador, in Mata Escura and Saboeiro. The rebels appear to have been influenced by Portuguese occupying the capital. In the words of Amaral, there was "fierce combat" in which Brazilian troops suffered many losses before pushing back the attackers. Many slaves were taken prisoner, and the French commander of the Brazilian troops, General Pedro Labatut, ordered summary execution for fifty-two of them and floggings for the rest. This was the most brutal punishment for Bahian slaves to date, and the bloody lesson did not go unnoticed. Most slaves realized that it was not a good idea to rebel when the adversary was so well armed and not particularly interested in sparing slave property but rather in winning a war at any cost. It is no coincidence that the massacre was the work of a foreign general with no roots in Bahian society.[21]

Slave Rebellions in Independent Bahia

After the war, unrest in the slave quarters became even greater than before. In 1824 on Felisberto Caldeira's Santana Plantation, in Ilhéus, slaves threw down their tools and formed a quilombo, which lasted until 1828, right on Caldeira's property. The slaves on that plantation, who were predominantly native-born, appear to have had a long tradition of organized struggle. Around the year 1780 they stopped working and wrote out a list of conditions under which they would go back to work. Nonetheless, they ended up victims of a treacherous armed ambush planned by their master, who pretended to accept peace negotiations.

On 25 August 1826, two years after the last uprising in Santana, a rebellion broke out in the Cachoeira district, but very little is known about it. Once again the leader declared himself "King of the Blacks," and his consort was the "Queen." The movement was immediately put down in a battle in which the queen fought to the death, and the king only surrendered after being wounded several times. Fearing reprisals from the capital, Bahian authorities censured the news of this rebellion. A chronicler of the times, an ex-soldier, claims he saw the leader being brought into Salvador in chains, but still wearing a crown decorated with ribbons and a cape of green duvetyn decorated with gilded hash marks, probably symbolic of his authority. They also confiscated a red flag among the rebels' objects. Perhaps it should be mentioned that red is a color symbol of orisha Shango, god of thunder and lightning, the ancestral king of Oyo, the powerful Yoruba kingdom.[22]

That year one of the many African enclaves in the outskirts of Salvador, the Urubu ("Vulture") Quilombo, revolted. The uprising was set off by runaway slaves who gathered first in Cajazeiras, in the Pirajá district. Their first victims were members of a farm family who, on the night of 16 December, happened upon some blacks transporting stolen meat and manioc flour to their hideout. In fear of being reported, they attacked these witnesses, including a mulatto girl between the ages of seven and eight named Brígida. She was seriously wounded. They then attacked several houses in the area and set out for Urubu, in the unvanquished district of Cabula. This revolt began ahead of schedule as others had.

On the morning of the seventeenth, some slave hunters tried unsuccessfully to take Urubu. Three of them died in the process, and their bodies were mutilated beyond recognition. One of the dead was an exslave, a cabra. Three other slave hunters were seriously wounded, two of them native-born blacks. Set in flight, these slave hunters came upon a scouting party of twelve police soldiers sent from Salvador to control the situation. A squad of twenty-five militiamen from Pirajá joined this patrol, and together they attacked the quilombo.

FIG. 5. Plantation slave hut (idealized). Slave life was rarely this peaceful. Drawing by John Moritz Rugendas, reprinted from his *Malerische reise in Brasilien* (Paris: Engelmann & Cie, 1835).

According to the deposition of one of the soldiers, the rebels—nearly fifty men and "also a few women"—fought back fiercely, using knives, machetes, swords, lances, razors, sickles, and small- and large-bore shotguns. Their war cry "Death to Whites! Long live Blacks!" rang throughout Urubu on that day. But after a brief encounter the legal forces triumphed, killing three men and one woman and taking the rest prisoner. Most of the rebels fled into the bush, however. That same afternoon, two hundred regular army troops arrived. They had been sent by the provincial president, who, because of sensational reports which this time reached Salvador, was under the impression that the revolt was more serious than it was. The troops arrived too late to fight. At an African religious gathering place *(candomblé)* they arrested an African with a deep wound in his throat and wearing long underwear. They dressed him in African ritual garb so as to mock the sacred vestments cult members wore during their ceremonies. These robes indicated divine presence among the faithful. The soldiers also reported finding the bodies of five rebels who "had obviously slit each other's throats"—doubtlessly, a unique method of collective suicide. Once again, it seems, soldiers, confident as they were of impunity, took the law into their own hands.

At Urubu they captured an extraordinary woman by the name of Zeferina. She had fought back with only a bow and some arrows. During the struggle she was a real leader, rallying the warriors, keeping them on the line. The provincial president, in an involuntary burst of praise, referred to her as "queen." Zeferina later declared that on Christmas Eve the insurgents expected many slaves to arrive from Salvador. On that date they planned to invade the capital, kill the whites, and gain their freedom. She also revealed that the majority at Urubu, both slaves and freed, were Nagôs. If that is true, the candomblé in the thickets of Urubu could have been Yoruba. According to the testimony of one sergeant, "dance paraphernalia used by blacks" were found inside three huts. Among the confiscated objects were shells, rattles, drums, "a cardboard crown decorated with sea shells" (which was fitted onto the wounded man's head), statues of "cows painted red, a red hat with three feathers," and so on. The cloths, torsos, and wands they found were predominately red, which suggests a candomblé dedicated to Shango. It could also suggest Yansan, his wife, a goddess with similar powers. But the feathers in the hat suggest Oshossi, god of hunting.

It seems beyond dispute that Urubu was one of those places on the outskirts of the city where quilombos and candomblés melded. Its very name could derive from African temples, since around these temples vultures abounded, attracted as they were by the remains of animals sacrificed to African gods and to ancestors. The habits of those birds are even part of Yoruba mythology: they believe vultures carry sacrificial offerings to their proper destination. In the lines of a divining ritual, the diviner god Ifá says:

> Vulture, come and eat sacrifice
> So that sacrifice may be acceptable to the gods.
> One does not always realize that without vultures,
> One cannot perform a sacrifice.[23]

Urubu Quilombo was quite likely a place with tremendous religious significance for the Africans in Bahia.

An interesting detail on the Urubu candomblé is that it belonged to a mulatto named Antônio, which seems to be one of those rare cases of Afro-Bahian cooperation in a slave revolt. Elsewhere, I have discussed candomblés' role in promoting interethnic alliances, including alliances between Africans and Afro-Bahians and even white Bahians. On the other hand, it could be that the mulatto was merely the unknowing pawn of the Nagô rebels; he may have been just the owner of the house they used as a temple. The existing "proof" about the relationship between Antônio, the candomblé, and the revolt appear in the testimony of José Joaquim de Souza, a sergeant in the Pirajá militia regiment:

> And asking if anyone knew who had given help or counsel to that meeting of armed blacks, he said he does not know who was present at that gathering, and he only knows through having seen it that there was a house known to be a candomblé. The house's owner was Antônio So-and-so, who did deal with the aforementioned blacks, which was proven by our finding there several articles of clothing drenched in blood and belonging to blacks.[24]

That the wounded rebels took refuge there does not prove Antônio's involvement in the rebellion, nor that of the candomblé. But even if the candomblé did not directly figure into the organization of the revolt, slaves and freed people who went there probably did, and they probably felt that they were protected by the Yoruba gods, or orishas. Be that as it may, the alleged priest, Antônio, was charged by the Bahian authorities. He and Zeferina seem to have been the only ones to receive regular sentences: they were both sentenced to prison with hard labor. Of the other ten accused (six slaves and four freedmen), two died in prison and some were returned to their masters, and about others nothing is known. Of the freedmen, Joaquim Duarte has been positively identified.

Duarte was a Hausa who in 1826 was arrested while selling "groceries." In an appeal he had someone write for him, he let it be known that in addition to Nagôs, Hausas were involved in the uprising. In his appeal he maintained that "he could not be implicated along with the schemers and insurgents because he was a freedman who lived among whites, whom he likes, and with whom he does business, peacefully buying and selling, with no conspiring with his people, since he has always refused to consort with them." Duarte was obviously trying to save his neck with this declaration of loyalty, and to this end he also summoned white neighbors, including his landlord, Antônio de Brito Aragão e Vasconcelos, a man totally above suspicion, a lawyer graduated from the University of Coimbra. He and two other residents of Tijolo Street told the police that their African neighbor was, as he said, gentle, law-abiding, peaceful, and friendly to whites. He never gathered his compatriots or other Africans in his house. There is no information on whether Duarte was able to convince the police of his innocence.[25]

After the Urubu revolt the provincial president, Manoel Ignácio da Cunha Menezes, whose slaves in Itapuã had revolted in 1814, complained to the imperial government that Salvador's police force of two hundred men was not sufficient to withstand African rebels, whose numbers were growing. Menezes begged the national leaders to support his plan to double the police force and create an additional force of sixty cavalry men and one hundred foot soldiers. The response to those appeals was an evasive suggestion to forward the plan to the minister of war, who on a daily basis bombarded Bahian rulers with requests for local recruits to serve in southern Brazil, where the emperor was undertaking an unpopular campaign to annex Uruguay. The campaign was led by the same Felisberto Caldeira who had protested Arcos's slave control policy. Bahia's military unpreparedness became a recurrent theme among the upper echelons every time the matter of slave insurgency loomed on their agendas. In addition to their small number, Bahian troops were poorly armed, poorly clothed, poorly fed, and undisciplined, and if all this were not enough, they, too, were given to insubordination and revolt.[26]

And the rebellions continued. Between 1827 and 1831 waves of minor uprisings upset the tenuous social balance in Bahia. With the exception of the urban unrest of 1830, disturbances occurred outside the city. In 1827 there were at least three revolts: one in Cachoeira on 22 March, one in São Francisco do Conde in April, and another in Abrantes, which seems to have been put down in September. The last one has been described as a series of lightning raids and robberies perpetrated by residents of quilombos. Nothing more is known about it. The one in São Francisco was extremely serious and involved slaves from ten plantations—Jacu, Canabrava, Boa Sorte, Retiro, Caju, Paciência, Água Boa, Pimentel, Felipe, and Pandalunga. It was quickly subdued, but no details, either of the rebellion or of its defeat, are known.[27] Concerning the revolt in Cachoeira, there are more details, which come from the local magistrate's and the Cachoeira city council's correspondence with the provincial president, but even this does not provide a complete picture.

Between 8:00 P.M. and 9:00 P.M. on 22 March, slaves rioted on Vitória Plantation, located just six kilometers below the town of Cachoeira on the banks of the Paraguaçu River. This property belonged to an extremely wealthy merchant and shipowner, Pedro Rodrigues Bandeira, who lived in Salvador. Founded in 1812, during the upswing of the sugar economy, Vitória was a tremendous plantation, with a water-powered mill, a two-story mansion, and hundreds of slaves squeezed into two small quarters *(senzalas)*. The rebels killed the overseer and one of his brothers, indicating, perhaps, their reaction to the tyranny of the whip. The uprising ended there, but soon news came that slaves on three other neighboring plantations also belonging to Bandeira (Buraco, Moinho, and Conceição) had colluded with the slaves of Vitória for a massive revolt. "The great uproar that was being made," wrote the frightened Cachoeira councilmen, "indicated it to be a general insurrection involving all four plantations belonging to said proprietor, because they are close together." It was a false alarm. When the few cavalry and militia men the magistrate had been at pains to recruit arrived, everything was calm. The officer in charge was

FIG. 6. Pedro Rodrigues Bandeira, the owner of Engenho Victória and hundreds of slaves in the Cachoeira district and elsewhere, ca. 1835. Portrait courtesy of the Santa Casa de Misericórdia da Bahia.

also put at ease: "Luckily the rioters only wanted to kill the overseer and his brother, and once that was accomplished, they returned to their quarters. So when the troops arrived and the attack was made, almost all the rioters were caught."[28]

A report by the French consul in Bahia, Jacques Guinebaud, offers additional and precious information concerning this uprising. He maintained that there were some three hundred slaves on the plantation but that only forty participated in the plot against the overseer, who, again according to Guinebaud, was killed because he was suspected of being a sorcerer and for having cast a spell on and killed the master's wife.

If this report can be believed, the slaves seem to have concocted a creative justification for their uprising that also reflected blacks' magical thinking. Sorcery was an important element in African social and power structures. In Africa people did not fall sick, suffer misfortune, or die merely at the mercy of ordinary people or of the gods. They could be hexed, and there were specialists to cast spells and to cure them. Often the same person performed both roles. In the African slave diaspora, both in the city and in the countryside, the sorcerer was feared and respected by slaves and quite often by their masters. The black sorcerer aimed his magic primarily at the great white wizard believed responsible for slaves' tragic status or at the designs they believed these white sorcerers had.

Many slaves crossed the Atlantic believing that terrible men were waiting at their destination, waiting to devour their bodies and possess their souls. In 1823 a group of Makwas on their way to Bahia from Mozambique mutinied in the mid-Atlantic because, according to one testimony, "if they didn't, whites would eat them once they got there." Since the overseer of the Vitória Plantation in 1827 was the agent who disciplined and punished slaves, he was the ideal character to assume the role of witch, since one of the definitions of a witch is malefactor of the community.[29]

Arguing as they did that the evil power of their overseer had struck down their master's wife, Bandeira's slaves cleverly placed themselves under their master's protection, linking their belief in witchcraft to paternalistic seigniorial ideology. They had not risen up against their master, but against one of his treacherous and disloyal subordinates. The slaves rose up in self-defense and to defend their master against an agent menacing both the big house and the slave quarters. The consul's report, however, needs to be amended. The sorcerer/overseer could have had no hand in Bandeira's wife's death, because Bandeira never married. He died a bachelor in 1835. Perhaps the victim of the overseer's spell was a woman married to some white man on the plantation, possibly an administrator; or perhaps Bandeira's sister, Maria, who according to a census made two years before the uprising was living on the neighboring Buraco Plantation.[30]

In spite of the limited nature of the uprising, punishment was prescribed so as to avoid greater evils. Around thirty slaves were arrested and publicly flogged "to serve as an example for other slaves who for some time had been raising suspicion among whites," the magistrate explained. The quick dénouement did not stop police and political authorities from bemoaning Cachoeira's weak defenses. Even though it was the largest town in the Recôncavo, its two regiments of civilian militia and its one cavalry regiment had among them only fifty firearms to use in such emergencies. As a stopgap measure private citizens and local hardware store owners had lent them arms. In the (possibly) overstated opinion of those men, Cachoeira could be easily taken by a band of one hundred determined slaves.[31]

In the following year, 1828, there were more rebellions in Cachoeira, on 17 and 21 April, but almost nothing is known about them. In June the slaves on the Santana Plantation, in southern Bahia, were finally defeated after four years in the bush. The most serious revolt of 1828, which took place in the vicinity of Salvador, was almost a reenactment of the 1814 rebellion. On 12 March in Itapuã, slaves from the city and neighboring plantations attacked and burned fishing marinas belonging to Francisco Lourenço Herculano and Manoel Ignácio da Cunha Menezes. Cunha Menezes's interests had suffered from other slave revolts. While some new slaves belonging to Herculano joined the rebellion, Cunha Menezes' more acculturated *(ladino)* slaves balked. From Itapuã the insurgents headed toward Pirajá, burning cane fields and sacking houses on their way. But before reaching Pirajá, in Engomadeira they were met by patrols sent out by the government. A bloody battle followed in which the rebels did not beat the soldiers only because the latter received reinforcements from militia troops. The uprising was subdued after twenty rebels were killed and eight privates were wounded.

According to all indications, only four slaves were captured; the rest, numbering more than one hundred, must have escaped into the bush and joined the maroon communities. During the previous year the French consul had written to his government: "There are still runaway blacks living in the vicinity of the city. Some of them grow crops, others live by stealing. It is very hard to catch them in Brazil's beautiful virgin forests, which they know so well and which, for ordinary soldiers, are impenetrable." Perhaps because of their prisoners' youth, the authorities were fairly lenient to those caught in the uprising. Only one of them, a Nagô slave by the name of Joaquim, was punished with 150 lashes. Meanwhile, José Pedro de Souza Alcamin, in spite of vouching for his slave Teófilo, asked the chief of police to have Teófilo punished with "150 lashes so as to set an example for the other slaves." Alcamin attended to the interests of his class, but not all slaveowners acted in that fashion.[32]

In September of the same year a revolt exploded in Iguape, in the heart of the cane-growing region. A group of slaves revolted on the Engenho Novo plantation, which belonged to the powerful Colonel Rodrigo Antônio Falcão. After burning down all the slave quarters, they attacked and sacked the big house. The nearly forty attackers destroyed furniture and other items and then searched for the mistress, who had managed to escape with the aid of one of her domestic slaves. Two mulatto slave children, aged six and seven, sleeping in one of the house's rooms were not as lucky: one was killed during the attack, and the other died later from wounds inflicted by the insurgents. After the big house, the Engenho Novo rebels sacked the house of Father Francisco Borja Santos, the plantation chaplain and a cane grower as well. Slaves from other plantations rose up, and together with Falcão's slaves or acting on their own (sources do not agree), they attacked the Acutinga, Campina, and Cruz plantations. They expected support on each plantation they attacked, but when they encountered resistance, they killed an old carpenter and an old blacksmith working on Acutinga; at Campina they killed the overseer and three slaves; and at Cruz they killed four freed Africans and more slaves. Native-born and African slaves refusing to take part in the movement were attacked and wounded on several other plantations.

Only after considerable mayhem were the free people of the region able to organize and counterattack. They wounded some rebels, killed others, captured some, and set the rest to flight. More than twenty rebels died. Those who survived regrouped in a cane field on Engenho Novo, apparently to counterattack, but troops soon arrived from Cachoeira and sent them running into the bush, catching only four more rebels. To avoid other uprisings, soldiers were billeted on the local plantations.

Unfortunately, today no one knows the exact reason for this uprising, although the existing information suggests that the slaves of Engenho Novo wanted to avenge abuses the mistress had inflicted on them. The burning of their own quarters suggests that they were also protesting their living conditions and that they had no intention of going on as slaves. The fact that slaves from more than one plantation may have participated in the uprising indicates that whatever the reasons were, they were not restricted to the slaves at Engenho Novo and their differences with their mistress. The evidence points toward the plan's being of ample scope. It seems to have failed because it did not get sufficient adherents to assure, if not victory, at least a major blow to Iguape's slave economy. At the heart of the matter is the familiar problem of schisms between the many native-born slaves and the Africans on Engenho Novo. Even Africans were divided: rebels comprised mainly recently arrived slaves. They were so new that people living on the plantation did not know their Christian names, which made the authorities' task even harder as they tried to identify the rebels.

More details on the revolt could have appeared in the police investigation, but it was hobbled by Colonel Falcão, who would not permit police officers or soldiers to arrest his slaves. Such a stance made the owner of Engenho da Praia, Judge Manuel Ignácio de Lima, protest to interim President Manoel Ignácio da Cunha Menezes, the victim of the March uprising in Itapuã. Other slaves belonging to other masters were accused of participating in the rebellion and were arrested. But in the face of Falcão's refusal to hand over his slaves, the other slaveowners protested, which created more dissension, when they needed unity. Most slaveowners wanted to avoid the additional economic setbacks the punishment of their slaves would cause them. They had been set back enough by the revolts. For that reason and because witnesses maintained they did not know who else was involved, only two slaves, Colonel Falcão's Florentino and Father Borja Santos's José, were arraigned. To avoid more losses and at the same time to protect their lives, planters supported the establishment of a preventive police structure in the Recôncavo to stop uprisings before they began. They needed more troops and well-armed soldiers and militiamen, because once again Cachoeira's police authorities were obliged to borrow weapons from local shopkeepers and distribute them among civilians, court employees, and orderlies gathered at the Town Council to go on their beats and protect the village from a surprise attack by the Iguape rebels.[33]

But for the time being the government in Salvador could do no more than send the Recôncavo more ammunition. There were not enough men to defend Salvador, since most recruits were being sent to Uruguay. According to Consul Guinebaud, the army's presence in the Bahian capital in March 1828 had been reduced to the Minas Gerais battalion, whose three hundred soldiers had been provisionally headquartered there. Provincial authorities could only instruct local authorities to keep careful watch over slaves. In the middle of April interim President Dom Nuno Eugênio recommended that the provincial commander of the army order troops headquartered in Santo Amaro use cavalry patrols to intensify their highway vigilance. He wanted to cut off communication among slaves on different plantations. All those off their plantations without signed permission from their masters were to be arrested. Plans like this one were only partially successful. They did not stop another revolt in the Santo Amaro district.[34]

After days of rumors, at 11:00 P.M. on 30 November, slaves on the Engenho do Tanque killed their chief overseer and several native-born slaves, after which they set off to attack the big house. The rebels beat the overseer's wife, but she managed to escape along with the plantation mistress, since loyal slaves escorted them to the neighboring Santa Ana Plantation. The insurrectionists burned some buildings on the plantation, but a downpour kept the fire from spreading. A magistrate in Santo Amaro marshaled troops and dispatched them to Santa Ana, where they met resistance that ended with some rebels' death and the wounding of one soldier by a stray bullet. This magistrate also ended his report of the repression complaining of the lack of men, arms, and ammunition "so as to defend Plantations, property, and even the town, which was threatened by an invasion of desperate, enslaved barbarians who have friends and relatives inside our very houses." These words show that masters feared an alliance between domestic and plantation slaves.[35]

After this uprising, the president, viscount of Camamu, under pressure from local authorities and planters in the Recôncavo, elaborated a plan of military assistance for the region. Dated 10 December, this plan, which was carefully thought out and argued over, aimed to combat both rebellious slaves and the highway robbers infesting the area. According to Camamu, "The plan, besides assigning over seven hundred effectively armed men to diverse detachments stationed close to one another for their mutual protection, as well as that of their families and property, also has the advantage of . . . purging the roads of thieves and scoundrels."[36] At a time when Bahians were unhappy with the national government, Camamu, as the emperor's faithful subject, argued that his plan would "let the landowners and residents know the government is concerned with their safety." Proof of Camamu's influence in the capital is the fact that his measures were endorsed at the ministry of justice on 20 March 1829.[37]

Planters throughout the Recôncavo applauded the president's initiative and asked that the plan be put into practice immediately, according to the law promulgated for that purpose. They also offered to contribute to the cost of its execution. In a manifesto to Camamu, they wrote:

> The detachments . . . even though they might not be sufficient to prevent a slave insurrection on their own, since there have been, recently, many such revolts, are sufficient to make slaves behave, especially since these detachments are on the alert and ready to intervene should there be a revolt. . . . On the other hand, since it is not the intent of the undersigned to burden the Treasury with the entire weight of such an expenditure, we shall attempt to provide funds to bear part of the expense.[38]

The signatures on that document included those of such local giants as Barons Itapororocas, Jaguaripe, Rio de Contas, and Maragogipe as well as those of Colonel Rodrigo Antônio Falcão, Antônio Calmon Du Pin e Almeida, Francisco Vicente Vianna, and Pedro Rodrigues Bandeira. Some of these men had had the peace and prosperity of their plantations shaken by slave uprisings.

In spite of a greater military presence, slaves continued to rebel. Even the sugar planters acknowledged that African unrest could not be completely eliminated. The president also agreed that troop reinforcements would not do away with insurrection. But it was necessary "to do all they could so that similar uprisings would never be more than partial and would be easily put down when and where they began."[39] The Bahian ruling class was not stupid, and it never nurtured the illusion of being able to live in peace with its slaves. Its goal was merely to keep rebellions within acceptable limits and to avoid at all costs a slave revolt like the one in Haiti.

A fate similar to Haiti's would be avoided in Bahia, but the fear of an overwhelming insurrection was kept alive by fragmentary rebellions, which became daily bread in the province, often in the form of nagging hearsay. On 1 January 1829, for example, a justice of the peace in Itaparica arrested a man named Silvestre for spreading false rumors of slave uprisings. Still, just to be on the safe side, that magistrate intensified patrols within his district. Later that year, on 16 October, someone looking across the Bay of All Saints from Itaparica would have seen a large fire. It was a real slave revolt in Cotegipe, on three plantations belonging to militia Colonel José Maria de Pina e Mello. It was only six leagues from Salvador. The rebels killed three people, and as in other cases, fire consumed one of the plantations before the local militia and armed civilians stopped the rebels. It is quite likely that in November of the same year there was one more revolt in the countryside, but the exact location is still unknown.[40]

In 1830 the scene shifted from the countryside to the city of Salvador. Early in the morning of 10 April, nearly twenty Africans assaulted three hardware stores on Taboão Hill Street, which linked the business district in the lower city to Pelourinho Square in the upper city. The shopkeepers fought back, but the attackers got away with over fifteen swords and *parnaíbas* (long knives imported from Germany and used extensively on the African coast and in Bahia). They immediately proceeded to the nearby slave market, owned and operated by Wenceslau Miguel de Almeida. There they freed recently arrived Africans waiting to be sold. The rebel group had swollen to over one hundred, although there is news that eighteen newly imported blacks were "eliminated" for refusing to join their liberators, which was, as we have seen, common in Bahian revolts.

After they left the slave warehouse, the Africans attacked a police station in the neighborhood and killed one soldier. The police fought back, and finally the arrival of reinforcements trapped the insurgents between two lines of fire. From a technical point of view, bullets against blades was an uneven fight. The Africans were dispersed, hunted down, and lynched by the same soldiers and the same urban crowds that so frequently rioted themselves. More than fifty were beaten to death, and others were wounded. These losses have only been surpassed by those in the 1835 rebellion.[41]

The 1830 rebellion was the first slave revolt to occur in the heart of Salvador and has never been given its proper place in Brazilian history. Its instigators may have concluded that the only way to succeed was to attack white power at its center. Up to then most attempts at attacking the city had come from without, with the exception of the 1807 plot, which after all never materialized. This time a vanguard of audacious, seasoned Africans mobilized newly arrived, inexperienced blacks in order to bring other slaves in Salvador into a fight already in progress. The stage was rapidly set, but it was just as rapidly cleared.

The 1830 massacre demonstrated to the rebels that an urban revolt could have sad consequences. In the countryside and in Salvador's outskirts slaves had the uninhabited bush to flee into. The city was made of stately, two- and three-story houses *(sobrados)* separated by narrow streets teeming with enemies. The white man's social and political center had quite a capacity to fight back. No matter how paralyzed Bahians may have been by the daring surprise attack from Africans within the city, they also showed themselves to be surprisingly quick and ready for a counterattack. They were also cruel. Future conspirators would have much to think about and plan before they attempted another adventure of that type.

With the 1830 rebellion squelched, the government tightened its hold on the city. The recently empowered provincial president, Luís Paulo de Araújo, initiated a set of measures to address what he considered "the most important matter in the province." He criticized owners of rebellious slaves for their relaxed attitude concerning law and order. He maintained that "because of this, slaves do not think twice when they want to start more trouble." With a fanfare of drum rolls, as was the custom, he had an edict proclaimed in the streets of the city. All slaves were to be off the streets by the 9:00 P.M. curfew. He also instructed the criminal magistrate to keep all slaves accused of participating in revolts in prison. Even those found innocent in a court of law could only get out of jail if someone from outside the province purchased them, which was not likely owing to Bahian slaves' rebellious reputation. Urban slaves' lives became more difficult. Patrols investigated any suspicious action. In early March at least eleven slaves of four different masters were arrested. One of the masters objected, saying that his slaves, "besides being peaceful, are not involved in the recent unrest stirred up by others." The government had them released, but only after confirming that there was no evidence against them.[42]

Also, outside Salvador, the viscount of Camamu's plan seemed to be working, notwithstanding occasional lapses. In September 1830 a justice of the peace in Pirajá Parish complained that of the six men posted at the outskirts of Salvador, on a road leading to the Recôncavo, four were often seen relaxing in the city. According to the magistrate, the soldiers were in charge of a key position: "It is a place insurgent blacks pass when they leave the city on their way to kill people and burn houses. And more than once many have been the victims of their wrath." A year later the Pirajá detachment was disbanded for lack of funds in the public coffers. Deep in the Recôncavo, in the heart of plantation territory, soldiers were often taken away for activities having nothing to do with slave control. Or they lingered in the towns, leaving the plantations unprotected. In the beginning of 1831, and only after a great effort, the justice of the peace in São Tiago Parish was able to place twenty men on Engenho Desterro, as Camamu's plan had called for. However, these men's weapons consisted solely of some vines to use as rope, which made them the laughingstock of both the local free inhabitants and the slaves. In view of this and other problems, the magistrate perceived "in said slaves a tendency to revolt." He cited an incident in which a slave of Engenho da Ponta used force to stop a man from punishing a slave from the Engenho Novo Santa Catarina. The slave walked off with the other right before the eyes of a detachment of soldiers, who did nothing because they were afraid of what the other slaves present might do to them.[43]

One of the few regiments that functioned according to plan was the one commanded by Colonel Rodrigo Falcão, who systematically refused to use it for any activity other than slave control. The regiment stayed on his plantation and was well-fed and disciplined. On one occasion, in October 1831, Falcão refused to use his troops against the mulatto Felizardo Pereira, one of the leaders of a motley group of bandits and millenarians. Pereira called himself an "Ambassador who, like Charlemagne, was a holy man," according to a police report. If it were up to Colonel Falcão, the millennium would get to the Recôncavo before any slave revolt did.[44]

The slave rebels did in fact calm down. Fear of rebellions burnt brightly, however. The province resonated with rumors of uprisings, which became clamorous during the year-end celebrations. In late November 1831 the news in Itaparica was that slaves from several plantations were planning to rise. The administrator of one of the plantations stopped a slave he believed to be one of the ringleaders, but another slave being questioned attacked the administrator with a sickle, wounding him but ultimately losing the fight. He was taken off, and everything calmed down. The justice of the peace meanwhile asked the president to send another detachment to guard the island's many plantations, since he could only count on a few militiamen scattered over the island on farms and villages.[45]

In December of the same year rumors reached the mainland, and in Salvador the president instructed all justices of the peace to be on the alert. News of an imminent revolt spread through the city and into the outskirts. But nothing happened. The French consul noted that rumors had been in the air for two months but became so intense around Christmas that the police were alarmed. "Many patrols," he wrote, "combed the city after sunset, interrogating all the blacks they could find and arresting those who looked suspicious." The plotters, supposedly led by freed slaves, were purportedly planning to burn down the Customs House on Christmas Eve, while slaves still at home would kill their masters and then attack the worshipers attending Mass in the various churches. The bishop reacted and ordered (in vain) parish priests to hold their masses all at the same time so that isolated groups of churchgoers would not be caught unaware. Arrests continued after Christmas, and suspicions would have grown even more intense with the discovery of a cache of arms and ammunition in a house owned by native-born blacks had these blacks not been gunsmiths. Whites had long known that Africans, rather than crioulos, were behind the slave uprisings in Bahia. Marcescheau claimed that Nagôs were the most militant: they were "generally big people, well-built, robust, and willing to face death in their best clothes, believing that such a death is a way to return to their fatherland."[46]

But contrary to what the French consul thought, Nagôs, even though they had made a desperate attempt in April 1830, were not suicidal. They would patiently wait a few years before rising again in Salvador. And when they did, they would rise with a daring never before seen in Bahia.

PART II

The Muslims and the Rebellion of 1835

· 4 ·

The Battle for Bahia

The 1835 rebellion had been planned to begin at dawn on Sunday, 25 January, the day of Our Lady of Guidance, then an important celebration in the Bonfim church's cycle of religious holidays. Bonfim, some eight kilometers from downtown Salvador, was still a semi-rural settlement consisting mainly of planted fields and orchards. Sunday, the day of Our Lady of Guidance, was a good day for slaves to rebel, since seigniorial vigilance would be relaxed somewhat. Staging revolts on Sundays and holidays was part of the standard pattern for slaves in Bahia and throughout the New World. Contrary to modern rebels, who mainly protest and strike on workdays, slaves used to rebel more frequently on days of leisure.

The feast of Our Lady of Guidance had, in fact, begun on Saturday. That evening a throng consisting both of worshipers and merrymakers gathered in Bonfim to pray or celebrate. This was one of the many public celebrations in which the dividing line between the sacred and the profane blurred and people from different social classes freely mixed. The world was thus symbolically turned upside down. But, at least in 1835, one group was conspicuously absent. While the masters were celebrating their saint on one side of the city, on the other side slaves also used religious faith and celebration to prepare a real turning upside down of the world the masters had made.

Saturday began with a buzz of rumor and gossip about an uprising said to be set for the following day. Salvador's business district, Conceição da Praia, and especially the port area were the rumor centers. Early Saturday evening, when Domingos Fortunato, a freed slave, reached home, he told his wife, Guilhermina Rosa de Souza, that blacks working on boats had spent the day whispering back and forth about an intense, unprecedented movement of slaves coming in from the Recôncavo. They were reputed to have come to join their leader, an African "chieftain" by the name of Ahuna, who was leading an uprising scheduled for Sunday morning in Salvador. Domingos went so far as to try to let his old master,

Fortunato José da Cunha, know what was up. He was afraid, perhaps even ashamed, to go in person to his master's house, but he had someone write da Cunha a message denouncing the revolt. This was how the first news of the uprising reached the ears of whites. There is, however, no evidence to indicate that Fortunato José took his ex-slave's warning seriously. From that denunciation, at least, the movement seems to have escaped.

It did not, however, escape a second warning from the ex-slave couple. It was now Guilhermina's turn. After getting the news from her husband, she went to the window, where she trained her ears on two or three Nagôs passing by. She heard that at the sound of reveille, 5:00 A.M., when slaves were to head for the public fountains to fetch water as they did every day, they would be called to battle. She also overheard something about the participation of people from Santo Amaro in the struggle. Later on she testified that "after conferring with her mate, she also went to tell her old master, Souza Velho." It was more proof of loyalty to her ex-master, and this loyalty was probably what got her freed in the first place.

Back home Guilhermina found her *comadre* Sabina da Cruz, another Nagô ex-slave, who had come to Guilhermina's to talk about the uprising. She specifically wanted to talk about one of the conspirators, her husband, Vitório Sule, with whom she had had a terrible fight that morning. When she had come home the night before, after a day's work selling food in the business district, she had found the house turned inside out. Vitório had left, taking some of her clothes with him. She left in search of "her children's father" and found him "on Guadalupe street, at the home of some Africans from Santo Amaro." It seems to have been the house of an ex-slave of African origin known as Manoel Calafate because of his trade (*calafate* means "caulker"). The house was almost at the foot of Praça Hill Street and thus near the square in front of Our Lady of Guadalupe Church. Vitório was there having supper with the "chieftain" and many other Africans who most likely were working out the final details of the following day's revolt. Sabina was unable to see her husband that evening, but she did have a bitter exchange with a black woman named Edum, who told her that she would only see him when Africans were masters of the land. Sabina replied that "on the following day they'd be masters of the whiplash, but not of the land." She had approached to talk to Guilhermina because she knew that her friend had access to whites.

Sabina's visit gave Guilhermina incentive to finish her duty to the seigniorial order. She went to the house of her white neighbor, André Pinto da Silveira, and told him what she knew. Antônio de Souza Guimarães and Francisco Antônio Malheiros were also at Silveira's house and took it upon themselves to transmit the news to the justice of the peace of the Sé Parish, José Mendes da Costa Coelho. The justice of the peace went immediately to the palace to let the president know the facts. He arrived in the company of the commander of the Permanent Municipal Guard, Colonel Manuel Coelho de Almeida Sande, and Comendador José Gonçalves Galião, a wealthy local proprietor. These events occurred between approximately 9:30 and 10:30 on the night of Saturday, 24 January.[1]

President Francisco de Souza Martins, a lawyer from Piauí who had been in power a little over a month, lost no time. By 11:00 P.M. he had already reinforced the palace guard with some of Colonel Sande's men and informed Chief of Police Francisco Gonçalves Martins of the situation. He ordered a general alert throughout the city's barracks and had the justices of the peace double the night patrols in their respective districts and alert their block inspectors. In addition to those measures, he ordered the frigate *Baiana* to watch the bay, probably to stop the rebels should they attempt to flee in the ships anchored in the harbor. Finally, a special order had justices of the peace in the first and second districts of Sé Parish organize extra patrols and search Africans' houses in the part of Guadalupe neighborhood Sabina da Cruz had indicated. One of those patrols was inspected by Gonçalves Martins before he headed to Bonfim with a cavalry brigade to protect the people there from a possible uprising of the slaves living on the farms and small sugar mills *(engenhocas)* in Itapagipe. The Bahian authorities demonstrated remarkable efficiency in their preparations to quell the imminent revolt.[2]

The fight began two or three hours after Guilhermina's denunciation. It was nearly 1:00 A.M. on 25 January when the justices of the peace and their patrol, having unsuccessfully searched some houses belonging to Africans, arrived at number 2 Ladeira da Praça, a two-story house. Custódio José Fernandes, the brother of a resident on the second floor, had also let the authorities know that he had seen suspicious goings-on among some blacks in the "loge" (a sort of basement that can still be seen in some of Salvador's colonial buildings). There were, in fact, two African ex-slaves living there as tenants of a mulatto tailor, Domingos Marinho de Sá. Domingos lived on the ground floor with his "concubine," a mulatto woman named Joaquina Rosa de Santana, the mother of an infant child. A Nagô slave known as Ignácio also lived there. Ignácio belonged to Domingos's brother, who lived in the Recôncavo and who had lent the slave to the tailor during the latter's convalescence from a recent illness.

That night the patrol found Domingos seated at the window. He was asked if there were Africans meeting in his loge. He answered somewhat nervously that the only Africans there at that time were his tenants, whom he considered very "capable" (i.e., well-behaved): Manoel Calafate and Aprígio, a sedan chair porter and bread seller. Domingos's nervousness was justified. A few minutes earlier, attracted by noisy voices, he had gone down to investigate. At the entrance to the loge, Aprígio had threatened to kill him with a "pointed knife" if he denounced the African meeting

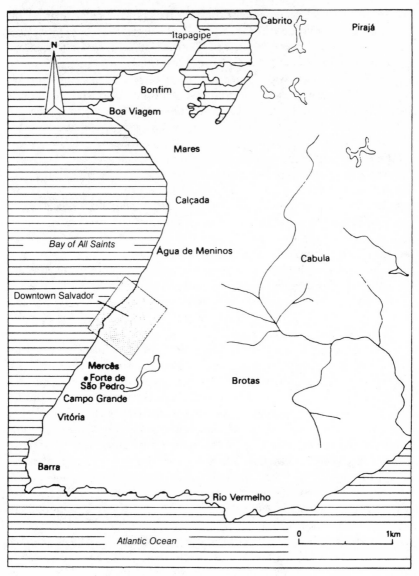

MAP 2. The City of Salvador

under way. He feared for his life, which is why he did not cooperate with
the patrol. But the justices of the peace insisted on seeing for themselves,
and the tailor got more mixed up and told them to come through the
window, since he did not know where the keys were. He got more and
more befuddled. The authorities then threatened to break the door down,
which made him get the keys and let them in.[3]

Inside the loge the final touches were being put on the plan for the
uprising. There was a supper, a ritual meal in the Muslim calendar. The
conspirators still had three hours to wait before they rose up in arms.
Some indication of what was going on in old Calafate's house appears in
the testimony of Pompeu, a slave who had fled to Salvador from a plantation in Santo Amaro in order to participate in the movement. He later
confessed that he had been brought there on a lighter by a slave who was
also from Santo Amaro:

> Clovis was the one who brought him by boat. Once they arrived at the
> city, he was taken, by Clovis, on Saturday, at seven in the evening . . . to
> a house next to a church on the road to Gravatá. Clovis had him enter
> that house, and when they went below into a large loge, they found many
> Africans armed with swords and lances. They gave him food and drink
> and told him what they were to do later that morning. After Pompeu
> had eaten and drunk, the soldiers arrived. At that point the other blacks
> said: "Let's do it now, there's no other way."[4]

After Domingos opened the door, Caetano Vicente de Almeida Galião,
justice of the peace of the Second District of the Sé Parish, Police Lieutenant Lázaro Vieira do Amaral, and two soldiers from the National Guard
entered the corridor and headed for the door to the loge. They were about
to break it down when it flew open and disgorged some fifty to sixty
Africans, who came out shooting, waving their swords, yelling "Death to
soldiers!" as well as orders in an African language. Another group escaped
the siege by jumping over the wall of the garden in back of the house. On
the other side two Nagô freedmen known as Joaquim de Matos and Ignácio Limeira were living. Twelve empty sword sheathes were found on
their premises later. Their house faced Verônicas Street, which is where
the Africans must have fled.

There was a scuffle in front of number 2 Ladeira da Praça. The rebels
put their surprised adversaries to flight with ease—a phenomenon that
would be repeated several times in the streets of Salvador that night. Later
on it was discovered that only two soldiers had their guns ready to fire.
Despite the 1830 rebellion, Salvador's authorities seem to have doubted
any possibility of another African uprising in their midst. On the hill insurgents wounded at least five people, among them Lieutenant Lázaro do
Amaral. One National Guardsman was killed. Another victim, a civilian
who was helping with the patrol, ended up with wounds that left his face

FIG. 7. Nineteenth-century view of Ladeira da Praça, where the Malê uprising began, as reproduced in a 1946 drawing by Octavio Torres. Reprinted from A. Wildberger, *Os presidentes da província da Bahia* (Salvador: Typographia Beneditina, 1949).

and head deformed. Among the wounded in this initial encounter was the wealthy comendador (an honorific imperial title) Galião, who later on reported having "received a blow from a sword that knocked him to the ground, where he remained, pretending to be dead."[5]

On the rebel side, one African was bludgeoned to death by young loyal slaves (one native-born, the other a Nagô) who had joined the patrol with Block Inspector Pedro José de Santana and Justice of the Peace Costa Coelho, their masters. Another rebel was brought down with a bullet in his head from a National Guardsman. One of the two Africans killed was Sabina da Cruz's husband. According to the Nagô freedman Gaspar da Silva Cunha, Vitório Sule "died in action in Guadalupe." Other testimony, from a slave known as Agostinho, of the Mercês Convent, confirms this.[6]

The rebels emerging from Manoel Calafate's house divided into several groups. The biggest group headed up the hill toward Palace Square (today Praça Municipal), at the top of the hill. The others headed in different directions, along Capitães, Pão de Ló, and Ajuda streets. Eyewitness accounts of the opening skirmish in the Malê rebellion are vivid. Luís Tavares Macedo, thirty-two years of age, a member of the National Guard, a solicitor for the court and for the treasury, reported what he saw and heard from the window of his house on Ladeira da Praça:

> He had heard shots and clamor, which brought him running . . . to the window to see where the noise was coming from. He saw a group of black Africans wearing white skullcaps and large smocks over their pants. They were armed with swords and heading toward Palace Square. A little in back of that group he saw another [group], also armed with swords. When this group saw the witness open his window, [one of them] jumped up and swung at him with his sword. Luckily, the blow missed, and the witness retreated inward, leaving the window he had opened.

He barely escaped. Another witness, young mulatto merchant João José Teixeira, twenty-seven years of age, who also lived on Ladeira da Praça, had his story thus recorded by the police scribe:

> Between one and two during the night of last January 24–25, the first Africans coming out attacked the justice of the peace, the troops, and the other people who were with them. They had knocked at the door and requested two torches before the breakout. When the door was opened and they had them [the torches], shots rang out and swords were being brandished. The Africans divided into two lots; one took off toward the Square, and the other headed up toward Capitães Street. He also saw that there were Africans fighting with soldiers over by the Church of Guadalupe.

Father Bernardino de Sena do Sacramento woke up in a fright:

> He woke up with the crackling of gunfire, which was right next to the house where he stayed. He opened the window to see where the shots were being fired, and he then saw come out of the house of Domingos Marinho de Sá a huge contingent of armed Africans shouting in their native ways and mercilessly wounding soldiers and civilians who had accompanied the justice of the peace in his search and whose shouts and cries were heartrending. Some pleaded for arms, whereas others complained of wounds received.

From his house on Tijolo Street, Pompeu da Silva, a thirty-year-old freed black street vendor, "heard the Africans' noise, that is, he heard the thunder of gunshots and of people running down the street."[7] It was the beginning of a long and tumultuous night.

After the skirmish on Ladeira da Praça, the rebels who went up to Palace Square did most of the fighting. However, notwithstanding that contingent's primacy, other groups were formed by the dispersed insurgents and by slaves and freedmen woken in the middle of the night by the racket. The first groups apparently went through the city beating on doors

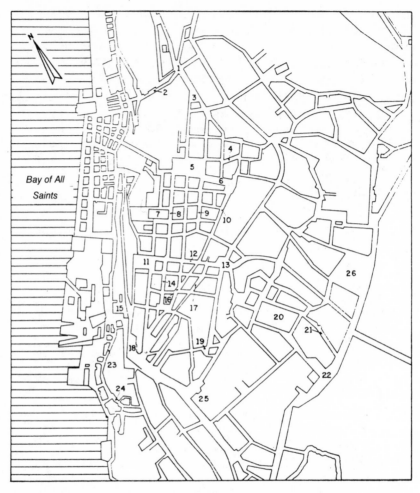

Places mentioned in the text:

1. Baixa dos Sapateiros
2. Ladeira do Taboão
3. Pelourinho Square
4. Laranjeira Street
5. Terreiro de Jesus
6. Cruzeiro Square
7. Sé Church
8. Colégio Street
9. Oração Street
10. São Francisco Street
11. Palace Square
12. Ladeira da Praça
13. Guadalupe Square
14. Ajuda Street
15. Conceição da Praia
16. Pão de Ló Street
17. Capitães Street
18. São João Theater
19. Barroquinha
20. Palma Barracks
21. Mangueira Street
22. Lapa Square
23. Ladeira da Preguiça
24. Ladeira da Gameleira
25. São Bento Convent
26. Campo da Pólvora Square

MAP 3. Downtown Salvador

FIG. 8. The Municipal Council House (city hall) and jail, ca. 1860. This was the first government building attacked by the Malês. Photograph by Benjamin Mulock, reprinted from Gilberto Ferrez, *Bahia: velhas fotografias, 1858–1900* (Salvador: Banco da Bahia Investimentos; Rio de Janeiro: Editora Cosmos, 1988).

and telling their companions of the uprising's precipitous beginning and calling them to war. Africans who were forewarned understood immediately, but one can imagine how surprised others were when only then did they find out what was going on. The president's report seems trustworthy: "Different groups of armed blacks spread out through the main streets of the city whooping and hollering, beating on their cohorts' doors entreating them to join in. The only opposition they encountered was from patrols who shot at them from time to time."[8] The whole city pulsated in the power struggle.

On Palace Square, Africans first attacked the city jail, located in the basement of the city hall. They were trying to free Pacífico Licutan, an esteemed Muslim elder, who was being held there. They probably also had in mind capturing the guards' weapons and setting free all the African prisoners, the latter probably a significant proportion of the jail population, especially among runaway slaves. A white jailer, Antônio Pereira de Almeida, forty-two years of age, living with his family in the jail itself,

FIG. 9. The Provincial Government Palace in Salvador ca. 1860, scene of skirmishes between rebels and soldiers. Photograph by Benjamin Mulock, reprinted from Gilberto Ferrez, *Bahia: velhas fotografias, 1858–1900* (Salvador: Banco da Bahia Investimentos; Rio de Janeiro: Editora Cosmos, 1988).

declared that he was abruptly woken up that night by the "noise of shooting coming from the Prison Guard. The soldiers said they were firing because someone was shoving from the outside and trying to break the door down."[9]

The attack on the jail failed, however. The Africans were suddenly caught between two lines of fire, one coming from the jail and the other from the palace guard, which was firing from the opposite side of the square. They assaulted the palace guard, killing one soldier and wounding others in hand-to-hand combat. It seems that no insurgent was killed in this clash, but many were wounded. The wounded, according to one witness, were carried off by their companions. Joaquim, a Hausa slave, was one of those taken out of action at Palace Square by a bullet in his leg. He later testified that "he was wounded at night by the soldiers of the palace guard, and he dragged himself away because he could not run and hid in the Preguiça shipyards." Joaquim, along with three other slaves, had rushed out of his master's house early that morning. "He does not know the names of those who called him, because there were many of them."[10]

The rebel group retreated from Palace Square under heavy fire. According to the president's report, they ended up on Terreiro de Jesus (Jesus Square), but even if some of them went there, the majority went down Ajuda Street and entered the Largo do Teatro (today Castro Alves Square). They were reinforced by Africans coming out of various alleys and neighboring streets. Together they attacked the small contingent of eight men posted in front of the theater, wounding five, taking their arms, and routing them. They then proceeded to a nearby National Guard barracks located in the São Bento Convent, where more people joined the rebels. The provincial president's report says that in front of the barracks, "the soldiers, after intense shooting, lost their composure and were obliged to close the gate against the fury of the brutal invaders." The report continues: "The battle went on from the barracks' windows, and a few Africans were killed and a few soldiers wounded."[11] If the object was to take that barracks, the Africans failed again. But they held the streets.

By this point the battle was heated. At São Bento, Pompeu, the slave from Santo Amaro, deserted. Even so, he did not escape. He testified that "he had been sleeping in the house of a short mulatto living on Ladeira de Guadalupe and went out onto the Square. And, since there was shooting there, he fled to São Bento, and from there, going down Ladeira da Gameleira toward Preguiça, he was wounded by a soldier."[12] Like Pompeu, others quit at São Bento. Those who went on fighting headed toward the Vitória neighborhood, in the southern part of Salvador, where there was a large colony of Muslim slaves within the English community there. Along the way they stopped off at the Mercês Convent, whose sacristan, a Nagô slave named Agostinho, was also a conspirator. The convent was a regrouping point as well as a rest stop. There the insurgents were soon harassed by a police patrol, which retreated from the rebels' swift counterattack to Fort São Pedro, only one block away. The Africans did not attack the imposing fort, within whose walls lived an unruly infantry battalion that, its dissident tradition notwithstanding, was as anti-African as any in town. The rebels stopped at the gate of the fort and retreated to the convent.

In the struggle at Mercês, National Guard sergeant Tito Joaquim da Silva Machado was stabbed to death with knives and swords. At least three artillery soldiers were wounded, one of them seriously. Some rebels were also put out of the fight, although it appears that none died there. One of the wounded was Eusébio, a Nagô slave from the Rosário Plantation, in Santo Amaro. He explained to the court that he had come to Salvador at 8:00 P.M. and later "joined up with his companions . . . at Mercês." He had probably been at the caulker's house as well. Eusébio had been shot in the foot and stabbed in the arm with a bayonet. Unable to go on fighting, he slipped off into the woods near the fort, where he hid for a week before giving up, since he could no longer withstand the pain from the open wounds on his body.[13]

Returning to the rebels at Mercês Convent, in a short time the people from Vitória arrived. The inspector of the fifth block of that parish, André Antônio Marques, an unmarried, thirty-two-year-old white civil servant and notorious persecutor of Africans in his neighborhood, claimed to have seen several slaves that he knew from his daily rounds:

> After the attack on the sidewalk corner of Mercês . . . Marques was watching from inside the wall of Fort São Pedro and saw and recognized without a doubt said Africans on the new highway coming from Vitória. They were armed with swords and wearing white tunics. Since they were fired on from the Fort, they quickly joined the other group over by Mercês.[14]

Some were wounded as they passed in front of the fort, among them Pedro, a Nagô slave of an English physician named Robert Dundas. Pedro's leg was fractured with a bullet wound. The British consul estimated that eighty attackers passed by Fort São Pedro, shouting and cursing.[15]

The insurgents' next advance reached the police barracks on Lapa Square (Largo da Lapa), exactly where the historic Central High School is located today. They must have come along São Raimundo and Piedade streets. The several hundred rebels in the contingent easily routed the thirty-two municipal police waiting for them in front of the barracks. In spite of their small numbers, the soldiers kept their post from falling into rebel hands. But they lost two lives and suffered other casualties. Once inside the barracks and protected by the walls, their gunfire beat the Africans back.

The rebels retreated down Barroquinha and reappeared on Ajuda Street, in back of the city jail, then headed off to Terreiro de Jesus. There they lost two men in an attack on the twenty soldiers posted in front of the former Jesuit school. On the government's side, two fell mortally wounded: an artillery soldier named Simpliciano Antônio and a civilian, a native-born black named Geraldo das Mercês. The rest of the guards took to their heels.[16]

The crazy chase coursed through the city. The insurgents went down Pelourinho toward the Baixa dos Sapateiros, where they killed two mulattos who got in their way. They continued down Ladeira do Taboão to the lower city. From there they headed toward Itapagipe. They were stopped halfway there, at the cavalry barracks in Água de Meninos, where the decisive battle in the 1835 rebellion took place.

The cavalry barracks was on the only land route to Itapagipe, Bonfim, or Cabrito. Cabrito, according to contemporary accounts, had been chosen as the place where the rebels would join slaves from plantations near Salvador. When the rebels met the cavalry in Água de Meninos, they had given up on the urban struggle, at least for the moment, and were trying the countryside. Another less likely hypothesis is that they were heading toward Bonfim to attack the free people gathered there.

The only detailed report of the confrontation in Água de Meninos comes from Chief of Police Gonçalves Martins, who emphasized his soldiers' bravery as well as his own. He proudly wrote that the only military corps to "take the offensive" was the one under his command. He had just arrived at Bonfim when three soldiers sent by the cavalry commandant, Francisco Teles Carvalhal, arrived to tell him the rebellion had broken out in town. The chief of police returned immediately to Salvador, leaving behind eighteen Municipal Guardsmen charged with making the people go into the church in case of danger. Gonçalves Martins arrived at Água de Meninos around 3:00 A.M. and was advised that the rebels were headed in their direction. The Africans' advance was probably heard at the post, given the clamor and the beating on a war drum the rebels carried. According to one account, "they went down Pilar Street armed with swords and [accompanied] by a drum and shouting."[17]

The first wave of rebels reached the post a few minutes after Gonçalves Martins. The foot soldiers and National Guardsmen around the post took immediate refuge in the barracks, whereas the men on horseback waited outside. According to Gonçalves Martins, there were some fifty to sixty rebels approaching and carrying lances, swords, clubs, and pistols. But they did not attack the barracks; in truth, all they wanted was to pass by. They were met by bullets coming from the barracks windows and by a cavalry charge.

The horses quickly routed the rebels, and the struggle soon turned into a human hunt, with Africans trying to escape the horses' hooves and make their way along the Noviciado Highway linking Água de Meninos to Calçada. Others huddled in front of the barracks, but they too were routed by Gonçalves Martins's cavalry. At this moment Commandant Carvalhal, who was on foot, was wounded and put out of commission. Then a second contingent of rebels appeared on the scene. The struggle then turned into a direct and desperate attack on the barracks. Gonçalves Martins and his men rushed into the fort and from inside, for fifteen minutes, shot from safety at their adversaries, who were falling dead and wounded. It made no sense to go on fighting. They soon gave up on the attack and fled. It was then that the cavalry's last charge administered their *coup de grâce*.

Many escaped into the woods and hills of the surrounding area. Others took to the water but drowned or were captured or shot by the sailors on the *Baiana*. However, Domingos, a slave who managed to swim to Pilar and escape, perhaps to embarrass the winners, later declared that "the majority fled." At dawn on 25 January, nineteen African dead were found

FIG. 10. Two views of Água de Meninos, the site of the final battle, 1860. Photographs by Benjamin Mulock and Camilo Vedani, reprinted from Gilberto Ferrez, *Bahia: velhas fotografias, 1858–1900* (Salvador: Banco da Bahia Investimentos; Rio de Janeiro: Editora Cosmos, 1988).

between Xixi Fountain and the cavalry barracks; another thirteen were taken prisoner during the fighting. Based on these numbers and on Martins's estimate of the size of the first rebel group he fought, it appears that nearly two hundred Africans fought at Água de Meninos.[18]

After the cavalry's victory, Gonçalves Martins returned to Bonfim with a force of seventy men, but all was calm there. The insurrection had not spread to rural slaves and fishermen on the Itapagipe Peninsula, but neither had it stopped completely in the city. At least two groups of Africans went into the streets between 5:00 A.M. and 6:00 A.M. on the twenty-fifth, according to the original plan. They may not have known that the rebellion had begun and failed. But it is also possible that they knew everything and gambled on mobilizing slaves in the city with another daring attempt in the light of day. One of these groups was formed by six slaves of a merchant named João Francisco Ratis. One of these slaves was denounced as an important leader of the uprising. They set fire to their master's house, which seems to have been according to their original plan. Armed with knives, swords, and pistols, they headed toward Água de Meninos. They were all killed in a matter of minutes. Another group set out in the Julião section of the lower city, but only half its story was recorded by the pen of the inspector of the eleventh block of Conceição da Praia Parish: "[At 6:00 A.M. on the twenty-fifth] a group of eight to ten armed blacks wearing strange garments appeared. They threw themselves furiously on some soldiers there. They were immediately repelled, leaving one dead, and the rest ran off, being chased by soldiers and other people."[19]

The French consul in Salvador in 1835 spiced up the story of the rebellion with assertions not to be found in any other source contemporary with the event itself. He maintained that rebels escaping the encounter in Água de Meninos were able to reach the swamplands on Engenho da Conceição, a league away. On the following day they proceeded to Engenho Novo, half a league from Conceição. They were later attacked by government forces posted there. In spite of many casualties among soldiers or National Guardsmen (the consul was not sure of their status), the soldiers won, killing some forty rebels and pushing the rest into the neighboring thickets.

Surely a fight like this would not have been omitted from official reports and the voluminous inquiry carried out afterwards. On top of this, these two plantations were not that close to one another, nor were they as close to Salvador as the French consul claimed. They were in the heart of the Recôncavo, many dozens of leagues from Salvador. Engenho Novo was in São Francisco do Conde, and Engenho da Conceição was in Cachoeira. It would have been impossible for the rebels to reach these places undetected, traveling on foot and tired as they must have been. It seems that the consul, describing these goings-on on the day after the uprising, passed off as truth one of the many rumors circulating through Salvador after the struggle ended.[20]

Against Great Odds

The other accounts contemporary with the rebellion indicate that the group meeting at Manoel Calafate's house on Ladeira da Praça may have been entirely responsible for the first act of insurrection on the morning of the twenty-fifth. Nowhere in the extensive police and trial records is there any evidence of a significant number of rebels grouped elsewhere. Of course, slaves living with their masters could not bring many people together for secret meetings. Many joined the fight quietly and on their own, without gathering people in their quarters. That was how the En-glishmen's slaves operated, and they contributed a significant contingent of rebels. Even for the houses belonging to freedmen other than Calafate, there is no information of gatherings on the night of 24 January. The original idea—that is, before the police discovered the plot—seems to have been to have a great explosion on Ladeira da Praça, followed by adhesions here and there throughout the city. The loss of the surprise element in the center of operations was an irreparable blow to the armed uprising, since it upset the basic strategy. The Malês barely escaped a knockout in the first round.

Even though Africans seemed to have taken the lead in the first en-counter on Ladeira da Praça, they were not yet ready to begin. They began because they "had no choice," as Pompeu revealed. The erratic march through the streets of Salvador reflected their lack of preparation. Of course, it is difficult to imagine exactly what happened. Why so many attacks in diverse parts of the city? On the one hand, they tried to rouse fellow slaves, but to do this it was necessary to course through the city's central parishes. On the other hand, they seem to have made deliberate attempts to take some government buildings, at least the city jail and the barracks in São Bento and Largo da Lapa. But that was not the case of Fort São Pedro and the cavalry barracks. The former, which they never actually attacked, was simply located on the road they took to meet up with the group from Vitória. The cavalry post was on the escape route from the city, and no one would suggest that the rebels had planned to attack it on their way out of the city.

There is one document that clarifies the apparently disjointed move-ments made by the rebels that night. It is the translation of one of the "Arabic papers," which was done on 7 February 1835 by Albino, a Hausa slave of a lawyer named Luís da França d'Athaide Moscoso. The text of what must have been written on a small piece of paper reads:

Everyone should come out between 2:00 and 4:00 A.M. stealthily [*in-visíveis*], and after doing what they could, they should gather at Cabrito opposite [*detraz de*] Itapagipe, in a large hollow there. There would be people from another nearby [*atraz e junto*] engenho, because they had been alerted. In the event they did not come, they [the rebels from the city] would proceed to the engenho, taking considerable care in steering clear of soldiers so as to take them by surprise, until they had all left town.[21]

This text is far from being a jewel of clarity, but it indicates that the plan was to call the city to arms ("doing what they could") and then take the movement into the Recôncavo ("all left town"). If this deposition is true (the original Arabic text has not been recovered), even with the revolt's premature beginning, it seems the rebels tried to carry out what had been planned originally. The cane-producing region, the center of the Bahian slave economy, was doubtlessly on the rebels' itinerary. Combatants came from the country to the city, and from the city they accompanied the rebel forces back out, to call the slaves on plantations to arms.

Their strategy had not been to occupy Salvador immediately. Perhaps that is why the rebels did not insist on taking barracks, palaces, or churches. They were trying to arouse the city. They had no intention of being stuck in Salvador waiting for the inevitable siege, as had happened with the Portuguese in 1823 and would happen later to the federalist rebels who occupied the capital in 1837. Everything suggests that they understood the strategic nature of the Recôncavo in Bahia's political and military geography. When they were stopped in Água de Meninos, they had "done what they could" and were trying to launch the second stage of the revolt. The rebel meeting place at the Cabrito Plantation, today a working-class neighborhood of Salvador, was practically on the border between the city and the rural Recôncavo.

One way to assess the rebels' action in the city is to consider what it might have occurred. In spite of all the confusion that night, they did not resort to indiscriminate violence. They did not engage in random violence against bystanders, nor did they pillage or vandalize houses. They did not submit the city to widespread terror. They did not even do violence to their masters and their families. The British and French consuls reported that the original rebel plan included setting fires here and there, even in their masters' houses, as a means of diverting the attention of the police and their masters. But except for the action of João Ratis's slaves, none of that happened, perhaps because the rebels were obliged to begin ahead of time and the confusion cost them some of their advantage. They lost the opportunity both to confuse their adversaries and to swell their ranks with more rebels. Still, they could have done more damage than they did, since it would not have been hard to throw some torches on roofs and break into houses and kill whoever was inside. Instead of this, they preferred an almost classic head-on confrontation with their adversaries. Even the president of the province acknowledged their military ethics with a hint of admiration. "It is undeniable that they had a political goal in mind, since there is no evidence that they robbed a single house or that they killed their masters on the sly." The French consul seconded the president: "Their plans seem to have been to take over the government, since they attacked sentinels, military bases, and even the Presidential Palace."[22]

The rebels were not prepared for a conventional fight. They had only a few men, most of whom were armed with knives (the best being the German parnaíbas), swords, and clubs, which would have worked well only in a general melee, in a truly massive uprising. But their adversaries avoided hand-to-hand combat as well as a generalized urban slave insurrection. As far as firearms were concerned, the rebels had only a few pistols to count on. Nothing expresses their frustration better than André did on Monday, 26 January, at his job (he was a meatcutter). He smashed a pistol with a hatchet and swore at it: "Devil! You were no help to me yesterday, you're through." Apparently the rebels even had a gunsmith among them, a Nagô ex-slave named Antônio Manoel do Bomcaminho, a man of sixty-four, who, it seems, was not able to get the arms to them in time. In his house the police found five rifles, two muskets, eight pistols, and eight swords. Not a lot. There were also a few weapons needing repairs of one sort or another. Old Bomcaminho (an ironic name for a rebel, *bom caminho* meaning "good road") and his arsenal would hardly have made a difference in the events of 25 January. Indeed, back in Africa, Yorubas, unlike other warriors in their region, rarely used firearms, preferring bows and poison arrows, which, evidence suggests, they planned to use in Brazil.[23]

For three hours nonstop, Africans ran and fought in the streets of Salvador. It is almost impossible to imagine that at the end there were people who had been fighting since the initial encounter on Ladeira da Praça. At any rate, when they met the cavalry at Água de Meninos, they were weakened and exhausted. And, of course, many had already given up. A seventeen-year-old Nagô slave, Higino, declared that "in the early morning he fled to his master's house because he could no longer fight the soldiers." It must have been pure hell in the streets for a slave to flee *to* his master's house. Another Nagô slave, Cornélio, from the Muslim group at Vitória, did not get very far. As soon as he arrived at Fort São Pedro, he turned around and went back home, frightened by the intense fire coming from the barracks. After the revolt a Jeje slave known as Alexandre was heard to tell a Nagô woman that "he wanted to join, but as he saw the others were dying, he did not."[24]

It is difficult to determine exactly how many Africans actually went into the streets to fight. The moonless night did not allow police to make an accurate estimate of the size of the enemy forces, but Consul Marcescheau estimated them to number four hundred to five hundred. The president of the province resigned himself to a vague approximation: "Their quantity exceeded two hundred individuals." (In today's terms this is tantamount to a Bahian governor's report of an armed rebellion of "more than nine thousand individuals.") In his famous report the chief of police did not risk a global estimate for the number of African combatants. His narration of the battle at Água de Meninos notes the presence of fifty to sixty rebels; further on he adds "a few more Africans." It appears to be a conservative estimate, but even if it is reliable, it does not help us count all those who fought on the African side: those who fought from beginning to end and those who fought only part of that time. Considering these factors, including the desertions along the way, the French diplomat's estimate of four hundred to five hundred rebels seems reasonable. I venture a number of about six hundred, although I do not believe that all six hundred were fighting at any one time during the uprising. Indeed, whatever their numbers may have been, few of the twenty-two thousand Africans living in Salvador at that time joined the rebellion. And it is likely that not even all those in on the conspiracy went to the streets and fought.[25]

Concerning the legal forces, Gonçalves Martins explicitly mentioned 182 men under his command. But his estimate did not include the artillery soldiers housed at Fort São Pedro, the cavalrymen temporarily under the command of the chief of police, the National Guardsmen, and the large number of civilians who formed patrols in their neighborhoods to accompany the justices of the peace and block inspectors. The British consul wrote that their numbers "could not be less than 1,500," to which one should add, according to him, the sailors on two warships. There were certainly more people on the legal side than on the rebel side, but the majority of them did not meet the Africans face to face. They defended their installations, shooting from a distance at their adversaries.[26]

The total number of deaths in the 1835 rebellion was more than seventy. The chief of police counted fifty Africans killed during the uprising or drowned in the sea. Perhaps to be different, President Martins estimated that "a few more than forty negroes were killed." But others died afterwards from wounds received during the fight. There is information on only four of the latter: A slave known as Henrique had his middle finger smashed by a bullet but was able to return home without being assaulted further. On 31 January, six days after the uprising, he was arrested and taken to the charity hospital (Hospital da Misericórdia) with "an advanced case of tetanus"; three days later he died. Noé, Hipólito, and Constantino, all Nagô slaves, also died in the hospital. Besides these, very few Africans who were killed have been identified, and news about them is vague. Typical are the words of a block inspector who wrote: "A barber who they say died on the night of the 24th of January [was killed] by the cavalry because he was with his companions, the evil Africans." No name. But a few names can be rescued from total anonymity: Flamé, Batanhos, Combé, Mama Adeluz, Vitório Sule, Dassalu, Nicobé, Gustard—most of them belonging to the English at Vitória—all lost their lives that night. The burial records of the local charity institution (Santa Casa de Misericórdia) list other African casualties: Roque, a slave, "who was killed by shooting"; Manoel, a Nagô slave, "who died from a shot"; Gertrudes, a Nagô slave woman, "who died from a shotgun firing." We also learn from these records that some Africans committed suicide after the defeat, like Baltazar and Cicero.[27]

The number of Africans wounded is even harder to estimate, but it must be considerably larger than the number of deaths, as is common in armed conflicts. Some ended up with woeful reminders of the revolt inscribed on their mutilated bodies. The slave Pedro had his leg fractured with a bullet. It was amputated later on. Almost all the African casualties had been shot from a distance by their adversaries.

According to Gonçalves Martins's account, only nine people were killed by the rebels. Among these were four mulattos and one native-born black, all civilians. The names of four appear in the records: José Luís de Sales, Inocêncio José Cavalcante (a carpenter), Joaquim dos Reis, and Geraldo das Mercês (the native black). The other people were Sergeant Tito Joaquim da Silva Machado and someone named Siqueira, both of the National Guard, the municipal policemen Fortunato José Braga and Francisco Joaquim de Castro, and the artillery soldier Simpliciano Antônio de Oliveira. All nine were free people, common folk. There were also some wounded on the legal side: Lieutenant Lázaro do Amaral, the first man to be put out of the fight on Ladeira da Praça. The lieutenant survived with deforming scars. Another who survived, but the worse for wear, was an Angolan ex-slave, Miguel Vitório, who bore a deep scar on his left cheek for the rest of his life. The corpses of the rebels' victims show that their wounds were without exception inflicted by "cutting tools"—swords, knives, and lances—which proves that the few firearms the rebels were able to gather did nothing more than weigh them down.[28]

· 5 ·

The Sons of Allah in Bahia

Allah desires no injustice to His Creatures
—Koran, 3:108

Beyond a shadow of a doubt, Muslims played the central role in the 1835 rebellion. The rebels went into the streets wearing clothes peculiar to practicers of Islam. And the police found Muslim amulets and papers with prayers and passages from the *Koran* on the bodies of fallen rebels. These and other characteristics of the revolt led Chief of Police Gonçalves Martins to conclude the obvious: "What is certain," he wrote, "is that Religion played a part in the uprising." He continued: "The ringleaders persuaded the unfortunate wretches that pieces of paper would protect them from dying." Another Martins, the provincial president, said: "It seems to me that there was religious fanaticism mixed up in this conspiracy."[1] Everyone writing about this revolt could not avoid the religious factor, be it to exaggerate it, be it to diminish it. Both positions have their merits, but both are incomplete.

Before making a detailed examination of Muslim involvement in the 1835 rebellion, one should take stock of Islam's presence in the Afro-Bahian community of the time. Quite likely the first big contingent of Muslim Africans arrived in Bahia at the turn of nineteenth century. It is true that during the more than two hundred years of slave trade preceding that time, many slaves coming from West Africa were Mohammedans. Most of these were Malinkes, known in Bahia as *mandingos*. During the first three decades of the nineteenth century, of the some seven thousand slaves imported annually to Bahia the immense majority were Hausas, Yorubas (Nagôs), and neighboring peoples—victims as they were of the severe political and religious disturbances in their countries. It was a time of Islamic expansion in West Africa, especially in the western part of present-day Nigeria. Islam went its way peacefully, except when traditional leaders sought to block it; then it went to war. Such were the circumstances that led the Fulani Muslim leader Shehu Usuman Dan Fodio (or Sheik Dan Fodio) to begin a jihad, or holy war, in 1804 against the hostile government of King Yunfa of Gobir, considered by jihadists to be a wayward Muslim. This conflict produced thousands of slaves, mainly Hausas, who ended up stocking the slave-gathering outposts on the Bight of Benin, especially the up-and-coming port known as Eko or Onim, today Lagos. The leaders of that jihad were Fulanis, who ended up organizing the powerful Sokoto caliphate in Fulani and Hausa territory. As an expansionist caliphate, it was always involved in local conflicts, which continued to produce slaves for the Atlantic trade. Many African slaves interviewed in the late 1840s by Francis de Castelnau, the French consul in Bahia, had been soldiers captured during wars. Others had been taken prisoner in raids on villages or along the highways.[2]

Parallel events in Yoruba territory also explain the presence of Islamic slaves in Bahia. The end of the eighteenth century was the high point of the Yoruba Oyo empire, which exercised hegemony over Yoruba-speaking subgroups and satellite states surrounding it, such as Dahomey and the Nupe kingdom. The Oyo empire began to disintegrate starting with a series of civil wars begun by the revolt of Afonja (ca. 1797). The rebel leader was nothing less than the *are-ona-kakanfo* ("commander in chief") of the provincial armed forces, which included Oyo's powerful cavalry. He was also the ruler of the city of Ilorin, in the north, on the border with Sokoto. The revolt occurred during a decline in power suffered by the alafin (the king of Oyo), whose position Afonja had tried in vain to occupy. Support from provincial leaders had been to no avail in this endeavor. The next twenty years were a period of gradual disintegration in the center of the Oyo empire. This gradual disintegration accelerated beginning in 1817.

During that year a widespread slave revolt broke out in the territory still dominated by Oyo. Its instigator had been Afonja, and it was made up mainly of northern slaves: Fulanis, Bornus, Nupes, and especially Hausas. Hausas comprised the greater part of the Yoruba slave labor force. They were especially famous as ropemakers, cattle herders, and physicians and surgeons. They also had a reputation for being competent veterinarians, which the Yorubas sorely needed for their cavalry. Some of those slaves also worked in agriculture or as their masters' agents and commercial assistants. Even though Yorubas kept most of these skilled slaves, they traditionally sold some on the coast to Atlantic slave traders. But only with Afonja's revolt were their numbers to swell in the trading posts along the Bight of Benin.[3]

Those northern slaves became the backbone of Afonja's rebel forces. From the beginning, however, Muslim Yorubas, including some wealthy merchants, rallied around the commander in chief in reaction to pressure from the powerful alafin, whose power derived from the traditional Shango cult. (In Oyo the supreme deity, or orisha, was Shango, the mythical fourth alafin of the kingdom and the god of thunder.) With the help of these allies, Afonja's strictly political rebellion, according to Gbadomosi, "became mixed up with Islamic ferment and agitation of the time."[4] The slave revolt widened its field of operations and created Muslim strongholds in the north. Ilorin became a virtual Yoruba Mecca. There Muslims took possession of "pagan" slaves captured in battle. The Yoruba historian Babatunde Agiri ironically comments: "The slaves who successfully rebelled against the Oyo government in 1817 now owned slaves of their own."[5]

Between 1817 and 1820, Afonja, who was not himself a Muslim and who had even refused to be converted, tried to form his own *jama'a*, or band of Muslim militants. Soon, however, the imperial capital (Oyo) was attacked and partly destroyed. But the old empire was still able to defeat its attackers. At this time Afonja began to have problems with his Fulani and Hausa allies, who were leaning toward Sokoto. The commander in chief tried in vain to convince them to leave Ilorin and settle to the east of the city, but he was soon murdered. This was the end of Yorubas' control of Ilorin, which would become an emirate subject to the Fulani caliph in Sokoto. The Fulanis' advance over Yorubaland was slow but thorough. It lasted ten years, crushing one *oba* (Yoruba chief) after another and transforming the region into an inferno of minor wars that were more political than religious and that spread out like waves. Society became militarized with the formation of numerous independent armed bands fighting over the spoils of Oyo and capturing one another to supply slaves for the Atlantic trade. People from all over the region were caught up in civil wars, jihads, and rebellions of kingdoms formerly under the thumb of Oyo. Great numbers of Nupes (known as Tapas in Yorubaland as well as in Bahia), Bornus, and the peoples from Dahomey came ashore in the New World as slaves. Many of those slaves were Muslims.[6]

Islam played an ambiguous role in the political and religious movements of West Africa during the first half of the nineteenth century. On the one hand, for mainly expansionist states, it provided an ideology and inspired governments. Here it was an ally of power, often a military instrument at the service of slaveowners and merchants. On the other hand, it offered refuge for the poor—spiritual and moral strength as well as organization to free men subjugated to powerful groups supported by traditional religion. It also kept the hope of freedom alive for thousands of

Muslim slaves. It was, then, an instrument of revolt as well. Concerning Yorubaland, Agiri sums up this contradictory movement nicely:

> Ilorin became the bridgehead for Muslim expansion to the south, but beyond its borders Islam played a far different role than it did in the emirate. In the independent Yoruba states, Islam was more often associated with slaves of Northern origin, and consequently this religion provided a potential rallying point for the consolidation of a distinct slave subculture. Many Yoruba chiefs saw this danger.[7]

It was mainly this second Islamic tradition that the Muslim slaves, whose ranks now included Yorubas converted to Islam, tried to recreate within Bahian slave society.

Muslims Become Malês

In 1835 Muslim Africans were known as Malês in Bahia. The origin of this term has been the object of protracted debate. Braz do Amaral, for example, has made the ridiculous suggestion that it derives from the phrase *má lei* (a Portuguese phrase meaning "bad law"), which has been rejected even by Etienne Brazil, a Catholic priest and militant anti-Muslim. Perhaps Amaral wanted to attach a pejorative connotation to the name to suggest that Muslims would reject it. This was, however, wrong, since the term *Malê* did not seem negatively charged, at least at that time. With a firmer basis, R. K. Kent has linked *malé* with *malām*, a Hausa word taken from the Arabic *mu'allim*, which means "cleric," "teacher," or "preacher"—like *alfa* in several parts of West Africa, or its Yoruba variant *alufa*, which has come to be spelled *alufá* in Bahia. (In the 1835 police and trial records the Malê preachers, or alufás, are called *mestres*, a Portuguese word meaning "teacher," "spiritual guide," or "master" but not *"slave master."*)

On the other hand, Raymundo Nina Rodrigues, the first competent student of the Malês, suggested that the term is derived from *Mali,* the name of the once powerful Mandinka Muslim state on the Gold Coast. Still, the explanation that seems more sensible and direct has been presented by Pierre Verger, Vincent Monteil, and Vivaldo da Costa Lima, who link the term *Malê* with *imale,* a Yoruba term for Islam or for a Muslim, which may also have influenced the formation of the Fon term *malinou* or, even closer, *malé. Imale,* in turn, is held to be derived from the word *Mali.* Rodrigues, Brazil, Bastide, and others who point toward the Mandinka as originators of the term seem to have overlooked a closer word. *Mali* would perhaps be the starting point, producing *imale* and finally *Malê,* which is a plausible etymology.

Malê, imale, and similar expressions seem to have been in use in the eighteenth century to describe African Muslim merchants in the slave trading posts of the Bight of Benin, from where most Bahian slaves were coming in the years preceding the 1835 rebellion. In the 1720s, for example, Jean Baptiste Labat linked the term *mallais* specifically to Hausa slave traders, who probably called themselves by the Hausa term *musulmin*. In the nineteenth century the term *Malê* surfaced in Bahia, probably because of the then greater presence of Yorubas (Nagôs) and Aja-Fon (Jejes) peoples, who imposed a word from their languages on the others. Nonetheless, it should be clear that in 1835 Bahia *malê* did not refer to any African ethnic group in particular, but to Africans who adopted the Islamic faith. And because of this there were Nagôs, Jejes, Hausas, Tapas, Bornus—that is, persons of various ethnicities—who were Malês.[8]

Islam was not the dominant religion among Africans in Bahia. Yet it is quite likely that it was a heavyweight contender in a cultural free-for-all that also included the Yoruba orisha cult, Aja-Fon Voodum, the Angolan ancestor spirit cult, among other African religious manifestations. Add to this a creole Catholicism, and you will have an idea of the religious plurality in the African and Afro-Bahian communities of the time. The only ethnic groups whose members seem to have wholeheartedly embraced Islam before coming to Brazil were the Hausas; their neighbors, the Nupes; and the Bornus. The majority of the Nagôs, the Bahian ethnic majority, continued to practice candomblé, the orisha religion. Even the Hausas, who were Islamicized, were still attached to their native spirit cult known as Bori, which is not to be confused with the candomblé ritual with the same name.[9]

Hausas were promptly identified with Islam in Bahia. Malê and Hausa became synonyms. In his report on the rebellion, the chief of police observed: "Generally almost all of them [the rebels] know how to read and write using unknown characters that look like Arabic and are used by the Hausas, who seem today to have combined with the Nagôs. The former nation was the one that rebelled quite often in this Province, but has been substituted by Nagôs."[10] And a slave named Marcelina, when asked about writings found in the house of an ex-slave, said: "The Malê prayer slips were made and written on by the others' elders, who go around preaching. These elders are from the Hausa Nation, because Nagôs do not know and are brought together by the mestres to learn, as well as by some from the Tapa Nation."[11] Among the Malê preachers in Bahia in 1835 were Dandará, the Hausa merchant whose Christian name was Elesbão do Carmo, and a Tapa slave named Sanim, whose Christian name was Luís. Both confessed to teaching Islamic doctrine in their homelands. Other Hausas admitted being familiar with Muslim writings. One of those, the slave Antônio, claimed to have attended a Koranic school in Africa.[12]

It is nonetheless incorrect to give the Hausas exclusivity in Islamic affairs in Bahia. As we have seen, Islam was a religion on the rise in Yoruba kingdoms, and most certainly hundreds of Islamicized Yorubas landed in Brazil as Nagô slaves. Around 1835, Malês in Bahia were probably for the most part Nagôs and not the offspring of minorities such as Hausas or the even rarer Tapas. At any rate, the Nagô Malês enjoyed power and prestige within the Muslim community. Ahuna and Pacífico Licutan, both slaves, were the two most important characters in the 1835 uprising, and both of them were alufás or preachers of Nagô origin. The alufá and rebel leader Manoel Calafate, a freedman in whose house the rebellion began, was also a Nagô. Several Nagôs confessed to having been initiated into Islam before crossing the Atlantic. A slave known as Gaspar to Bahians and Huguby to Africans declared he "knew how to read and write back in his homeland." During his arraignment, he even read some passages in Arabic for the justice of the peace, who wanted to know what a book the police had confiscated dealt with. But Huguby, according to the scribe, "was not able to or did not know how to tell it in our language." Another Nagô slave, Pedro, when asked about the contents of some papers and a book he had, answered that "the book contained prayers from his native land, and the papers contained doctrines whose words and meaning he knew before leaving his country." Pompeu, a freedman, was more cautious. He claimed to "have learned [the Arabic writing] in his native land, as a small child, but now he remembered almost nothing." One can see that like the Hausas, the Nagôs had Muslims of long standing in their ranks whose prestige, influence, and dominance cannot be underestimated.[13]

Malês of long standing tried to attract new Malês. Documents from the 1835 inquiry indicate vigorous proselytizing and conversion in Bahia during the 1830s. The label of passivity Bastide applied to the Malês is thus inapt. The slave community varied in its commitment to Islam. On a superficial level we find the adoption of external symbols of Islamic culture. Malê amulets and good-luck charms were especially popular. Students of African Islam are unanimous in recognizing Africans' esteem for these amulets, which prevail despite opposition from puritanical leaders, who throughout time have criticized them as elements of traditional, backward religion, as signs of pagan atavism. Though a pagan, Afonja put considerable trust in those magical amulets during his military campaigns. Even religions that had been unaffected by Islam acknowledged the virtues of those charms. The English traveler John McLeod, who visited Dahomey in 1803, wrote that Arab merchants "carried about with them scraps or sentences of the *Koran* which they distributed to the natives, who generally fastened them on the ends of sticks near their doors as charms against witchcraft."

In Bahia, because they were reputed to have strong protective powers, Malê charms were *de rigueur* adornments for Muslims and non-Muslims alike. And Rodrigues observed that at the end of the nineteenth century,

Bahian blacks generally considered Malês to be "wizards familiar with high magical processes." Yorubas gave amulets the name *tira* (in Bahia, *tiá*, according to Etienne Brazil), and whites likened them to Catholic scapularies containing prayers, so they called them "briefs" *(breves)* in the 1835 proceedings. These amulets spread beyond the Malê group because they did not signify a strong commitment to Islam on the part of their wearer. They posed no threat whatsoever to the magical beliefs of "pagans" whose relationship with the supernatural was conceived largely in terms of solutions for immediate, day-to-day problems. Tiras promised protection for all and functioned well as a vehicle of Islamic propaganda in Bahia. From Bahia their influence spread to other ports in Brazil, especially Rio de Janeiro.[14]

The written word, which the Malês used, had a great seductive power over Africans whose roots belonged in oral cultures. The amulets consisted of pieces of paper containing passages from the *Koran* and powerful prayers. The paper was carefully folded in an operation that had its own magical dimension. It was then placed in a small leather pouch, which was sewn shut. In many cases, besides the paper, other ingredients appeared in those charms. A police scribe described the contents of one amulet as follows:

> Little bundles or leather pouches were opened at this time by cutting them at the seams with a penknife. Inside were found several pieces of insignificant things such as cotton wrapped in a little powder [*sic*], others with tiny scraps of garbage, and little sacks with some seashells inside. Inside one of the leather pouches was a piece of paper with Arabic letters written on it.[15]

The "insignificant" substances referred to here likely included sand moistened beforehand in some sort of holy water, perhaps water used by some renowned and pious alufá or water used to wash the tablets on which Malês wrote their religious texts. In the latter case, this water could also be drunk, since the ink was made of burnt rice; such a drink was believed to seal the body against outside harm. Some of the amulets were made of West African fabric; leather was used more often, since it provided better protection for both the sacred words and the other charms. There is a remarkable similarity between the Bahian Malê talismans and those still in use in black Africa, although the Bahian amulet seems to have had more "pagan" ingredients. According to Vincent Monteil, "In general the Islamic Talisman is a leather case, sewn together and containing a piece of stiff cardboard . . . and inside this is a folded piece of paper on which are written phrases in praise of God and cabalistic symbols—that is, Arabic letters, pentacles, and the like."[16] Kabbalistic drawings such as the ones mentioned here were found in several amulets confiscated in 1835.

The Magrebian Arabic in the Malê amulets found on the bodies of dead rebels or in Muslims' houses has been studied and translated by Vincent Monteil and Rolf Reichert.[17] Reichert took stock of twelve amulets, some of which contained kabbalistic shapes. This is the description of what he found in one:

(1) in the name of God the merciful the compassionate God praise be . . . later prophet. . . .

Next there is a rectangular magic figure divided into 11 x 13 = 143 squares filled with individual letters, to each of which one attributes a numerical value. Below the square:

(2) in the name of God the compassionate the (merciful) . . . God
(3) . . . God's help and imminent triumph gives the good news
(4) for believers God's help and imminent triumph gives the good news.
(5) for believers God's help and imminent triumph gives the good news.
(6) for the believers

To the left there is a horizontal line:

They love us as God is loved but those who believe love God in a stronger way and. . . .

This is a sentence extracted from verse 13, sura 61, of the *Koran*. It seemed to have been tailored for the rebellion and repeated several times. Another example:

(1) in the name of God the compassionate the merciful
(2) God will protect you from all men
(3) God will not (guide) the infidel people God
(4) [He] will protect you from all men God will not (guide) the infidel
(5) people God will protect you from the
(6) All men God will not (guide) the infidel people
(7) if God wills and with God goes victory.

This text (verse 67, sura 5) is accompanied by several circles, each with the word "flight" (*fuga*) inside it. Besides that word Reichert found "master," "owner," and "alone." This could be a fugitive slave's magical passport. Other amulets scrimped on words:

(1) in the name of God the compassionate, the merciful

Next comes a magical rectangular figure, divided into sixteen square fields, each one filled with three, four, or five isolated letters.

(2) gabriel michael

This is a request for help from the archangels, who are also part of Islamic doctrine.[18]

The magic in the Islamic texts and drawings worked as protection against various threats. The Africans arrested in 1835 said little about their magic, and when they did say something, they avoided linking it to the

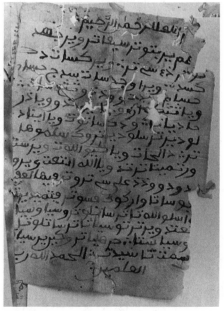

FIG. 11. Malês' spiritual arsenal: Koranic verses, Muslim "powerful" prayers' magic figures were used as amulets. Photographs courtesy of Arquivo do Estado da Bahia.

revolt. However, besides their obvious political function, these amulets were especially designed to control daily life. A freedman named Silvestre José Antônio, a merchant, was arrested with five amulets in his case. He declared they "were prayers to save [him] from any unfortunate happenstance in his travels through the Recôncavo." Whether in Africa or in Brazil, a good Muslim merchant never traveled without a considerable number of protecting charms. A booklet of Islamic prayers could also work to protect its holder against evil spells. It was for that reason that a freedman named Pedro Pinto asked a literate Malê to make one for him, so he could "be free from wagging tongues." Pedro, by the way, was not a Malê.[19]

Besides protecting against human evildoers, these amulets helped their owners control the uncertain terrain of the spirit world. The *isköki,* for example, are Hausa spirits who, like all spirits, need to be cared for according to a specific protocol. Their essence is the air—*iska,* the singular of *isköki,* literally, the "wind." With the advent of Islam, these Hausa spirits dispersed and, as agents of good and evil, became confused with Muslims' jinns. These spirits, known as *anjonu* or *alijano* in Yoruba, are also formed from air when air is joined with fire. This helps explain why, in 1835, Lobão Maxado, a freedman, explained that several of the amulets found in his house were "to protect him from the wind." Likewise, José, a Nagô slave, said he bought his tira from an African negress "because she told him it was good for the wind." José had been living for ten years in white man's land but to a great extent still traveled his own cultural route. Interestingly, in popular wisdom wind still inspires fear. It is said to carry specific illnesses and to leave a body deformed should someone feign deformation either innocently or maliciously. Today it is the actual wind that does this, but the motivating force for these beliefs can be found embodied in the iska, jinns, anjonu, and other beings born by air.[20]

As a general rule, Muslim amulets were made and sold by alufás, whose mystic power, or *baraka,* was embodied in their product. In Africa the manufacture of talismans constituted (and still constitutes), in some cases, the main activity and an important source of income for literate Muslims. The belief that more amulets mean greater protection creates an ever-expanding market. (Of course it also creates an ever-expanding likelihood of fraud.) It is doubtful that in Bahian slave society the Malê preachers, especially those who were slaves, could live exclusively off the highly specialized occupation of manufacturing magic charms.

Even so, one Malê fisherman made a good living from amulet making. According to one witness, Antônio, a Hausa slave residing in Itapagipe, "wrote prayers in his language and sold them to his partners making 4 *patacas* [1,280 réis] a day doing that." When he was arrested, a writing quill was found in his room: "Asked . . . by the justice [of the peace] why he kept such a quill, the same slave answered that he kept it so as to write things having to do with his Nation. He was then asked to write and he made a few scribbles with the phoney quill and the justice asked . . . what he had written. He answered that what he had written was the name of the 'Hail Mary.'" This Islamic-Christian melding does not seem to have impressed the justice of the peace. Antônio calmly went on telling his questioners that "when he was a young boy in his homeland, he went to school," and there he had learned Arabic so as to write "prayers according to the schism of his homeland."[21]

A somewhat more innovative and daring amulet maker also melded Christianity and Islam. Consul Marcescheau reported having seen one document written half in Arabic and half in Latin, with the Latin section being a transcription of a passage from the "Song of Songs." This talisman may have been used in a lover's conquest rather than a military maneuver. Be that as it may, this is one more example of the Malês' scriptural sincretism, which challenges the notion that they were cultural separatists.[22]

Another sign of Islamic presence in the African community was the wearing of a totally white garment, a sort of long frock called an *abadá* in Bahia, an *aqbada* or *agbada* in Yorubaland. The abadá of Bahia was worn only in private so as not to attract attention or persecution from the officers of the law, who were always on the lookout for anything out of the ordinary among the blacks. It was only during the 1835 rebellion that the spectacle of hundreds of sons of Allah dressed in white first occurred in the streets of Salvador. For this reason police authorities called the abadás "war garments." As we have seen, the French consul observed early on that Nagôs wore their best clothing when they made war in Bahia, believing that if they died, they would reappear in their native land. During peacetime, Malês only wore white clothing at home, far from curious eyes, during their prayers and rituals. Thus, José, a slave from the Congo, belonging to a Nagô freedman, Gaspar da Silva Cunha, declared under questioning that his master only donned the "white petticoat" when "he went to talk in the attic" with fellow Muslims.[23]

Some Africans considered the abadá a symbol of social superiority. Bento, a Nagô slave, affirmed that "concerning those clothes, in his country important people, such as the King and his nobles, are draped in them." And the slave Higino said: "Those clothes come from the same place *pano da costa* [West African cloth] comes from, and whoever wears them is important and on the warpath."[24] These are curious affirmations, even if one takes into account that they might have been made in attempts to confuse the investigator. Could it be that Malês were seen as "important people" by the rest of the African community and that their clothing indicated their special status? This could also be a veiled allusion to the powerful Muslim warrior chiefs of Ilorin and other northern cities in the forefront of the conflict with Oyo. But any interpretation can only be tentative given the existing documentation. It is possible that both Bento and Higino belonged to a group of slaves who considered the Malês important because they were unaccustomed to Islamic ways. The Malês' need for secrecy helped maintain their image of importance, which they may have enjoyed, given their wishes for superiority. If the abadá only had (peacetime or wartime) ritualistic functions in Bahia, its use can be considered one more African cultural adaptation or shift in the face of restrictions established by a slaveholding society.

Since they could no longer wear traditional clothing in public, Bahian Malês had a special way of identifying each other on the streets. They wore rings of white metal, silver or iron, on their fingers. Similar rings, known as *kendé* in Africa, were worn by the Muslim allies of the rebel Afonja. According to Samuel Johnson, these rings were worn on the thumb and the third or fourth finger of the left hand. When rebels greeted one another, they struck their rings. Johnson maintained that this was "a sign of brotherhood." This custom appears to have crossed the Atlantic. In Bahia, according to the testimony of a Nagô freedman, João, "white rings . . . were the badge worn by members of Malê society to recognize each other." The police confiscated dozens of those objects after the uprising. It seems that with their defeat even that symbol disappeared because everyone now knew what it meant. One witness testified that "immediately, on the day after the blacks' insurrection, everyone took the rings off their fingers." Much later, at the beginning of the twentieth century, the pioneering ethnologist Manoel Querino wrote that Bahian Malês wore silver rings only as wedding rings.[25]

The Growth of Islam in Bahia

Salvador's urban environment in many ways facilitated Islamic activities. The relative independence of urban slaves, the presence of a large number of African freedmen, and the interaction between these two groups helped create a dynamic network and community for proselytizing and mobilizing. Whether slaves or freedmen, Malês who knew how to read and write Arabic passed their learning on to others. They gathered on street corners to offer their services, and while they waited for customers they concerned themselves with their religion and their rebellion. Besides reading, writing, and talking, they also sewed abadás and Malê skullcaps. One witness, a native-born black woman named Maria Clara da Costa Pinto, who lived on Mangueira Street, opposite one of those African gathering points, or *cantos,* claimed that Aprígio (a freedman living with Manoel Calafate), along with other Malês, "for a long time had been making notes of the sort that appeared or were found on the insurgents, using totally strange letters and characters, and bringing together at that place others of their Nation . . . to whom they taught to write with pointers dipped in ink they had in a bottle, as she had witnessed many times. They even taught them prayers in their language."[26] A second lieutenant and also a poet, Ladislau dos Santos Titara, when he was not busy writing patriotic verse, also kept an eye on the same gathering and acknowledged that "he had seen them, principally the latter [Aprígio], making huge shirts and skullcaps, which the insurgents donned as uniforms. He also heard that Aprígio taught others of the same nation how to read."[27]

The houses of African freedmen also provided space for Malê worship, meals, celebrations, and of course conspiracies. This was the case with Manoel Calafate's house, where, according to the testimony of the slave Ignácio, Malês frequently met, under the command of mestre Manoel. Another locale regularly frequented by Malês was the tobacco shop belonging to mestre Dandará, in the Santa Bárbara market. There, according to a confession made by the elder himself, he brought African young people together to teach them the word of Allah. One of the prosecution's witnesses declared that Dandará organized twice-daily prayer sessions *(salah)*, which were a local adaptation of the five daily prayers of Islamic tradition. Such adaptations were necessary given the rigors of daily work under slavery. A Malê mestre named Luís Sanim in turn taught the faithful who gathered in the house of a Nagô freedman, Belchior da Silva Cunha. This house was located on Oração (meaning "prayer") Street, a short distance from Calafate's house.

In some cases slaves took advantage of their masters' largesse and met in their own quarters, where they received friends and spent time reading and writing. That went on in the house of an Englishman named Stuart. Another Englishman, Abraham, let his slaves James and Diogo construct a hut on his property. In 1835 this hut was perhaps the most important Malê community center in Bahia. Pacífico Licutan, the popular alufá, was not as lucky concerning his master, who was quite intransigent. Licutan and some other slaves pooled their money to rent a room where they could meet in peace. The majority of those "private mosques" (*machachalis* according to Etienne Brazil) were in downtown Salvador, except the one run by Dandará and the one in Vitória. Alufás Manoel, Sanim, and Licutan operated in a tiny area from Ladeira da Praça to Terreiro de Jesus.[28]

There is no detailed documentation concerning what went on behind those doors, but the little that exists is suggestive. The Malês met to pray, to learn to read and write Arabic, and to memorize verses from the *Koran*—all of which are important and indispensable tasks in Muslim education, regardless of time or place. Conversion through revelation in reading is expressed as follows in the *Koran:* "The unbelievers among the

People of the Book [Jews and Christians] and the pagans did not desist from unbelief until the Proof was given them: an apostle from Allah reading sanctified pages from eternal scriptures" (98:1).[29]

It is quite impressive that the experience of reading and writing riveted the interest of slaves and freedmen, who always found time for these activities. During the searches begun after the revolt was put down, the police confiscated dozens of writing slates used by Malês. These slates were wooden rectangles with a handle at one of the narrow ends. They were called *allo* by the Hausas and *wala* or *patako* by the Yorubas; *wala*, one more Yoruba word, displaced the others in Bahia. They wrote directly on the wood using ink made of burnt rice. Of course, they also used the slate as a desk for writing on paper, and their ink was sometimes black, sometimes red. Malês practiced their Arabic and religious lessons by copying prayers and passages from the *Koran*. Again, the water they used to erase the words was believed to have magical powers, especially if the words had been written by some prestigious Malê preacher.[30]

Not all the words were washed away, however. In spite of the high price of paper back then, Malês used it extensively to record matters of their faith. The police found many papers covered with Arabic writing, and these papers made a deep impression at the time. In a society where even the dominant whites were largely illiterate, it was hard to accept that African slaves possessed such sophisticated means of communication. However, these papers revealed that among their slaves were people highly instructed in the language of the *Koran,* people who left their marks in perfect calligraphy and correct grammar. These were Africans who, even though they were slaves in Bahia, had certainly been members of an intelligentsia in Africa, if not members of the wealthy merchant classes. They had enjoyed social privileges that allowed them to spend much of their time in intellectual pursuits.

One of the flawless texts Reichert found is a copy of the *Koran*'s opening sura, the Exordium:

   (1) in the name of compassionate merciful God !" praise
   (2) God master of the worlds !" the compassionate the merciful
   (3) Lord of judgement day !" we love thee
   (4) and from thee we ask for help !" lead us in the path
   (5) of righteousness !" in the path of those thou
   (6) didst favor and who are not the object of thy
   (7) wrath and not the wayward amen

But it was not just the hands of educated Malês that produced the famous "Arabic papers." Much of the writing came from inexperienced hands of students being initiated into Islam, or at least into its language. It is they who give witness to the dynamic pace of Muslim conversion and education in Bahia on the eve of the 1835 rebellion. Following is an example of a beginner's work:

(1) in the name of compassionate merci-
(2) ful god, may god protect thee
(3) from evil. he will not tell them
(4) all about . . .
(5) . . . from them amen

Here, according to Reichert, "the author made obvious errors, omissions, clumsy letters, etc."[31]

All this writing was to help them memorize prayers and texts from the *Koran*. This was an important step toward Islamic integration, because it let the initiate participate fully in collective prayers, and it added his voice to the ritual drama. It signaled a deeper commitment to the Malê community and its projects. According to Gaspar da Silva Cunha, "he did not join the prayers because he was a beginner." Whoever did pray always had, in addition to a wala and the white abadá, pieces of paper and the Malê rosary *(tessubá)*, which Querino describes in the following manner: "50 centimeters long, with 90 crude wooden beads, ending in a ball instead of a cross." In 1835 a scribe described it as "a string of 98 coconut beads on a cotton . . . cord." Whites and anti-Malê blacks maliciously called it a "pagan's rosary." Many of those rosaries were confiscated by the police during 1835.[32]

Women were conspicuously absent from Malê rituals. References to their role are rare in the inquiry. This is hardly remarkable; women's subservient role in the Muslim world is well known. In the words of Trimingham: "Women, seen as being in a constant state of ritual impurity, are not allowed to enter mosques." Although Islam does not formally forbid women to enter mosques, their inferior position is revealed in the *Koran:* "Women shall with justice have rights similar to those exercised against them, although men have a status above women" (2:228). Or: "Men have authority over women because Allah has made [men] superior to the others, and because they spend their wealth to maintain them. Good women are obedient" (4:34).

Doctrine is, of course, never carried out 100 percent in practice, and black Islam, both in Africa and perhaps mainly in Bahia, was obliged to make concessions to its feminine sector. In the 1835 goings-on alufá Dandará's companion, a slave by the name of Emereciana, handed out Malê rings like a general decorating meritorious recruits, an activity for which she was later sentenced to four hundred lashes. Emereciana was an exception, but as time went by, women became more and more integrated into Islamic rituals. Querino considered them to be totally incorporated into what he called "Malê masses." Also, in Rio de Janeiro at the end of the nineteenth century, women participated in funeral ceremonies; they ate and danced in an Islam of a more open variety.[33]

Even though the Malês of Brazil had to innovate with regard to Islam, they tried to maintain its basic characteristics. They tried to observe its food taboos and celebrate the most important dates on the Muslim calendar. Of course, it was not easy for the slaves to follow the Malê diet, since they could not always choose what they ate, even in the relatively flexible ambience of urban slavery. But matters pertaining to black Islam's eating practices appear throughout the inquiry. Malê suppers functioned as rituals of group solidarity. Communal dinners nourished dreams of independence and rebellion. Even if revolution itself is no banquet, as Mao Tse-tung wrote, the 1835 rebellion began with one at mestre Calafate's house.

Several witnesses saw Malês gather regularly to eat. One woman claimed that her neighbor, an ex-slave named Jacinto, "often had night meetings with dinner included at the house of his mistress Isabel, who lived on the Vitória road." (During the revolt Jacinto commanded a group of blacks who began their activities at Vitória Square [Largo da Vitória].) The slave sacristan at the Mercês Convent, Agostinho, invited Muslim companions to Christian quarters to, in his words, "just talk and eat." Ellena, a black woman, claimed that a slave known as Joaquim, who shared the rent of a room with alufá Licutan, "used to kill rams and have get-togethers during the day with his friends in his room, because at night they probably had to be in their masters' houses." Ellena was a Jeje ex-slave who lived in the same house. Further on, Ellena amended this and said the Malês "often came there to eat and have a party" only on Sundays and holidays, which was when slaves got time off.[34]

These suppers represented the Malês' effort to commit themselves to the Islamic precept of only eating food prepared by Muslim hands so as to avoid the danger of ritual pollution. They ate mutton frequently, which suggests ritual sacrifices. In Africa the ceremony in which a newly born child is given a name, on its eighth day of life, entails the sacrifice of a ram, which is then eaten. In some areas the same ritual is used when recently converted adults (newly born Muslims) receive their Islamic name. Quite likely these practices continued in Bahia. Querino also reports that Malês commemorated the end of Ramadan, the month of fasting, by sacrificing rams. Indeed, during 1835, at the request of a justice of the peace, a slave translated a text that was, according to the slave, "a sort of calender which the Malês use to keep track of their fasts and to know when to slaughter their rams." Querino also wrote: "When they sacrificed a lamb, they stuck the point of the knife into the sand and bled the animal saying the word *Bi-si-mi-lai*." (*Bismillah*, in its complete form *Bismika Allahumma*, opens all the suras of the *Koran* and means "In the name of Allah, the Compassionate, the Merciful.") This author also tells us that during Ramadan Bahian Malês lived on a diet of yams, bugloss *(efó)*, rice, milk, and honey.[35]

It was also at the table that Malês celebrated their main religious holidays, including Lailat al-Miraj (Mohammed's ascension into Heaven), which in 1834 was celebrated at the end of November, less than two months before the uprising. In that year, the twenty-sixth day of Rajab (the seventh month in the Islamic calendar), the traditional date to celebrate Lailat al-Miraj, fell on 29 November. That day many people met in the hut behind Mr. Abraham's house on the Vitória road. In the words of the slave João, "There was a dinner where all the Nagô slaves belonging to Englishmen met, plus some boatsmen [*escravos de saveiro*] who came to town, as well as some belonging to Brazilians." This great meeting seems to have been the first time Muslims shed their traditional reticence, and for this they paid dearly.[36]

In the midst of the Malê celebrations, there came an unexpected visit from a well-known enemy, Inspector Antônio Marques. He had come to stop the "disturbance of the peace" on his block. He acted arrogantly, dispersing the celebrants and running them off. On the following day he informed the justice of the peace of Vitória Parish, Francisco José da Silva Machado, of the goings-on, and the justice of the peace then complained to Mr. Abraham. To avoid problems with the Brazilian authorities, the Englishman obliged the builders of the hut, Diogo and James, to destroy it. Later on James would say that this coerced gesture brought him resentment from the Nagôs: "The master made them take the same house down, which made some of his countrymen who used to meet there refuse to greet him." In another part of his testimony, the slave was to tell the building's history: "Built some five months earlier, it had been made . . . so that other partners and friends could enjoy themselves, getting together to eat, drink, play, and talk." The loss of the building, a veritable black mosque, was doubtless a sad event for the Malês.[37]

This incident in Vitória is not the only example of religious persecution to be found in the court records prior to 1835. If there were some masters who were tolerant of their slaves' religion, there were others who prohibited them from practicing Islam. From time to time some masters repented their past tolerance and began to prohibit slaves' religious ceremonies, as seems to have been the case with the English merchant Frederick Robelliard. At one point he had permitted his slaves to learn Arabic, but he later prohibited it, having concluded that their lessons kept them away from their work. Carlos, who learned to read with other slaves, said: "At one time the master did not stop them, but later, when he checked the boxes belonging to his teachers *(mestres),* he had the contents gathered and burnt, scolding them and intimating that because they had nothing better to do they spent their time learning and teaching the language of their land." A twenty-seven-year-old merchant, Teodoro Barros, reported that a Hausa slave, Antônio, used to teach "a slave belonging to José Vieira to write, and for that reason Vieira punished him because he did not want his slave learning that language." On the other hand, on the same occasion Antônio's master defended his slave's activities, "because such writing is pursuant to his prayers."[38]

The feast of Lailat al-Miraj was a sign of Islam's success in Bahia, an Islam on the rise and daring to be public. At that time Mohammedans were a well-defined segment of the Bahian black community; they had a charged identity and provided a strong point of reference for Africans living there. Slaves and freedmen flocked to Islam in search of spiritual comfort and hope. They needed it to establish some order and dignity in their lives. The *Koran's* texts were especially appealing because of their sympathy for the discriminated, the exiled, the persecuted, and the enslaved. But if Allah is there to protect the weak, He also wants their fidelity and commitment to spread His word and the Islamic way of life. This militant aspect of Islam gave the Malês special distinction and attracted many Africans to them, but it also pushed others away.

Malês wove a web of complicity with other blacks using their amulets and their still incomplete rupture with the ethnic religions from Africa. This complicity aided the 1835 rebellion. There was, however, tension between the Malês and non-Muslim blacks who complained about the pride, the intolerance, and the orthodoxy of their Mohammedan brethren. A Yoruba-Ijebu slave by the name of Carlos made the following comment: "The Nagôs who can read, and who took part in the insurrection, would not shake hands with nor respect outsiders. They even called them *gaveré.*" The word *gaveré* was the scribe's attempt at writing *kafiri* or *kafir* (plural *kafirai*), the Arabic word for "pagans." In the case in point, the word designated Africans still associated with traditional ethnic religions such as Candomblé. The Malês treated Catholics even worse. Marcelina, the slave of a nun living in the Desterro Convent, complained that they harassed her saying "she was going to Mass to worship a piece of wood on the altar, because images are not saints." In spite of the relative openness of black Islam in Bahia, the religious fervor of many Muslims and their moderate habits could seem excessively disciplined to Africans weary of discipline and more inclined to embrace the polar opposite movement toward worldly pleasure. Ezequiel, an African freedman, criticized the Malês for not eating pork and said of their life of self-denial: "They all want to be priests."[39]

One must regard these declarations with reservations, however. After all, it must not have been difficult for the authorities to hear arrested Africans utter words against the attitudes and customs of the Malês, since such utterances were means of saving one's skin. Still, those declarations cannot be considered bald-faced lies. In that context they are valuable insofar as they reveal tension and contention among Africans, but this animosity should not be blown out of proportion. Even Marcelina, the Catholic slave who complained about the Malês, did not let their behavior drive her from the room she rented from a well-known Islamic militant, Belchior da Silva Cunha, where she came into daily contact with many Muslims.

Bahian Muslims were in no way the fierce separatists many students of the 1835 rebellion have claimed them to be. They may have gone to some extremes in the defense of their religious point of view, but life had other facets for them, too. Besides religious communion, there were other forces of social solidarity and integration in Africans' lives: their Africanness, their ethnicity, their very situation as slaves and freedmen who were exploited and discriminated against. These forces were significant for all Africans without exception. Seen in this light, religious contention represented a dynamic element within the African community, which contained immense cultural variety and a plurality of world and otherworldly views. The Malês never posed a threat to that plurality, and there is no proof that a monopoly on religion was their principal objective in 1835, or at any other time.

· 6 ·

A Bahian Caliphate?

THE MALÊS AND THEIR REBELLION

That night is peace, till break of dawn.
—*Koran,* 97 : 5

The 1835 rebellion was neither a spontaneous explosion nor the result of a hasty decision, as had often been the case in earlier slave revolts. It was quite likely long in planning. There are not, however, sufficient data to describe with precision either the period or the measures that led to the revolt. Under questioning the rebels were all silent on this matter. The few who said anything at all were not part of the conspiracy's central nucleus and not in on the whole story. Nonetheless, it is possible to piece the existing testimony together and construct an outline of events leading to 1835.

From Religion to Rebellion

When Malês met privately and, less often, publicly to carry out the precepts of their religion or just to share other aspects of their lives, they used those occasions to envisage a better world. They did not, however, rule out the use of force to attain this better world. According to a black woman named Agostinha, "When they got together they talked about making war on whites."[1] But for a long time Malê warriors' battles were little more than rhetorical warfare, a metaphor of real social conflict, angry expression of their desire for reparation rather than the conceiving of an actual revolt. Of course, after two decades of slave rebellions, prior insurrections would influence any speculation, no matter how unobjective it might be. But the idea of a specific, planned rebellion on a specific date must have emerged little by little.

The rebellion occurred at a time of Islamic expansion among the Africans living in Bahia. It is difficult to establish whether it was a natural consequence, a sort of climax to that expansion, or whether the search for new Malês could have been part of the plan to break with the status quo. Perhaps it was a little of both. The Malês' success in forming a relatively cohesive and attractive religious community must have inspired ideas of making even greater inroads on the limits imposed on them by the powers that be. These rebellious ideas, once they came to term, made the Muslim leaders want to widen their base of support as one step in their plan to take power.

It is, admittedly, futile to separate religion from rebellion in cases such as this. Rebellion begins when a religion sides with the oppressed. The very fact that African slaves opted for Islam proclaimed a schism, a radical separation from the seigniorial ideology, and, by extension a rebellion. In the 1824 Constitution, Catholicism had been declared the official state religion, and the only one allowed public ceremonies and clearly marked temples. *European* foreigners were conceded the right to religious freedom, provided they worshipped in private. Slave religions were illegal. They were police business rather than a matter of constitutional law. The Malês were outlaws.

The chasm between Islam and Bahian society was especially wide because Islam was an exclusively African religion that brought together slaves and freedmen. Besides, like Catholicism, Islam was a universal religion. And since it was not an ethnic religion, Islam could possibly unite diverse ethnic groups, nullifying the slaveholders' political advantage derived from Africans' diverse ethnicities. Islam was not just a class ideology, not just a slave ideology; it was, rather, the ideology of many peoples of non-European civilizations. It confronted the Brazilian master with a full-length portrait of an undivided Other. In Bahia, the very existence of Islam and of other African religions at least symbolically subverted the dominant order.

The 1835 rebellion clearly shows that Malês went beyond symbolic subversion. They began to structure a political rebellion. It is likely that 1835 was not the first experience of revolt for many of them. Even though it may be wrong to seek Muslim dominance in prior rebellions, especially those considered to be led by Hausas during the Ponte and Arcos governments, Muslims were certainly involved in at least some of them. One of the mestres to go on trial in 1835, Elesbão do Carmo (Dandará), appears in the records as a participant in the insurrections during Arcos's term. One witness testified that "because Dandará was clever, he always avoided being captured."[2] He was surely not the only clever Malê around. But there is no proof that Malês were exclusive actors or even part of the privileged vanguard of movements other than the 1814 uprising discussed above.

But 1835 was different. The first five years of the 1830s were tumultuous throughout the province: street riots, anti-Portuguese protests, ransack-ing, federalist revolts, barracks revolts, slave revolts—all in the midst of an economic crisis. At the same time, the Malê ranks were growing. The rush to Islam did not necessarily mean a rush into revolution. It was, at its beginning, a search for channels of solidarity in the crisis that slavery itself represented, for spiritual security, and possibly for upward mobility and social prestige within the African community itself. The factor of prestige cannot be underestimated. To be known as a Malê was an honor. It meant being respected for Malês' written culture and magical powers, or merely for membership in a group known to express strong African identity. As we saw in chapter 5, Muslim pride was a mechanism of power in daily interactions, and Malê pride created animosity between Malês and other Africans. There were, then, both vertical and horizontal vectors involved in becoming a Malê. One vector challenged seigniorial power; the other strove for power among the Africans. Both obviously crisscrossed, since for those who did choose Islam, among the many available options, be-coming a Malê must have seemed the best way to beat the white master, here or in the next world. But evidently not all Africans agreed.

This point in Bahia's history seems to have been extremely rich. It was a time replete with discussion, innovation, and political, cultural, and ideo-logical shifts. Keeping matters in their proper perspective, to call it a pe-riod of revolutionary effervescence is no exaggeration. Bahian society breathed politics, shook in unrest, and the black community was not out-side this process.

Among Africans' many political and cultural alternatives available at the time, Islam took the lead. It was the right moment. Not because it had always promoted social revolution, which is hardly obvious in its history, but because it fostered a revolution in the lives of its followers. It made them want not to be slaves or inferiors; it gave them dignity; and it created new personalities for its members. Only at a specific time did the Malê leaders redirect their disciples from an individual religious commitment to a commitment to an organized, armed rebellion. The French consul un-derstood this strategy: "The organizers were very clever. They began by leading people astray by inviting them to come and practice their religion. Then they brought them in on their plans, which were known to all those [Africans] who did not take part in the rebellion. The latter group, bound either by their oaths or by their beliefs, or by the hopes of sharing in the spoils without running the risks, kept the Malês' secret."[3]

The leaders put together a shrewdly organized revolutionary struc-ture. While the number of converts and sympathizers continued to grow without any concrete promise of revolt, the leaders evaluated their ranks, studied the political situation, and pondered when to revolt. It was im-portant for them to find a time when secular strategy would combine with

Allah's will. They also needed the confidence and unwavering respect of disciples who would follow them unflinchingly and wherever they led them. They also needed less committed disciples who could keep their secrets. Only the alufás or malāms knew exactly when they would attack. Perhaps that is why only on the eve of the revolt—when news of the conspiracy traveled from mouth to mouth throughout the city—were the authorities to learn of the Malês' plans. Concrete plans for the revolt seem to have begun around the end of 1834. Only then did the work begin: defining tactics, establishing methods, forming alliances, increasing contacts, assigning tasks, setting dates.

The enthusiastic celebration of Lailat al-Miraj in November was a watershed (see chapter 5). That day demonstrated Islam's success as well as its limits. When the feast was interrupted and dissolved by Inspector Marques, one chapter of Bahian Islamic history ended. This episode was sealed shut by the later destruction of the Vitória "Mosque," which produced discord and distress in the Malê community. Its pride was hurt, and its weakness exposed to the entire city. The Muslims needed to act immediately, to do something to avoid a falling off of membership and a lack of confidence in their cause. In addition to the drama during Lailat al-Miraj, two other incidents must have influenced the leaders' political reasoning. One was the imprisonment, also in November, of Alufá Pacífico Licutan for reasons having nothing to do with the revolt. The other, more or less at the same time, was the imprisonment and public humiliation of another important preacher, alufá Ahuna. (On these men and the circumstances leading to their arrests see chapter 7.) The decision to revolt on 25 January 1835 was quite likely made in November 1834. It was a calm, calculated political decision designed to harness the high-strung emotions of the crisis. The twenty-fifth of January coincided with a propitious date in the Islamic calendar.

From Rebellion to Religion

At that point Malê leaders began to define their objectives more clearly. Their radius of action was to extend beyond Salvador. It seemed clear to them that a strictly urban revolt had little future, since it would leave out the better part of the African population, which was concentrated on the plantations and villages throughout the Recôncavo. Once again the rebellion's strategy had been preceded by religious expansion. The Malês had gained followers and created a base in the countryside. "Throughout the Recôncavo," the slave Carlos confessed, "everywhere they have commissaries charged with widening the bases of Malê society . . . and he heard other blacks on several occasions say that when the time came for a widespread outbreak, people in the Recôncavo would come and help those in the city." Even if their contacts in the countryside were not new, they were increased during the weeks before the rebellion. The role of Malê freedmen was fundamental in that effort. Manoel Calafate was one of the "commissaries." Joaquina, the mulatto woman who lived in the same building as Calafate, informed the justice of the peace that three days before the revolt Calafate returned from Santo Amaro, and from that time on the coming and going of Africans in and out of his loge intensified. Another commissary for the area around the Bay of All Saints was the tobacco merchant Dandará. According to the testimony of Pompeu, a plantation slave from Santo Amaro, Dandará gave him spiritual assistance on his visits to Santo Amaro. Santo Amaro seems to have been the main nucleus of conspiratorial activities in the countryside. Pompeu and some others left that town to fight in the streets of Salvador.[4]

For nearly a month, perhaps, the Malês were in a state of alert. The rebellion could explode at any moment. Word on the exact date only reached the rank and file a few days (for some, a few hours) beforehand. This security measure was certainly employed to reduce as much as possible any likelihood of betrayal. It makes sense that the freedman Belchior da Silva Cunha only "heard talk of making war against the whites . . . Saturday morning as he was on his way to buy lime." A slave known as João was told the afternoon of the twenty-fourth, and Agostinho, at 8:00 that night. The testimony of João, one of Abraham's slaves, provides an excellent example of how the news reached the ears of most rebels: "He was told, however, the afternoon of the 24th of January by some partners, whose . . . names he no longer remembers, that they would all meet, so as to kill all whites, mulattos, and creoles. The prisoner, at midnight, more or less, with his partners Diogo, Jaimes, and Daniel, went to join the others, who by that time were at Fort São Pedro." The declarations of Pedro, a slave of English physician Robert Dundas, complement João's:

> At 7:30 P.M. on the 24th of January he had left his master's house and headed for the Graça road. Along the way he spoke with Jaimes and Diogo, slaves belonging to the Englishman José Mellors. These slaves invited him to be ready for the frolic, for killing whites. They went on, reaching the Graça road and the house of another Englishman, Frederico Robelliard, and there they spoke with two of his slaves, Carlos and Thomaz, telling them to be ready to frolic. From there he headed toward Barris and on the way he met Pedro and Miguel, also Mellors's slaves, as well as many others who were gathering. Once in Barris, at Mellors's house, he met his partner Carlos, and they came to join [the others] at the Mercê Convent, where in the midst of the shooting Pedro was wounded.[5]

The majority of these Africans, slaves of Englishmen, were Muslims of possibly long standing, yet they were only "invited" to the uprising at the last minute.

One might object that such testimony comes from suspects' efforts to hide greater involvement in the rebellion. Perhaps, but not in every case. It is hard to imagine that Belchior da Silva Cunha would have only found out about the rebellion the night before, since he lived in one of the most active Muslim centers, and with another dedicated Malê, the tailor freedman Gaspar da Silva Cunha. But it seems unlikely that detailed and self-accusatory testimony such as João's and Pedro's could be made up. There were some clever Malês who denied everything or made up stories, but there were also those who, for their own reasons, told the simple truth.

Apparently only a small rebel group knew all the information. This group consisted of the mestres and their closest associates. It seems beyond question that the final call to arms came from them. This is what one learns from the testimony of a Nagô slave woman, Marcelina, as she heard it from a Nagô freedwoman, Agostinha, who told her that her companion Belchior da Silva Cunha "had been invited by his mestre, the aforementioned slave Luís [Sanim], just as the other mestres had invited their disciples to make war on the Whites." (Belchior's testimony is different.) The lead role played by the mestres or alufás has been supported by a singular ritual that took place in Manoel Calafate's house. According to Justice of the Peace Caetano Vicente de Almeida Galião's report, in Calafate's room "they found a rod and a white handkerchief with a purple border, like a flag with six little bags made of leather and cloth in front of which black Ignácio declared they swore not to die in bed but [to die] alongside Father [Pay] Manoel Calafate."[6] It may be that this loyalty oath sworn on a Muslim war banner was repeated before each leader on the eve of the revolt, at least by their most favored and committed disciples.

Even if each mestre led his disciples into revolt, the final word was probably given by an African known as Mala Mubakar. According to a contemporary translation of a manifesto written in Arabic, whose original unfortunately has not survived, this was the man who must have summoned all Malês into battle, guaranteeing them physical invulnerability when they met the enemy. Mubakar was not mentioned by that name by any prisoner; nor was he taken prisoner, or if he was, he managed to keep his identity a secret. One could perhaps consider him to be a character of the police's fantasies at the time, a convenient attempt to exaggerate the Malês' organization in order to justify the excessive repression later on. However, Mubakar's existence was also mentioned sixty years later. Rodrigues heard from an old alufá that Mubakar was known as Tomé in white man's land, and in 1835 he was Bahia's *almami* (*iman* in Arabic), that is, the supreme spiritual leader of the Bahian Malê community.[7] Nonetheless, it is intriguing that a rebel star of such magnitude only appears as a signature on a manifesto that has vanished. It may be that the distance maintained between this leader and the rank-and-file Malês typifies Bahian

Islam and the rebellion itself. Hidden forces always seem more powerful. (The next chapter suggests that this apparently mysterious personage may have been someone quite well known in the African community.)

The date chosen for the beginning of the rebellion was Sunday, the feast day of Our Lady of Guidance. This choice had obvious strategic advantages and proves that the men who made it were sufficiently integrated into Bahian society to know its habits, in this case to know that the celebration would take many people, especially free men, off to the distant locale of Bonfim. A good part of the police force would also head in that direction in order to keep the celebrators in line. Given both the distance and the precarious transportation and highways of the period, people went to Bonfim with the idea of spending the entire weekend in celebration. Emptied of its able-bodied men and its police, Salvador would be easy prey. This was the first plank in the rebels' plans.

One other reason for choosing that date was that it offered greater ease in mobilizing urban slaves. A Sunday holiday would help them slip out from under the watchful eyes of their masters, as well as from the eyes of their guardians on the streets, the police. They could leave their quarters more freely and meet their co-conspirators as well as encourage the participation of slaves not in on the planning. Some testimony indicates the plotters planned to enlist whatever African slaves were in the streets fetching water at the public fountains on the morning of the twenty-fifth. From a practical point of view, the day seemed perfect for the outbreak of a massive urban revolt.

But there were other, less worldly reasons for choosing that date. The rebellion had been planned to come off at a very special moment in the Muslim religious calendar, in fact at the most important time of all—Ramadan. With the exception of Rodrigues, no other author has given this element of the timing its due importance. Even Rodrigues only refers in passing to "fasting as a propitiatory measure." However, the records furnish definite indications of the propitious timing. The testimony of the jailer at the city jail, Antônio Pereira de Almeida, maintains that a few days before the revolt a meeting between alufá Licutan and some African visitors took place in the jail. On that occasion his visitors told him that "when the fast was over, they would get him out of jail once and for all." Another police report chronicles the disappearance of peanut flour and unrefined sugar blocks *(rapadura)* from Salvador's markets, foodstuffs eaten by Malês after nightfall during Ramadan.[8]

Converting 25 January 1835 of the Christian Era into the Muslim calendar gives the twenty-fifth of Ramadan, A.H. 1250. It was near the end of the month of fasting, and the Malês may have been celebrating one of the feasts that end the holy month, Lailat al-Qadr, which means "Night of Glory" or "Night of Power." The exact date of Lailat al-Qadr is not fixed but occurs on one of the last ten nights of Ramadan. In West Africa the most popular date is the twenty-seventh of Ramadan. The Malês may have celebrated it on the twenty-fifth, a Sunday and slaves' day of leisure, without feeling they betrayed its holiness. Perhaps the Malês planned to celebrate their victory on that very day of glory and power. It is more likely, however, that they wanted to celebrate that glorious night using their newly gained spiritual power base to further the revolt.[9]

Lailat al-Qadr commemorates the revelation of the holy scriptures to Mohammed and is thus a celebration of God's proximity to mankind. It is also known as the "Night of Destiny," because on that night humanity's fate is cast for the coming year. In West Africa people believe that on Lailat al-Qadr Allah imprisons jinns and with a free hand reestablishes order in the world. The *Qadr* is the ninety-seventh sura of the *Koran*. It is brief and beautiful. Reading it must have inspired the rebels in one way or another:

> We revealed the Koran on the Night of Qadr
> Would that you knew what the Night of Qadr is like!
> Better is the Night of Qadr than a thousand months.
> On that night the angels and the Spirit by their Lord's
> leave come down with His decrees.
> That night is peace, till break of dawn.

"Till break of dawn." Could the Malês have tried to follow the *Koran*'s word to the letter? Could they have been breaking their fast and celebrating the "Night of Glory" at Calafate's house and waiting for daybreak to challenge the slaveholding order? It is a plausible understanding of the movement and of the records, which explicitly name dawn as the hour set for the uprising and the breaking of the fast as the moment of liberation for alufá Licutan.

Even if the revolt might not have followed the ritual itinerary entirely faithfully, it is certain that Ramadan was not an accidental aspect of this event. It does not matter that Ramadan is traditionally considered a time of truce, contemplation, and purification, since there is always leeway to adapt to local circumstances. The Malê uprising is a typical case of "the intrusion of sociopolitical tensions into the sacred calendar."[10] In fact, any time during Ramadan would be appropriate for dangerous adventures, since, as one author has observed, "it is believed that during this period many evil spirits and powers are largely neutralized."[11] Once the forces of evil embodied in their enemies were neutralized, the Malê rebels believed they were ready for whatever came their way.

Beyond a doubt the 1835 rebellion was part of the Malês' program for the commemoration of Ramadan. This celebration was to be the first act of a new era. The festive air is expressed in the terms used by many to define the rebellion, terms such as "frolic" *(folguedo)*, "rumpus" *(brinca-*

deira), "toying" *(brinquedo)*, and "spree" *(banzé)*. Playful language, an aspect of the African cultures recreated in the New World, makes one believe that religion, politics, and celebration were melded in the Malê worldview, as in that of other Africans. It is necessary to underline this point, especially because it does not jibe with the point of view of those who interpreted African Islam in Bahia as being a stubborn, sad variety. The testimony of prisoners and witnesses so often mentions feasts, dinners, eating and drinking, that one can only conclude that in Bahia Islam was quite festive, notwithstanding its dietary, sexual, and other taboos, which, as in all religions, were probably not obeyed rigorously by all. Thus, from the Malê outlook, in 1835 the serious defenders of and participators in the white slave society were on the side of evil, whereas the apocalyptic Islamic militants were on the side of good, and were joyous because they were working for a just transformation of the world.

Nonetheless, sura 97 is not among the surviving papers seized by the police, nor does it appear in any trial record. As Reichert has noted, however, some passages in the existing papers address the plight of the oppressed and promise believers better days if they were ready to do their part. Some amulets sent from Salvador to E. de la Rosière, the French representative in Rio de Janeiro at the time, were written in the same spirit. According to de la Rosière, they all read:

> In the name of God the merciful, the compassionate! May God have compassion on our lord Mohammed! Praised be the name of the giver of salvation = blood must be shed: we must all have a hand in it = Oh God! Oh Mohammed! Servant of the Almighty! We hope for success if it be God in the highest's will. Glory be to God! Amen.

The diplomat added: "The versicle on the shedding of blood was repeated 210 times on 42 different lines of each piece of paper carried by each black." It is unlikely that every rebel carried an identical text, since none of the surviving Arabic papers is an exact copy of any other, but there is no reason to doubt that at least one such text existed.[12]

A Bahian Caliphate?

Protected by their amulets, their abadás, and their religious guides' words, and acting in tune with a favorable cosmic event, the Malês went into the fray with great hopes for success. "Victory comes from Allah. Victory is near. Glad tidings for all believers," promised the millennial text in one amulet confiscated by the police.[13] But victory over whom? And what would they do with that victory?

It is hard to imagine what Bahia would have become with the Malês in power. The testimony of the accused says nothing about this matter directly. The documents in Arabic that have been recovered contained no plans for a government. That does not, however, make it impossible to establish some of the rebellion's important characteristics and objectives. In the first place, the revolt envisaged a Bahia for the Africans. According to one of the Arabic documents translated by a Hausa slave known as Albino, "They were to have come from Victória taking the land and killing everyone in white man's land." Not only whites were marked for death; mulattos and native-born blacks were marked as well—"everyone in white man's land" meant all those born in Brazil. Other sources are more explicit. A slave known as João confirmed that the rebels' objective was "to kill all whites, mulattos, and native-born blacks." On the other hand, Guilhermina Rosa de Souza's testimony offers an important variation. She claimed that her husband, Domingos Fortunato, had heard on the waterfront that the rebels planned to take the land, "killing whites, cabras [i.e., 'faded' blacks], creoles, as well as any other blacks who might not side with them. They would keep the mulattos as their slaves and lackeys." On top of this, they entertained the possibility of other Africans' taking sides with the locals. Those Africans would have the same fate as the locals. The most interesting part is their plan to enslave mulattos.[14]

In the event the Malês actually planned to enslave mulattos, such a plan would not be out of character with the logic of the times. In Africa prisoners of war were partly spared to serve the winners or to be sold as slaves. Slavery existed throughout West Africa, even among those who came to Bahia as slaves, such as the Yorubas, the Hausas, and the Aja-Fon. It is true that the institution was different in Africa. Captives enjoyed greater social mobility, and slaves could become generals, ministers, advisers to kings, and local chiefs. Of course, as in all slave societies, the majority of slaves remained in lower social echelons. One must also remember that Islam accepted enslavement of heretics and pagans, and even if such people converted to Islam, that did not mean automatic freedom. In Africa Muslims had a hand in all business, including the slave trade. It is quite likely that many Bahian Malês' pasts were somewhat sullied. A man named Mohammed (known as Manoel in Salvador), a Hausa malām from the city of Katsina, was interviewed by the French consul in the late 1840s. He claimed to have been captured by Fulanis while taking his own slaves to a market. The Fulanis sold him too. The famous story of a Fulani Muslim Job Ben Solomon, captured in similar circumstances and sold by Mandingos during the first half of the eighteenth century, is similar.[15]

In addition to what they knew about African slavery, Africans learned more about the art of enslavement in Bahia. They learned not only from the white master's example but also from Africans' desire to turn the tables on the power structure. Besides, in Bahia it was not rare to see an ex-slave become a slaveowner, and there were even a few cases, albeit rare ones, of slaves owning slaves. It must be made clear, however, that the Malê community was not particularly known to have slaveholding members in it. Among the prisoners to stand trial, only *one* freedman, Gaspar da Silva Cunha, owned *one* slave, a Congo by the name of José.[16]

Coming from slave societies in Africa, and having been plunged into another society even more profoundly structured around slavery, the rebels may have considered slavery an inevitable social relation. Their plan for Bahian slavery might be unique (e.g., mulatto slaves), however it was no exception to the contemporary rule in the world they were familiar with. They did not envisage an egalitarian utopia, which may come as a disappointment for those wanting to find altruistic heroes in the history of rebellions. The Malês were men of flesh and blood, limited by the outlook of their time, circumstances, and human nature. After all, what slave has never dreamed of being a master?

Even though it is not outlandish for the rebels to have planned a new system of slavery, one must point out that there is scant evidence for all this. Indeed all the evidence comes from Guilhermina. It may be that the people who talked to her husband about enslaving mulattos were just voicing their own opinions, which may have had little or no resemblance to mainstream tendencies within the movement. The rebels certainly planned to end white domination, and they considered mulattos and native-born blacks accomplices in domination rather than victims. (This matter is discussed in greater detail in chapter 8.) If, however, history had been on the Malês' side, once in power Africans probably would have ended up establishing a modus vivendi with Afro-Bahians. Peace with whites was probably beyond consideration. Whites were the principal target of rebel rage. The movement was defined from the beginning as a "white-killing frolic." "War on whites! Kill the whites!" and other, similar expressions were the most frequent in the testimony of African prisoners. Neither mulattos nor creoles were the object of great attention among the 1835 insurgents.[17]

If on the one hand rebels considered all people "in white man's land" adversaries, on the other hand they based their rebellion on the principle that all Africans were potential allies. This interpretation clashes head-on with the opinion of those who saw (or see) the rebellion as a jihad of the sword, a classic Muslim holy war against the infidel of whatever color or origin. Authors sharing this opinion are, among others, Etienne Brazil, Arthur Ramos, and Pierre Verger. The jihad tradition was begun by Rodrigues, who, in spite of not using the term *jihad* and not presenting the slightest evidence, claimed that rebels planned to "massacre . . . pagan Africans" along with whites and native blacks. In his classic book on African religions in Brazil, Bastide maintains that the rebels' only adversaries were the Catholics. He has also pointed out that some pagan Africans may have participated in the revolt. In contrast, Goody has recently underlined Islam's role as a literate, universal, proselytizing, and intolerant religion.

He maintains that Bahian Malês sought to protect and expand Islam as Fulani holy warriors in Africa had.[18]

The Malês may have planned to set up an exclusive caliphate in Bahia, but they could not have been so stupid as to imagine they could take on so many different fronts at once. Religious illumination did not blind their reasonable political intelligence, demonstrated in the movement's organization. While the movement was doubtlessly headed by Malês, the uprising itself needed non-Muslim participation. Islam may have furnished the predominant ideology and language, but other factors contributed to the mobilization, among them ethnic solidarity (see chapter 8).

The rebellion was to be an alliance among Malês and other Africans, and Malês were not the only Africans to go into the streets that January morning. The uprising attracted Africans of diverse origins and religious persuasions, and its organizers counted on having an African front. Such a plan was inevitable, not because of their religious tolerance, but simply because the Malês knew they were a minority among Africans and an even smaller minority in the total population of Bahia. All alone they would not even take a parish, much less the entire province. They needed to recruit all African slaves that Sunday morning, and thus they would not check to see whether everyone joining the "frolic" was a Malê. If they had a jihad in mind, it was a jihad conveniently diverging from the classic holy war, including as it did people from outside the Islamic community.

The religious overtones of the rebellion's preparation did not scare off non-Muslims. For an outsider who believed in Islam's powerful magic, this was a good opportunity to try it out. Others, perhaps the majority, would join the struggle without caring about its religious meaning. They were there for come what might. If there was to be an African revolt, they, as Africans, would be in on it. Those who did not take part did not necessarily disagree with Islamic directives (although some may have); they did not participate either because they were unaware of the revolt or because they did not believe it was a solution to their predicament. They may have been afraid to participate or have been at odds with someone in the movement. In the testimonies all of these positions were expressed.

Malês dominated the rebel bloc, but they were not alone. A Malê vanguard was responsible for conceiving and beginning the revolt. A second group of workmates, friends and Malê sympathizers, became mobilized in a few hours or during the heat of battle. And people joined the insurrection on the spur of the moment: they woke up to the noise in the streets, went out, looked around, figured out what was going on, and participated. In this scenario Malês fought alongside kafirai, especially orisha people, who were Nagôs, as were most of the Malês. In a nutshell, this was a *Malê* plot but an *African* uprising.

Nagôs were predominant in the movement. Beyond the "jihadist" perspective, what other reasons motivated Nagôs to join a project initiated by its Mohammedan sector? Many Malês, perhaps the majority in 1835, were Nagôs, and several contemporary observers understood the rebellion to be a Nagô undertaking. As chapter 5 makes clear, there was also considerable cultural intercourse between Islam and traditional African religions, including orisha cults. The widespread use of Malê amulets reflected this. Another example would be the syncretism between tribal spirits (anjonu) and Muslim jinns. There were, however, others.

Members of orisha cults reserved a special place in their mythology for the sons of Allah. They thought of them as people on the side of the white divinities *(funfus)*, especially the great Orişalá, known as Oxalá in Bahia. The white abadás and Muslims' use of water in public ceremonies as well as in their private rituals, such as their daily bathing and their washing of the dead before burial, were evidence of parentage with Oxalá, whose symbolic color is also white and one of whose vital elements is water. A large white sheet, coincidentally called an *alá,* is Oxalá's most important emblem. His most important feast day is known as the Waters of Oxalá.[19] Even certain taboos united the faithful of both cults. Neither Muslims nor the followers of Oxalá should drink alcoholic beverages. For the Yorubas this peculiarity was linked to their myth of creation, which establishes their divine being as the representative of ethic and ritual purity.[20]

Using these symbolic and ritualistic links, the priests of Ifá, the divining god, identified African Muslims as the sons of Oxalá. These priests would send to alufás people whose problems seemed more likely to be resolved by Islamic wisdom. It became common for *babalawos,* which is what those Yoruba priests are called, to direct people toward Islam when this advice emerged from their divinatory practices. According to Stasik, "*Imale* was eventually found in the 12th of the 16 *odu* or 'chapters' of Ifá wisdom, in *otua meji* which was the traditional sphere of *orisatalabi,* the orisha associated with whiteness and ritual washing, the two most identifying traits of Muslims."[21] In this tradition the *otua meji* recommended conversion to or initiation into Islam.

In his classic work on West African geomancy, Maupoil maintains that the sign of *tula-meji* relates to Muslims. "The 'marabouts' and all who wear long shirts come into the world under the sign, which is symbolic of everything that is Malê, everything Islamic."[22] Malês are also present in the divination system using the sixteen cowries, which is simpler than Ifá and, perhaps because of its simplicity, more widespread. One of the verses in the ten-cowry play actually explains the origin of Ramadan. It says that Nana, the old water goddess and the mother of all Malês according to a Yoruba tradition, had fallen sick. The cowries revealed that her children should make sacrifices to the gods. But instead of feeding the gods, Nana's children fed her cornmeal mush every day. After thirty days,

> Nana was finished and about to die; she called her children.
> She said, "From today on
> "You will begin, when the year has gone around,
> "For thirty days you should go hungry.
> "You must not eat during the day, and you must not drink water."
> This is how fasting began, that Muslims must not break their fast;
> This is the origin of fasting.[23]

From this one can see that a fundamental Islamic practice could be interpreted within the orisha religious system.

The incorporation of Islamic elements into Yoruba religion is one more example of the latter's well-known malleability and tolerance. But the establishment of friendly ground for Muslims in the orisha universe was not without its own purpose. Power was at stake here. Stasik rightly suggests that babalawos actually gained more power by incorporating Islam into their divinatory system, since it allied them with a successful religion that was becoming more and more popular among Yorubas. The diviner achieved authority in two different religious schemes. He became a precious asset in the spread of Islam, a true ally who at the same time strengthened orisha belief as well. A brilliant lesson in politics. Muslims, notwithstanding the conflicts and tensions they must have had with practitioners of ethnic religions, "tried to accommodate their preaching to the prevailing cosmological vision so as to avoid direct confrontation with orisha people."[24]

Crossing the Atlantic does not seem to have obliterated that alliance. While Bahia brought more changes in the relationship between these two religions, their relationship is clouded now that African Islam as a distinct, organized religion has disappeared in Brazil. Bastide has pointed out Malê elements in the Brazilian candomblé ceremonies. Terms such as *Malê, Allah, alufá,* and so on, appear sprinkled throughout religious chants and in representations of spiritual entities. On the other hand, Bahian Islam must have incorporated important elements from the Yoruba pantheon. This was the case with Olorum, the supreme Yoruba deity, who must have been associated with Allah, for he was also called Olorumuluá, for some the Malê supreme being.[25]

It is more difficult to identify Bahian Malês as sons of Oxalá; nonetheless, there are interesting associations to be made. The day dedicated to the deity is Friday, the same day Muslims set aside for prayer and meditation. (In Salvador the custom of wearing white on Fridays is widespread.) It may be that Yoruba imales in Africa had a special relationship with *Ojo-*

Obatalá, the fifth and final day of the Yoruba week, which they dedicated to Oxalá. A more striking association of Malês with Oxalá may occur on the most important popular festival in Bahia (after Carnival) and is linked to the well-known relation between Oxalá and the city's patron saint, Senhor do Bonfim.

In 1835 Senhor do Bonfim and other Catholic saints were honored in a cycle of festivities on Bonfim Hill, the most important of which occurred on the first Sunday after Epiphany. On the Sunday after that, people celebrated Our Lady of Guidance, a week later Saint Gonçalo—both in grand style and with popular participation. As time went by, a Thursday celebration became more important, and Senhor do Bonfim for all intents and purposes took over that cycle of feast days. Our Lady of Guidance and Saint Gonçalo faded into a distant background, and Oxalá had a hand in this. There is, in fact, evidence that this was the case back in 1835. Shortly before the uprising, on 14 January, an African freedman by the name of Vicente Pires, along with other Africans, asked Salvador's city council for permission to "celebrate Senhor do Bonfim with dances and drums."[26]

The washing of the temple *(lavagem),* in the beginning a simple ceremony controlled by the church, slowly became custom and turned into an Afro-Bahian celebration. This feast, for a long time persecuted by the police and ecclesiastic authorities, demonstrates a victory of African folk mythology over that produced and promoted by the Church. It would be interesting to know how and when this happened. The celebration of Senhor do Bonfim occurs on a day very close to the twenty-fifth of January. Perhaps the Bahian Malês are at least partial beneficiaries of the conjunction of Oxalá and Senhor do Bonfim, the most celebrated case of Nagô-Catholic syncretism in Bahia. It may be that with the waning and ultimate disappearance of black Islam, its traces and traditions have found other forms of expression, for example, the use of Nagô-Malê syncretisms such as the conjunction of Oxalá and Allah. Thus, even though they may have been excised from Bahian collective memory, Malês may have persisted in Bahia's collective unconscious and may be victorious in the ongoing celebrations. With its water and white clothing, the Bonfim celebration could actually be a hidden Muslim holiday.[27]

Symbolic structures are part of social structures. They bind and express social relations. For that reason one can consider them symptomatic of underlying historical phenomena. There are no explicit written data concerning formal political alliances between Malês and non-Malês. There are, however, clues suggesting that not just Malês rebelled in the 1835 uprising and that the union between Malês and non-Malês had historical and cultural roots prior to the act of rebelling that made the alliance in the revolt possible. In this light the notion that the 1835 revolt was a "holy war" against all non-Muslims cannot be maintained. The rebellion did of course have its religious side, and for many it was even a holy war, but it was not a classic jihad of the sword.

The rebellion was not directed against African kafirai, nor, *malgré* Bastide, was it directed against Christians as such. Bastide adopted the European model of Christian-Islamic antagonism in his analysis of the 1835 scenario. This model, which asserts that Islam is fanatic and intolerant *in principle*, fails to account for historical specificity, in this case the intense symbolic intermingling of African Islam with ethnic religions both in Africa and in Bahia.

Goody takes a different route to reach a similar conclusion. He maintains that Muslims' ability to read and write was instrumental in the conspiracy and that the role of a universalistic Religion of the Book created both a strong ideological bond among its followers and an intransigence vis-à-vis non-Muslims. Literacy was one of the Malês' goals, as it is for all Muslims, but the evidence suggests that few of them could write or read Arabic with ease and that the conspiracy was planned and organized primarily through word of mouth. Perhaps because he lacked more detailed information on the rebellion, Goody underestimated—although he did not deny—the role of the written word as magical protection among African slaves in Bahia. It is therefore difficult to accept that a struggle based on the West African jihadic models, mainly the Sokoto jihad, took place in Bahia. Not because the jihad is necessarily a form of state imperialism, as Raymond Kent has argued. The jihad begun by Usuman Dan Fodio, for example, did not attempt to expand an existing Muslim state; it was, instead, a revolution aimed at replacing specific state institutions purportedly deviating from the Islamic path as well as a struggle against heterodoxy among local Muslims.[28]

In any case the Fulani-Hausa precedent is a weak candidate for the role model of a rebellion planned and led by Nagô slaves in Bahia. Nineteenth-century Islam in Yorubaland did not follow the Hausaland pattern either. Indeed, the Yorubas had no tradition of jihads. The wars following the collapse of the Oyo empire were political struggles between successor states, and while they were exacerbated by Islamic tensions in the area, they were not primarily religious. In fact some alliances were made across religious boundaries. On the other hand, coreligionists fought on opposing sides. It seems unlikely that the Nagôs would have started a holy war tradition in Brazil, not having had one in Africa. It is equally unlikely that the proud Nagôs would have accepted absolute Hausa leadership in their uprising, and they did not. Malês, including Muslim Nagôs, did follow the guidance of Hausa preachers, but as we shall soon see, the most important Muslim leaders in 1835 were Nagôs.

Despite Islam's central role in the Malê uprising, there is no reason to assume that the movement was experienced as a jihad by its rank and file or declared to be one by its leaders. Doubtless, rebels derived strength and fervor from Islamic rituals and from Muslim collective solidarity. In addition, Muslim and non-Muslim alike counted on the Arabic amulets for supernatural help. But the presence and even predominance of Muslim ideas, rites, and symbols in a movement does not in itself make it a jihad.

· 7 ·

Malê Profiles

By this point it should be obvious that the political and religious leaders of the 1835 rebellion were the same people. Seven important Muslim leaders involved in the movement have been identified: Ahuna or Aluna, Pacífico Licutan, Luís Sanim, Manoel Calafate, Elesbão do Carmo (Dandará), Nicobé, and Dassalu. The quantity and quality of archival information on each of these men vary but are sufficient to map their political and religious activities, their visibility in the African community, and, in a few cases, some of their personality traits.

Ahuna was perhaps the most wanted man in Bahia during 1835. He was of "ordinary build," according to one description, and he had four scars, tribal marks, on each cheek. He was a Nagô and the slave of an unnamed man who lived on a plot of land near Pelourinho Square, where, contrary to Islamic principles, drinking water was sold.[1] He seems to have traveled rather frequently into the Recôncavo, or to be exact, to Santo Amaro, where his master had a sugar plantation. In fact, a few weeks before the rebellion, Ahuna had been sent to the plantation handcuffed. He had been accused of some petty domestic crime. On that particularly humiliating occasion, his friends and disciples formed a cortege and followed him to the port from where he was to travel to Santo Amaro. The word of his banishment quickly spread through the African community. Dadá, a Nagô slave, claimed that he "had heard from other negroes that Ahuna had been sent there by his master, the reason [for the quick spreading of the news] being that he is a negro whom the others love." The freedman Belchior da Silva Cunha also testified that "[Ahuna] was loved by all his Brethren."[2]

A few days before the uprising Ahuna was in the news again. He had come back from Santo Amaro. Many Africans taken prisoner testified that Ahuna was an extremely important link in the conspiracy's chain of command. When Guilhermina betrayed the plot, she said the Africans referred to Ahuna as the "straw boss" *(maioral)*. He was probably the same "straw boss" Sabina found with her companion, Vitório Sule, and the others on the evening of 24 January. Belchior confirms this: "Some negroes working on lighters said that 'Ahuna' had come back from Santo Amaro and was living in Guadalupe." It is almost certain that he was in the house belonging to Manoel Calafate, where the rebellion began.[3]

Oddly, Ahuna was the only Malê leader Africans called a maioral in their testimonies, notwithstanding their many comments about other alufás. He may have been the key man. Belchior's testimony is revealing: "He heard talk about making war on whites, but only on Saturday . . . during the morning, on his way to buy limestone, since he is a mason, did some blacks tell him 'Ahuna' had already come back from Santo Amaro."[4] The word "already" suggests that only Ahuna's presence had been lacking for the rebellion to begin.

If there was an almami in Bahia at that time, it may have been Ahuna, who could also have been the Mala Mubakar mentioned in chapter 6. One other possibility is that he may have been a *bábbá malāmi*, that is, a "great malām," as the Hausas would have it.[5] Rodrigues confused him with another Ahuna taken prisoner in 1835. This Ahuna, a Mina freedman with the Christian name of Pedro Lima, had been the slave of a priest in Santo Amaro. Obviously, if the two Ahunas had been suspected of being the same person, the authorities in Bahia would not have failed to follow up on Pedro, because they carefully investigated all the other leaders. In addition, the two characters were fundamentally different: one was a Nagô slave, the other a Mina freedman. "Straw boss" Ahuna is still an enigma.[6]

Pacífico Licutan has been described as an aged man, tall, thin, with a sparse beard and small head and ears and "perpendicular and horizontal marks on his face." Without doubt an impressive figure. He was a Nagô slave working as a tobacco roller on Dourado Wharf and living with his master, a medical doctor by the name of Antônio Pinto de Mesquita Varella. During his interrogation Licutan added a personal touch to his testimony: Varella "treated him poorly as a slave." This hints at how important the matter of experience under slavery was in the decision to join the rebellion. Dr. Varella really was a scoundrel. Out of sheer seigniorial pride he had refused to free Licutan both times Malês offered to pay him a fair price for his slave's freedom. Varella needed the money too. He was in arrears concerning a debt he had incurred with some Carmelite friars. This debt was the reason Licutan was in prison at the time of the rebellion—he had been confiscated as part of Varella's property, which was to be auctioned off to pay his creditors. Another sign of Varella's poor treatment of his slave was that when Licutan went to trial, Varella refused to defend him.[7]

Pacífico Licutan was a highly esteemed alufá and a man of great influence and power within Bahia's African community. The testimony of a slave known as Francisco, who had decided to cooperate with the police, is telling:

> He often saw Licutan, a negro from the Nagô nation, gather people around his door, and everyone said that he summoned them and then went with them into his room. . . .
> . . . the name of said "Licutan" was on the tip of many blacks' tongues, who spoke of him with secrecy.
> . . . he would not hesitate to go and point out Licutan's master's house, but he will only go at night, because he does not want to die.

At this point the questioning is interrupted, and the scribe notes:

> Right then the Justice of the Peace saw that the negro was very frightened after glancing at the stairway where the ones waiting to be questioned were. He stopped the interrogation, sending the witness under guard to a prison, where he could be questioned further.

On the following day Francisco was again questioned.

> He answered that he is afraid to talk about Licutan because that negro is a grandee among his Nagô brethren and also because the witness had spent considerable time with two negroes who talked about Licutan and his group. They had told Francisco that if he were to tell or even talk about this, he would die.
> He was frightened when he spoke yesterday because he feared one of those waiting there might go back to jail and tell "Licutan," who, in spite of being in jail, got visits from and bestowed blessings on almost all Nagôs [in Salvador], who had collected enough money to buy him when he would be auctioned.[8]

The head jailer at the city jail, Antônio Pereira de Almeida, confirms the final part of Francisco's testimony. According to him, on the day after Licutan's incarceration,

> said negro had many negroes and negresses visiting him. And it went on like that day after day and hour after hour. [These visits were allowed] because he was in jail for safekeeping. There was also the following singularity: everyone kneeled before him with great respect to receive his blessing. And it was known to the witness that the others had the money ready to buy his freedom when he went on the auction block.[9]

Some of this happened during Ramadan, a time of constant fasting and prayer, which may have increased the baraka (the spiritual power or blessedness) of the distinguished prisoner.

All the pertinent testimony indicates that the revolt had been planned while Licutan was in jail, and it supports the hypothesis that the planning was done around the end of 1834, since Licutan was incarcerated in November. For a time during Licutan's incarceration, Malês planned to buy his freedom at his auction, but once the date of the rebellion had been set, Licutan was told he would be liberated "once and for all" at the end of Ramadan. And during the uprising rebels actually tried to liberate him forcibly, but they failed.[10]

Licutan was a strong, daring man, but not without feelings. Paulo Rates, a Mina freedman in jail at the same time as Licutan, witnessed his sorrow when the revolt failed: "On that same Sunday he bowed his head and never raised it. He became upset and cried when the other negroes taken prisoner that morning were brought in. One of them brought him a book, or a folded piece of paper with letters on it, like those that have been found lately, and Pacífico read it and began to cry."[11]

But the old Malê's spirit was not entirely broken. On 11 February 1835, during his interrogation, Licutan refused to reveal the name of any collaborator or disciple of his. He even denied being a Muslim, in spite of all the proof to that effect. At the same time, he maintained both his personal dignity and his Malê identity for all to see—his interrogators as well as his fellow Africans waiting to be questioned. He told the judge his name was Bilāl, and the judge responded in a fury, saying that he knew his true African name was Licutan. The slave answered him with insolence: "It was true he was called 'Licutan,' but he could call himself whatever he wanted." Owing to his own ignorance, the judge was unaware that Bilāl is a very common Islamic name, which in Licutan's case, was loaded with special symbolic meaning. In Muslim tradition, Bilāl is the name of Prophet Mohammed's black assistant, or *muezzin*. In West Africa *bilaal* has come to mean *muezzin* (literally, the assistant who "calls" the faithful toward prayer). The revolt was still alive in Licutan's (or Bilāl's) heart, despite its failure on the battlefield.[12]

The next character is Luís, known to Africans as Sanim. Sanim was also along in years. He was a man of "average build," with a wide forehead, white hair, thick beard, and "chestnut-colored hands." Like Licutan, he was a slave and worked as a tobacco roller. (These two Malês were also close friends; Sanim brought food to Licutan while he was in prison.) Sanim lived on Pão de Ló ("Sponge Cake") Street with his master, Pedro Ricardo da Silva. Notwithstanding his lengthy enslavement in Bahia (judging from his apparent old age), he could scarcely speak Portuguese. However, according to several witnesses, he spoke both Hausa and Yoruba fluently, in spite of being born a Nupe. He was a versatile, cultured individual with experience in several cultures.[13]

Sanim performed his duties at the house of two freedmen, Gaspar and Belchior da Silva Cunha. He was the latter's as well as other Africans' "Malê prayer teacher," Belchior told the judge. But Sanim was also a practical person. He organized a pool or savings fund into which each member, presumably on a monthly basis, contributed 320 réis, at the time a day's pay for slave labor (see chapter 9). The money in the pool was divided into three parts: a part for buying cloth to make Muslim garments; a part to pay masters' portions of slave wages (conceivably the amount to be paid masters on Fridays by all Malê slaves since Friday is a Muslim holy day); and a third part to be used to help buy letters of manumission.[14]

Sanim had little to say during his interrogation. In spite of all the evidence, he denied being an alufá. He insisted that he had never entered Belchior's house, although he did admit to knowing him and Gaspar, whose sartorial services he had used. One passage in his testimony suggests that he had been an alufá in Africa ("when he came to white man's land, he had nothing more to do with it"), but beyond that declaration, the scribe lamented, he "denied absolutely everything." Still, Sanim's master was familiar with his slave's Malê convictions. In contrast with Licutan's owner, Pedro Ricardo defended in court his slave's right to practice his religion, a constitutional guarantee according to Sanim's attorney's interpretation of the law.[15]

Almost everything known about Manoel Calafate has been said already. The fact that he was formally addressed as "Father" *(Pai)* Manoel by his disciples indicates he was also along in years. He was a freed Nagô and a caulker by trade. He lived in the house at the foot of Ladeira da Praça street, where the insurrection began. He lived with another freed Nagô, a sedan chair porter by the name of Aprígio. Their house was a busy meeting place for Muslims.

Manoel was undeniably an important person in the scheme. He traveled to Santo Amaro to mobilize rebels on the eve of the uprising. His disciples made a powerful oath—to die fighting alongside their teacher. "Father" Manoel may have been the only alufá to take an active part in the struggle, and he appears to have died from wounds suffered on Palace Square a few minutes after the uprising began. This is what can be gleaned from the testimony of João José Teixeira, a mulatto merchant: "Alexandre José Fernandes . . . had seen the black man, Manoel Calafate, going up Ladeira da Praça and stabbing a soldier, then returning wounded to the insurgents' house."[16] But these are all the details concerning the fate of this Malê leader.

A Hausa freedman, Elesbão do Carmo, or Dandará, was the most prosperous of the elders. He lived on the New Gravatá road, near Guadalupe neighborhood, with a Nagô slave woman, Emereciana. She was his companion, not his slave. Dandará owned a tobacco shop in the Santa Bárbara market of the Conceição da Praia Parish. At his store he gathered his disciples for prayers, readings, and Arabic lessons. In the entire investigation Dandará was the only man to acknowledge having been "a teacher in his Land," and he added that "he has been teaching young fellows here, but not to do evil." Contradicting Dandará's alleged "good" intentions,

Domingos, one of the few slaves who openly admitted taking part in the rebellion, confessed to "having studied with Dandará." Dandará also carried Islam to the Recôncavo, which he was constantly visiting on business.[17]

The authorities produced six witnesses to testify about Dandará's Islamic activity. One of the witnesses, a mulatto tailor by the name of Luís da França, who resided above the shop in Santa Bárbara, used to spy on Dandará through the loose floor boards, "and he often saw him with some large prayer beads, rubbing them in his hands and shouting to heaven." However the most incriminating accusation against Dandará was one that alluded to a large number of parnaíba knives a witness had seen stashed in the Malê leader's shop. These weapons were surely used during the fight.[18]

There seem to have been more alufás in Bahia at that time. Among the slaves of Englishmen living in the Vitória neighborhood, there was someone known as Sule or Nicobé. A slave by the name of Carlos testified that "he did not know how to read, but was still learning from mestre Dassalu and Nicobé, as well as [from] Gustard." Dassalu and Gustard were probably just more advanced students in the Malê reading and writing classes, but Nicobé (or Sule) appears in the testimony of another slave, João, who referred to him as "the captain of them all" during the celebration of Lailat al-Miraj, in November 1834. Nicobé was never captured. He may have been killed in one of the skirmishes.[19]

There was also Luís, a Nagô slave, a tailor accused of sewing Muslim garments and being treated by his countrymen with suspicious deference. Luís does not seem to have played a significant role in the rebellion nor in the overall Malê movement. Indeed, his name was never mentioned in that context by any of the more than two hundred blacks questioned. Luís probably told the truth when he claimed that "it was because of his age that he was respected by his partners, who approached him to receive his blessing."[20]

The profile of the Malê leadership is an example of the democratic tendency generally attributed to Islam in recruiting its spiritual and political spokesmen. Islam may be male-dominated, which greatly limits its democracy, but it is not aristocratic. In West Africa, with the exception of women and slaves, anyone could become an *alim*—a knower of Islam, a cleric—all one needed was to "receive sufficient training to be socially legitimated."[21] In Bahia "Malê democracy" was broader, since not just free men had the privilege of guiding the sons of Allah.

In fact the positively identified alufás were mostly slaves. As one would expect of people considered close to the gods, they were respected and honored by the African community. Ahuna, Licutan, Sanim, and Nicobé, all of whom were slaves, were men with baraka, and that was all that mattered. Their advanced age increased their prestige, for Africans have great respect for the wisdom of age. Any prejudice freed Africans in Bahia may have had against slaves in general evaporated in the presence of these Malê elders.

That most of the Malê leaders were slaves must have exacerbated tensions between Malês and Bahian slave society. Forced into slavery, these men did not have the time they wanted for studying doctrine, for preaching, and for teaching. This state of affairs certainly frustrated eager disciples and followers looking for guidance. Moreover, the leaders were always subject to their masters' humiliating whims, which could not help but enrage the Muslim community. It is hardly coincidental that the rebellion occurred when Licutan was incarcerated and shortly after Ahuna's master sent him handcuffed to Santo Amaro. These incidents were provocative in themselves and abetted the Malê revolution.

Besides the political and religious "high command," other Malês stood out, either as agitators for the cause or as providers of infrastructure, without which neither organization nor planning could have been possible. Other students of the Malês have considered many of those ancillary agitators to be important leaders in the insurrection.[22] Even the most superficial reading of the court documents reveals that whenever the prosecutor was able to show any physical proof (wounds, blood stains, etc.) of an African's having participated in the uprising, the jury considered him a "ringleader" in the insurrection. These prisoners were melded in with those who appeared in the testimony as Malê preachers. Of course, people such as Belchior da Silva Cunha, Vitório Sule (a peddler), and others were more than just dedicated followers—some of them allowed their houses to be used as meeting places, others were indefatigable agitators—but they never had the last word in Malê goings-on.

As is the case in any minimally structured movement, the rebellion depended on a hierarchy of leaders, but this hierarchy already existed, in outline form, in the Muslim community. It was not unique to the rebellion. The more advanced students and the most committed Malês had greater access to the elders and consequently more information about the rebellion itself. Their role in the movement should not be downplayed, however. For example, Aprígio, who shared Calafate's residence, was beyond a doubt an important man in the movement. Witnesses for the prosecution testified to his being an avid proselytizer and an educator of Malê initiates. But he was not an alufá. Other dedicated Muslims of his rank deserve mention: Diogo and Jaime, who by themselves erected the makeshift mosque in Vitória. There was Thomas, whom Inspector Antônio Marques described as "a reading teacher." There was also an anonymous "slave of João Ratis," who, according to the testimony of a slave known as José, was "one of the principal seducers of the Malê sect or religion."[23]

The list of these African fighters could be lengthened, which is not surprising, since spreading of the faith is one of the fundamental duties of all good Muslims. Many people were probably commissioned for specific tasks, such as coordinating and mobilizing forces before and during the fight, but, unfortunately, there is insufficient information to describe their activity in detail.

PART III

The African Community in Revolt

· 8 ·

Roots: Ethnic Motivation in 1835

*Even though they are all Nagôs, each one has his own
homeland.*
—Antônio, a Nagô slave

As noted earlier, the slave population in Bahia included few women, which meant that it could be replenished mainly by importing more Africans. At the turn of the nineteenth century, when a wave of prosperity washed over the Recôncavo, slave imports were stepped up to satisfy the demand in the cane fields and in the urban areas—both of which were rapidly expanding. The already numerous African population grew even more, and newly arrived slaves came from different "nations," as African ethnic groups were rightly called in Bahia.

The first three decades of the nineteenth century witnessed a restructuring of the African ethnic scheme in Bahia. During these years, the African population swelled with Yorubas (known as *nagôs* in Bahia) and Hausas (*haussá, uçá,* etc.), as well as with other ethnicities, mainly Aja-Fon-Ewe groups (known as *Jejes* in Bahia), living in the area of the Bight of Benin and farther inland, particularly from old Dahomey, today the Republic of Benin, and present-day Nigeria. It has been estimated that up to 183,700 slaves were exported from that region to Bahia between 1801 and 1830.[1]

Between the years 1820 and 1835, Nagôs, Jejes, Hausas, and Tapas (Nupes) made up 57.3 percent of Bahia's African-born slave population (see table 5, last two columns). As mentioned in chapter 5, these slaves were victims of armed conflicts in their homelands, especially of the Oyo empire's internal struggles and Islam's military expansion in that region. Once landed in Bahia, these same slaves inevitably and fundamentally altered the African community's way of life. They also changed its internal

Table 5

ETHNICITY OR REGIONAL ORIGIN OF DEFENDANTS AND OF SALVADOR'S BLACK POPULATION

Region, Ethnicity, or Port of Departure	1835 Defendants								Samples of Black Population			
	Slaves		Freed		Unknown		Total		Freed[a] 1819–36		Slaves[b] 1820–35	
	No.	%	No.	%	No.	%	No.	%	No.	%	No.	%
Nagô (Yoruba)	143	76.9	53	46.1	3	42.9	199	64.6	275	11	424	19
Hausa	8	4.3	23	20	0	0	31	10.1	111	4.5	141	6.3
Jeje (Aja-Fon-Ewe)	4	2.2	6	5.2	0	0	10	3.2	288	11.6	240	10.8
Tapa (Nupe)	1	.5	5	4.3	0	0	6	1.9	45	1.8	43	1.9
Bornu	3	1.6	4	3.5	0	0	7	2.3	24	1.0	21	1.0
Gurma	0	0	3	2.6	0	0	3	1	0	0	0	0
Calabar	1	.5	1	.9	0	0	2	.6	15	.6	26	1.2
Mina	2	1.1	5	4.3	0	0	7	2.3	180	7.2	89	4.0
Bagba	1	.5	1	.9	0	0	2	.6	6	.2	0	0
Mundubi	1	.5	0	0	0	0	1	.3	0	0	0	0
Congo	3	1.6	1	.9	0	0	4	1.3	16	.6	46	2.0
Cabinda	2	1.1	2	1.7	0	0	4	1.3	21	.8	111	5.0
Angola	0	0	0	0	0	0	0	0	97	3.9	165	7.4
Benguela	0	0	1	.9	0	0	1	.3	22	.9	35	1.6
Other Africans	0	0	0	0	0	0	0	0	107	4.3	139	6.2
Native-born	1	.5	4	3.5	0	0	5	1.6	1281	51.6	752	33.7
Unknown	16	8.6	6	5.2	4	57.1	26	8.4	0	0	0	0
Total	186	99.8	115	100	7	100	308	100	2493	100	2232	100

Sources: AEBa, *Insurreições escravas*, maços 2846–50; Mattoso, "A propósito de cartas de alforria," 38, 39; Andrade, "A mão de obra escrava," app. table 4.

[a]Based on manumission certificates.
[b]Based on probate records lists.

structure, its sociocultural hierarchies, its strategies of alliance and inter-ethnic conflict, and so on, as well as its relationship with the seigniorial class and the native inhabitants. This period (1800–1835) saw the Jeje-Nagô culture sweep over Bahia and become its dominant African culture. Also during these decades, African rebellions shook Bahian slave society.

The count of Ponte was not totally wrong when he declared, in 1808, that most Africans arriving in Bahia at that time would pose a great threat to the slaveholding system. According to the count, they belonged to "West Africa's fiercest nations."[2] Nagôs brought with them either the Oyo militaristic tradition or their experience resisting that tradition. As the empire crumbled during the first two decades of the nineteenth century, local inhabitants entered a period characterized by small, independent, mutually hostile armed factions formed and led by all-powerful warrior chiefs—*ologuns* or *oloroguns*.[3] Many slaves coming to Bahia had been leaders in Africa. The 1835 rebels were stirred not solely by religious fervor but also by men with experience in intra- and interethnic warfare, that is, in civil and national wars. These men, besides having lived peacefully within their ethnic traditions, had put their ethnic and native identity on the line in the most extreme case of political contention—war. Ethnic identity continued to be an organizing and sociopolitical cornerstone of African life in Bahia.

Table 5 lists the origins of slaves and ex-slaves accused of taking part in the rebellion. Samples of the black population include representative data on the ethnic makeup of Salvador's slaves and freed people and help put each ethnic group's participation in the revolt in the proper perspective.

The Absence of Crioulos

Brazilian-born slaves and ex-slaves made up around 40 percent of the population (see also chapter 1). However, the police only arrested two mulattos and three native-born blacks. The creoles were held for questioning but were never put on trial. The mulattos were Domingos Marinho de Sá (who had rented the loge on Ladeira da Praça to Manoel Calafate) and his companion, Joaquina Rosa de Santana, both of whom certainly had nothing to do with the conspiracy.

The absence of Brazilian blacks in the rebellion is not unusual. Native-born blacks and mestiços did not take part in any of the more than twenty Bahian slave revolts prior to 1835. This creole pacifism was typical of the many different slave societies in the New World. Although some revolts of native slaves did occur, they were most frequent in areas where African-born slaves were the majority, such as in the Caribbean and Bahia.[4]

To put it mildly, relations between Afro-Brazilians and Africans were strained. Afro-Brazilians' failure to participate in the 1835 revolt can be explained largely by their tensions with the Africans, which derived from their different positions in the local slave society. With a few exceptions, throughout the Americas, native-born blacks did not get involved in slave revolts when they were a minority among slaves. When they constituted a majority, they took more risks but never as persistently as Africans did. Perhaps creole and mulatto slaves felt more threatened by possible but unknown African dominators than they did by the familiar rule of the white master. Their position was based on established social practice, on their peculiar socialization. Afro-Brazilians had been born and raised in slavery and, contrary to the Africans, had no other reference point, much less a radical contradiction between part of their lives lived in freedom and another part in slavery. This is not to say that Afro-Brazilians were happy, well-adjusted slaves. They confronted another set of contradictions within slavery.[5]

Culturally, native-born blacks were caught between Western and African ways of life. There was much linking them to the white man and to the New World. They spoke the same language, which was a fundamental tie with the master. It was easier for them to have families and even to become in some way coopted into the master's family (the family being a major contributor to social integration or, at most, to peaceful protest). Bahia had no lack of females in the *Brazilian* sector of the slave population, which made sexual contact and the creation of (albeit unstable) families much easier among creoles. Masters often had their female slaves' children baptized, and these children (black or mulatto) were eventually manumitted, only to form a network of seigniorial dependents and clients. In fact these manumitted children were often the sons and daughters of masters who acknowledged their several links with female slaves in their letters of manumission. Mestiços were especially favored. Lígia Bellini reports that 64 percent of the "affective" letters of manumission were for mulattos, 21 percent for native-born blacks, and 15 percent for Africans. Since slave women were predominantly Afro-Brazilian and children almost exclusively Afro-Brazilian, gender and age, in addition to origin, played a role in the formation of relationships between masters and slaves. It was not uncommon for a male or female master to declare that a child was being given liberty because it "was born in their bed" or because "it had been raised as a child of the family." On the other hand, even in cases where there was no emotional attachment, native-born slaves fared better in manumissions, as one can see clearly in table 5: native-born slaves made up 37.7 percent of the total slave population but 51.6 percent of those manumitted. Africans lagged behind the native-born either in buying their freedom or in having it granted to them. Manumission was one of the few avenues of upward mobility for slaves.[6]

Daily life in Bahia reflected a paternalistic ideology that in principle excluded Africans who refused to renounce their Africanness. While Bahian seigniorial paternalism had its origins in the local microcosm, where master and slave stood in opposition, it was not far from being a system of political and ideological hegemony. The seigniorial class wielded its power not only with a whip but also by fostering the belief that slavery provided slaves (some more than others) with security and even a modicum of leeway. It is true that during the crisis following independence, which included a crisis of hegemony, the social framework and power structure seemed on the verge of crumbling, but a basic trump card could always be played, namely, the anti-African pact among all Bahians— masters and slaves, blacks, whites, and mulattos.

An especially important part of this pact was that mulattos, cabras, and crioulos made up the bulk of those employed to control and subdue Africans. These people did the whites' dirty work: they kept order at the fountains, on the squares, and in the streets of Salvador. It was they who raided and destroyed religious meeting places *(terreiros)* in the suburbs, who tracked down fugitive slaves throughout the province, who quelled slave rebellions wherever they started. City police, slave hunters, regular army troops, a good part of the civilian contingent in the National Guard (created in 1831) consisted of free people of color born in Brazil. Their commanding officers were white. Indeed the planter class could always count on Afro-Bahians during crises created by foreigners, be they African or Portuguese. The crioulo often was on their side in daily life—in customs, values, and traditions. But even if the seigniorial class was successful in systematically thwarting the union of Afro-Bahians with rebellious Africans, it did not succeed in keeping them from living together, from forming bonds, or from sociocultural exchanges.

The expectations of whites, the ambiguity of crioulos, and the boldness of Africans in matters of ethnocultural politics can be seen in the 1829 correspondence between a justice of the peace in the Brotas Parish and the provincial president. Giving a wealth of detail and attempting to justify the police's habitual high-handedness, Antônio Gomes Guimarães tells of a raid on a Jeje religious gathering. Guimarães was responding to a charge, made by an African known as João Baptista to the president, that during the raid pieces of African cloth *(panos da costa)*, a hat, and 20 mil réis, as well as other items, had been stolen by the police.

The magistrate registered the prisoners taken in his blitz: "They caught three African blacks [*pretos*], but the others got away. They caught a slew of black African women [*pretas*], and *worse than that,* a lot of crioulas born in the country [Brazil]." (Note the crystal-clear racial language of the time: *preto* always referred to African blacks; Brazilian blacks were always referred to as *crioulos*.) The unexpected presence of native-born black women in an African gathering celebrating African deities shocked the justice and seemed to be a break with social norms, a serious detour from the straight and narrow. Still the women were treated paternalistically, perhaps because they acted like repentant daughters: "Seeing how they cried, after scolding them, I sent them on their way because they were crioulas and also so as not to vex their masters." While the African women went to jail, the crioulas were treated better. Their crying was a typical crioulo self-preservation strategy. They were masters of dissimulation, experts at fooling whites and getting personal favors from them.[7]

Crioulos and, to an even greater extent, mulattos had their own ways of bucking the system. At times their strategies were scarcely distinguishable from out-and-out conformity. They were very good at what has come to be known as "daily resistance," what some North American authors have rather crudely deemed "creole rascality." Under the heading of daily resistance, one can find individual insubordination, work slowdowns, the damaging of tools and seedlings, feigned illness, petty thievery, flight, and clever manipulation of the paternalistic mentality such as the crioulas' weeping. Dona Maria Bárbara, herself a plantation owner, understood the ploy. In 1822 she had the following to say about her slaves: "The good negroes come from the [African] Coast. All the others are infernal." Speaking of Pernambuco at the beginning of the nineteenth century, Henry Koster, also a seasoned plantation administrator, agreed wholeheartedly.[8]

No matter how free of conflict their relationship with the master may have been, crioulos frequently ran off, although never as often as Africans did. In a sample of fifty-four escapes announced in Bahian newspapers during the 1830s, seventeen were cases of native-born fugitives. Antônio, a tailor, whose master claimed "he loved to play cards," seems to have taken flight in order to enjoy this pastime more freely. Maurício, between sixteen and eighteen years of age, had fled Salvador three months before the notice was published; he had headed for the town of Cachoeira, in the Recôncavo. A crioulo by the name of João, an eighteen-year-old journeyman cobbler, was a slave in search of adventure: he had fled Iguape, in the Recôncavo, for Salvador, "where he intended to join the army or go to sea." Carlos began his career as a fugitive early on, as can be seen in an announcement his master had put in the *Gazeta comercial* on 18 September 1838. His first flight from slavery occurred when he was ten years old. Carlos had been away for seventeen days. A nineteen-year-old slave known as Casimiro was described by his mistress as so "given to escaping and stealing" that she could not give him away. Casimiro was finally manumitted because his mistress could not control him. These little slices of creole slave life show that their position in the slaveholding society of the time could not be described as out-and-out conformity.

Crioulos could at times even join Africans in devising a common culture, as was the case at the Brotas religious meeting. But even in their cults to African gods, they often kept their distance. At the end of the nineteenth century, Rodrigues met an old African woman watching from a distance a candomblé gathering at Gantois, one of the most prestigious orisha temples in Bahia today. He asked her why she did not join in. She answered that her "temple [*terreiro*] was for people from the [African] Coast and was located in the Santo Antônio neighborhood. The Gantois temple was for the native-born."[9] Any "betrayal" of white values on the part of crioulos did not necessarily imply an alliance with Africans. This was the case even when native-born blacks led revolts.

The incident in Ilhéus, at the Santana Plantation, is relevant once more. The slaves on that plantation, most of whom were native-born, rebelled on at least two occasions. Once, at the end of the eighteenth century, they ceased working, ran off into the woods with their tools, and presented their master with a list of demands to be met before they would return to work. Even in this struggle against their master, crioulos did not refrain from discriminating sharply against their African comrades. One of their demands read: "You shall not oblige us to fish in the tide pools nor to gather shellfish, and when you wish to gather shellfish have your Mina blacks do that work."[10] That is, let the Africans ("Mina blacks") do the dirty work—a parody of white attitudes toward blacks. When these slaves rebelled another time, they occupied the plantation for four years, between 1824 and 1828, but there is nothing to suggest any anti-African content in that revolt.

It is, however, important to point out that crioulos and mulattos, both free and slave, also set off their rebellions when they felt betrayed by abrogations of what they considered their rights and legitimate aspirations. Afro-Bahians were mainly urban rebels. They were behind most of the plebeian revolts in Salvador. The well-known Tailors' Conspiracy (Conspiração dos Alfaiates) of 1798 was a predominantly mulatto conspiracy in which rebels sought Brazil's independence from Portugal and racial equality. Then, two decades later, during the 1820s and 1830s, crioulos and mulattos, slave and free, went into the streets to protest against the government, to ransack stores, and to attack military garrisons. Rebellious soldiers were mainly blacks and mestiços. In many movements of the urban poor, such as the anti-Portuguese riots in 1831, crioulos and mulattos probably protested and rioted alongside poor whites and Africans.

While the abolition of slavery was always present in the minds of slaves, who expressed their feelings on several occasions, such as the war of independence in Bahia during 1822 and 1823, native-born activism in

Salvador and in the towns of the Recôncavo was generally more closely linked to the struggles of the poor (including the slaves) than to the question of slavery per se. During the war of independence, the free populace in Bahia had been drawn into a bloody local process of decolonization. Native-born slaves and nonslaves sought to carve out places for themselves in the new nation, since they had been born in Brazil and felt their interests should be considered in restructuring the former colony. They shared the nationalistic sentiments present at every anti-European demonstration. If Africans organized according to their "national" ties, crioulos and mulattos would not be outdone. However, their "nation" was Bahia and not Oyo, Dahomey, or the Sokoto caliphate.[11]

Africans in the Fray and on the Sidelines

Rebel prisoners' testimony clearly indicates that the Malê rebellion was an exclusively African undertaking. But the African nations in Bahia did not all have the same level of commitment to the movement. The majority on trial were Nagôs, which partly, but only partly, reflected their greater numbers among all Africans. Indeed Nagôs were disproportionately present in the movement. They made up 28.6 percent of the African slaves and 22.7 percent of manumitted Africans in Salvador. On the other hand, of those on trial, they made up 76.9 percent of all slaves and 46.1 percent of ex-slaves, counting five Afro-Bahian prisoners. If one leaves out prisoners of unknown origins, these figures rise to 84.1 percent and 48.6 percent. More succinctly, Nagôs made up 68.1 percent of *all defendants* (or 70 percent, excluding the "unknowns"), whereas they were around 26 percent of *all Africans* in Salvador.

Naturally, the most preponderant African nation in Bahia would be able to outdo the others in mobilizing its members. And beyond their majority status, Nagôs were also culturally dominant, if one can believe the claim that Nagô worked as a sort of lingua franca among Africans in Bahia. Even so, they did not constitute the overwhelming majority one often imagines when faced with their impact on Bahian culture. To repeat: Nagôs were 26 percent of all Africans. Their great presence in the revolt can be explained by the large percentage of Muslims among them. I maintained in chapter 6 that the Nagô strength in the Malê community was reflected in its priestly class, primarily Nagô elders. Conversely, (Nagô) Malês—to be exact, the imales—were influential throughout the Nagô community, including "pagan" countrymen. The numerical and moral preponderance of Malês within the Nagô community must have helped it to attract many adherents to the rebel cause. This is why the rebellion seemed to be a uniquely Nagô product in the eyes of its beholders.

Questioners, questionees, and spectators insisted on blaming the uprising on the Nagôs. "A Nagô disturbance," was what José, a freed Hausa, and Claudina, a freed Tapa called it. Pedro Pinto, a freed Nagô, agreed, calling the revolt a "Nagô riot." A Congo slave known as Luís declared that he had been wrongly arrested and had gone to jail "because Nagô blacks had revolted." Another African from the Congo, José, a slave of a Nagô Muslim, Gaspar da Silva Cunha, claimed in his testimony that the people who used to get together at his master's house were "all Nagôs." Even Licutan, a Nagô Malê preacher, admitted that "he did not realize *his countrymen* [*parentes*] wanted to rebel."

British consul John Parkinson wrote that "an insurrection broke out yesterday morning among the Nagô blacks, who compose the chief part of the slave population of this city." A.-J. Baptiste Marcescheau, his French counterpart, referred to the uprising as a "complot des nagôs"; and in another communiqué he added: "The large mass of Nagô blacks in Bahia puts this province in constant danger thanks to this nation's unanimity of language, will, suffering, and hatred [*haine*], which joins this group of men, who, let it be said, are intelligent, strong, and courageous."

The language of the courts was similar. In the text of a corpus delicti the uprising is described as an "insurrection brought about in this city by Nagô blacks." Chief of Police Gonçalves Martins blamed the revolt on "Africans, in particular, Nagôs." A magistrate in Vitória Parish in essence agreed, calling it "a slave insurrection, mainly Nagôs." Antônio Pereira de Almeida, the jailer at the city jail, claimed that he had found out about the rebellion "when he saw that Nagô blacks had revolted." João Crisóstomo, the master of a rebel known as Manoel, bemoaned "the disastrous Nagô episode." One witness claimed that the call to battle heard the night of the uprising was: "Death to whites! Long live Nagôs!" [12]

The available documentation reveals that at the time, both the authorities and the rebels saw the 1835 rebellion as largely an ethnic movement. The religious factor was acknowledged, but it was considered secondary. Only later on were students and others interested in the matter to give extraordinary, almost exclusive emphasis to religious motivation for the revolt, perhaps because they considered it a more exotic and more compelling view of the uprising.

Clearly, however, more than just Nagôs took part. Contemporaries often intimated that Hausas were there too. "The blacks who rebelled were their Nagô countrymen and Hausas," declared Manoel. A Nagô slave called Pompeu offered an almost perfect diagnosis of the revolt: "There were no whites, no mestiços, no crioulos—there were only Nagôs and Hausas." [13] Hausas, who made up 9 percent of the urban African slave population, were only 4.3 percent of slaves arrested. On the other hand, almost 20 percent of ex-slaves arrested were Hausas, even though Hausas were only 9.1 percent of freed Africans in Salvador.

Nagôs and Hausas made up 81.6 percent of prisoners whose origins have been ascertained. In addition, people from twelve other African nations were also indicted; however, together they made up only 18.4 percent of the prisoners, excluding "unknowns" (see table 5). Jejes did not contribute to the rebellion in proportion to their numbers. The same can be said about other West African groups, such as Tapas and Minas, who may have been intimidated by the Nagôs, who dominated the movement. "Long live Nagôs!" was, after all, a discriminatory call to arms. Beyond this, the African kingdom of Dahomey, the home of Bahia's Jejes, had waged protracted and constant war with Yorubas. Hausas, although enemies of Yorubas in Africa, may have joined more readily in view of both groups' strong commitment to Islam.

The rebel leaders planned an African front that never materialized, even among neighbor nations who were culturally and linguistically related. The deciding factor in this failure may be owed to the hostility between Jejes and Nagôs, who together made up nearly 45 percent of urban African slaves and almost 47 percent of manumitted Africans. Nagôs and Jejes divided the so-called Sudanese Africans (i.e., West Africans) living in Bahia in 1835.[14]

The most striking absence in the rebellion was, without a doubt, that of Bantu speakers (from southern Africa). Conspicuous among them were the Angolas, a populous and visible African group in Bahia. Quimbundos, Umbundos, and Ovimbundos were known in Bahia by more generic, geographic, slave trade names. The so-called Cabindas, Angolas, Congos, and Benguelas together constituted 24 percent of African slaves in Salvador and 13.4 percent of manumitted Africans. Nonetheless, they made up only 3 percent of those arrested during the 1835 rebellion, and there is no record of their involvement in other uprisings of the period. Why were these Southern Africans so far outside the rebellious African currents in nineteenth-century Bahia? Their absence evokes that of the Afro-Bahians, who doubtless had much in common with these Africans.

Colonial and provincial authorities in Brazil, as well as plantation owners, foreign travelers, and native chroniclers, often portrayed Bantus, and especially Angolas, prejudiciously. They maintained that Angolas were mentally slow, physically weak, and uncivilized and thus more submissive and less anti-white than West Africans. From the seigniorial point of view, Angolas were model slaves. They were considered excellent field hands, because, according to the racist delirium, their inferior culture made them unsuitable for any more complex type of work. They were considered good domestics owing to their supposed docility and facility in learning the master's language. This was about as far as seigniorial anthropology and psychology could go. Unfortunately, this portrait was later appropriated by historians and anthropologists committed to specific notions of evolution, which is how the master's point of view became the modern explanation for Bantu absence in 1835.[15]

In other parts of the New World, Europeans tried to classify Africans according to personality profiles. They did not, however, always agree on the traits they assigned to specific groups. In Spanish America slaves from Upper Guinea were considered submissive.[16] In Brazil, the fugitive slave community of Palmares, made up mainly of Bantus, did not stop the Portuguese and later Brazilians from creating the myth of the cordial Angolan. The common term for a maroon community, a symbol of slave resistance, was *quilombo,* which is of Bantu origin. It may even be that the myth of passivity was concocted to deflate or stem Angolas' tradition of forming quilombos.

Recent work has shown that there were no striking differences among African ethnic or linguistic groups as far as their tasks within the slave work force were concerned. That Bantus were more suited to certain types of work is simply one more historical myth. There were, however, occupational differences between African and Brazilian slaves. Brazilians were prevalent among domestics and in specialized occupations—a normal consequence of crioulos' and mestiços' socialization and training. It had nothing to do with any ethnic, cultural, or racial superiority; it came from their being natives.[17]

This is not to say that there were no differences between West and Southern Africans. They came from different historical experiences in Africa, and once in Brazil, they developed different ways of dealing with one another, as well as with the seigniorial class and Bahian society in general—its social groups, its culture, and so on. In Africa, Angolans had been targeted by Portuguese Christian missionaries from an early date. Many of them, like other Bantu peoples, had been catechumens and knew some Portuguese before landing in Brazil as slaves. In fact, they often used their earlier exposure to European ways to improve their lot in the New World. They organized themselves according to white institutional precedents and used these structures to cope with slavery and discrimination, to go on living with whatever dignity they could manage, and to preserve part of their African identities.

Black Catholic lay brotherhoods, for example, were preeminent in the lives of Angolans, helping them recreate ethnic identity and forge interethnic alliances. Brotherhoods were perfect façades for important and profound ethnic conclaves; they were African ethnic mutual-aid societies; they offered loans and donations; they bought members' freedom; they organized and financed burials and masses for their dead. Brotherhoods were also centers for culture and leisure. On Christian holidays, especially

FIG. 12. Coronation of black kings and queens, a ritual of inversion in the Afro-Catholic feast of Our Lady of the Rosary. Drawing by Johan Moritz Rugendas, reprinted from his *Malerische reise in Brasilien* (Paris: Engelmann & Cie, 1835).

on a brotherhood's patron saint's day, the brothers gave parties and costume balls that included coronations of African kings and queens, in a symbolic revival of their lost world. If in the beginning the seigniorial class and the church hoped black brotherhoods would incorporate members into the white man's world, at a later date they came to acknowledge the formation of a unique religiosity and culture among the Africans, very different from what whites had tried to pass on.

In Salvador, a brotherhood such as Our Lady of the Rosary, located on Pelourinho Square, is an interesting case of ethnic dynamics. It was Angolan in its seventeenth-century beginnings, and for a long time it only accepted members who were Angolan. However, beginning in the second half of the eighteenth century, it started admitting others, in particular Jejes and crioulos. By the first decade of the nineteenth century, Jejes had become numerically dominant. But perhaps because of the threat their numbers posed, bylaws prohibited them from being on the board of directors, whose membership was restricted to Angolans and crioulos, which perhaps indicates, on a micropolitical and institutional level, wider social allegiance between these two groups.[18]

Native-born blacks and Angolans seem to have devised similar strategies for coping with slavery. This may be because Angolans came to Brazil during the earliest stages of colonization. They were the mothers and fathers of the first Brazilian blacks and mestiços. As more continued to arrive from Angola, the ones already in Brazil initiated them into the ways and wiles of white man's land and through their experience eased in the new arrivals. When, in the nineteenth century, West Africans began to arrive in large numbers, there was already a long Angolan tradition of contact with Brazil and its inhabitants, including crioulos.

The majority of Africans from West Africa, the so-called Sudanese, stressed other forms of cultural and institutional behavior and were perhaps more faithful to their origins. This is not to say that they flatly refused to belong to any Euro-Brazilian organization whatsoever or that they were above using elements of white culture. That was simply impossible. Jejes, for instance, besides being the bulk of the Rosário Brotherhood, had their own brotherhood in Salvador: Lord Sweet Jesus of the Needy, Redeemer of the Black Man (Senhor Bom Jesus das Necessidades e Redenção dos Homens Pretos). Even the belicose Nagôs set up a brotherhood known as Our Lady of Good Death (Nossa Senhora da Boa Morte), but it only admitted Nagôs from the kingdom of Ketu. Moreover, both Jejes and Nagôs belonged to brotherhoods originally established by other Africans.[19]

The point here is that at the historical moment under consideration, West Africans were not as attracted to European institutions and ideas, probably because unlike the Angolans, Nagôs and Hausas were new arrivals who had come in numbers unprecedented in the history of the Brazilian slave trade. This mass migration must have favored their maintaining a more cohesive African identity.

Islam and especially what became known as Candomblé played an important cultural and political role among West Africans during the first half of the nineteenth century. In 1829, when the Brotas magistrate raided the candomblé meeting place in his parish, he reported having caught blacks celebrating "the so-called Voodum God," which indicates that it was a Jeje or Dahomey meeting place. He went on to say: "On top of an elaborately prepared table [was] a heap decorated all over with ribbons and seashells, and a big African gourd full of seashells, and some copper coins mixed up with the alms. Male blacks were playing barrel drums and gourds decorated with seashells. Some black women were dancing; others were off in a room sleeping, or pretending to be asleep."[20] To this day in

Salvador, offerings to the gods, barrel drums, rattles (or tambourines), ritual dancing, and initiation chambers are essential to a candomblé. Such cultural practices under slavery challenged white values in a way black brotherhoods never could, no matter how Africanized they may have been. With the law on his side, the magistrate met the challenge head-on:

> It is true that the Sacred Political Constitution offered by His Majesty the Emperor says in Article 5 that "the Holy Roman Catholic Church will continue to be the Religion of the Empire. All other Religions will be permitted, but their practice will be kept indoors and private [and] the buildings designated for worship [kept] with no external sign of a Temple." This is understood to apply to Europeans, never to black Africans, who, coming as they do from their country to ours, are brought up in our religious fold. How could we dare allow them to apostatize and feign Catholicism only to turn the other cheek and worship their Gods in public?[21]

In contrast with European nationals, the "ethnic nationals" of Africa should not be permitted religious freedom. This faithful vigilante of Christian values, this master of cultural intolerance, this political follower of the count of Ponte line, even abhorred religious syncretism. Such a position was most certainly counterbalanced by other, more tolerant ones on the part of other authorities. It was, after all, the provincial president who demanded a justification for the justice's heavy-handedness. The magistrate's attitude betrays the presence of a repressive, anti-African stream in Bahia, and it suggests the effort Africans had to exert to keep their culture even partially alive.

Could it be that there is no information on Angolans' African cultural practices? What about the Angolan candomblés? Their survival into the twentieth century certainly suggests cultural resistance among Bantus, but one must still explain phenomena such as the Bantu absence from nineteenth-century rebellions. For the purposes of this study, their absence can be explained by taking into account the different behavior patterns and the different social relationships set up by each community in the New World. Many of the differences between the West and Southern Africans in Brazil obviously came from the different sociocultural and economic structures they left behind.

Hausas and Nagôs came from highly urbanized, politically independent, socially complex patrilineal societies that were integrated into wide-ranging commercial networks. Hausas were traders who roamed all over Africa, reaching both the Mediterranean Sea and the Middle East. The Sokoto caliphate, under Fulani leadership, united them in a more or less homogeneous body politic. Oyo Yorubas had built a mighty, longstanding empire with cities where commerce, metalworking, and textile manufacture had become famous. Both Nagôs and Hausas came from militarily structured societies in densely populated cosmopolitan areas and were in constant contact with other peoples and other civilizations.

Angolans were different. They were basically matrilineal farmers and shepherds. They were spread out in unstable kingdoms that had suffered profound economic, political, and cultural incursions from Europeans. It may have been that the contrast between the Angolans' peasant tranquility and the Hausas' and Nagôs' urban-commercial arrogance made planters think that inherently one group was peaceful, whereas the other was warlike. In addition to these "structural" differences, West Africans had left their homelands during a period of total war, when violence had become the daily norm in their societies.[22]

Coming from such different societies, West and Southern Africans developed different patterns of behavior and thought in the New World, and this made each group resist slavery and ethnic oppression in its own way. Southern Africans chose to deceive their masters, cloaking their culture in the white cape of religious brotherhoods, through which they ended up transforming both their culture and white culture. West Africans, mainly Nagôs and Hausas, followed the path of cultural confrontation, changing when it helped them cope with slavery or when they were forced to change. While the greatest expression of Angolan revolt was their creation of an independent rural life on a quilombo, Nagôs and Hausas opted for violent revolts against the power structures on plantations and in the cities. This is not to imply that no Angolans rebelled or that there were no Nagôs on quilombos. These are, of course, gross generalizations. In addition, there is no reason to consider either form of resistance superior. Rather, one must identify the differences. Neither strategy was victorious. Both gave a modicum of dignity to Africans' lives by keeping the prospect of freedom alive and by obliging masters to put some limits on their exploitation.

Signs of Ethnicity

It would have been hard for Africans to entirely forget their native values in nineteenth-century Bahia. They were there in great numbers, and more were always arriving. In spite of the cultural adaptations and innovations slavery demanded of them, in spite of their contact with diverse peoples in a new environment, Africans retained, or at least tried to retain, strong links with their past. This should not be understood to be a mechanistic theory of African "traits" or "survivals" preserved and unchanged in the New World. Cultural transformations were imperative to the survival and resistance of African slaves and their descendants. Price and Mintz have argued convincingly that notwithstanding the undeniable presence of an

African cultural matrix (which tinges all black cultures in the New World with some Africanness), Afro-American slave cultures began with Africans' interacting with each other's cultural experiences as well as with their masters and their European or Brazilian culture. As time went by, European culture also changed. Whatever "traits" remained, and many did in Bahia, they never survived unadulterated. They followed from specific choices on Africans' parts, and these choices were made based on their importance, functionality, and efficacy in organizing community or even personal life under slavery. This was clearly the case with Bahian candomblés.[23]

African slaves turned their past into an instrument of identity and transformation. Ethnic identity was strengthened daily by interaction among people of the same nation. Africans refused to be treated as a homogeneous, uniform group of human beings. Each had a history and genealogy that supported and reinforced his or her ethnic awareness in exile. That is, the term *Nagô* identified a group of African Bahians before the word *Yoruba* identified their brethren in Africa. Such a change was in itself an adaptation to their new surroundings. During questioning, Africans insisted on contrasting "white man's land" with "black man's land." Such phrases appear over and over again in prisoners' testimonies. Bahia was "white man's land"; Africa was "black man's land." One rebel said he had taught Arabic in his homeland, but never in "white man's land." Others claimed to have arrived in "white man's land" on such and such a date. A huge number of them said they had one name in their homeland and another in "white man's land."

But sometimes detainees made very specific references to their African origins. A slave known as José claimed to be Nagô-Jabu, that is, an Ijebu, one of the Yoruba subdivisions. An ex-slave, Sabina, referred to a black woman named Edum as being a *Nagô-Ba,* that is, a Yoruba from the kingdom of Egba. After ten years in Brazil, José, also a slave, continued to insist that he was from the Egba Yoruba nation. "Even though they are all Nagôs," the slave Antônio told the judge, "each one has his own homeland." Antônio likewise described himself as an Egba, and José, a fellow sedan chair porter, claimed to be from Oyo. All this means that the term *Nagô*—which was originally used by the Fon to identify native speakers of the Yoruba language—was too broad to be accepted outright by Bahian Nagôs. These "nations" included minorities with more real, deeper identities. For this reason it is in many ways confusing to go on working with terms such as *West African, Sudanese,* or *Bantu.* The African community was much more complex and varied in reality.[24]

Each individual bore various signs of ethnic identity. One of the strongest was the African name preserved alongside the one the master provided. For Africans a personal name had special symbolic power. Among Yorubas a name can have several meanings: how an individual appeared at birth; the circumstances of birth; the individual's position within the family lineage; or the family's prosperity or lack thereof. People born with the umbilical cord around their neck are named Ojo. A child born facing downward is called Ajayi. A male child born after several females is called Alade. Ajadi is said to have won the spoils of battle. Yorubas all have a birth name *(amuntoruwa)*, an official name *(àbiso)*, and an intimate name *(oriki)*. On top of this, Yorubas initiated into orisha cults have another name, which often must be kept secret and only uttered in specific rituals.[25]

Once in Bahia, Africans were given Christian names and from one day to the next became José, Manoel, or Antônio. This was, for them, symbolic of their tragic passing from being Africans to being slaves. By preserving their old ethnic or Muslim names, they tried to hold onto an important and very meaningful part of their personal memories. Their Christian names were only used in their dealings with whites. They were names from "white man's land." Among themselves they went on using the ethnic or Muslim names from their homeland. During questioning, they insisted on the difference, as if to affirm that inside each slave there was a person. One slave said "he was called Matheus . . . but in his homeland he is Dada." A black known as Faustina referred to a "black Nagô named Ajahi, known as Jorge in white man's land." Ajahi, in turn, mentioned a "black named Aliara who is called José in white man's land."[26]

In many cases Africans did not even bother to memorize the Christian names of their closest associates. Mama Adeluz was a very good friend of Gaspar and gave him a precious Malê prayer book. However, Gaspar, a Nagô slave, according to a disappointed scribe, "did not know [Mama's] name in our language." And this was not to protect him. Gaspar, whose real name was Huguby, knew Mama had been killed. Concerning the plotters meeting at the house of Belchior da Silva Cunha, on Rua da Oração, Agostinha, a Nagô freedwoman, claimed not to "know their slave names . . . because there they were known by their African names." These names were Ova, Dada, Ojou, Namonim, and Aliara. André, a Nagô freedman, gave his work address and that of the master of an African with whom he shared a room. He could not, however, give his roommate's Christian name. "In his language he was called Ojou." That he knew.[27]

Thirty-seven Africans questioned, or at least mentioned in testimony, whose ethnic or Muslim names have been identified are listed in table 6. The twenty-one without Christian names, other than Edum, never appeared in court; that is, they were mentioned by third parties. Exclusive use of African names was more frequent among slaves than among ex-

Table 6
DEFENDANTS AND SUSPECTS WITH AFRICAN OR MALÊ NAMES
IN THE 1835 COURT PROCEEDINGS

African or Malê Name	Christian Name	Ethnic Group	Legal Status	Occupation
Ahuna	—	Nagô	Slave	Domestic
Ajadi	Luis Doplê	Nagô	Freed	Sailor
Ajahi	Jorge da Cruz Barbosa	Nagô	Freed	Porter
Alei	João	—	Slave	—
Aliara	José	—	Freed	Porter
Alade	Joaquim	Nagô	Slave	Chair porter
Aluna	—	Nagô	Slave	—
Arruecu (?)	—	Nagô	Slave	—
Baquim	—	Hausa	Freed	Merchant
Batanho	—	—	Slave	—
Buremo	—	Nagô	Slave	—
Campara	Benta	Hausa	Freed	Hawker
Combé	—	—	Slave	Domestic
Cubi	Adolfo	Nagô	Slave	Stevedore
Dada	Matheus	Nupe	Slave	Blacksmith
Dandará	Elesbão do Carmo	Hausa	Freed	Merchant
Dassalu	—	Nagô	Slave	Domestic
Edum	—	Nagô	Freed	Domestic
Flamé	—	—	Slave	—
Gala	Urbano	Bornu	Slave	Gardener
Gonso	Antônio	Nupe	Freed	Chair porter
Huguby	Gaspar	Nagô	Slave	Chair porter
Licutan/Bilal	Pacífico	Nagô	Slave	Tobacco roller
Liu	—	Nagô	Slave	Domestic
Mama Adeluz	—	Nagô	Freed	—
Manco	—	Nagô	Slave	—
Manura	—	Nagô	Slave	—
Mongo	—	Cabinda	Slave	Cook
Namonim	—	Nagô	Slave	Hawker
Nicobé	—	Nagô	Slave	Domestic
Ojo	José	Nagô	Slave	Chair porter
Ojo	—	Nagô	Slave	Chair porter
Ova	—	Nagô	Freed	—
Sanim	Luís	Tapa	Slave	Tobacco roller
Sule	Vitório	Nagô	Freed	Peddler
Sule	—	Nagô	Slave	—
Sumeno	—	—	Freed	—

slaves, suggesting perhaps a greater integration of the latter into Bahian society. Freedmen often had surnames inherited from ex-masters. One such case is the by now well-known pair Belchior and Gaspar da Silva Cunha, who bore the family name of their deceased owner, Manoel da

Silva Cunha. Still, despite their greater integration, freed slaves did not desert their old ethnic allies. Together with their countrymen, they married, lived, worked, and conspired against the white man.

The struggle to maintain ethnic and cultural identities helped Africans consolidate and widen their field of resistance in Bahian society; at the same time, it exacerbated preexisting differences among the various nations. The relatively paltry participation of the Jejes and the total absence of Bantus in the 1835 rebellion were due at least partly to ethnic animosity. Indeed, on several earlier occasions, authorities and colonial chroniclers observed that ethnic differences among Africans guaranteed social stability. As seen in chapter 3, the count of Arcos chose to permit African "drum dances" because these celebrations kept diverse ethnic groups apart. In addition to acknowledging slaves' rights to leisure, the count feared that cultural repression would create pan-African unity against the interests of slaveowners. On the other hand, his predecessor, the count of Ponte, considered African celebrations essentially subversive because they gave slaves a taste of independence, stimulated self-confidence, and promoted licentiousness and scorn for Western notions of morality and decorum. For him, these celebrations were more like pressure cookers than safety valves.

Matters such as these continued to divide officials during the postcolonial era. Perhaps ethnic celebrations may have been more conducive to solidarity than armed rebellions were, but the latter both benefited from and melded with the former. The Brotas magistrate, whose view of slave control followed the Ponte tradition, had been struck dumb by the presence of native-born black women at the Jeje candomblé site he invaded. This mixing, according to him, was clearly subversive. On the heels of this episode, he severely criticized a colleague for adopting the Arcos line. This magistrate, "from Engenho Velho, [which is] outside my jurisdiction," often let blacks gather for festive occasions. On one of these occasions, according to the magistrate, "so many people came that in just one day they killed a steer and ate it, on top of which there were people of all colors there." He ended by saying, "That is how rebellions begin." As a segregationist, Antônio Gomes considered feasts to be forces that unified rather than divided people of diverse ethnicities, colors, and races. As far as he was concerned, segregation meant order. Five years later Inspector Antônio Marques was to adopt this principle in Vitória when he forcibly brought the commemoration of Lailat al-Miraj to an end.

However, neither feast, religion, nor rebellion was able to erase interethnic tensions entirely. Africans questioned in 1835 had much to say about these tensions. The proud and predominant Nagôs were the favorite object of criticism. A Jeje freedman, João Duarte da Silva, claimed to have nothing to do with them and not to speak their language. In fact, "because they are enemies of Jejes, if he were to have been outside on that occasion [the uprising], he would certainly have been killed." Another Jeje freedman, José da Costa, argued in his own defense that "he was from a Nation that was wholly inimical to the blacks who disturbed the city's peace."[28] This is one more example of Nagô-Jeje rivalry. In Africa the Aja-Fon kingdom of Dahomey was the traditional adversary of the powerful Yoruba empire of Oyo and paid tribute to that empire or fought against it for decades. Their mutual animosity crossed the Atlantic with them.

Slaves and ex-slaves from other ethnic groups also tried to exonerate themselves by appearing hostile to Nagôs. A Hausa freedman, João Borges, declared that with Nagôs he had "no dealings whatsoever that would let him know about their goings-on." Mongo pleaded innocent, saying "he was of the Cabinda Nation and had no truck with Nagôs." Even more resentful was another Hausa freedman, Domingos Borges, who lived with João and had the following to say: "While still a slave he was stabbed twice by a Nagô companion who wanted him to join the first Nagô uprising here. He is to this day gravely ill from the wound and hates those people, with whom he has no dealings. Such [is his animosity] that even though a Nagô lives below them, neither he nor his friends ever paid this Nagô a visit . . . nor did they say hello to him."[29]

These declarations, however, should be put in their proper perspective, since much of the anti-Nagô sentiment expressed therein was a stratagem on the part of those questioned. They wanted to convince their questioners that they were innocent vis-à-vis a revolt officials believed was caused by Nagôs. It is hardly haphazard that Nagôs were put on the firing line by other Africans. Rather, it supports the thesis that the rebellion was largely ethnic in motivation, that it was principally a Nagô affair. The hostility prisoners expressed against Nagôs in their testimony could even be discarded as rebel lies designed to escape justice. This hostility had a real basis in the daily life of Salvador, but it was played to the hilt during the trials.

One should not overemphasize the importance of disunity in the African camp. The goals of the 1835 movement show that the rebels' worst enemies were not African. Various African nations may have been adversaries, but in Bahia this never brought them to blows with one another. Collective violence on the part of Africans was always aimed at one target: the enemies from "white man's land." This was the case in 1835, notwithstanding Nagô dominance in the revolt.

Ethnic identity, however, should not be understood as an alternative to religion in explaining the revolt. The relationship between ethnicity and religion was complex. Even though Islam is not an ethnic religion, aiming as it does toward universal status, it may have been ethnic in the 1835 scenario. In Bahia, Islam was linked to specific ethnic groups, mainly Hausas and Nagôs. Nonetheless, one should remember that becoming a Malê did not seem to diminish the convert's ethnic awareness, precisely because to an important degree Islam melded with indigenous African ethnic religions. Many of the Africans entering the rebellion did not know exactly whether they were there as Nagôs or Malês. Some were merely Nagôs who got swept up in the struggle their Malê countrymen had organized.

· 9 ·

Workers, Slave and Freed

OCCUPATIONAL PROFILE OF THE ACCUSED

*Just you wait. Before you know it, you'll look for a black man
in this place and you won't find one—then it'll be you who
has to heft these chairs.*
—African sedan chair porter to a drunken customer, five days
before the 1835 rebellion

Salvador and its export docks ran on black labor. To speak of African labor was, however, not to speak solely of slave labor. Salvador's businessmen hired both slaves and ex-slaves off the street for many different tasks. Scholars have privileged research on slave labor, perhaps because it has left more lasting marks on history and in the available documentation, but the present portrait is broader. The investigators of the Malê rebellion collected data on everyone indicted in the uprising, and these data shed light on the work of freedmen as well as of slaves. While the data show that belonging to similar ethnic and religious groups provided solidarity and collective identity for Africans, they also show that the workplace performed this function, too. It actually facilitated the development of traditional ethnic and religious identities, which helped fuel the rebellion.

African Workers in Action

Africans filled the streets of Salvador. They worked in the open air as artisans, washerwomen, tailors, street vendors, water bearers, barbers, musicians, artists, masons, carpenters, stevedores, and sedan chair porters. Almost every foreign visitor remarked about the variety of occupations exercised solely by blacks, both free and slave. Visitors were surprised that a society controlled by whites could be so totally dependent on black labor. Mattoso found forty-two different professions or livelihoods in a sample of 582 slaves she studied. Andrade listed eighty-nine different ones based on a considerably larger number (6,974) of slaves. They did all kinds of work, certainly giving urban slaves a wider world-view, eventually including visions of individual manumission and occupational mobility.[1]

Relations among slaves and masters in Salvador were based on a system of "earnings," or *ganho*. On a daily or weekly basis, slave "earners" *(ganhadores)* were obliged to give their masters a previously set quantity of money. Whatever else they earned they kept, and masters usually obeyed that rule, although no law obliged them to. Nonetheless, the ganho system was far from being a seigniorial blessing. "In Salvador," wrote Spix and Martius, who visited in 1818, "those who have to earn a certain amount (some 240 réis) every day for their masters have a sorry plight; they are considered live capital in action, and as their masters want to recuperate their investment and interest within a certain time, they do not spare their slaves." Quotas varied from one occupation to another and depended as well on the age, health, and other attributes of the slave in question. The chief element in calculating quotas probably was the average productivity of specific occupations within the marketplace. Andrade gives some examples of quotas for the year 1847: a sedan chair porter paid out 400 réis per day, as did a shoemaker. Next came other porters and stevedores, who paid their masters 320 réis per day. Rachel, a slave washerwoman, only paid 240 réis, which was the average quota noted thirty years earlier by Spix and Martius.[2]

With three years of productive work, masters recuperated the capital they invested in a slave. Slaves were an excellent investment during times of economic prosperity, when jobs for ganhadores abounded. During slow times they still paid, because as a rule these slaves could support themselves. They ate, dressed, and often lodged on their own account.

The majority of female slaves worked as domestic servants or in related occupations, such as seamstress, washerwoman, or cook. But many of them worked on their own, as *ganhadeiras,* and were indistinguishable from freed black women, who also worked on their own. Small-time street businesses were almost monopolized by these women. During the colonial period many different laws were passed in vain attempts to restrict their activities. Shortly before the turn of the century, Vilhena observed, somewhat worried and irritated, that for all intents and purposes, the ganhadeiras monopolized the sale of fish, vegetables, and contraband. They gathered in open-air markets (at the time called *quitandas*) and, in the words of the illustrious chronicler, "got together to sell all they had, be it fish, half-cooked meat (which they call *moqueada*), salt pork, whale meat (when available), greens, what have you." Using ingenious systems of market speculation and smuggling—which they called *carambola* ("somersault") or *cacheteira* ("mockery")—ganhadeiras, often in cahoots with their former or current mistresses, controlled the supply of basic foodstuffs

FIG. 13. Chair porters bearing a woman of ill-repute. Drawing from Johann Baptist von Spix and Karl F. von Martius, *Viagem pelo Brasil, 1817–1820: excertos e ilustrações* (São Paulo: Melhoramentos, 1968).

in the city. Some forty years after Vilhena's observations, the situation had not changed, according to an American missionary.[3]

A large portion of adult male slaves (nearly 16 percent) were also employed in domestic service, but the majority, beyond doubt, worked in the streets as earners. Both slave and free earners worked mainly as stevedores and sedan chair porters. The latter made up the majority of Africans working in the streets of Salvador. Sedan chairs were the most common form of transportation in Salvador, where the hilly topography, not to mention the high price of horses, did not allow the widespread use of carriages. The important coming and going between the upper and lower parts of Salvador was done in these chairs. Carrying sedan chairs was obviously a grueling occupation. In the early 1820s Maria Graham described Bahia's sedan chairs as follows: "They consist of a cane armchair, with the footboard and a canopy covered with leather; curtains, generally of moreen, with gilt bordering and lined with cotton or linen, are contrived to draw round, or open at pleasure; and the whole is slung by the top to a single pole, by which two negroes carry it at a quick pace upon their shoulders, changing occasionally from right to left."[4]

African workers assumed their daily tasks in an organized manner, in their own fashion. This also impressed foreign visitors:

> Immense numbers of tall, athletic negroes are seen moving in pairs or gangs of four, six or eight, with their loads suspended between them on heavy poles. Many more of their fellows are seen sitting upon their poles, braiding straw, or lying about the alleys and corners of the streets, asleep. . . . The sleepers generally have some sentinel ready to call them when they are wanted for services. . . . they often sing and shout as they go, but their gait is necessarily slow and measured, resembling a death march.[5]

In the early nineteenth century Sir Robert Wilson, who saw blacks such as these carrying enormous boxes of sugar up a hill in ninety-degree heat, claimed that it was "scarcely possible to imagine a more distressing toil."[6]

The music, the cadenced steps, the collective organization, all indicate that Africans imbued urban toil with elements of their native culture. Their singing does not mean that they were unaware of being exploited in the "death march" Kidder compared their gait to. Actually such an attitude toward work functioned both to ward off sorrow and to put limits on their exploitation. James Wetherell, an English merchant who lived in Salvador for a time, despite his ethnocentrism, was able to provide interesting observations on the work habits of Bahian Africans:

> During the time of carrying heavy burdens through the streets they sing a kind of chorus, a very useful manner of warning persons to get out of the way. This chorus generally consists of one of the blacks chanting a remark on anything he sees, and the other comes in with a chorus. . . . I have noticed, too, that when the work is heavy, or the burden is being carried uphill, that they become much more vigorous in their shouts, aiding their labour and varying their song with an expressive long grunt. Although thus collectively, the blacks carry very heavy burdens, yet one man will not carry nearly as much as a European, and they are extremely independent, they would rather lose the chance of gaining a wage than carry more than what *they* thought proper.[7]

This precapitalist attitude was also typical of street vendors, who "preferred to throw out perishable merchandise rather than sell it for a price deemed too low."[8] As far as Africans were concerned, market pressures did not always have the last word.

Both Wetherell and Kidder came upon a work pace, ethos, and aesthetic that were foreign to them. Wetherell went even further, contrasting the collective independence of African workers in Bahia with the muscular but submissive individualism of the English salaried worker. At least to some extent, Africans got to do what they believed to be in *their* interest. And it appears that they were not about to trade chattel slavery for wage slavery. They had their own traditional, African notions of labor relations, and it was according to those notions that they wanted to guide and even overcome Bahian slavery, at least in the urban environment.

In many ways African labor in the New World, in spite of being inserted in a commercial system, kept time according to the task at hand rather than by the clock. This is different from capitalistic logic, where workers sell their labor at a certain price, and it is consumed at a specific time, with no regard to what is being done. In factories machines control the pace of labor and separate it from daily life. Among Salvador's Africans there seems to have been minimal "demarcation between 'work' and 'life,'" because "social intercourse and labour are intermingled," just as E. P. Thompson suggested for European preindustrial workers.[9] This did not eliminate slavery's dehumanizing, crude, and violent aspects; it did, however, attenuate some of them. Furthermore, it was not thanks to seigniorial generosity that Africans behaved that way; it was an African conquest in the urban environment. The master might control the output of slave labor, but the slave decided where, how, and with whom to work. Together with freedmen, African slaves in a way controlled their entry into the labor market.

The ganho system created *cantos,* literally "corners" of freed and slave laborers, institutions formed by earners organized by ethnicity. They were called "corners" because of the places where they gathered in the city to attend their customers. Each canto bore the name of the locale where its ganhadores gathered: Calçada Square, Portão de São Bento, Mangueira Street, and so on.

Little is known about the internal structure or dynamics of these cantos. Each one had a leader known as *captain (capitão do canto).* Such a designation may suggest some sort of linkage with a type of African military organization. But it also could be related to the *parakoyi,* the person who administered open-air markets in Egba and who probably existed in other Yoruba towns; or to the *bale* in Yoruba craft compounds, usually an elder who led other craftsmen. In Salvador canto captains mediated between the earner and the contractor: they arranged jobs, set prices, and paid Africans under their management. No one knows whether they also shouldered loads as the others did, or what exactly qualified someone for the job. Experience, freed status, and knowledge of local customs were quite likely important. Captains were elected, but historians do not know how. According to Manoel Querino, "when a captain died, they would try to elect or acclaim his successor, who would take the job immediately." Querino goes on to describe the inauguration ceremony for the new captain:

> The members of a canto would borrow an empty keg from one of the warehouses on Julião or Pilar Street. They would fill it with sea water, bind it with ropes, and stick a long board through the ropes. From eight

to twelve Ethiopians, usually the strongest of the lot, would lift the keg, on top of which the new canto captain would ride, holding the branch of a bush in one hand and in the other a bottle of white rum.

The entire canto would parade toward the Pedreiras neighborhood. Porters would intone a monotonous air, in an African dialect or patois.

They would return, in the same order, to the point of departure. The recently elected captain was then congratulated by members of other cantos, and on that occasion, he performed a sort of exorcism with the liquor bottle, sprinkling a few drops of its content out.

This confirmed the election.

The inauguration ritual gives some idea of the importance of the institution. The captain seems like a king in a coronation ceremony. The barrel full of salt water might associate the work of an African with the crossing of the Atlantic on the way to slavery in the New World. Africa is evoked as well. As Bastide has mentioned, the sprinkling of white rum on the ground is an offering to African gods. It is the "saint's share" that candomblé practitioners always proffer before they take their first drink. The captain's confirmation ceremony, in Bastide's words, represented "communion in their ancestral religion."[10]

Cantos helped establish solidarity among the African workers. They restricted individual competition among them; they kept the tradition of collective work alive; and they fought back against slavery's destruction of the African spirit of community.

The ganho system allowed urban slaves, by dint of great effort, to buy their own letters of manumission. While there was no law in the mid-1830s to force masters to free their slaves, if slaves offered them their market price, masters customarily freed them. Letters of manumission could be paid for in cash or, and this was more common, in installments. Slaves could also buy other slaves, train them in a skill, and give them to their masters in exchange for their freedom. There were also free manumissions, but masters tended to favor mulattos and native-born blacks, who, let it be said, also outdid Africans in buying their own freedom.

Africans tried to obtain manumissions collectively by forming credit unions called "manumission pools" *(juntas de alforria),* which they formed within their ethnic groups. The pool consisted of a fund into which both slave and freed members contributed. On a revolving basis members would be entitled to the amount necessary to buy their freedom, but they continued to pay whatever they owed until they paid off their debt plus whatever interest was necessary owing to inflation. The origin of these pools is not known. However they are very similar to a Yoruba credit institution called *esusu,* which Johnson describes: "A fixed sum agreed upon is given by each at a fixed time (usually every week) and place, under a president; the total amount is paid over to each member in rotation. This enables a poor man to do something worth while where a lump sum is required."[11] Ellis called these associations *eşu* societies, noting that they were spread out all over Yorubaland. He maintained as well that members met every fifth working day to collect quotas and distribute credit.[12]

The Defendants as Workers

Tables 7 and 8 correlate occupations with legal status and ethnic origin. Most Africans were employed in urban services, which constitutes 34 percent of the occupations identified with any accuracy (i.e., excluding those unknown). Sedan chair porters were the majority within this sector (fifteen slaves, fifteen ex-slaves). Seven slaves and one ex-slave worked in sugar and tobacco warehouses along the docks. There were six meatcutters (four slaves, two freedmen); five porters (three slaves, two freedmen); one freed washerwoman; a slave employed as a clerk; and a slave who was a lamplighter.

Slaves and freed persons were almost equally represented in these urban services. The same cannot be said, however, about other types of work. Although domestic service was the second largest category (after urban services), among the prisoners only five ex-slaves worked as domestics, all of them as cooks. On the other hand, twenty-five slaves were domestics, of whom many were Malês serving the foreigners living in Vitória. (Since he watched over Christ's house, one Nagô slave, Agostinho, working as a sacristan has been included in the category of domestic. Such a task must have been less than honorable for a good Muslim.)

Slaves were also predominant among African farmworkers and seamen. In this group there were seven lighter rowers (six slaves, one freedman); four field hands (three slaves, one freedman); one slave who was a fisherman; and another slave who was a shepherd. On the other hand, peddlers and street vendors were rarely slaves. There were only four slaves selling food and one selling cloth. Of the ex-slaves working in markets in Salvador as well as towns and plantations in the Recôncavo, eight dealt in African cloth *(panos da costa)* and other products. Another eight sold food in the streets, two had stands, and the rest dealt in many other items (charcoal, whitewash, bread, etc.), selling from little stands or going door to door. There were also some owners of slightly bigger businesses: four tobacco merchants and one boat owner, as well as one landlord.

Finally there were specialized artisans and other professionals, the majority, but not the overwhelming majority, of whom were freed. There were three tailors and one seamstress (two slaves, two freedmen); five masons (three freedmen, two slaves); three barbers (two slaves, one freedman); three caulkers (two ex-slaves, one slave); one blacksmith, one shoemaker, and one tanner (all slaves); one gunsmith, one carpenter, one

Table 7
DEFENDANTS' OCCUPATIONS

Occupation	Slaves	Freed	Total
Merchant	0	6	6
Peddler	5	22	27
Artisan	10	17	27
Urban service	29	23	52
Domestic	25	5	30
Farmworker/sea worker	11	2	13
Unknown	106	40	146
Total	186	115	301

Source: AEBa, *Insurreições*, maços 2845–50.

Table 8
DEFENDANTS' OCCUPATIONS AND ETHNIC ORIGINS

Occupation	Ethnic Origin							Total
	Nagô	Hausa	Jeje	Tapa/ Bornu	Bantus[a]	Other Africans[b]	Native- born	
Merchant	1	2	0	0	0	3	0	6
Peddler	8	10	2	5	0	2	0	27
Artisan	11	3	3	5	2	2	3	27
Urban service	34	6	2	4	2	4	0	52
Domestic	23	1	2	0	2	2	0	30
Farmworker/ sea worker	7	3	1	1	0	0	1	13
Unknown	115	6	0	0	4	1	1	127
Total	199	31	10	13	10	14	5	282

Source: AEBa, *Insurreições*, maços 2845–50.
[a] One Mundubi, one Benguela, four Congos, four Cabindas.
[b] Seven Minas, three Gurmas, two Calabars, two Barbas.

baker, one excavator *(caboqueiro),* three weavers who made hats, mats, and figures (all African freedmen).

Of the 185 people whose trials have been examined, twenty-six were women, nineteen of them freedwomen. They worked mainly as street vendors. One of them, a Jeje ex-slave known as Ellena, told the judge about her daily struggle. "She spends all day in the street selling fish and hunting up fishermen. She retires after dark and gets up early." Marcelina, a slave of Mundubi origin, "lived off selling dry goods."[13] More than half the prisoners considered street vendors (i.e., fourteen out of twenty-seven),

FIG. 14. A woman buying fish on the beach to resell. Blacks controlled street commerce in Salvador. Drawing by Johan Moritz Rugendas, reprinted from his *Malerische reise in Brasilien* (Paris: Engelmann & Cie, 1835).

were women, which supports the claim that women dominated that profession.

Among the women, there was one washerwoman, one hairdresser, and ten others whose occupations have not been determined. Perhaps many of those of unknown occupations were domestics, which was a category of employment surprisingly absent among these prisoners. But this absence could also be explained by the small number of slave women arrested in 1835. According to Andrade, the most prevalent female occupation in Salvador was domestic service, which employed 58 percent of female slaves. Female ex-slaves seem to have refused to go on working as they had while they were slaves.[14]

Africans (other than Hausas) of different ethnicities do not appear to have flocked toward specific occupations in Salvador. Hausas maintained the commercial proclivities that distinguished them in Africa. On both sides of the Atlantic, they were good Muslims and good businessmen, confirming the Islamic proverb, "Merchants are the messengers of this world and God's faithful trustees on Earth." Nearly half the Hausas arrested were in business, either with small establishments in Salvador or as peddlers doing business in different parts of the province. Caetano Ribeiro, a freedman, claimed to come "to the city to sell tobacco and other goods which he buys in the Recôncavo to sell in town." The Malê preacher Elesbão do Carmo (Dandará) bought and sold tobacco in a store at the Santa Bárbara market. Raimundo Nunes de Barros had established credit with three white merchants (probably Portuguese) in Salvador, and these men trusted him with cloth that he would take and sell throughout the Recôncavo. All these merchants were Hausas. There were many Hausas among the freedmen indicted, but few among the slaves—a total of twenty-three freedmen and only eight slaves—which may explain their near absence from the less specialized occupations, such as domestic service.[15]

One of the survival strategies Africans commonly used in Bahia was to work at more than one job. Masters doubtless often obliged slaves to work at different activities, but slaves themselves often devised ways of making extra money, be it to live a little better on a daily basis or to save and buy their freedom. Among those arrested in 1835, ten slaves and eleven freedmen claimed to have more than one job (see table 9).

Of course there were many more Africans doubly and triply employed, but this small sample suggests that both slaves and freedmen worked hard to complement their meager incomes, or just to get by. More people must have worked at more than one job during times of economic hardship—Bahia of the 1830s. Kidder saw black porters "weaving straw" in their cantos while they waited for customers. Manoel Querino provides a long list of crafts and other activities done in those niches. "They made rosaries from *coquilho* berries with tassels made of colored thread; leather wristbands decorated with seashells or others made from oiled Morrocan leather; wire chains for parrots; *ouricori* straw mats and hats; as well as *piassava* palm leaf brooms; they weaved Panama and other straw hats; and they repaired parasols." Aprígio, a Muslim slave and chair porter working in the Mangueira canto, passed his waiting time making clothing. Chair

Table 9
PRIMARY AND SECONDARY OCCUPATIONS

Principal Occupation	Secondary Occupation	Legal Status
Domestic service	Sedan chair porter	Slave
Domestic service	Sedan chair porter	Slave
Domestic service	Sedan chair porter	Slave
Domestic service	Sedan chair porter	Slave
Domestic service	Oarsman	Slave
Sedan chair porter	Peddler	Freed
Sedan chair porter	Stand owner	Freed
Sedan chair porter	Tailor	Freed
Sedan chair porter	Bread seller	Slave
Sedan chair porter	Shepherd	Slave
Tailor	Stand owner	Freed
Tailor	Landlord	Freed
Mason	Field hand	Freed
Mason	Landlord	Freed
Meatcutter	Sedan chair porter	Slave
Meatcutter	Porter	Slave
Tanner	Field hand	Slave
Barber	Musician	Freed
Sailor (*saveirista*)	Cook	Freed
Whitewash salesman	Hatter	Freed
Cook	Sailor (*saveirista*)	Freed

porters, it seems, were adept at combining their main activity with all sorts of other jobs. Paulo da Silva Guimarães was a chair porter and a Hausa merchant who often traveled to Africa, bringing back cloth and palm oil, which he sold in Salvador.[16]

There was also a marked tendency for domestic slaves to acquire other occupations. When this happened, their master got not only their housework but also their daily earning. It must have been much more difficult for domestic slaves to save money for manumission given that housework paid them nothing. But it also may be that they were on a better footing with their masters, which allowed them to do better at both tasks. Oliveira suggests that "sporadic or part-time ganhadores who worked mainly as domestics or artisans did not make enough money to live on their own and lived with their masters and were entirely supported by them."[17]

Combinations of ordinary jobs were common. Much less common were combinations of ordinary work with activities that only a privileged few could perform. Such was the case of José, a man of forty and a semi-freed Jeje, who in 1835 was still paying installments on his letter of manumission. He worked as a meatcutter, but his true calling seems to have been, according to one witness, that of "witch doctor" (*curador de feitiço*).

Even though he was a Jeje, José testified to having "been brought up in Nagôland," where he had probably learned about orishas and their herbs. Several witnesses claimed that he had a reputation for curing "spells." One told the judge a story going through her neighborhood. "A mestiça by the name of Thomazia so-and-so sick, and said black [José] made her believe she was under a spell and set out to cure her." Ana Rita, a Bornu freedwoman living on Ladeira de Santa Teresa with her husband, a Bornu known as Miguel, was also a witch doctor *(curandeira)*. She had gained the confidence of masters who sought her out to cure their slaves. A slave woman, Marcelina, arrested in Ana Rita's house on the night of the uprising, claimed to have been sent there by her mistress, Dona Ana Joaquina, "to get her foot treated." Also active at the time of the rebellion was someone named Lessa living in Cabula, a suburb of Salvador. Lessa worked a tract of land and also helped sick people. One must not overlook the Muslims who sold amulets to heal spiritual ills and ward off bodily danger. Antônio, a Hausa slave fisherman living in Itapagipe, made four patacas a day selling protective prayers he wrote for his African clientele. Since a pataca was worth 320 réis, which was about the daily quota paid to a slaveowner in 1835, Antônio could be said to be doing well. Similarly, a twenty-three-year-old Nagô slave belonging to a Frenchman had an interesting source of supplementary income. "Said black performed marriage ceremonies for all the negroes and negresses who went to the Barris fountain. After the ceremony, he would give them a ring . . . and he then got an amount of money or certain other things." According to one witness, blacks called him a priest.[18]

As a rule, freed slaves stayed at the same job they had done as slaves, but it was also common for them to change. To change their legal status and their job probably made them feel doubly free. Raimundo de Barros had lived in Bahia for twenty years when he was arrested in 1835. During his days of slavery he had worked as a clerk in the taverns of three different masters. His last owner had bought him at an auction as part of the confiscated property of a Portuguese tavernkeeper who had left the province in 1823, at the end of the war of independence. Five years later he acquired his manumission for 340 milréis—40 milréis in cash plus a slave worth 300 milréis. Having spent thirteen years of his slavery as a clerk, he knew his way in business, and once freed, he started his own business, selling cloth throughout the Recôncavo.[19]

Other freedmen stayed with the jobs they had had as slaves until they were forced to find new ones because of their age, health, or other vicissitudes of life. When Domingos and João Borges, Hausas, ex-slaves of the same master, were manumitted, they went on with their old sedan chair partnership until João broke his leg and had to earn his living making mats at the entrance to the Gomes warehouse. Domingos went on until he suffered a "hernia on the left side," at which time he became a cloth merchant. The "medical" history of these two men shows the bodily harm that could come from being a chair porter. Daniel da Silva became a rope and mat maker ("he braided") after the stand where he sold whitewash fell apart.[20] Many manumitted Africans simply resumed the work they had done in their homeland. Commerce was a Hausa trademark, especially of Muslims. Another Hausa specialty was ropemaking, which, according to Oroge, was typical of Hausas enslaved in Yorubaland.[21]

Some of the African defendants could not adapt to their new circumstances or had no opportunity for less grueling tasks. In spite of their advanced age, four Africans (aged fifty-five, sixty, seventy, and seventy-one) went on carrying sedan chairs. The oldest prisoner, Domingos, an eighty-year-old Hausa slave, had been a chair porter until age seventy-eight. In his testimony he declared to the judge that he had lost "the use of his faculties" in a fall and had quit working. However, notwithstanding his age, judging from his long, coherent explanations, Domingos had not lost his mind. Insanity seems to have been a new occupation Domingos cleverly devised for the end of his life. He deceived the white man by pretending to be crazy. "While he retained his faculties, he served his master. But once he lost them, over a year ago, he is only good for being fed by his master," the slave declared. Domingos, by the way, was acquitted.[22]

If age did not exempt the majority of Africans from work, it also did not exempt them from rebellion. The data dispel the idea that only the young rebel, but then most rebels of any age did not have restraining family obligations, as we shall see. Almost 30 percent of the fifty-two prisoners whose ages have been discerned were over forty, and 20 percent were over fifty. Considering that they belonged to a population with very short life expectancies, it appears that older generations were well represented among the rebels. Ex-slaves were older than slaves, since manumission took time. Most slave prisoners (52.8 percent) were between twenty-one and thirty years of age, as were, most likely, most African slaves in Bahia at that time. The youngest prisoner was Higino, a seventeen-year-old Nagô; the oldest was Domingos, who was eighty.[23]

The youngest prisoners were employed mainly in domestic service. There, under the master's watchful eyes, they learned their early lessons about being a foreigner and slave in Salvador. As time passed, and with age, most men went outside the house to work in the streets, while women stayed behind. Older prisoners were largely artisans, perhaps because of the time needed to learn a trade but also because these occupations required less physical strength and energy than others.

Urban slavery and the workplace had much to do with the rebellion in Salvador. The ganho system clearly demonstrated how masters ex-

Table 10
DEFENDANTS' AGES

Age	Slave	Freed	Total
Under 21	4	0	4
21–25	7	0	7
26–30	12	3	15
31–35	2	2	4
36–40	4	3	7
41–45	0	2	2
46–50	2	1	3
Over 50	5	5	10
Total	36	16	52

ploited slaves' labor. Slaves' daily contact with freedmen clarified things even further. While freedmen pocketed all their earnings (be they from transporting passengers in sedan chairs or from lugging barrels of white rum), their slave partners were obliged to hand the bulk of their earnings over to their masters. This was the weak link in the political economy of urban slavery, as well as a point of great stress.

Domestic slaves did not have the same amount of contact with freedmen, but they experienced other types of friction in the system. The pressures they felt within the master's house and within his family (too much work, petty humiliations, constant vigilance, etc.) could be greater than those felt by black earners. Either way, slavery was always at the root of African rebelliousness. "His brethren complained of bad treatment as slaves," Muslim preacher Licutan told the judge in 1835.[24]

Freedmen also faced a disturbing dilemma. For them, slavery was a sad memory reexperienced daily in the bondage of friends, wives, relatives, countrymen, spiritual guides, and partners in work. Their adversaries were aware of this. A petition signed by dozens of Bahians of different social statuses argued for the expulsion of manumitted Africans with the following words: "They are the . . . surest support for slave conspiracies, since they once shared their lot. Being freedmen, they can judge the hardship of slavery better than anyone, and for this reason they can describe the pleasures of freedom to those still enslaved."[25] Most freedmen were far from content, however. They still worked at slave occupations, and their personal wishes for change and upward mobility were checkmated by prejudice, in addition to the nature of the economy itself. They were stigmatized and treated as inferiors by the really free sectors of the population. Whites, mulattos, and even native blacks reminded African workers on a daily basis that they had come to the New World to work and obey. That is why, five days before the 1835 uprising, Aprígio, when obliged by a bailiff and a soldier to take a drunken customer in his sedan chair, reacted by saying: "Just you wait. Before you know it, you'll look for a black man in this place and you won't find one—then it'll be you who has to heft these chairs."[26] An African, even a freed one, could not refuse to serve a white man, even a drunken one.

One cannot underestimate the political role of freedmen in this movement, and in others. In addition to opening their houses for planning sessions, they could move conspiracies along thanks to their greater mobility and the distances they covered in their professions. Certain occupations principally filled by freed slaves helped undermine Bahian slavery. Peddlers wove networks of complicity among their customers. They took news from one place to another. Their wares whetted customers' appetite for novelty. They created hope for something better. They maintained contacts. Traders involved in transatlantic commerce brought fresh news back from Africa and maintained links with the old countries. Others spread the word of Allah along with their merchandise, or they made those words their merchandise, which they sold in the form of protective amulets. Peddlers brought Africans out of isolation and regularly gave them the feeling of belonging to a community wider than that of the plantations, the towns of the Recôncavo, and the suburbs of Salvador. Finally, in the case of the rebellion, they carried a concrete message: the transformation of the world in favor of Africans. Thus was Vitório Sule, who exuded energy "selling cloth from a basket" and who was "one of the main enticers of people into the Malê sect."[27]

One cannot downplay the new dimensions work added to African identities or its role in creating new bonds of solidarity. When they founded cantos and manumission pools, and when they gave their work a cultural flavor of their own, Africans realized that they could have an impact on the daily workings of the system, which they made more bearable at the same time that they exposed its shortcomings. Their independent organization on the job gave them a glimpse of a Bahia free from masters and their allies. Between the time they realized this and their rebellion, much more happened, of course. But beyond a doubt, labor organization and labor exploitation in the urban environment workplace were fundamental in the formation of a collective African will to oppose white man's rule. African labor was not to be separated from daily life and cannot be separated from the revolt. Those who try to explain the uprising strictly on the basis of religious motivation (and a disembodied religion at that) are in error. Even if the Malê rebellion were found to be a jihad, it is important to remember that historically jihads have also risen out of socioeconomic oppression.

· 10 ·

Making Do: Africans away from Work

Very few studies examine how Africans in Bahia led their lives away from work.[1] Where and how did they live? Whose company did they keep? Did they have families? children? relatives? The lack of detailed urban censuses for the 1830s makes it hard to carry out a broad, in-depth study on this subject, and this makes information on matters in the court records of the 1835 rebellion all the more important. Gleanings from the court records furnish glimpses into how the men and women in Bahia's African community got on and why they opted to revolt.

Residential Patterns

Addresses of African defendants reflect the urban nature of the movement. The parishes in which defendants' inquiries were held are presented in table 11. In the main, because most people brought to trial were not arrested on the night of the uprising, their trials were presided over by magistrates from the parishes where they lived.

The majority of the accused lived in Sé Parish, the oldest part of the upper city, where Pacífico Licutan, Manoel Calafate, Gaspar and Belchior da Silva Cunha, Luís Sanim, and other important characters in the Malê movement lived. Rua da Oração, Ladeira da Praça, Palace Square, the city jail, the cathedral, and the city hall were all in that parish. Residential, governmental, and ecclesiastic buildings stood side by side. Almost half the freedmen charged with rebellion lived there, with the rest scattered among the city's other parishes.

Only seven freedmen were brought to trial in Vitória, which was a neighborhood primarily inhabited by European foreigners, mainly English merchants. However, 27.3 percent of the slaves accused of participating in the rebellion lived there. Other slaves lived in the parishes of Sé (21.5 percent), Conceição da Praia (14.5 percent), Pilar (14 percent), and

Table II

RESIDENTIAL DISTRIBUTION OF THE 1835 DEFENDANTS

Parish	Slaves		Freed		Total	
	No.	%	No.	%	No.	%
Sé	37	21.5	52	47.3	89	31.6
Vitória	47	27.3	7	6.4	54	19.1
Conceição da Praia	25	14.5	16	14.5	41	14.5
Pilar	24	14.0	0	0	24	8.5
Santo Antônio	12	7.0	8	7.3	20	7.1
São Pedro	11	6.4	11	10.0	22	7.8
Passo	6	4.1	8	7.3	15	5.3
Santana	3	1.7	8	7.3	11	3.9
Penha	4	2.3	0	0	4	1.4
Brotas	2	1.2	0	0	2	.7
Total	172	100.0	110	100.0	282	100.0

Source: "Rol dos Culpados," AEBa, Insurreições, maço 2849.
Note: Only defendants whose legal status and trial parish have been identified are included.

Santo Antônio (7 percent). Of the slave defendants, 84.3 percent lived in these five parishes.

The defendants had relatively stable residences. Of the forty-nine who declared a period of residence at their current address, thirty-one had lived in the same house for more than three years. Notwithstanding the limitations of such a small sample, a few conclusions can be ventured. The trial proceedings especially lead one to conclude that recently arrived Africans, for all intents and purposes, did not take part in the rebellion. In addition, the only two slaves who claimed to have lived at the same address for less than two years had moved shortly before, and with their masters—or they had been purchased by new owners. It is significant that 60 percent of the slaves had lived more than six years at the same address. Such stability of residence may suggest, among other things, that these slaves were growing old and had given up any hope of buying their freedom.

On the other hand, 45 percent of the freedmen claimed to have lived at the same address for less than two years, which may mean that ex-slaves had less stable residences; that they moved more often from one house or parish to another. It may also mean that they had acquired their freedom and left their masters' houses less than two years before the rebellion. In support of the second hypothesis, data in other studies show that the first five years of the 1830s was a period marked by an increase in manumissions, and this tendency was linked to masters' difficulties in supporting their slaves during an economic crisis.[2]

Whether because they moved often or because they had recently acquired their letters of manumission, freedmen were clearly the more mobile and transitory group. They were perhaps more anxious about the future and what they expected (in vain) to become. Even though they had succeeded in freeing themselves, they still had fresh memories of their own enslavement and had not had time to fit into their new roles. The economic crisis reduced their chances for employment and probably exacerbated the discrimination against them. These newly freed slaves could have had good reasons both for maintaining and for destroying the system.

Whether they were slave or free, sedentary or nomadic, the defendants were all seasoned urban dwellers. Their familiarity with the city's streets and alleys was evident in the skirmishes. They had also become well acquainted with their masters and their neighbors and may have wanted to point their weapons at a few personal enemies: excessively arrogant whites, mestiço soldiers who had harassed them repeatedly. In a society such as Salvador's the line between personal and social vengeance was a blurry one. Equals and unequals lived close to one another, watched each other, kept tabs on and feuded with one another. During the trials defendants' Brazilian neighbors were especially efficient in identifying the most militant Africans and knew specific details about how and with whom they lived. For the Africans there were unexpected disadvantages in living in a residentially unsegregated society. That is, unsegregated relatively speaking.

Salvador's racial and social hierarchy becomes crystal clear if we examine the distribution of tenants inside city buildings. There was, so to speak, a sort of indoor segregation. On the topmost floor of the building on Ladeira da Praça where the rebellion began lived Major Alexandre José Fernandes, a government employee who worked at the ministry of finance. Fernandes was fifty-six years old, white, married (in the church), a father, and brother of the chief surgeon, Custódio José Fernandes. On the next floor down lived a mulatto couple: Domingos Marinho de Sá, a tailor, and his "concubine," Joaquina Rosa de Santana. With them lived an infant child of Joaquina and a Nagô slave, Ignácio, who belonged to Domingos's brother living in the Recôncavo. Domingos, in turn, sublet the basement, or loge, to Manuel Calafate and Aprígio, the bread peddler, both of whom were freed Nagôs. They, in turn, rented a room at the back of the loge to a slave, Belchior, who was also a Nagô. As one can see, the distribution of space in this building mirrors Bahian society and its inequities.[3]

Slaves and freedmen lived in loges. An 1855 census found only 8 percent of people living in loges to be white. Some freedmen also lived in rented hovels. A few, such as Belchior da Silva Cunha, went so far as to become urban landlords. Oliveira has identified 108 homeowners in a sample of 259 freedmen living in Salvador between 1790 and 1850. However, since these were people who left wills, this group of property owners,

41.7 percent of the total sample, was an elite subsection consisting of successful ex-slaves, rather than ordinary freedmen, as most of the defendants
under study here were. Even so, the houses belonging to this freed elite
were shabby, according to Oliveira:

> The great majority can be described as "thatched hut dwellings," impro-
> vised [*de bofetão*], "mud huts," or made of stone and whitewash. They
> were generally one-story, with a door and a window, almost always on
> rental lots belonging to convents, churches, or important urban land-
> owners. Some only own half of the dwelling they live in. The other half
> belongs to someone else with whom their relations do not go beyond
> that of cotenants.[4]

Part of that meager space was also often rented to slaves trying to escape
the stifling environment of the loges.

Loges were basically urban slave quarters. While masters' families
lived on the first and/or second floors of old colonial buildings, slaves lived
below in the loges, in an area often crowded with people. They had little
ventilation or light, no division into separate rooms, no privacy. Loges
were little more than one big room also known as the "storeroom" (*armazém*), and what they stored was people.

When the police searched those places for suspects and proof of participation in the rebellion, they never tripped over a piece of furniture.
Slaves slept on mats stretched out on the ground or, in rare cases, on mats
spread over planks. Some of them owned a single wooden crate in which
they kept their paltry possessions: clothes, tools, money, amulets. At night
masters locked their slaves in—to make sure they obeyed curfew as well as
to keep them from fleeing. But such strict vigilance was not always possible or desirable. Slaves in Salvador commonly found other dwellings.
Secretly, and often authorized by their masters, they would rent rooms or
parts of rooms from freed comrades willing to be impinged upon in exchange for some extra money. That is where they spent the day. They
returned at night to the master's home to sleep. They usually kept their
crates at their rented rooms.

Once they left their master's basement, slaves had more control over
their lives. Ova, Namonim, and Marcelina were slaves who rented rooms
from Belchior da Silva Cunha at 3.5 patacas (1,120 réis) per month. Marcelina (the slave of a nun from the Desterro Convent), who was arrested
along with Belchior and other Africans, testified that she lived in "the
house where she was arrested only during the day so that she could sell
her cloth, which is how she makes her money since the troops came in
from the Recôncavo [in 1823]. Even so, every night she returns and sleeps
at the slave quarters next to the convent." Marcelina had enjoyed that sort
of independence for twelve years, since the Bahian war of independence!
Another Belchior, a Nagô sedan chair porter and slave of José Joaquim

Xavier, confessed that for a year and a half he had been renting a room in Manoel Calafate's loge because he did not trust a slave Xavier had recently purchased.[5]

Indoors there was considerable variation in living arrangements. On a specific Sunday Joaquim, a slave of Francisco Lopes, borrowed a room rented by another slave to spend a few hours alone with "the mother of his children." This back room of a house on Laranjeiras Street had been rented by a group of slaves from "Father" *(Pai)* Ignácio, an old African ex-slave. The renters were Roque, Joaquim (a slave of Brigadier Manoel Gonçalves da Cunha), and Pacífico Licutan, the famous Malê preacher. They used it for religious meetings, dinners, celebrations, and, obviously and quite likely simultaneously, to plan the rebellion. They also used it for amorous encounters.[6]

Some slaves lived entirely on their own, with the consent of their masters, who were really only interested in their daily earnings. Emereciana, a Hausa slave, told the judge that she lived alone and supported herself selling food in the Santa Bárbara market and "had permission from her master to pay him on a weekly basis." Antônio, a Calabar slave, lived in Salvador, while his master lived on the island of Itaparica. The master defended his slave's autonomy: "The prisoner lives solely on his ganho work. His master receives part of his profits. . . . And so that he could get work [his master] let him live in the city, where it was easier for him to be useful and profitable to his master." Antônio's independence was "useful and profitable" to a master who did not have to be bothered about his slave's clothing, food, or lodging. Antônio lived in a rented room near the Santa Bárbara market.[7]

There were slaves who shared rented rooms with their men or women. For 800 réis per month a Nagô freedman, Luís Vieira, a sedan chair porter, rented a room in the back of a house on 61 Rua Direita de São Pedro, where he lived with Felicidade, the slave of a freed Mina man. Another room, connected to theirs, was home for Jacinto, a freedman, and his wife, a slave known as Firmina. They were both Nagôs. On the other hand, Urbano, a Bornu slave called Gala in his native land, for all intents and purposes lived with his girlfriend Benta, a freedwoman. He would only leave the premises early in the morning, when he would sneak back into his master's house.[8]

· Many different factors contributed to Africans' choice of housemates. Amorous unions were one obvious reason for living together. A few former slaves ended up living with their ex-masters out of necessity, convenience, or loyalty. Shared ethnicity and religion also was a motivating factor for living together, although it did not play an exclusive or excluding role in such arrangements. It was rare for West Africans to share a roof with Southern Africans. On the other hand, Nagôs, Tapas, Bornus, and (rarely) Jejes lived under the same roof. At 8 Ladeira da Palma, five Nagôs, one Tapa, one Bornu, and one Hausa, all freedmen, lived together and probably prayed together to Allah. The Hausa was the only one responsible to the landlady. (There was also mention made of an Angolan freedman living there, although there is no record of him in the trial proceedings.) Another house on Laranjeiras Street was occupied by four freedmen (two Nagôs, one Hausa, and one Gurma). Of course, many residences housed people from the same ethnic group. Three Hausa peddlers lived at 40 Rua de Baixo, in São Pedro Parish. And all those living with Manoel Calafate were Nagôs.[9]

Many freed Africans who had been slaves together shared houses after getting their freedom. Of the four Oliveiras sharing the house on Laranjeiras Street—Fortunato, Brás, Julião, and Felisberto—two were Nagôs, one was a Hausa, and the other a Gurma. They were all bachelors, and each had a different occupation: Fortunato was a sedan chair porter; Brás, an excavator; Felisberto, a mason; and Julião, a carpenter. They all carried their old master's name. Belchior and Gaspar da Silva Cunha at one time belonged to the same master, Manoel da Silva Cunha, and in 1835 they lived together on Rua da Oração. A few houses farther on lived two Hausa partners: Domingos and Jorge Borges, who also shared the family name of their former master.[10]

This short account of Africans' living arrangements already says something about the home life of the majority. Since there were few African women in Bahia, most dwellings were inhabited predominantly or entirely by men.

Bonds of Affection

The marital status of the defendants, that is, whether or not they were living with a person of the opposite sex, can be seen in table 12. As one might expect, slaves had scant opportunities for affectionate relationships, either episodic or long-lasting. More than 27 percent claimed to be bachelors, and that number could be raised to 98 percent if we consider those whose marital status is not known to have been single. Of the four male slaves who had marital ties with women, at least two had only intermittent contact with their partners. Joaquim, who borrowed friends' rooms to meet with a woman who had even borne him children, and Urbano (Gala), who returned to his master's house early every morning after spending the night with Benta, exemplify this pattern.

The other two lived apart from their masters. One of these was a woman: Emereciana, who declared she was the "lover" (*amazia*) of Elesbão do Carmo (Dandará), another Malê preacher. They appear to have had a stable relationship. José was the other one. He lived like a freedman,

Table 12
MARITAL STATUS OF THE 1835 DEFENDANTS

Marital Status	Slaves	Freed	Total
"Married"[a]	4	32	36
Not married	52	33	85
Widower	0	1	1
Unknown	130	49	179

Source: AEBa, *Insurreições*, maços 2845–50.

[a]Included here are all people in a marital arrangement but not necessarily under the same roof.

even though he had not yet finished paying for his manumission. This man was a famous witch doctor. He appears to have divided his amorous moments between Lucinda and Felicidade, since he identified his residences as being two different rooms, where these women lived. This man had two lovers, whereas the overwhelming majority of African men had none at all. Of course, how many of them possessed José's magic power? [11]

Freedmen had more chances to female partners. Almost 90 percent of the "married" defendants, including the women, were ex-slaves. From another perspective, exactly half the freed men and women whose marital status is known were, or had been, living in a marital arrangement. Even if we consider the "unknowns" as unmarried, a healthy 29 percent of freed slaves were or had been married. Of course, this is still a small percentage compared with those found in populations having a relative balance between men and women, which was not the case among the Africans in Bahia.

Surprisingly, there were no cases of slave men and women cohabiting. Male slaves typically had relationships with freed females, and vice versa, as in the cases of Urbano and Benta, Emereciana and Dandará, and the José-Lucinda-Felicidade triangle. African couples were mainly freed men and women. Of the nineteen unions in which the legal status of both people could be positively identified, only four had different statuses. There were obvious advantages for a slave to find a free person to live with. A Jeje freedman named José da Costa bought his wife's freedom.[12] Although there was not a single case of this in the 1835 trials, where, of course, there were so few women, this sort of assistance did not come only from men. Certainly many hard-working, compassionate women ransomed their men from slavery.

In spite of the lack of women in the African community, African men rarely took up with Brazilian women—or were refused by them. There is not a single case of a union between an African and a native-born black or mulatto in the 1835 records. Recent research points to the existence of powerful endogamy, which could have carried over to second-generation Afro-Brazilians. For instance, in the early nineteenth century, a crioulo wrote to the archbishop of Bahia complaining that after he had become engaged to a woman, her Nagô mother all of a sudden and in bad faith started to accuse him of being already married and an escaped slave to boot. In his missive the crioulo challenged his mother-in-law, and to strengthen his argument, he maintained that for all intents and purposes he was living at his fiancée's house. He ate there; they washed his clothes; and he and the young woman even slept together. According to him, the woman's mother became opposed to their marriage because of pressure from the Nagô community, who wanted to see the woman married to a Nagô man.[13]

This incident is corroborated by Oliveira's research on marriage among ex-slaves. Of the 167 marriages between ex-slaves that she considered, 150, or 90 percent, were marriages of Africans with Africans. Unfortunately, her documentation does not identify these people's ethnic origins. Were there marriages between Hausas and Nagôs, or between Jejes and Angolans? For the time being the answer can only be perhaps. While there is no record of marriages between West Africans and Southern Africans in the 1835 documents, there are records of marriages between West Africans of diverse origins. José, a Jeje freedman, expressed an attitude that must have been idiosyncratic: in his defense he swore that he had never slept with, nor would he ever sleep with, a Nagô woman. It is unlikely that the majority of Africans would have taken ethnic differences quite so seriously.[14]

The documents provide both partners' ethnic origins for sixteen couples; in thirteen of the couples, both partners were from the same ethnic background. Nine couples were Nagôs, which may only reflect their preponderance among the defendants rather their endogamous behavior. The other cases of intraethnic unions are one Hausa couple, one Bornu, and two Jeje couples. Two mixed marriages involved people from neighboring regions in Africa: a Bornu man with a Hausa woman, and a Bornu woman with a Hausa man. Another mixed union was that of Gaspar da Silva Cunha, a Nagô, with Teresa, who claimed to be from "the Tapa Nation next to the Nagôs," that is, from the border area between Yorubaland and Nupe country in Africa.

Aside from the nine Nagô couples, there were four intraethnic unions and three interethnic ones, which is too small a sample to allow one to draw any definitive conclusions about the role of ethnicity in the relationship between African men and women in Salvador. Bringing in the Nagô couples suggests a *tendency* toward ethnic endogamy. It is, however, safe to say that Africans rarely married native-born blacks or mulattos. On the other hand, there is no information on how ethnic origin influenced the choosing of same-sex partners. Homosexuality is an important factor in any analysis of the sexual behavior of Africans in Bahia at that time, precisely because one sex, the male sex, was numerically predominant.[15]

Tensions between Africans and Afro-Brazilians could perhaps diminish when African couples had Brazilian offspring. But as in the case of the unfortunate crioulo whose marriage was being checkmated by ethnic prejudice, being born in Brazil did not necessarily solve the problem. At any rate, children were not a major presence in the nineteenth-century African community in Salvador. They are rarely mentioned in the police reports, which carefully listed all residents in every house the police searched after the uprising.

There were, however, three children belonging to a Nagô couple, Ajadi Luís Doplê and Felicidade Maria da Paixão, who lived in the house at 8 Ladeira da Palma. A young girl known as Maria also lived there. She was the daughter of Efigênia, a Nagô ex-slave who sold rice cakes and rice pudding. A black woman named Edum, who lived in a focal area of the conspiracy, between Ladeira da Praça and Guadalupe Square, had an infant child. And Joaquim, a slave, was involved with a woman he called "the mother of his children." In addition, an old Nagô freedman, Ignácio de Santana, and his wife (whose name was never mentioned in the proceedings) had three children. These most likely were the only children having anything to do with the defendants. Very few indeed—only ten children for more than three hundred people questioned or mentioned in the investigation.[16]

Evidence from other sources does not reveal a situation so bereft of offspring, so direly adult, but it still points to a very small number of children within the African community. In her study of 259 freedmen, Oliveira found that 70 percent had no children. Of those having children few had more than two, and the great majority had only one. Very small families by African standards, especially by Muslim African standards. While Muslims in Africa were prolific, few could compete with their famous role model, Muslim leader Usuman Dan Fodio, who had thirty-seven children. One of his sons, Bello, had no fewer than seventy-three, doubtlessly by several different wives. It may be that when a slave woman in Salvador attained her manumission, she was too old to have or want children. In 1835 Agostinha and Teresa had been living with Belchior and Gaspar for three years and one and a half years, respectively, yet had no children. It may also be that African slave women and ex-slaves in the city had some understanding of birth control. The fact is that beyond their being few in number, African women had few children.[17]

In some cases African families extended beyond the nuclear husband, wife, and occasional children. Belchior da Silva Cunha had a brother known as Manoel, who was safely off in Africa during the revolt, having gone on a business trip. And another Belchior, this one a slave, felt threatened with prison after the revolt, so he hid with a brother who lived in the slave quarters on a farm in Boa Viagem, on the outskirts of Salvador. Links deriving from ritual kinship were no less important. Beyond the affinity between Catholic godparents or among orisha worshipers, other bonds were deeply rooted in the shared experience of slavery. The documents reveal a deep friendship between a slave known as Mateus Dada and Belchior da Silva Cunha. This friendship grew from their having been *malungos,* that is, from their having made the fearful crossing of the Atlantic on the same ship. They were such close friends that Agostinha, Belchior's wife, thought they actually were brothers.[18]

Family and emotional ties were sources of solidarity and conflict, love and hate. Men cared for their children when the women worked. They took care of the women too, when they needed care. In Ajadi's testimony he claimed that he watched their three children when Felicidade was at work. Ignácio Santana, an aged Nagô, testified that he "was busy having one of his children learn carpentry; having another in school; and taking care of the third, who was very young and still at home." When Gaspar da Silva Cunha was arrested, the police found him "making cornmeal mush [*mingau*] for his comrade, who was sick." His "comrade" was Teresa. She and many other African women passionately defended their men and cared for them while they were in jail.[19]

But jealousy and conflicts between men and women were also part of African life in Bahia. Efigênia, a peddler, made life difficult for her ex-boyfriend Belchior when she claimed that the Muslim papers and rings found in her house belonged to him. She was getting back at him for having abandoned her for a certain Ana Rita. The story of Sabina da Cruz is even more tragic. Vitório Sule abused her. According to an African neighbor's testimony, "[He was] a hot-headed Nagô married man who was always fighting with his wife." On the morning of 24 January they had a quarrel that jeopardized the revolt set for that very night. The quarrel started again that night, when Sabina set out to find Sule and get an explanation for the mess he had made at home while she was out. When she found him in a nearby house, he flatly refused to leave and talk with her because he was discussing the impending revolt with the men. Her pride wounded, Sabina went and spoke to her comadre Guilhermina, who denounced the plot. Sule was killed that night.[20]

While revenge played its part in Sabina's actions, this was more than just a personal vendetta. She was worried about her man's safety and was trying to keep him off the streets and out of the fight. Guilhermina testified that her comadre had asked her specifically to "tell some white person in charge . . . so that she could have two soldiers and retrieve her children's father—Sule—who was off conspiring and had taken some of her clothes and personal effects with him."[21] Her motives were quite likely ambivalent, but they do not prove her loyalty to the system, nor are they merely a betrayal of her children's father's revolution. Her story must be told in its entirety because students of the rebellion have been silent about Sabina's personal conflict, her emotions, and finally the complex love-hate relationship that drove her to betray the movement. One cannot simply state in passing that Sabina betrayed the rebellion. Had the rebellion not appeared as a threat to her man's safety, she probably would have seen it with different eyes. Between her family and the revolt she chose her family, which almost anyone would do—especially when raising a family seemed even more difficult than trying to bring down a government. Sule, of course, had taken the opposite option.

Thus far I have examined the African family in Salvador as if it were the conventional Western, bloodline family. But the kinship systems coming from Africa at the time of the Malê rebellion entailed polygamy, patrilinearity, patrilocality, extended families—none of which could be rebuilt in Bahia. In Bahia African patriarchy suffered a tremendous blow, partly because of women's new economic independence and because of the slave trade's devastation of families and kinship networks. In Bahia Africans redefined and expanded their notion of family and kinship, adding an ethnic factor. The word *parente* ("relative") was the one Africans took from their masters' language to mean "countryman" *(patrício)*. The members of a specific ethnic group considered themselves each other's "relatives." It is also significant that even today candomblés are divided into "nations" and their members belong to "saints' families." In the absence of bloodlines, ethnic groups took on the features of family, and ethnic identity became perhaps the principal channel of solidarity and daily routine for the majority of Africans living in Bahia at the time of the rebellion.[22]

These observations on the living arrangements of the 1835 defendants shed some light on the rebellion. As urban dwellers the rebels were often neighbors. Their propinquity helped make community ties and aided communication and the conspiracy itself. In addition, rebels resided near the symbols of institutional power: the palace of government, Catholic churches, prisons, the city hall, and forts; they also rubbed shoulders with free inhabitants benefiting from that power. Such an urban cocktail was potentially explosive. Salvador was a typical rebellious city: "In the ideal insurrectionary city the authorities—the rich, the aristocracy, the government or local administration—will be as intermingled with the central concentration of the poor as possible."[23]

Inside their hovels, loges, and shabby, crowded rooms, slaves and freedmen sought to redefine their lives and live in a manner somewhat different from what masters and authorities wanted for them. Not all slaves had even this meager luxury, since not all masters allowed their captives very far outside their sphere of influence. Nonetheless, urban slaves in many ways had much more autonomy in their goings-on than did their plantation counterparts. This autonomy was liberal enough to allow them to long for a better life and to strive for one through peaceful means, through manumission and social mobility, as well as through violent means, in collective revolt.

Their opting for revolt was made easier by their difficulty in establishing families and progeny, both of which were very dear to them. Having their own families would have helped them accommodate, as it did in other slave societies. Families would have helped weaken more extensive networks of solidarity. Gutman argued that bloodlines and extended family networks inhibited the development of class consciousness and the prevalence of revolt among slaves in the United States.[24] In Salvador rebellion did not come exactly from a "development of class consciousness" among African slaves, but the absence of families and progeny among Africans helped foster stronger notions of ethnic identity and strengthened independent African institutions such as religious groups. Ethnic and religious ties were made even easier by work and living arrangements in an urban environment, and all these factors combined led Africans to choose a radical break with the white man's world.

PART IV

The Anti-African Backlash

· II ·

The Repression after the Uprising

None of them has the rights of a Citizen,
nor the privileges of Foreigners.
—Francisco Gonçalves Martins, chief of police,
on freed African slaves

With the defeat of the rebellion, Bahia was shrouded in an atmosphere of at times almost hysterical fear, with persecution of and violence toward Africans. In a letter to Wellington, after mentioning that plantation owners expected a massive slave revolt in the Recôncavo, John Parkinson, the British consul, added that "the white population narrowly escaped a great disaster." Throughout the Recôncavo and the islands in the bay, rumors of slave revolts ran rampant during the weeks following the Malê uprising. In early February people were sure that slaves from several different plantations on Itaparica Island, along with others coming from Cachoeira, would rise up in revolt on Carnival Sunday. These rumors were repeated in Salvador. On 31 January the president was told that blacks together with dissatisfied mulattos in the nearby suburb of Rio Vermelho would attack Salvador that evening. The French consul described the situation as a case of "each man for himself." The president called out the troops and armed civilians, both European and national; and a contingent of marines on an American gunboat (the *Erie*) came ashore to safeguard American lives. In Vitória Parish many families abandoned their dwellings and spent the night offshore in canoes. Salvador appeared to be in a state of siege. In Parkinson's words, "A sleepless night was passed under arms. Not the shadow of a rebel appeared, and at sun-rise one hundred and twenty-five thousand souls had the gratification to find that they had laboured under a panic fear." Notwithstanding Parkinson's exaggeration of the number of souls in "panic fear," his testimony is indicative of the general state of mind after the rebellion. A few days later, celebration of the fishermen's feast day in Rio Vermelho (2 February) was canceled to avoid any gathering of crowds. Whites went so far as to consider putting an end to the slave trade, which, in spite of being against the law, was operating at full tilt. Over three months later, in May, rumors still circulated concerning free men inciting slaves to rebel once more.[1]

This climate of fear egged the victors on in their campaign for vengeance, in which they beat and killed peaceful, innocent Africans. Even Gonçalves Martins, the chief of police, expressed his concern about the goings-on. He wrote to the president of the province:

> The strange conduct of some soldiers in the army and in the Municipal Guard who, in total scorn of discipline and orders, have been killing or wounding peaceful blacks obliges me to request energetic measures from Your Excellency on their [the blacks'] behalf, because certainly these murders of peaceful Africans lead me to believe that at a later date other types of people will become victims. This barbarity and lack of discipline will not be prejudicial just to blacks. It . . . is a most serious state of affairs. Murders without motive go on in public; just a short time ago there was one right on my street.[2]

Martins's reaction to anti-African violence came not solely from humanitarian motives. He knew those soldiers belonged to the poorest free sectors of Bahian society and had tradition of insubordination. To permit their arbitrary acts against Africans could lead to social chaos and to similar acts against privileged groups. The chief of police wanted the rebels to be handled by the local authorities and not by a group of undisciplined ruffians in uniform. These individuals, in venting their wrath on African slaves, were also jeopardizing seigniorial property. Martins was not speaking just as a provincial leader but as the slaveowner he also was.

The French consul reported that soldiers, besides arbitrarily arresting blacks and beating them, had begun to pick on whites who opposed their actions in any form. When masters showed up at garrisons to demand the return of their slaves, they were met with insults from the soldiers, who also talked back to officers "if they tried to attend to the [masters'] complaints."[3]

In addition to the soldiers' reactions, several incidents show that retaliatory sentiment, the product of fear more often than of real danger, had spread to a large portion of the free civilian populace. On the day after the rebellion, unfounded rumors of another uprising caused merchants in Conceição da Praia to close their doors at noon. Armed civilians occupied the streets and took potshots at blacks, killing at least two of them. H. S. Fox, the British representative in Rio de Janeiro, reported "the cruelty of the white inhabitants, and of the soldiery, towards the unoffending part of the blacks." No testimony was as damning, however, as the one registered twenty-five years later by Robert Ave-Lallemant, who claimed, "An eyewitness told me terrible things. Blacks were bludgeoned to death in broad daylight, like dogs." This witness went on to claim that mulattos were even more avid than whites in their violence against blacks, which, if true, may be explained by the fact that they formed the majority of the police forces.[4]

Even the lawyers defending the insurgents were inhibited in their work by the mob that surrounded them shouting insults, curses, and threats. One lawyer, fearing for his life during the frenzy accompanying the trials, filed a complaint with the city judge in charge of the courts. Some of the rebels were forced to defend themselves in writing because they could find no one willing to face the fury of the mob. José da Costa, a freedman, wrote: "Since I could find no lawyer whatsoever willing to be subjected to the riffraff's insults, to their wisecracks, I present to Your Grace . . . my response to the accusation with its final allegation . . . in writing." Some compared the persecution of Africans to that suffered by the Portuguese after independence; however, such a comparison is invalid, since slaves had neither the material resources nor the powerful allies the Portuguese did.[5]

The Assault on the African Community

The authorities did not let up. During the two days following the rebellion, 25 and 26 January, they arrested at least forty-five slaves and fifty freedmen, 51 percent of the people whose trials are used in this study. The president of the province and the chief of police worked together to control the repression. On the parish level, justices of the peace headed police operations. These justices, along with their subordinates, the block inspectors, took groups of National Guardsmen, Municipal Guardsmen, and army troops, as well as armed civilians, on their searches of Africans' houses.

The president of the province, Francisco de Souza Martins, was thirty years old at that time. He was a native of the province of Piauí, the son of a rural political boss *(coronel),* and a nephew of the powerful viscount of Parnaíba. His family had wanted him to be a priest, but Martins abandoned ecclesiastic life in Rio de Janeiro when he quit the São José Seminary and left for the University of Coimbra, in Portugal. He spent only one year there, since like most Brazilians, he was forced to leave when Dom Miguel, an enemy of Brazil's emperor, became king. Back in Brazil he obtained a law degree in 1832 and was immediately appointed district judge of Oeiras, in the province of Piauí. He was elected to the Brazilian legislature for the term 1834–37. In 1834 he was named president of Bahia. He took office on 10 December of that year and left in April 1835 to take his seat in Parliament. During his short administration the first session of the Provincial Legislative Assembly met, under the leadership of Archbishop Dom Romualdo Seixas. The first law promulgated by this assembly and sanctioned by the president on 28 March 1835 permitted police to search houses without warrants for thirty days in order to facilitate the repression of African rebels.[6]

On the day after the revolt, President Martins ordered the chief of police to "waste no time" in arraigning the insurgents, especially the leaders and those found "bearing arms." He advised the chief to be zealous in the collection of evidence and to subpoena witnesses who could help reconstruct the movement in its entirety and punish all conspirators.[7]

Francisco Gonçalves Martins (no relation to the president), the chief of police, was also young—twenty-eight years old. He was born on the Papagaio Plantation, the son of its owner. Martins began his career in law precociously, in 1823, at the University of Coimbra, where he remained until 1828, as did President Francisco Martins. Back in Brazil, after stopovers in France and England, he joined the liberal movement. In 1831, at the age of twenty-four, he incited a crowd in Santo Amaro to protest against the Portuguese. At the same time he was elected justice of the peace of Sé Parish. He would later repudiate his radical phase, attributing it to youth and inexperience. At any rate, power fell into Gonçalves Martins's hands early on: in 1833 he was named judge of law *(juiz de direito)* for Salvador's city council. Soon thereafter he would become chief of police and alternate deputy to the General Legislative Assembly in Rio de Janeiro. In addition to all these posts, he was also elected as a representative for the Bahian Assembly in 1835. His election was most certainly facilitated by his reputation as being the key man in the quelling of the 1835 rebellion.[8]

Gonçalves Martins instructed justices of the peace to have block inspectors "enter every house and loge belonging to black Africans and search them rigorously for men, arms, and 'written papers.'" He also insisted that all citizens be mobilized—by force in the event "their patriotism and self-interest have not already motivated them to join." Patrols must have been increased, since the chief demanded that "attempts such as that of the twenty-fifth should end rigorously and once and for all." The chief of police seemed upset by the police violence against Africans, but at the same time he created conditions that could justify violence. Concerning manumitted slaves he declared: "None of them has the rights of a Citizen, nor the privileges of Foreigners." He wrote this notwithstanding their letters of manumission, which stated that they were "free for ever and ever as if from a free womb they had been born." In fact freed Africans had no rights; they were no more than inhabitants.[9]

Justices of the peace followed their superiors' instructions to the letter. The office of justice of the peace had been created by liberals after a long

FIG. 15. Francisco Gonçalves Martins, viscount of São Lourenço. As a young man and chief of police, Gonçalves Martins led the fight against the Malê uprising and oversaw the anti-African backlash that followed. Portrait courtesy of Instituto Geográfico e Histórico da Bahia.

struggle in Parliament. It was part of their scheme to demolish the legal system Brazil had inherited from Portugal, as well as to weaken the emperor's centralized government. Justices of the peace usually had no background in law. They were "respectable" citizens, often merchants, petty landlords, or slaveholders elected to office by their peers. For example, Caetano Vicente de Almeida Galião, in 1835 justice of the peace of the Second District of Sé Parish, owned a small plantation and a little farm in Brotas, a suburb of Salvador.[10]

Justices of the peace played an important role in the repression. They were responsible for law and order in the ten parishes of Salvador—Sé, Conceição da Praia, Santana, Vitória (these first four, because they were heavily populated, were divided into two districts with separate justices of the peace), Pilar, Passo, São Pedro Velho, Santo Antônio, Brotas, and Penha, the last two being suburban parishes. Each parish was for police purposes divided into blocks, and each block had an inspector named by the justice of the peace.

Under order from the justices of the peace, patrols formed by inspectors, National Guardsmen, civilians, and soldiers occupied the streets and invaded Africans' residences. The most common modus operandi was to cordon off houses (or entire blocks) so that no one could escape. Then groups of five to seven men, which always included a justice of the peace and a scribe, would carefully inspect each house and question all residents. Any "suspicious" religious objects (an amulet, Arabic writing, Malê garments, etc.) meant the immediate arrest of their owner.

When they knocked and no one answered, the police broke down the doors of rooms, houses, and loges. On 27 January a block inspector in Conceição da Praia reported "having a barbershop door broken down [because] the barber was said to have died on the night of the twenty-fourth at the cavalry [fort]." Nothing suspicious was found, however, just the tools of his trade. Another barbershop in another parish (Passo) would be searched on the twenty-eighth, and there police found copious Muslim literature, Malê garments, and four knives. The barber, a slave, was arrested on the spot. On 29 January, this time in the loge of a two-story house at 2 Rua Direita de São Pedro, there was another forced search. More than six men, among them a justice of the peace, a scribe, a cavalry colonel, an officer of the law, and Municipal Guardsmen, "did the necessary cordoning . . . around the door of the house, then invaded the garden in back, where they found two hiding places that appeared to be likely places for African blacks to hide out. The justice had two doors knocked down, and they found two small hovels, but no blacks inside either of them." They did find 88,640 réis, one spoon, a frock, three Muslim skullcaps, and three empty burlap bags. The owners of this material, freedmen named Luís Vieira and Jacinto, were arrested later and ended up with sentences of eight years in prison.[11]

The authorities arrested any black who when questioned point-blank failed to answer to their satisfaction. They did not even consider that Africans might be intimidated given the situation and their individual difficulties with the master's language. Only later on, during their trials, were some able to say, as Pompeu did, that "his master is the one to defend him because he [Pompeu] does not know the white man's language."[12] Of course, many pretended not to know Portuguese. Some masters instructed their slaves to feign ignorance.

In some cases everybody in certain households landed in prison. At the house of Belchior and Gaspar da Silva Cunha, the owners, their female companions (Agostinha and Teresa), José (Gaspar's slave), and Marcelina (a slave woman renting a room from Belchior) all went to jail. At the two-story house at 9 Ladeira da Palma, fourteen people were arrested, including three children and their mother, Felicidade, who was several months pregnant at the time.

The police only respected houses belonging to masters, who as a rule cooperated with the operation, even though they were to defend their slaves in court later on. In spite of a protest from the French consul, the search of one of his countrymen's houses during the owner's absence was carried out properly, in the presence of two French nationals who were neighbors. Most foreigners cooperated with the police, even those who later on defended their slaves in court. Few masters were as helpful to their slaves as João Baptista Fetal. He let Conrado escape, believing him to be innocent. Some English residents felt the searches violated their rights as foreigners, but these few were rebuked by the Foreign Office, and the majority cooperated. Frederick Robelliard, the son-in-law of Consul Parkinson, handed over two of his slaves without complaint. On 26 January an English merchant named Joseph Mellors Russell personally handed over to Inspector Antônio Marques a crate containing Arabic texts, books, writing tablets, rosaries, and silverware found in his slaves' rooms.[13]

Generally, however, the confiscation of "subversive" material was carried out by justices of the peace, who had their scribes make note of everything. The following account of a search at the house of José Pinto Novais is typical:

> The Justice had Novais take us to where his slaves slept, which was where they kept their boxes and baskets or whatever they used to store their belongings. Religiously obeying, Novais handed over a box and claimed it belonged to Torquato, a Nagô slave of his. In this box the necessary search turned up the following: a string of glass beads of different colors, some small scapularies in leather covers, some of which contained cotton soaked with unknown potions and others containing the following five pieces of paper.

This document, which was a term of search and confiscation *(termo de busca e apreensão)*, contained signatures of the justice of the peace, a nineteen-year-old soldier, a tailor from Sergipe, who accompanied the patrol, and the scribe himself. For his possession of these objects Torquato was sentenced to 250 lashes.[14]

Local residents generally went along with the campaign. They not only joined search parties but also denounced Africans they knew personally, including slaves whose owners may have tried to cover up their participation in the rebellion. The same thing happened to manumitted Africans living among white, mulatto, and black Bahians. Africans who taught Arabic and distributed Islamic literature were turned in, as were people who did nothing more than have visitors in their dwellings. Some accusers made great efforts to put suspects behind bars. Leonardo de Freitas accused two freedwomen, Maria das Chagas and Maria da Conceição, of supplying food to alleged insurgents living in a house on Ladeira da Praça. The justice of the peace, however, saw no proof for Freitas's accusation and did not arrest them. Freitas was furious. He requested intervention from the chief of police and accused the justice of the peace of protecting these women. But the chief of police also thought Freitas was overzealous. The episode seems to have been either a personal vendetta or one more case of the paranoia running rampant at the time. On the other hand, the fact that more than two hundred people testified against the African rebels shows to what extent the authorities gladly received the cooperation of informants. The testimonies of two eyewitnesses were needed to prove a person guilty.[15]

There were, nonetheless, a few witnesses who, although they had not been summoned by the defense, appeared and gave favorable declarations concerning their African neighbors. One such witness was the sexagenarian widow Jacinta Rosa de Mello. She was white and lived upstairs in the house in whose loge Luís Vieira and Jacinto lived. On 11 February, during a hearing against the two freedmen, Dona Jacinta declared that "during . . . the time that she lived there, for the last two years, she had always noticed that the black man known as Luís and his companion lived there quietly. They left every morning to work." She went on to say that on the night of the rebellion "Luís had retired peacefully to his room." On the other hand, she let it slip out that she saw him wearing the white Muslim gown (abadá) and "cutting and sewing those frocks that they ordered and paid him for." Even a sympathetic witness such as this one could destroy a defense when he or she innocently passed on information such as this about Africans with whom she rubbed shoulders on a daily basis.[16]

Police raids during the first half of 1835 brought in hundreds of Africans, both slave and freed. Prisoners were distributed among five prisons: the city jail; the Sea Fortress, where the majority were put so as to be safely surrounded by water; the cavalry garrison in Água de Meninos; Fort São Pedro; and in the Presiganga, an extremely unhealthy prison located in the hold of a ship. Prisons were so full that their administrators claimed it was impossible to feed all the inmates with the meager resources at their disposal. In response the authorities determined that all freedmen should furnish their own food. Those who were so poor they could not feed themselves would be fed by the hospital of the Santa Casa. Slaves were to be sustained by their masters.[17]

Interrogations and Trials

In mid-February, newspapers announced the formation of a tribunal that would judge the rebels. Rebels would face a newly created jury system—one more innovation of the empire's liberals. In this new system, trials were divided into two main parts: First, prisoners faced the Júri de Acusação ("accusation jury"), also known as the Primeiro Conselho de Jurados (First Council of Jurors). If the jury delivered a verdict of guilty, prisoners' names were added to the Roll of the Guilty, and they were then transferred to the tribunal where they faced the Júri de Sentença (Sentencing Jury). The First Council of Jurors consisted of twenty-three jurors selected from a pool of "citizens in good standing" *(cidadãos ativos)*. A citizen in good standing was a voter—a man twenty-five years of age or older with a modest yearly income (at least 200 milréis or 150 alqueires [1 alqueire = 18.135 liters] of manioc flour). The jurors' role was to examine the dossiers *(autos)* on the prisoners prepared by the justices of the peace. These autos contained the terms of search and confiscation and transcripts of interrogations of prisoners and testimonies of witnesses. They also contained the concluding remarks of the police concerning the guilt or innocence of the accused.[18]

The Sentencing Jury was made up of only twelve jurors, who also fulfilled the requirements for being citizens in good standing. On the day of a trial, a child (always a boy) drew their names by lot. This jury was headed by a judge of law, this time a professional magistrate. Sessions proceeded in the following manner: the judge questioned the prisoner in a cursory fashion; the court scribe read the proceedings; the district attorney *(promotor)* read the accusation; the defense responded; the jury offered its verdict; and the judge declared the sentence.

After being arrested, the accused individual was questioned either in jail or, more often, at the residence of the local justice of the peace. There were always at least two witnesses facing the "respondent" during these sessions besides the justice of the peace and the scribe. The justice of the peace asked the questions and always began by asking for the prisoner's name, "nationality," legal status, and, in the case of a slave, the names of his or her master. A few interrogators also requested the names of ex-slaves' ex-masters, their length of residence in Bahia, and/or their current address. They then tried to learn prisoners' "professions or means of support." Matters such as these opened the interrogation ritual and were followed by questions more directly related to the insurrection: questions on participation, names and addresses of suspects, Malê paraphernalia found at their residence, and so on. This was the basic model for interrogations.

Perhaps because of their haste in punishing the rebels, as a rule both justices and judges were incredibly superficial and pragmatic in their questioning. Few of them asked questions of substance, even about the rebellion. One exception may have been the justice of the peace of São Pedro Parish. During some of his sessions, he asked prisoners when and by whom they were first purchased, how many masters they had had, and what work they had done since arriving in Bahia. If sessions with this sort of questioning had occurred more regularly, historians today would have complete life histories; unfortunately the authorities evinced a surprising lack of interest in these matters. Even the police reconstruction of the entire movement was more a product of deduction than one of direct information collected in interrogations. Many aspects of the rebellion remained obscure in large part because the right questions were not asked. And even when they were, the occasion and the specific person questioned did not seem to be the right ones. On 25 January the justice of the peace in Vitória asked a slave named Lino some interesting questions: How long had they been preparing for such an attack? And how many took part in the attack? And who were the leaders? And what was their objective? Where did they meet? And what sort of arms did they possess? Lino, however, caught red-handed at Água de Meninos along with thirteen other rebels, only answered the standard questions: name, nationality, and so on. He had nothing more to say, the scribe lamented, "no matter how much said justice was to insist before the undersigned witnesses."[19]

The police never learned the whole story of the movement, thanks to attitudes such as Lino's. Arrested Africans cannot be described as having cooperated with their interrogators. Specific circumstances in the interrogations, as well as personal determination, made police work difficult. Some interrogation sessions were directed at several suspects at the same time. This was the case with Lino and the thirteen others caught at Água de Meninos. These men were tense, worn out, and wounded. They were lined up and called one by one to be questioned in each other's presence. Being questioned in that manner helped bolster their morale and helped them to avoid giving information to the police. Beyond this, no one wanted to lose face in front of the others. They all gave no more than their name and ethnic origin.

Collective interrogations kept potential turncoats in line. While any sign of weakness or cooperation with the authorities might save a person some punishment from the whites, it would indict them with the rebels. Under the menacing eyes of other Africans, the slave Francisco supplied his interrogators with alufá Pacífico Licutan's address as well as information on his religious activities. The scribe noted that the man seemed "afraid and frightened." Later on Francisco reported that he had received death threats from an African waiting alongside him in a line. There is no proof, however, that rebel justice sentenced Francisco or anybody else in 1835. If it did, it did not sentence many, because few confessed to having participated in the movement, and those who did rarely gave anyone else's name. A few merely gave the names of Africans known to have been killed during the struggle.[20]

There were, of course, some cases of African collaboration in the repression. These rebels—indeed, rebels in general—were not always the men of steel they are made out to be in fiction. Pressure under questioning frightened and upset many. Some justices probably resorted to violence and threats in their interrogations—without, however, registering this in their dossiers. There is, in fact, only one concrete accusation of torture. The lawyer of a slave known as Manoel accused the justice of the peace in Vitória of having tortured his client, "since he applied force when he questioned the prisoner." Violence, fear of imprisonment, or the simple desire to save one's skin made a few prisoners submissive and cooperative. But in general, on an individual basis, rebels gave out very little information. Given the size of the conspiracy, this represents quite an achievement in rebel loyalty.[21]

Prisoners had the right to court-appointed legal counsel *(curadores)* during the investigation. Poor freedmen and slaves abandoned by their masters had this privilege. However, such legal aid scarcely went beyond mere formality and sometimes not even that far. Innumerable, perhaps even most, interrogations were carried out illegally, without the presence of any counsel, and this often occasioned protest from masters. On the other hand, privately contracted lawyers did in fact help change the fate of some prisoners.

Once the Sentencing Jury was constituted, the dossiers read, and the prisoner cursorily questioned, the district attorney took the floor. District attorney Angelo Muniz da Silva Ferraz's charges clearly show how Bahian society, especially its rulers, apprehended and understood the rebellion and the rebels:

> The prosecution will prove that a considerable number of Slaves over a long period of time met in different parts of this City and settled on a plan to take their freedom by force.
>
> The prosecution will prove that so as to achieve their goal the Authors of this Insurrection diligently plotted in absolute and unprecedented secrecy. They imbued their followers with the Religion of their Country and taught them to read and write the Arabic language. They also circulated papers written with Arabic characters, special rings, garb, and skullcaps in their style. This was not just so that conspirators could recognize one another; it was also a sort of shield whose impenetrability had been prepared by their God to help them over obstacles in their way as well as shield them from danger.
>
> The prosecution will prove that with this in mind and with the help and guidance of freed Africans, they designed in their hideaways the most horrible of plans, which, had they succeeded, would bring about the extinction of whites or mulattos, the destruction of the National Constitution, the loss of our property, the burning of public Edifices, the profaning of our altars, the burning of our Temples, and of all monuments of our splendor and glory. . . .
>
> The prosecution will prove that after having concerted with other

Africans residing in some of the towns of this Province, where they used to send their emissaries, they set up meeting places determined by their leaders, who had already obtained weapons and ammunition, which they had distributed competently. They were to meet at 2:00 A.M. on the day of January 25th to carry out their plans. . . .

The prosecution will prove that thanks to Police vigilance, or rather thanks to Divine Mercy, such horrifying plans were discovered before their execution, which hindered the massive gathering of insurgents and thwarted the attempts of those who burst onto the field [of battle] on the night between January 24th and 25th and which kept most of the conspirators indoors on that occasion.[22]

In addition to providing the official version of the events of 1835, this text presents Bahian leaders' political definition of the conflict.

The revolt and the trials, it should be remembered, took place during an early period in the formation of the Brazilian nation state. It was a time when the privileged sectors of society struggled to determine the political, cultural, and racial content of the new nation. Who constituted the nation under attack? In Ferraz's opening statement he claimed that Africans sought to obliterate only whites and mulattos. Of course, from the rebel perspective, the main enemy was the whites, but secondary adversaries were not only mulattos but also native-born blacks. Ferraz, however, excluded crioulos from among the Africans' enemies, which was tantamount to excluding them from the Brazilian community. The "our" in Ferraz's speech—"*our* property . . . *our* altars . . . *our* Temples . . . *our* splendor and glory"—was exclusive. It left blacks born in Brazil without a country. This exclusion is, however, understandable. For the Bahian ruling class it would have been outlandish to name as co-citizens a part of the population that was still largely enslaved and so similar in color and custom to the African enemy. As far as the rulers were concerned, governments, constitutions, and property were beyond the comprehension of blacks, even those born in Brazil.

The theme of a struggle between civilization and barbarism comes out in various parts of Ferraz's speech. The Brazilian nation was vouchsafed politically by a "government" and a "constitution." It was legitimated historically by its "monuments of our splendor and glory." All this would go up in smoke thanks to some treacherous African rebels whose political sophistication was limited to conspiracy and violent, armed struggle. They had a different set of ethics—as well as a different set of esthetics.

The rebels brought a remarkable ensemble of anti-Brazilian colors, sounds, and shapes from their hideouts. They wore amulets around their necks, rings on their fingers, "strange" garb that covered bodies decorated with tribal markings. They beat on drums and spoke strange languages. During the execution of those "horrifying plans" Bahians saw revolutionary esthetics in action. But Ferraz the ideologue also saw the spiritual significance behind that exotic and hostile political esthetic.

Malê amulets, papers, rings, and garb were material signs the rebels carried in the name of the "their God." They were all part of a code. They represented uncivilized analogues of Catholic images about to be profaned and of the temples about to be burned down. Through these tokens their God guaranteed that such deeds could be safely done. Luckily, the prosecutor goes on to affirm, the Brazilian forces were also backed by a powerful celestial ally. In their victory against the Malê rebels, Bahians did their part by putting an efficient police force into action, but Divine Christian Providence was the deciding factor. Only it could have determined the outcome. Brazil's God had beaten Africa's, and this allowed the new nation to maintain its spiritual bases.

Ferraz's opening argument set the tone for all the rebel trials that year. It was a patriotic, Christian campaign of Brazilian citizens against a foreign and barbaric enemy—"dangerous guests," in the words of President Martins. In such a context any Africans seeking acquittal would have to convince the jury that they conformed to the seigniorial ideal reserved for them. They would have to prove their loyalty to the country's whites, to white man's culture, religion, and way of life. Africans should be Brazilianized, acculturated in their inferior and submissive position, and always deferential to the white man and his civilization. Obviously, good behavior and obedience to masters were expected from slaves. But slaves' reverence for their masters should be extended to all white people. And Africans, even those who were freed and prosperous, could not even think of being equal to a Brazilian who was free and white. Bahian rulers made sure the proceedings of 1835 would be a ritual reaffirmation of their social, national, and ethnic superiority over Africans.

The prisoners' masters understood the purpose of the trials, and whenever they could, they defended their rebels with the rhetoric of African submissiveness. Former slaves (or their lawyers) used the same tactic in their petitions. João Crisóstomo Pinto da Silva, the master of Manoel, argued that his slave "has always been submissive and extremely obedient, both to the petitioner [Pinto da Silva] and to all whites and other people of the same status he meets." This would be supported by an important member of the white community, Antônio José do Amaral, a priest, appellate judge, and a knight in the Imperial Order of the Southern Cross. Amaral declared that the prisoner was "very submissive to Pinto da Silva and in general to all whites, for which everyone prized him." (Even so, Manoel was condemned to seven hundred whiplashes.) Another slave, Sabino, maintained under interrogation that "because of the love he had for his master, he had no reason to rebel against him." A witness for the defense of Belchior testified that "he always acted so humble, so much so that it seems impossible that he could have joined the insurrection." Another witness declared: "Said slave was always very obedient, careful in his work, and very close not only to his master but also to all White people." On top of this, both witnesses claimed that Belchior, a sedan chair porter, was a "baptized Roman Catholic."[23]

These declarations were long on rhetoric and short on information concerning real relationships. Many masters undoubtedly had financial reasons for making their slaves out to be docile. Still, this does not mean that there were not some who defended their slaves because they sincerely believed in their innocence and were grateful for the loyalty, obedience, and good service their slaves had given in the past. These masters seemed not to understand how a habitually submissive slave might suddenly rebel. As Eugene Genovese wrote concerning law-abiding slaves in the New World, "Dangerous and strong currents run beneath that docility and adjustment."[24]

For many masters, economic interests really were secondary. This seems to have been the case with Pedro Ricardo da Silva, who for over two years spent time and money trying to free his old slave Luís Sanim. He even took this slave's case to the Appeals Court in Rio de Janeiro, where in addition to pointing out several irregularities in his trial, he defended his slave's right to freedom of worship. On the other hand, there were masters who cut their slaves adrift, often in punishment for their former unruliness. When Antônio de Araújo was summoned to appear before the judge and defend his slave Joaquim, a Nagô barber, he answered that "he did not care [about Joaquim], nor would he act on his behalf given his crime and his having tried to kill him [Araújo] . . . with poison." It turns out that Araújo was himself an African freedman.[25]

If defense arguments such as the one on behalf of Sanim or responses such as Araújo's did not exactly typify the courtroom spirit in the 1835 trials, other texts mirrored it beautifully. It is not by chance that one of the best examples comes from the efforts of one freedman to acquit himself in the eyes of his jurors. As a freedman speaking on his own behalf, without the advantageous intervention of a master, he had to make an especially good impression on the jurors and convince them that he was worthy of living among free Brazilians. More than any slave had to, he needed to show that he had not only repudiated his African background but accepted his (inferior) place in Brazilian society.

A Jeje freedman, José da Costa, thirty-eight years old, presented himself to the jury claiming to be a "scrupulous" individual who belonged to "a nation that was entirely inimical to the blacks who upset the city." To prove his rivalry with Nagôs, he went so far as to declare that he was friends with none of them and that "not even out of human frailty [sexual desire] would he have relations with black women of that nation." His innocence could be proven by the fact that he was not wearing the feared white frock (abadá) or any other African garb when he was arrested. Quite to the contrary, he was arrested "wearing a calico frock coat and other Brazilian attire." As an artisan at the Naval Arsenal, he portrayed himself as a good and faithful worker ("steady in his work as a caulker"), as "a well-known friend of the land that had graced him, as obedient to his superiors in color and to the Authorities, and as an abider of the laws." On top of this, he was "observant in matters of the Roman Catholic Church . . . and zealously inclined toward the customs and the citizens of the Empire, with whom he always got along." The only thing "against him [was] his misfortune in being born in the Country of Africa." His true affection, he maintained, was for Brazil, the "Country in which he was raised" and on whose side he would have fought had he been called to do so. José da Costa was sentenced to fifteen years in prison. He appealed and was acquitted but was obliged to leave the country in July 1835.[26]

After the uprising Bahian authorities spent many weeks turning the African community inside out. It is impressive how the presence of Africans and their cultures challenged the world-view, the daily habits, and even the psychological stability of many Bahians. The so-called African customs, which before had seemed so typically Bahian, suddenly emerge in the documents as alien and subversive and in need of prohibition and, if possible, extinction. Down with African Bahia! There is no other way to interpret labeling as illegal any African object the police found in their searches. Indeed, in the heat of the anti-African backlash, not just the abadás, the Malê rosaries, and the Arabic writing constituted proof of rebelliousness. Musical instruments, necklaces, and African cloth were also considered harmful to law and order. The old current of anti-African sentiment, dubbed in this book the "count of Ponte line," seems to have prevailed in the court proceedings of 1835. But in post-independence Brazil this attitude had a new meaning. Having expelled European colonizers, Bahian rulers joined forces with national elites in building a nation that they hoped would be closer to the European model.

This should explain why the reforms of the Brazilian judicial system inaugurated in the early 1830s were methodically tested during the repression and in the definition or reiteration of norms of thought and behavior expected from Africans living in Bahia. French consul Marcescheau, himself a European, was amazed that Bahians went to so much trouble in trying blacks who had no constitutional rights.[27] Carried out in grand style, the trials exceeded the mere punishment of rebel slaves; they aimed at exorcizing anything African. Any Africans wanting to stay should leave their roots behind. As far as the Bahian ruling elite was concerned, this was not just the only road to peace for their slave society, it was also the road toward a more "civilized" future. Whoever disagreed with such an aim, even if they were considered barbarians, needed to be made an example of—under laws established in a civilized manner.

· 12 ·

The Punishment

Article 113 of Chapter 4 of the 1830 Criminal Code defined the gathering of "twenty or more slaves aiming to take their freedom by force" as a crime of insurrection. The harshest penalty for leaders of such a gathering was death; the mildest was fifteen years' forced labor. Midway between these extremes were sentences to forced labor for life. (Forced labor [*galés*] was performed in chain gangs, where men worked on governmental projects.) Slaves following such leaders would be punished by flogging, the exact amount to be determined by the judge. Article 114 extended these sentences to free individuals leading rebellious slaves, and Article 115 sentenced free people to twenty, twelve, or eight years of prison at hard labor when they were guilty of "helping, inciting, or advising slaves to rebel and furnishing arms, ammunition, or other means to that end [rebellion]." This was the legal text used to punish slaves and freedmen accused of participating in the 1835 rebellion.[1]

Unlike other slave societies, where the state punished rebel slaves more severely and paid reparations to their masters, Brazilians chose a different strategy. Proprietors still preserved their interests, but in a different way. Slaves were flogged and then immediately put back to work. Only leaders were sentenced to death or prison. In these cases, which were seen as matters of security and maintenance of the slave society itself, the law made no concessions to masters' well-being. Rebel leaders, be they slaves, ex-slaves, or free, received equal treatment before the law. In the case of ordinary rebels, however, the law distinguished between slaves and non-slaves. Article 115's only objective was to attach a special dangerousness to free men, especially to freedmen, in order to justify harsher sentences for them. The principal target of this section of the law was African freedmen, since they and their slave countrymen were the ones who most often rebelled throughout Brazil, as well as in Bahia.

Sentences

The range of sentences is shown in table 13. Most of these sentences are the final ones laid down after standard appeals were made. Only for cases in which such sentences were not available are those given during the first trial included, and some of these may have been changed by courts of appeal. In many cases it has not been possible to identify any sentence whatsoever, since many trial records are incomplete. Included in the table are individual trials as well as the names of people in the Roll of the Guilty, which lists 289 prisoners, their names, ethnicities, legal statuses, masters' names in cases of slaves, the parishes where trials were held, and, less often, prisoners' sentences. I have omitted defendants tried *in absentia*.

If we take the Criminal Code as a guide (and exclude deportations), freedmen appear either as heads (Article 114) or as instigators (Article 115) of slave revolt. All sentences leading to imprisonment fell on freedmen. On the other hand, except for nine slaves sentenced as leaders, slaves were overwhelmingly deemed ordinary participants in the rebellion. The judges and other Bahian authorities did not, however, follow the code down to the letter. Deviations from strict observance benefited prisoners in some cases, but in general they made matters worse for them, especially for freedmen.

Sentences to prison, forced labor, and floggings varied. The most common prison terms were five and eight years (for 5 and 4 prisoners, respectively). Less common were sentences of fifteen years (2 prisoners), ten years (1 prisoner), and twelve years not at hard labor (2 prisoners). Alexandre, a freedman who lived on Ladeira da Palma, was sentenced to a term of twenty years. Of the eight Africans sentenced to lifelong forced

Table 13

THE RANGE OF SENTENCES IN 1835

Sentence	Slaves		Freed		Total	
	No.	%	No.	%	No.	%
Acquitted	28	15.0	0	0	28	9.3
Death	3	1.6	1	0.9	4	1.3
Prison	0	0	16	13.9	16	5.3
Forced labor	6	3.2	2	1.7	8	2.7
Flogging	43	23.1	2	1.7	45	15.0
Deportation	0	0	34	29.5	34	11.3
Unknown	106	57.0	60	52.2	166	55.1
Total	186	100	102	100	301	100

Source: AEBa, *Insurreições*, maços 2845–50.

labor, six were slaves, but as often happened, their masters probably appealed their sentences. Floggings ranged from fifty to twelve hundred lashes. Pacífico Licutan was sentenced to one thousand lashes, since his being in jail during the uprising meant he could not be sentenced as a leader. Floggings commonly consisted of five hundred lashes (9 slaves), six hundred lashes (5 slaves, 2 freedmen), eight hundred (7 slaves), and two hundred (6 slaves). Other Africans received two hundred fifty (2 slaves), three hundred (5 slaves), four hundred (4 slaves), and seven hundred (2 slaves). Emereciana, a female slave and the companion of Dandará, received four hundred lashes. The only two freedmen to receive floggings were Gaspar and Belchior da Silva Cunha. In their initial trial they were sentenced to death, but on appeal this sentence was reduced to six hundred lashes. In this as in other cases, such as the five-year prison sentences, the Criminal Code was not respected, since it did not prescribe this type of punishment for freedmen. Indeed, five-year prison sentences were not ordered for any crime of this sort.

The greatest deviation from the code was beyond doubt deportation, which was the most common punishment for African freedmen. In fact, the numbers in table 13 reveal very little of what really happened: hundreds of freedmen brought in as suspects were arbitrarily expelled from the country even though the authorities could muster no incriminating evidence against them. More than three hundred Bahians of various social classes signed a petition arguing that the expulsion was justified because of the support and guidance freedmen provided for rebellious slaves. They neglected the fact that most alufás were slaves. The petitioners called all Africans barbarians who "have no place [*não representam*] in the Political, civilized World."[2]

Deportations were sustained by a hastily contrived casuistry Bahian authorities used to flaunt the law of the land. In his communiqué of 15 February to the minister of justice, ex-judge Martins, now president of the province, requested permission to "have those black African freedmen in custody and under suspicion of being accomplices in the rebellion deported outside the Empire [even though] they might not be sentenced by the Jury. The same fate [should befall] all those who in the future might be considered dangerous."[3] Quickly, in a decree on 4 March, Minister of Justice Manuel Alves Branco approved President Souza Martins's request. On the local level this measure was reinforced by Law 9, of 13 May 1835.[4]

The press also argued in favor of deportation. On 11 June 1836 the *Diário da Bahia,* a daily founded by Police Chief Martins, published a piece on the trial of the Hausa Malê freedman Silvestre José Antônio. The initial tone of the text seems almost sympathetic: "All they had against the detainee were some papers written in Arabic, some rings, and other things

similar to those found on the insurgents. They also found a pointed knife."
As far as the *Diário* was concerned, the three lawyers who defended Silvestre José were trying to prove him innocent of two different crimes—
participating in the insurrection and owning a pointed knife, a forbidden
weapon. The trial of this Muslim, held on the premises of Salvador's cathedral, lasted all afternoon, and only at nightfall did the jury find "the
detainee not guilty of both crimes." The *Diário* made the following comment: "We consider the verdict just, as far as his participating in the insurrection is concerned; however, this prisoner should be deported because
he is entirely suspect." That is, his being suspected of participating in the
rebellion was not the reason for deportation; he was suspect because he
was a Hausa freedman who owned a knife! The *Diário* did not bother to
quote the answer Silvestre José gave when he was asked about the knife:
"He replied that the knife was absolutely necessary for everyone who travels and he . . . makes his living traveling through the Recôncavo." The
prisoner sold cloth on these travels. His answer convinced the jury but not
the *Diário da Bahia,* which appeared to adopt the slogan of the moment,
namely, that all Africans were suspect and there was no proof to the
contrary.[5]

Commutations

Of the 34 freedmen listed in table 13 as subject to deportation, 31 had
originally been acquitted by the first council of jurors or by the Second
Council. Around the end of March, even before the promulgation of Law
9, prison administrators had made a list of 154 freedmen who should be
immediately deported. On this list were 67 Nagôs, 21 Hausas, 21 Jejes,
16 Bornus, 7 Tapas, and 22 other Africans of diverse origins, some of
whom were members of ethnic groups having nothing at all to do with
the rebellion—Angolans, Congos, Mundubis, and so on. During the years
that followed, ships leaving Salvador for Africa carried off many more
Africans.[6]

Initially at least seventeen of the accused, twelve of them slaves, were
sentenced to death. This may appear to contradict what was said earlier,
that the law sought to exempt slaves from sentences that would entail
definitive financial losses for their masters. Nonetheless an example-setting
elimination of rebels was more important than the preservation of the
immediate interests of a few masters. The eleven slaves sentenced to death
were deeply involved in the uprising—or their masters had failed to defend them. These slaves included Carlos and Tomás, two Nagôs who had
been left to fend for themselves by their English owner, Vice-Consul Frederick Robelliard. Another, by the name of Gonçalo, belonged to someone
registered on the Roll of the Guilty merely as Lourenço so-and-so, which

suggests that he never came forth to defend his slave. The other eight, even though not all of them were leaders, were notoriously guilty and thus strong candidates for suffering the maximum exemplary penalty eagerly sought by provincial leaders and slaveowners. They were the Malê preacher Luís Sanim and Pedro, the latter belonging to Mellors Russell; Lino and Belchior, who were caught red-handed; and Cornélio and Ignácio. All these men confessed or were mentioned in others' testimony as zealous agitators. There were three more: Pedro, a slave of English physician Robert Dundas; Joaquim, a slave of Luís Mefre; and Germano, a slave of João Lourenço. Germano was from Cameroon and had been denounced in what appears to be a vendetta by his master's wife, a seventeen-year-old mulatto woman who gave the police a pointed knife supposedly belonging to this slave.[7]

Concerning the freedmen sentenced to death, they included the by now well-known pair Belchior and Gaspar da Silva Cunha, who opened their house for Malê meetings; Aprígio, a housemate and assistant to Preacher Manoel Calafate; Ajadi Luís Doplê, accused on very shaky bases by the police; and Jorge da Cruz Barbosa, who had the bad luck of being wounded and then arrested the day after the revolt. They were all Nagôs.

The choice of victims for the death penalty may be the best example of the courts' erratic behavior in 1835. According to the Criminal Code, only leaders would be subject to such punishment, but the notion of leadership was "redefined" by the judges to suit their objectives. From the records one can conclude that of the sixteen Africans sentenced to death, only Luís Sanim can really be considered a Malê leader. The others, although they were implicated in the uprising, were only ordinary rebels; at most they were agitators dedicated to the cause. The legal travesty was so obvious that most of these sentences were commuted.

There were several avenues of appeal for the modification of a sentence. In successive order they were: (1) a jury in the most populous jurisdiction of the province after Salvador, either Santo Amaro or Cachoeira; (2) the Appellate Court (Tribunal da Relação) in Salvador; (3) the Supreme Court of Appeals in Rio de Janeiro; (4) imperial pardon—by the monarch or, in his stead, by the regents, since Dom Pedro II was still a minor. Prisoners accused of rebelling in 1835 appealed to all these channels.

A sample of twenty-three prisoners (ten slaves, thirteen freedmen) who appealed their sentences is given in table 14. Ten had been sentenced to death, thirteen to prison terms and forced labor. In none of the cases was the original sentence changed to absolution. Ex-slaves received deportation, and slaves received floggings, continuing the pattern set in 1835.

As a rule, neither the courts nor the majority of masters appealed floggings. There is no record of a sentence of this type being commuted

Table 14
COMMUTED SENTENCES
(SAMPLE)

Name	Origin	Status	Original Sentence	Parish	New Sentence	Legal Recourse
Ajadi Luís Doplê	Nagô	Freed	Death 10 Mar. 35	Santana	8 yrs. prison 26 July 35	Cachoeira
Felicidade M. da Paixão	Nagô	Freed	5 yrs. prison 10 Mar. 35	Santana	Deportation 1 June 37	Emperor
José da Costa	Jeje	Freed	15 yrs. prison 7 Feb. 35	Conceição da Praia	Deportation	Emperor
Teresa	Nagô	Freed	5 yrs. prison 10 Mar. 35	Sé	Deportation 31 July 35	Cachoeira
Joaquim de Santana	Nagô	Freed	8 yrs. prison 27 Apr. 35	Sé	—	Cachoeira
Ignácio	Nagô	Slave	Death 29 Mar. 35	Sé	Deportation	—
António Bomcaminho	Nagô	Freed	8 yrs. prison 29 Apr. 35	Sé	300 lashes 13 Aug. 35	Cachoeira
Joaquim J. Matos	Nagô	Freed	8 yrs. prison 29 Apr. 35	Sé	—	Cachoeira
Ignácio Limeira	Nagô	Freed	8 yrs. prison 29 Apr. 35	Sé	Deportation 22 Sept. 36	Emperor
Aprígio	Nagô	Freed	Death 29 Apr. 35	Sé	Deportation 22 Sept. 36 Forced labor 22 Sept. 36	Emperor Santo Amaro

Higino	Nagô	Slave	Forced labor 17 Aug. 35	Conceição da Praia	400 lashes 23 Aug. 36	Santo Amaro
Pompeu	Nagô	Slave	Forced labor 17 Aug. 35	Conceição da Praia	400 lashes 23 Aug. 36	Santo Amaro
Nécio	Nagô	Slave	Forced labor 12 Feb. 36	Vitória	700 lashes 23 Aug. 36	Cachoeira
Luís Sanim	Nagô	Slave	Death 12 Feb. 35	Sé	600 lashes	Cachoeira Relação, Rio
Tomás	Nagô	Slave	Death 10 Mar. 35	Vitória	800 lashes 20 June 35	Cachoeira
Carlos	Nagô	Slave	Death 10 Mar. 35	Vitória	800 lashes 20 June 35	Cachoeira
Tomé José Alves	Nagô	Freed	8 yrs. prison	Passo	Deportation 29 May 36	Emperor
Domingos da Silva	Nagô	Freed	8 yrs. prison	Passo	Deportation 29 May 36	Emperor
Belchior da Silva Cunha	Nagô	Freed	Death 2 Mar. 35	Sé	600 lashes	Cachoeira
Gaspar da Silva Cunha	Nagô	Freed	Death 2 Mar. 35	Sé	600 lashes	Cachoeira
José	Nagô	Slave	Forced labor 2 Mar. 35	—	Sold outside province 12 Aug. 42	Emperor
Cornélio	Nagô	Slave	Death 10 Mar. 35	Vitória	800 lashes 20 June 35	Cachoeira
Lino	Nagô	Slave	Death 9 Mar. 35	Vitória	800 lashes 31 July 35	Cachoeira

Source: AEBa, *Insurreições*, maços 2845–50.

or even of the number of lashes being reduced. There were, however, a few masters who appealed. For João Crisóstomo Pinto da Silva, thwarting his slave's sentence to seven hundred lashes became tantamount to a matter of personal honor. According to Pinto da Silva, his thirty-two-year-old slave, a chair porter by the name of Manoel, was a good, respectful, loyal, obedient man. Pinto da Silva accused the justice of the peace in Vitória of having tortured the slave to get information, and for this reason he believed the sentence should be dropped. However, the Appellate Court deemed his appeal inconsistent and upheld the sentence. José da Silva Romão appealed on behalf of his Hausa slave, Joaquim, a shoemaker who had been sentenced to five hundred lashes. He claimed to be appealing because he was "convinced of his slave's innocence." He alleged that there were irregularities in the slave's trial, but once more the court considered his arguments invalid. Some slaves came upon other obstacles when they appealed flogging sentences. A twenty-five-year-old Nagô slave, Manoel, was sentenced to three hundred lashes. His master, an African known as José Monteiro, who was poor himself, claimed that he had not appealed the sentence because he did not have the "means to pursue the appeals permitted him by law."[8]

Masters who tried to save their slaves from floggings usually did not do so out of mere economic motivation, since the risk of death existed but was minimal and did not justify the time and money spent on judicial appeals. Rather, it seems that they considered it their responsibility to look after their slaves' well-being, perhaps to pay them back for their loyalty and good work. Such attitudes should not be confused with those of people who appealed sentences that would entail irrecoverable financial losses, such as in the case of Higino and Pompeu.

Two lawyers argued the appeals of Higino and Pompeu in the court of Cachoeira. Higino was a seventeen-year-old Nagô. He worked on a lighter *(saveiro)* and belonged to a merchant named José Maria da Fonseca. Pompeu was a twenty-four-year-old plantation worker who belonged to José Pinto de Carvalho e Albuquerque, who, in turn, was a member of a powerful family of planters and whose brother was the famous viscount of Pirajá. These two slaves were among the few who openly confessed to having taken part in the rebellion. In fact, Pompeu had been wounded in the head and caught red-handed. He confessed to having escaped from his master's plantation in Santo Amaro in order to join the uprising. In a veiled admission of guilt, Higino testified that he had been severely beaten by his master for not having slept at home the night of 24 January. In view of such testimony, the jury condemned both men to life sentences of forced labor, as if they had been leaders. Their masters appealed to the court in Cachoeira, where on 23 August 1836 they were defended by Francisco Olegário Rodrigues and João Baptista de Farias.

Seeing that there was no doubt concerning these men's guilt, the lawyers tried a line of argumentation that they felt would resonate harmoniously in the ears of slaveowning jurors. They alleged that their clients did not deserve such light sentences. Being sentenced to forced labor would bring their lives as chattel slaves to an end, and this would almost be a reward for these criminals. The sentence was more a punishment for their masters, who in the future would be deprived of the slaves' services. The lawyers asked the jury for a verdict that would punish the "delinquents" and no one else. Higino's and Pompeu's sentences were reduced to four hundred lashes and two hundred lashes, respectively, and after their punishment they were able to return to their lives as slaves. Defending masters' interests worked perfectly.[9]

There are only two cases of slaves who initiated their own appeals: two Nagôs, Carlos, a cook, and Tomás, a stable hand, both slaves of Frederick Robelliard, the English merchant. These men had been seen at the feast of Lailat al-Miraj in Vitória in November of the previous year. Carlos confessed to be learning to read and write Arabic. Tomás did not confess, but he had been arrested wearing blood-stained garments. Robelliard had deserted them pure and simple. His indifference contributed to their being sentenced to death. Not happy with such a fate, they appealed to the court in Cachoeira, which commuted their sentences to eight hundred lashes. Once they had saved their own lives, Robelliard went before the court and demanded the return of his slaves, which he obtained. On 15 April 1836 he paid 159,468 réis for their imprisonment and for the treatment of the wounds on their backs. Three days later they were back in his possession.[10]

Only two freedmen had their death sentences reduced to floggings. It is not known exactly why Belchior and Gaspar da Silva Cunha were treated in this way, since freedmen seem only to have gotten their harsher sentences commuted to deportation. It may be that the Bahian authorities decided that given both men's degree of involvement, their expulsion would be preceded by a flogging of six hundred lashes.

There were cases of freedmen who were tried and convicted and had their sentences commuted in record time. José da Costa was sentenced to fifteen years' forced labor in a most summary trial that took place on 16 February—less than a month after the uprising. Immediately thereafter, in several petitions, he claimed to be an entirely acculturated African, loyal to whites and to Brazilian customs and a practicing Catholic. He also claimed that the justice of the peace had distorted crucial parts of his initial testimony. By the end of March his name had been entered on the first list of 154 Africans to be banished from the country. This must have been an unsettling development for a man who had vehemently argued for his being well integrated into Bahian society (see chapter 11).

Eight of these sentences were commuted by imperial pardon. Ignácio

Limeira and Joaquim José Matos, Nagô freedmen who lived and worked together as chair porters, were both sentenced to eight years in prison, which must have seemed to be overly harsh sentences for two men over seventy. There was strong incriminating evidence against them, including six knife sheaths found in the hovel where they lived. During those terrifying days of persecution, the coincidence of their being backyard neighbors of Manoel Calafate was also important, since one witness had sworn that he saw many rebels jump into their garden during the raid on Calafate's loge the night of the rebellion. They spent a year in prison, and then on 4 August 1836 their petition was sent to the imperial court in Rio de Janeiro. In two months' time the government substituted deportation for their prison sentences, as the two old freedmen had requested.[11]

In at least two cases imperial pardon benefited African families. Ajadi Luís Doplê was a Nagô freedman, the owner of a lighter, a married man, and the father of four children. He was also functionally literate in Portuguese. His wife, Felicidade da Paixão, peddled cloth throughout the city. They lived at 8 Ladeira da Palma, where until 27 January 1835 they shared a two-story house with nine other Africans. Felicidade was pregnant with her fourth child. Three days after the rebellion, she, her husband, and the other residents were arrested because a patrol had found some Malê writing, a quill, four writing slates, and several rings hidden in one of the rooms. When questioned, these Africans gave contradictory testimony concerning the ownership of those articles. Ajadi later claimed that the items belonged to a freedman named José, who was traveling on business in Africa and had asked him to take care of his things. He testified that he had hidden them "because he had heard [the police] were killing blacks who had such things." He also confessed to possessing a Malê frock, but he claimed that he did not use it to pray or to make war on whites—"he used it as a night shirt."[12]

Obviously, such a story did not convince the jury of Ajadi's innocence. On 10 March 1835 he was sentenced to death. Felicidade received a five-year prison sentence. Ajadi appealed immediately and was tried again in Cachoeira, on 28 July. His sentence was reduced to eight years in prison at hard labor. After serving two years, in May 1837 Ajadi and his wife appealed to the throne and asked to be deported to "Amim" (doubtless Onim, today Lagos, Nigeria). They declared that they could pay their passage, as well as that of their four children, one of whom had been born in prison. In a decree dated 16 June 1837 the representatives of the young emperor allowed the African family to leave. On 6 July the president of the province instructed the local judge to prepare the documents for their release. Unfortunately, there is no record of their leaving for Africa.[13]

Tomé José Alves and Domingos da Silva, two Nagô brothers both of whom had been sentenced to eight years in prison, also profited from royal pardon. The initiator of their appeal to the emperor was their mother. Her name, Francisca da Silva, indicates that only she and her son Domingos had been slaves of the same master. Cases such as this—of families divided by slavery in the New World—while rarely documented, were quite common. This mother is a good example of the strong, independent women who filled the streets of nineteenth-century Salvador. These were women who would not abandon loved ones to an unknown fate. Francisca da Silva had not been arrested in 1835. In her petition she claimed that Tomé and Domingos had been arrested "because of false accusations by their enemies," which seems to have been quite common that year. Francisca asked to be allowed to return to Africa with her sons, saying that she would pay all expenses. She was successful. Their deportation decree was signed on 29 May 1836.[14]

Execution of the Sentences

Any discussion of the sentences meted out to convicted prisoners in 1835 would be incomplete if it did not include a discussion of their execution. Each act of punishment was carried out with its proper ritual and had its own political significance.

In the opinion of Bahian rulers, the death penalty was by far the weightiest sentence, politically speaking. The president of the province, under pressure from influential members of Bahian society, felt that it was important to put on a public spectacle and hang prisoners as soon as possible so as to intimidate would-be rebels. With this in mind, on 6 March 1835 Francisco de Souza Martins wrote to the minister of justice:

> It seems fitting, as has been suggested to me by many Citizens of this Capital, that the Government of His Majesty the Emperor, so as not to diminish the healthy effect of an execution as soon as possible after the crime, should have the sentences carried out on the two or three main leaders, at the same time declaring that these individuals should not have any recourse or appeal; that is, such a measure is thought to be both efficacious and necessary in the present circumstances.[15]

In a decree dated 18 March 1835 the central government accepted this suggestion and ordered that the death sentences be "immediately carried out without being allowed to go before a Court of Appeal, after the remaining legal steps had been taken."[16] A month later, on 14 May, one day after the publication of the law on deportations, and without having taken "the remaining legal steps," the government put four Africans to death.

There was only one freedman among those executed: Jorge da Cruz Barbosa, a hod carrier *(carregador de cal)* whose African name was Ajahi. Ajahi had been arrested on the day after the uprising, in the house of some fellow Nagô acquaintances, Faustina and Tito. Tito was also involved in the rebellion and had left home some days before the twenty-fifth, never to return. On the morning of the twenty-fifth, Ajahi showed up wounded and hid under a bedframe *(estrado)*. Faustina turned him in to inspectors Leonardo Joaquim dos Reis Velloso and Manoel Eustáquio de Figueiredo, who arrested him. Under questioning Ajahi declared that he lived on Rua da Oração and was a neighbor of Belchior and Gaspar da Cunha, whom he used to visit regularly. Concerning the meetings they had there, he claimed: "Everybody prattled on and on or just stopped in to say hello." He denied being a Malê and having participated in the revolt. He tried to convince the judge and jury that the bayonet wound in his right leg "had been inflicted by soldiers . . . while he was at the window, [and] not because he was outside fighting with anybody." Ajahi was apparently just an ordinary rebel. Indeed none of the Africans questioned in 1835 suggested he had played an important part in the Malê organization. Even so, on 2 March 1835 he was sentenced to death, along with other important prisoners. His sentence had been set by Francisco Gonçalves Martins, the chief of police, now presiding over the jury as a judge: "In light of the previous declaration . . . on behalf of the Sentencing Jury I sentence prisoners: Belchior da Silva Cunha, Gaspar da Silva Cunha, and Jorge da Cruz Barbosa (all freedmen), as well as Luís Sanim, a slave of Pedro Ricardo da Silva, to natural death on the gallows." With the exception of Jorge Barbosa (Ajahi), all those listed by Martins had their sentences commuted. Ajahi appears to have escaped from prison, but he was quickly recaptured. Perhaps the maintenance of his sentence comes from his being considered an incorrigible rebel.[17]

Little is known about the others sentenced to death. They were all Nagô slaves. One of them was Pedro, a slave of Joseph Mellors Russell, the English merchant. It seems that all of this man's slaves took part either in the rebellion or, at least, in the Malê conspiracy. On his own Russell had turned over to the justice of the peace a crate containing a great number of Malê objects belonging to his slaves—Nécio, João, Joãozinho "the urchin," Tomé, Miguel, and Pedro. Of all these men João was the most militant, and his final sentence is not known. No one knows why Pedro was singled out for the death penalty. I could not find the records for his particular trial.[18]

The other two slaves executed were Gonçalo, whose owner appears in the records as Lourenço so-and-so, and Joaquim, who belonged to Pedro Luís Mefre. About them all that is known is that they were among the thirteen rebels wounded and taken prisoner during the confrontation at Água de Meninos. It may be that they were both abandoned by their masters, since nothing suggests that they might have been leaders and none of the other eleven taken prisoner in the same circumstances received similar punishment.[19]

These were, then, the four Africans put to death in 1835. Rodrigues began a tradition claiming that five Africans were executed, but there is no evidence for it. He names a freedman by the name of José Francisco Gonçalves as the fifth victim. This African actually existed. He was a Hausa and lived in the Maciel de Baixo neighborhood. According to his testimony, he earned his living "bringing out samples of sugar from the warehouses for Merchants." His name appears on the Roll of the Guilty with this observation: "sentenced and acquitted on 4 June 1835." On that same roll the names of Jorge da Cruz Barbosa, Joaquim, Pedro, and Gonçalo appear, with the following observation after each one: "sentenced to death and executed on 14 May 1835."[20]

Like all public executions, this one had its share of pomp and ceremony. The victims were paraded through the streets of Salvador in handcuffs. At Campo da Pólvora new gallows had been constructed to replace the old ones, which had rotted from lack of use. At the head of the cortege marched the council "doorman," José Joaquim de Mendonça, who cried the sentence out to the ringing of bells. After him came João Pinto Barreto, the execution scribe, and Caetano Vicente de Almeida, a municipal judge. On both sides of the prisoners marched a column of armed Municipal Guardsmen. The Santa Casa da Misericórdia was also present, since the bylaws of that important philanthropic institution obliged its members, who were recruited from the local elite, to march along with people condemned to death as an act of Christian piety. The execution itself was to be witnessed by the interim chief of police (Martins had already gone to Rio de Janeiro as a congressional deputy), Judge Antônio Simões da Silva, and by the commandant of the Municipal Guard, Manoel Coelho de Almeida Tander.

Much to the authorities' disappointment, the new gallows could not be used to hang the prisoners. No one would act as executioner. On 13 May, one day before the execution, the vice-president of the province, Manoel Antônio Galvão, in response to a request from the chief of police, offered 20–30 milréis to any ordinary prisoner in Bahia's many jails to act as executioner. Even though that was four months' earnings for the average urban slave, no one came forward. The chief warden, Antônio Pereira de Almeida, expressed his disappointment in a communiqué to the chief of police that afternoon: "I have offered the job to the inmates, and no one will take it. I did the same thing today at the Barbalho and Ribeira dos Galés jails, and no one will take it for any amount of money; not even the other blacks will take it—in spite of the measures and promises I have offered in addition to the money." Either because of prisoners' solidarity or out of fear of retaliation from the African Muslims, an executioner could not be found. For this reason, still on 13 May, the president of the province had a firing squad formed to carry out the sentences. Then, on the fourteenth at Campo da Pólvora, the four men were executed by a squad of policemen and immediately buried in a common grave in a cemetery run by the Santa Casa, next to the gallows. Without the hangings, the didactic value Bahian leaders envisaged in the spectacle was lost.[21]

Less pomp surrounded floggings, although they too were public. Here, as well, the chief of police insisted (20 March 1835) that the "punishment should immediately follow the crime." He argued that haste was necessary "so that the prisons would not overflow," a practical more than a political reason.[22] The scenes of torture could not have been more degrading. The victims were undressed, tied, and whipped on their backs and buttocks. Floggings were held at two different sites: the Campo da Pólvora and the cavalry garrison at Água de Meninos, where the last battle of the uprising had been fought. At times the authorities worried that these public spectacles would themselves disturb the peace. Alufá Licutan's sentence to one thousand lashes would be carried out in public, "but not on the streets of the city."[23]

Prisoners received fifty lashes per day, "for as many days as it took to undergo the entire sentence . . . provided there was no risk to a prisoner's life." The victims' suffering was closely watched by armed guards and carefully supervised by officers of the law, as well as by a court scribe who on a daily basis recorded the date, names, and numbers of lashes. From time to time, doctors visited the victims to check on their health and to advise whether the whipping should be continued or suspended for a while. These doctors' reports are shocking testimony to the physical state of the tortured individuals. On 2 May 1835 Dr. José Souza Brito Cotegipe told Caetano Vicente de Almeida, the municipal criminal judge: "I have only found two who are well enough to continue serving their sentences. The rest cannot because of the enormous open wounds on their buttocks." In a report on 19 September he said: "Having proceeded in the examination . . . of the Africans being flogged, I can inform Your Grace that the blacks [named] Carlos, Belchior, Cornélio, Joaquim, Carlos, Thomas, Lino, and Luiz (at the Relação Jail) are in such a state that if they continue to be flogged, they may die."[24]

On that very day Luiz was admitted to the Santa Casa da Misericórdia Hospital, where he stayed for two months. On 3 November he went back to the stocks, and two weeks later he completed his sentence of eight hundred lashes. Narciso, another slave, was less fortunate. He was caught red-handed during the uprising and did not survive the twelve hundred lashes of his sentence. He is the only African known to have died from that terrible punishment, but there may have been more.[25]

Floggings were not the final punishment for these slaves. Once they served their sentences, they were to be rigorously watched over by their masters, who were obliged to assume legal responsibility for the future comportment of slaves released from prison. Moreover, many, perhaps all, of the slaves released had to wear a *gargalheira,* a heavy iron rack in the form of a cross, around their neck, which was how runaway slaves were punished. Masters paid for these racks. Other slaves were hobbled in chains. The length of this additional punishment varied. Luiz, already mentioned above, wore the frame around his neck for two weeks. Joaquim received six hundred lashes, and his master only got him back when he agreed to "keep him in a leg-iron for two months." Malê leader Luís Sanim, whose death sentence had been reduced to six hundred lashes, was obliged to wear the gargalheira for two months. José Monteiro was obliged to keep a slave of his who had received one thousand lashes in irons as long as the slave resided in the province.[26]

There is very little information to be found concerning the terms spent in prisons or at forced labor. According to Rodrigues, Antônio Feijó (the imperial regent from 1835 to 1837) might have changed all those sentences to deportations, but there is no governmental decree to that effect. If such a decision was ever made, it did not include Domingos Marinho de Sá, the mulatto who tried to bar the police from the house where the uprising began. Domingos had been sentenced to eight years in prison at hard labor and served his entire sentence. In 1843 he applied for release. He also presented documents describing part of his life as an inmate. He had been in the Relação Jail, where, according to one employee, "he had always done what he was told" and, in the words of another, "he was always obedient [and did] any job he was assigned in prison." Domingos was often requisitioned to work in some of Salvador's other jails. In Fort Barbalho he repaired rooms, cleaned, toted water, and so on. In Forte do Mar he also "helped with repairs and with setting up cannonry." In the Casa de Correção (House of Correction) he worked "on the cells and on their cleaning." That was how Domingos spent his eight years in prison. His release was signed on 18 May 1843.[27]

João Clegg, a Nagô slave, served thirty-three years of a life sentence at forced labor. In 1835 he belonged to a partnership of two English merchants named Clegg and Jones, who seem to have abandoned him. He, in turn, pretended to be a freedman and took Clegg's name. In 1857, at the age of nearly fifty, he petitioned the chief of police, claiming to be in prison without ever having been convicted of a crime *(sem culpa formada)* and "doubtlessly because of some lapse on the part of the authorities, since . . . he was a poor, low-class individual." He told of having been in several jails in Bahia:

> When (1835) he was arrested, they sent him to the Cavalry Garrison, then to the old Relação Jail, then to the galley of the Naval Arsenal, where he remained until 1838, which was when the Sabinada [a liberal, separatist rebellion] took place and the prisons were opened so prisoners could take

up arms. Because he was an African, he was sent to Fort Barbalho, where
he is today, in the service of the Colonel commandant. . . . Thus . . . he
is neither [legally] imprisoned nor released.

Unfortunately, he was indeed legally imprisoned. The warden at Barbalho
showed the chief of police the court records of his sentence to life at forced
labor. Only in November of 1868, as a sexagenarian, did this man receive a
pardon from Emperor Dom Pedro II. Aprígio Geraldo, a freedman, was
serving a life sentence at forced labor along with João. The same year João
was released, Aprígio also asked to be released, maintaining in one petition
"that he was over sixty, poor, and feeble" and in another that "[Brazilians]
have nothing to fear from a sixty-year-old man who has been worn out by
working on chain gangs." Nothing is known about this man's release.[28]

Deportation sentences were more than a little troublesome for Bahian
authorities. The major difficulty was a dearth of vessels to carry out the
large-scale deportations the government had planned. The official end of
the slave trade in 1831 had reduced the traffic between Salvador and Africa
considerably. The legitimate trade in tobacco, palm oil, and cloth did not
launch as many ships as human trade did. On top of this, the sea captains
seemed reluctant to cooperate with Bahian authorities, either because they
were not paid enough or because they were afraid to cross the Atlantic
with these supposedly dangerous passengers on board. The fact is that
they did not obey Article 5 of Law 9, which obliged them to carry Africans
and levied a fine of 400 milréis for "each suspect who cannot be shown to
disembark at the proper Port." The chief of police was infuriated by a
captain who alleged that he was already overloaded and refused to take on
any banished Africans. The chief gave the head of customs orders to inform him of all captains asking permission to set sail for Africa. He also
used that occasion to register a complaint against shipowners, whose failure to cooperate was making it impossible to expel African freedmen.[29]
During the second half of 1835, provincial authorities decided to charter
the *Damiana*, which left Salvador with two hundred Africans on board
heading for Ouidah (Benin). However, most deportees left the country in
small groups—six, ten, eleven people—and they had to pay their own
passage.[30]

Another problem associated with deportations was preparing Africans
to leave. The prisoners needed to be released at least long enough to
gather their belongings and make whatever arrangements were necessary
for the trip. There is, however, no evidence that they were allowed to do
so. At the end of April interim chief of police Antônio Simões explained
why he was afraid to loosen his grip on the Africans: "if I did, it would
not be easy to get them together later and send them off." Later on, in
October, Simões still thought it "inconvenient" to let out one Angolan
who had requested permission to settle his affairs before leaving.[31] There

are records of two female ex-slaves who managed to be released on bail before their deportation. In fact, one of them, Felicidade, a Mundubi, was not being deported for her seditious activities, but for her sexual ones: "She had been arrested on moral grounds." As often happens, in the wake of political repression came the repression of mores. Felicidade was given twenty days to get ready to leave. The other woman, an ex-slave known as Luísa, was let out of prison on bail and "out of deference to her sex." She was being released "so as to get her affairs in order and be gone."[32]

But where? This was a matter of concern for the authorities, and even more so for the Africans about to be repatriated. In May 1835 the Provincial Assembly recommended many security measures to Parliament, among them that Brazil should establish a colony in Africa "where we can repatriate all those Africans who gain their freedom, or at least those freedmen who appear to threaten our safety." As nothing was decided on this matter, a few months later President Martins suggested that the imperial government negotiate with the United States to have the ex-Bahian slaves admitted to Liberia, but nothing seems to have come of that idea.[33]

The existence today of a considerable colony of descendants of Brazilian slaves in Lagos, Nigeria, and in neighboring Dahomey indicates that at least the Nagôs, the majority of convicted Africans, went home. But this does not mean that their return to Africa was easy. Their region had undergone deep political changes during the twenty to thirty years they had been away. It had also been devastated by war. Few, if any, found old acquaintances or family members still alive. Besides their frustration on arrival, these people left more than a trifle back in their port of departure. They had been in Bahia a long time. They had worked hard; they had bought their freedom; they had lived as freedmen; and they had formed ties with the place and people left behind. One must keep in mind that the overwhelming majority of these returnees did not take part in the rebellion. They were peaceful Africans who had adapted to life in Bahia. They were, pure and simple, victims of persecution. Even the rebels had set down roots and devised the rebellion to change lives they would live in Bahia rather than on the other side of the Atlantic.

Few Africans left Bahia happily in 1835. Freedmen such as João Duarte da Silva (a Jeje), Paulo da Silva (a Nupe), Ivo (a Bornu), Jorge Samuel (a Mina), and Eleutério Requião (a Nagô) refused to be included among those "acquitted for lack of evidence" and for that reason subject to deportation. As far as they were concerned, acquittal meant that they were found innocent and could stay, as others were able to. The chief of police, however, turned down their petition. Paulo, another freedman, tried to forge his name onto a baptismal certificate to avoid deportation.

While these men had succeeded in freeing themselves from slavery in Bahia, none of them had been as successful as Luís Xavier de Jesus had been before 1835. During a stay of over thirty years he had acquired property worth more than 60,000 milréis and had received the title of captain *(capitão de entradas e assaltos)* in 1811 from the royal government, which put him in charge of destroying maroon communities. In spite of his record, he was exiled. He wrote in his 1836 petition that he had been "forced to embark for African ports as [if he were] a suspicious brigand and dangerous to the land that held the fruits of his labor!" He blamed the accusations against him on people after his wealth. He was not at all happy with being deported, since "as a man of considerable wealth, he preferred to live in a civilized country, which was conclusive proof that he had not conspired to turn his adoptive country into a wasteland [run by] savage Africans." Luís Xavier, or his solicitor, had understood the "civilizationist" logic of the anti-African repression and sought to sway whites by repudiating his Africanness. He also argued for his return on the grounds that although he had come to Brazil a slave, he had become well-off, the sort of man civilized countries should recognize as useful. He also promised to provide the authorities references: "wealthy, law-abiding citizens" and important whites who would vouch for his conduct and character. His efforts were, however, fruitless. In 1841 he once again petitioned Bahian authorities to let him return.[34] Most, however, resigned themselves to staying in Africa and facing for the third or fourth time a radical shift in their way of life.

While deportation was the fate of manumitted Africans, many slaves were also victims of a type of deportation. After the rebellion many masters, fearing that their slaves might get involved in more disturbances or that they might be arrested or killed in the aftermath, decided to sell their slaves to people outside Bahia. In order that no rebel slave might escape justice, as well as to safeguard other regions of the country, no slave was allowed to leave the province without police permission. Police authorities attended many masters with documents proving their ownership of specific slaves and with witnesses swearing that these slaves had not rebelled. Masters often requested passports for their slaves, alleging that they were going with them on trips to the south. The Africans went south, never to return. Reading these documents gives one the impression that everyone was trying to get rid of their slaves, especially if they were Nagôs. In April 1835 the secretary of the government presented a list of 380 slaves (136 of them Nagôs) to the Provincial Legislative Assembly. In the two months following the rebellion, the owners of these slaves had received police permission to sell them outside the province.[35]

Like the freedmen, slaves considered exile from Bahia cruel punishment. They too had ties to the land. Slaves at least knew their masters, and their masters' quirks and foibles, and this knowledge aided them in their daily battles with and resistance to slavery. To leave Bahia was to voyage once more into the unknown, to have to adapt one more time. Changing masters always gave slaves anxious moments, since one way to punish slaves was to sell them. One can see this in an advertisement published in the *Diário da Bahia* in 1836. A master clarified that he was not selling his slave to get back at him: "For sale, *not out of vengeance,* one handsome, strapping lad." After the rebellion the tension created by selling slaves almost turned into conflict. In February some slaves of the powerful merchant and ex-slave trader José de Cerqueira Lima threatened to revolt because their master planned to sell them outside Bahia. Slaves working in Cerqueira Lima's house as well as on a farm he owned near Salvador participated in the conspiracy. The police, however, were still on the alert and arrested them all.[36]

Controlling Africans after 1835

The Africans remaining in Bahia were saddled with a gamut of legal and police measures designed to control and harass them. Less than a month after the uprising, on 21 February, Chief of Police Martins signed an edict that was to become one of the principal instruments the police used against them. In its preamble it set down two objectives: to end the rumors of slave conspiracies, which were "constantly keeping families on edge," and, more important, to keep these rumors from coming true and "to prevent that a happening such as the one [they had undergone] before should again darken the peaceful days of the City's inhabitants." The chief of police believed that African unruliness was facilitated by masters' "negligence," since they let their slaves "out into the streets at night on a regular basis."

The edict of 21 February established that all slaves found outside after 8:00 P.M. must have a pass signed by their masters indicating what time they had left and the hour they were expected back. All slaves arrested without passes would receive fifty lashes and would only be returned to masters after police expenses were paid. With this measure the authorities guaranteed that masters would have use of the night work of their slaves, while at the same time they made masters socially more accountable. Concerning freedmen found outside after 8:00 P.M., "their fate would be appropriate to the circumstances"—a vague statement that depended on the whims of power. After this edict freedmen's liberty became totally fictitious. Even slaves (provided they possessed the required seigniorial permission) could get around more easily than freed individuals could. The decree, on the other hand, repressed slave collective life, since it permitted any policeman or civilian to arrest slaves gathered in groups of four or more unless they were working. The rest of the edict deals with holding free individuals for questioning when they had disturbed the peace by spreading rumors of slave rebellions in Salvador.[37]

No free man, indeed no Brazilian, was taken to jail because of this edict. According to a sample of the daily police rounds between 1835 and 1837, all the 143 people arrested under this law were Africans. These arrests represent 21 percent of all arrests made on routine rounds during that time, which means that more than one-fifth of the police activities after the 1835 rebellion were designed to make Africans respect their curfew. In addition to these arrests, almost 40 percent of all arrests were of African men or women.

The year 1835 seems to have been a watershed. A small sample of thirty arrests for the previous year gives the following racial and ethnic profile: seven Europeans, eight native-born blacks, eleven mulattos and cabras, and only four Africans. Africans might be social rebels, but they were not given to crimes such as fighting and stealing, which attracted the police. After 1835 police activity turned into ethnic persecution and cultural repression. In October 1835 the justice of the peace in Vitória acknowledged receipt of an order from the president of the province not to permit "any gathering whatsoever for dances or drum parties which might disturb the peace and tranquility of families."[38]

The justice of the peace of Penha Parish protested to the president in defense of his authority over undisciplined National Guardsmen. Apparently, even before curfew some police arrested and beat Africans they found on the streets. The officers behaved in that manner "right under my nose," the justice complained. While some policemen harassed Africans before curfew, others waited until morning to harass them. The justice of the peace in São Pedro Parish reported officers who, once relieved of their night beat, between 7:00 and 8:00 A.M., "took to grabbing all and whatever black-skinned people they could." The justice feared that this brutality could disturb the "public peace" if the victims were to fight back. But if some blacks did fight back, most of them did so nonviolently, by engaging in some sort of civil disobedience. As the statistics demonstrate, Africans did not comply with the new legislation. In July 1836 the justice of the peace in Brotas asked the government to enlarge the patrols in his parish because the slaves there systematically disobeyed the curfew and roamed about "in large bands and even shouting."[39]

The chief of police's edict seems like child's play when compared with the other legal provisos set up to make life difficult for Africans: Law 9, of 13 May 1835, and Law 14, of 2 June 1835. Law 9 controlled the deportation of freed Africans. It also decreed that all freed Africans living in Bahia (be they suspects or not) must leave the country as soon as the government could find a place in Africa that would take them. This was clearly a plan for large-scale deportations. Those who tried to return to Bahia or even any ill-advised African ex-slave who wandered in from other provinces would be tried for insurrection and, if acquitted, be deported. Article 8 of Law 9 required that during the time it took for the deportations to do away with the freed African community in Bahia, Africans had to pay a yearly tax of 10 milréis, which at the time was the price of one arroba (15 kilos) of beef jerky, 24 liters of beans, or five liters of manioc flour. The only people exempted would be (1) those who denounced a conspiracy, (2) invalids with no resources, and (3) sugar mill workers or ranch hands, provided they had work contracts for three years and resided on their master's property, so that he could watch over them. As Manuela Carneiro da Cunha has astutely observed, this law sought to reconcile security and large landowners' need for a dependent, if not slave, labor force.[40]

Africans' dwellings would be carefully watched over. Justices of the peace would be required to make lists of freedmen living within their jurisdictions. This would facilitate the collection of taxes, and at the same time it would establish a more resolute watch over Africans' movement through the city. Those who failed to register with the justices of the peace would be subject to penalties ranging from six days to several months in prison, depending on why they did not register. From that time on, Africans could not acquire real estate of any kind. Anyone wanting to rent rooms or dwellings to freedmen would need special permission from the justice of the peace. On the other hand, renting rooms and loges to slaves was strictly forbidden.

Another article of the law obliged masters to instruct their slaves "in the mysteries of the Christian Religion and have them baptized." Their conversion should be complete within six months, after which a fine of 50 milréis would be levied "for each pagan slave." How they tested slaves' religious faith is not known. Other articles of the law dealt with rewards for slaves who denounced a conspiracy: freedom, once the master was compensated, and exemption from the tax on Africans. They also provided remuneration for the justices' of the peace extra work registering Africans residing in their parishes.[41]

Similar to their reaction against deportation, Africans also protested other provisos of Law 9. While there is no record of any collective protest against it, many individual petitions reached the Provincial Legislative Assembly. In their petitions freedmen were too diplomatic to deny the validity of the repressive legislation; instead, they invariably argued that they should not be affected by it. The reasons they gave for their exemption always included their love of the established order and their adaptation to the country's ways.

Felippe Francisco Serra was a Jeje over the age of fifty. He had lived in Bahia for forty years and owned a barber shop. On 28 February 1835

Serra took up a new activity: he left for the coast of Africa, where he was to administer a trading post belonging to Joaquim José Duarte, a merchant. During that time Law 9 was passed, prohibiting him from returning to the province where, according to Serra, he had "a house, children, and all else that mattered in his life." Besides, he went on to say, he had nothing against the Brazilian government, "since he had been brought up in that country [and] he had learned Christian Doctrine there. He had also been one of the defenders of the Constitution and of Brazilian Independence, doing his duty as an armed soldier and subject of His Imperial Majesty." Serra had in fact served in the Third Militia Regiment in Bahia during the war of independence and was considered, as he maintained in his petition, "a Brazilian Citizen with all rights" and privileges. The assembly did not agree, however, and did not let him return to Bahia and to his family.[42]

The tax of 10 milréis occasioned many objections. The year after the rebellion, two old fishermen, José Simões (a Jeje) and Manoel Bomfim (who only identified himself as from the "West Coast"), individually petitioned the Legislative Assembly. They claimed to have spent many years in Bahia; to be married, with children born in Brazil; to have always obeyed the laws of the empire; and to have never been involved in African uprisings. Similar to Serra, both of them had been in Salvador's Ninety-second Militia Battalion and had taken part in the entire independence campaign, "up to the retaking of this city, then occupied by Lusitanian bayonets," according to Simões. As far as they were concerned, this final detail in their biographies (which implied their "exposing their breasts to bullets in the interest of independence") should count much higher in exempting them than denouncing a conspiracy, disability, or a job at a sugar plantation would. The assembly's justice commission, however, one of whose members was Chief of Police Francisco Gonçalves Martins, did not agree and turned down their petitions.[43]

Two other protests against the new tax are worth noting, coming as they did from Brazilians rather than Africans. The first came from a mulatto named Francisco José de Santana, who was married to Antônia Maria da Encarnação, a Jeje woman. They lived in the Recôncavo town of Jaguaripe. According to the husband, people such as his wife should not be subject to that legislation because they were economically dependent on as well as politically obedient to their husbands, who were Brazilians and consequently against African subversion. He argued: "one could never imagine that the petitioner, a mulatto and a native of this city, might contribute to its destruction by allowing his wife to get involved in an African Insurrection. In fact, what is going on is that I, the petitioner, and not she the accused, am the one who will have to pay." This petition was also turned down by the assembly's justice commission in an opinion dated March 1836.[44]

Even though the legislators interpreted the law rigidly, many Africans did escape it, and they escaped deportation, thanks to the help of powerful individuals, according to an accusation published in November 1837 by *O censor*. This monthly newspaper protested that while some Africans got off easy, others were cruelly punished. It tells the story of an aged African woman who could not pay the tax. She was dragged off bodily to a justice of the peace, who sent her to the city jail to be "thrown into a dungeon." The poor old lady would only be released once she paid the 10 milréis by begging through the bars of the jail. A "monstrous spectacle," *O censor* called it.[45] Bahian authorities, however, never applied all of Law 9—nor could they. But it hung like a sword of Damocles over the community of freed Africans.

Law 14 was, if not more efficient, at least a more viable attempt at controlling Africans after 1835. It regulated the labor world of blacks in the streets of Salvador and deeply altered the autonomy of the cantos. The law created the post of overseer *(capataz)* as a substitute for the canto captain, and it divided the city into *capatazias* ("overseerdoms"), which were to take the place of cantos. The capatazias would be charged with "watching over earners . . . be they slaves, freedmen, or free [*ingênuos*] . . . working either on land or at sea." The overseer was to receive a "reasonable salary," to be paid by the earners under his jurisdiction. The overseer's specific duty was to ensure his workers' good behavior and job performance. In its second article, the law recommended "the observance of strict registration of all workers, their residences, the districts to which they belong, (in the case of slaves) their masters' names, the quality and type of work they normally do." Registration, with all this information on Africans, was to be updated on a monthly basis so that no change or irregularity might elude the authorities' scrutiny. Article 3 made offenders pay a fine of 100 milréis, double that amount in the case of repeat offenders.

A year after the publication of Law 14, on 16 April 1836, the government issued a sixteen-point ordinance detailing the operation of the new system of control over African laborers. Justices of the peace were required to name inspectors for each capatazia within their parish or district. These inspectors were to be literate Brazilian citizens with a record of good conduct and residents of the district where they were to work. Their duties included registering earners and naming overseers. In addition, they were to "keep an eye on the conduct of individuals within each capatazia," making sure that items did not get lost in transit and passing on "any news whatsoever that might interest the police and [threaten] public security." The inspectors were obliged to keep in constant contact with the justices of the peace, who were to judge workers' infractions and punish them adequately, with fines or prison terms.

The overseer, as the principal element of this mock canto, continued to be an African, as was the captain whom he replaced. This time, however, the African chosen was one whites felt they could trust. His job was to ensure that blacks worked regularly. He would note those who missed work and find out why. Any irregularity, no matter how insignificant, was to be relayed to the inspector. In fact paragraph 3 of Article 11 of the ordinance established that the overseer's duty was "to carry out the inspector's orders." Overseers were to collect a maintenance tax for their capatazia: 60 réis per day from each dry land worker and 80 réis from a maritime worker. Two-thirds of this money went to the inspector; the rest belonged to the overseer. Each capatazia was to have at least ten members; smaller ones would be absorbed by other groups. After being registered into a capatazia, earners would be given a metal bracelet bearing their registration number and the number of the capatazia. Overseers would wear identical plaques, bearing the same information, around their necks on a black leather thong.[46]

This legislation attempted to create a system of labor control in the city similar to the one on the sugar plantations. It tried to turn Salvador into a sort of immense urban plantation. After all, the term *capataz* echoed the control structure of rural labor. It is known that the capatazias did not work according to plan. Evidently, justices of the peace tried to put the new system in place, but even whites doubted its viability and fairness. The *Diário da Bahia* criticized the use of identification tags and the tax on capatazias, among other things. The Africans reacted to it, challenging the overseers' authority and reaffirming the canto system. The authorities were not able to enforce the law at all. Nearly twenty years later, in 1857, they tried once more to make workers pay taxes and wear the identification tags, which was now a city law. On that occasion blacks went on strike for almost two weeks, upsetting the transportation of merchandise in the city.[47]

Before 1835 the state had never tried to interfere as profoundly with the organization of urban slave labor. African street vendors, who at that time were a veritable institution in Salvador, also suffered persecution after the uprising. On 4 October 1835 the Junta de Paz, a sort of council made up of justices of the peace in Salvador, published an edict prohibiting Africans "from engaging in the buying and selling of staples." Police Chief Martins was quick to oppose the measure, however, and reminded the justices that a similar edict in the past had resulted "in a sudden rise in prices and in mass confusion concerning enforcement of such a measure." This is tantamount to a confession of Salvador's dependency on African petty merchants. The police chief did not seem to realize that the people he had been banishing from the province were the ones who supplied its foodstuffs. Similar difficulties may have hindered the enforcement of Laws 9 and 14, whose political urgency totally ignored (or deliberately tried to destroy) social institutions, work habits, and African solidarity networks rooted in the community.[48]

The repression following the 1835 rebellion expressed Bahian leaders' and the rest of the population's fear and anguish vis-à-vis the African community. The rhetoric in the accusatory discourse described the recent conflict as a battle between two irreconcilable worlds and the repression as a just national reaction against "treacherous guests." This was a convenient way to defend slavery in a recently independent nation. The behavior of freedmen seemed particularly unforgivable, since in the masters' eyes their existence was living proof of the liberality and benign nature of Brazilian slavery. Their "treachery" gave the ruling elite an excellent opportunity to begin an effective program to whiten free society in Bahia. In the discourse of government authorities, deportations and legal persecution of Africans did not make them feel guilty, because Africans had shown themselves to be so antagonistic that they did not deserve the privilege of living in Brazil.

The formula for punishing Africans was clear: floggings for slaves, deportation for freedmen. Both Africans and Brazilians understood the implications of such measures: Africans were only of use to Brazil if they served as slaves or if they continued to behave as slaves when freed. Since obedience and submission were not obtained with the desired ease, the authorities tried to rid Bahia of its freed Africans and to keep the remaining Africans under strict surveillance. Their goal was to make life so unbearable for Africans that those freed would leave on their own and slaves would give up wanting to seek freedom. Unlike North American or Jamaican slaveowners, who chose to kill rebel slaves, the men controlling Bahia could be cruel without being bloodthirsty.

Although life after the rebellion was harder than before, it went on for Africans. In spite of everything, there were still a few who saw the good side of things. Paulo, a freed canto captain, seventeen years a slave in Bahia, was heard to say: "The sentences for the black criminals were announced, [and] freed slaves were to go back to their native land and slaves were to get floggings . . . but that was better than dying."[49] Better than dying—who will argue with that?

Beyond Bahia, the Malê rebellion engendered repressive measures throughout Brazil. It created panic in Rio de Janeiro. The British representative, H. S. Fox, informed his government that the minister of justice had assured him that "more than usual precautions have . . . been adopted, through the department of Justice and the department of Police, to watch the coloured population." Indeed, the Legislative Assembly of the province of Rio de Janeiro later voted in a law of exception that facilitated house searches and restricted freedom of speech. Moreover, it authorized the president of the province to deport manumitted Africans, just as in Bahia, and it prohibited the constitutional right to gather in secret societies (such as masonic lodges) that had members who were "foreigners of color." The most well-known law of all was applied nationally. Promulgated on 10 June 1835, this law established the death penalty for any slave who killed a master, an overseer, or members of their families. Many slaves, including Bahian "troublemakers" who were exported to the prosperous regions of southern Brazil, ran afoul of this law.[50]

Epilogue

In Bahia of 1835, Malês found fertile soil in which to sow rebellion and try to change society to Africans' advantage. Bahia was riddled with social and racial inequities and was undergoing a profound economic and political crisis. Revolts of the poor free classes, as well as those of the liberal dissidents on the one hand and the Africans on the other, threatened slavery and the hegemony of the ruling classes.

The Malê plotters certainly took the divisions among free men and the tradition of African slaves' rebelliousness into account when they mapped their strategy. Africans had a strong sense of ethnic identity, and while this ethnicity divided them, it constituted the focal point for their break with the white man's world. Using their African roots, they devised a unique culture of resistance in which Islam flourished.

Organized around a militant and multiethnic religion, Malês believed they were ready to start the fight, as well as lead it. Bahia would be taken by mobilizing the slaves in Salvador and then mobilizing those on the plantations. The final victory, however, would also and especially depend on the mobilization of spiritual forces. The Malês hoped to combine the weakening of seigniorial power on a Christian holiday one Sunday with the spiritual strength they acquired during the holy month of Ramadan.

Rebels prepared as best they could for the fight, but it was clear that they could not win. The reasons are many, beginning with their bad luck in being denounced. It may also be that they would have performed better had they achieved greater unity and mobilization among the Africans of diverse ethnicities and religions. The main obstacle, however, between them and victory was doubtless the nature of their enemy.

Whereas free Bahians were divided on numerous issues, they always joined forces to quell slave revolts. Maintaining slavery was the strategic foundation for solidarity among the free, both rich and poor. But there was more to this. The cultural moat separating Brazilians (including slaves) from Africans (both slave and freed) also kept people apart in this conflict. Cultural and national ties brought the most powerful and the most abject Brazilians together against African-born slaves. It did not even matter that some of them had no slaves, or that some were slaves themselves.

The Malê rebellion, for all intents and purposes, brought the cycle of African revolt in Bahia to a close. Except for unfounded rumors of a Malê conspiracy in 1844 in Salvador and another slave conspiracy in the Recôncavo in 1845, there is no news of further revolts. The reprisal seems to have been successful in intimidating would-be rebels. It did not, however, usher in complete accommodation on the part of Africans. The tradition of resistance would no longer be expressed in collective violence, but it would continue to characterize the relationship between master and slave. The end of rebellions did not mean the end of resistance.

Notes

Archives and series frequently cited are identified by the following abbreviations:

AEBa	Arquivo do Estado da Bahia, Salvador
AMRE	Archives du Ministère des Relations Exterieures, Paris
AN	Arquivo Nacional, Rio de Janeiro
ANTT	Arquivo Nacional da Torre do Tombo, Lisbon
APMC	Arquivo Público Municipal de Cachoeira, Cachoeira
ASCMB	Arquivo da Santa Casa de Misericórdia da Bahia, Salvador
BNRJ	Biblioteca Nacional, Rio de Janeiro
CP/Brésil	*Correspondence Politique. Brésil*
FO	*Foreign Office*
PRO	Public Record Office, London

Chapter 1 Hard Times

1. [I often translate *engenho* as "plantation," although this is somewhat misleading. *Engenho* actually means "sugar mill," but in Brazil this word implied both the mill and the plantation.—trans.]

2. Sir Robert Wilson, "Memoranda of S. Salvador or Bahia," in *Life of General Sir Robert Wilson,* by Herbert Randolph, 2 vols. (London: John Murray, 1862), 1:342.

3. These figures come from Luís dos Santos Vilhena, *A Bahia no século 18,* 2 vols. (Salvador: Editora Itapoã, 1969), 1:503, 505; "Cadastro da população da província da Bahia coordenado no anno de 1808," Arquivo Público Municipal de Cachoeira (hereinafter APMC), *Documentos para embrulhar, século XIX* (the latter is the reference of the APMC in 1980; I thank Professor Catherine Lugar, who kindly furnished me a copy of this document).

4. A. J. R. Russell-Wood, "Colonial Brazil," in *Neither Slave Nor Free: The Freedman of African Descent in the Slave Societies of the New World,* ed. D. W.

Cohen and Jack P. Greene (Baltimore: Johns Hopkins Press, 1972), 97; Ignácio Accioli, *Memórias históricas e políticas da Bahia,* ed. Braz do Amaral, 6 vols. (Salvador: Imprensa Oficial do Estado, 1931), 3 : 228 n. 26. Thales de Azevedo shows that population estimates for Salvador in 1775 ranged between 35,635 and 40,932 inhabitants (*O povoamento da cidade do Salvador* [Salvador: Editora Itapoã, 1969], 191–93).

5. Herbert Klein, "Nineteenth-Century Brazil," in Cohen and Greene, *Neither Slave Nor Free,* 316.

6. João José Reis, "A elite baiana face aos movimentos sociais: Bahia, 1824– 1840," *Revista de história* 108 (1976): 381. Even in the plantation districts the slave population in 1835 was not a big majority. A census for that year of the important sugar-producing São Tiago do Iguape Parish counted 7,426 inhabitants, only 54 percent of them slaves (see Arquivo do Estado da Bahia [hereinafter AEBa], *Polícia. Recenceamento,* maço 6175). I thank Bert Berrickman for this information. Figures on the Bahian slave trade between 1786 and 1853 are in Herbert Klein, "A demografia do tráfico atlântico de escravos para o Brasil," *Estudos econômicos* 17 (May–August 1987): 133. More detailed estimates for 1811–51 are in David Eltis, "The Nineteenth-century Transatlantic Slave Trade: An Annual Time Series of Imports into the Americas Broken Down by Region," *Hispanic American Historical Review* 67 (1987): 114–15.

7. "Carta de José da Silva Lisboa a Domingos Vandelli, Salvador, 18 October 1781," *Anais da Biblioteca Nacional do Rio de Janeiro* 32 (1910): 502.

8. Stuart B. Schwartz, *Sugar Plantations in the Formation of Brazilian Society: Bahia, 1550 –1835* (Cambridge: Cambridge University Press, 1985), 348; João José Reis, "População e rebelião: notas sobre a população escrava na Bahia na primeira metade do século 19," *Revista das ciências humanas* 1 (1980): 197.

9. See Kátia M. de Queirós Mattoso, *Bahia: a Cidade de Salvador e seu mercado no século 19* (São Paulo: HUCITEC, 1978), 161–69 and passim.

10. F. W. O. Morton, "The Conservative Revolution of Independence" (Ph.D. diss., Oxford University, 1974), 46–58.

11. Mattoso, *Bahia,* 235 n. 477.

12. I am grateful to Mattoso for the raw data from probate records. To my knowledge, she was the first to tap this historical source in Brazil (see Kátia M. de Queirós Mattoso, "Um estudo quantitativo de história social, a Cidade do Salvador, Bahia de Todos os Santos, no século 19: primeiras abordagens, primeiros resultados," *Estudos históricos* 15 (1976): 7–28.

13. "Carta de Silva Lisboa," 505.

14. James Wetherell, *Stray Notes from Bahia, Being an Extract from Letters during Residence of Fifteen Years* (Liverpool: Webb & Hunt, 1860), 16.

15. See Stuart B. Schwartz, "Patterns of Slaveholding in the Americas," *American Historical Review* 87 (February 1982): 55–86.

16. For an excellent study of the fluctuations in the Bahian economy between the years 1750 and 1835 see Schwartz, *Sugar Plantations,* esp. chap. 15. On the African connection with Bahian tobacco see Pierre Verger, *Flux et reflux de la traite des nègres entre le golfe de Benin et Bahia de Todos os Santos* (Paris: Mouton, 1968) as well as his *O fumo da Bahia e o tráfico de escravos do Golfo de Benin* (Salvador: Universidade Federal da Bahia, 1966). On the Portuguese

connection see Catherine Lugar, "The Portuguese Tobacco Trade and To-bacco Growers of Bahia in the Late Colonial Period," in *Essays Concerning the Socioeconomic History of Brazil and Portuguese India*, ed. D. Alden and W. Dean (Gainesville: University of Florida Press, 1977), 26–70. On the end of the slave trade see Leslie Bethell, *The Abolition of the Brazilian Slave Trade: Brazil and the Slave Question, 1807–1867* (Cambridge: Cambridge University Press, 1970).

17. For slave prices in the province of Bahia see Kátia M. de Queirós Mattoso, *Etre esclave au Brésil, 15e–19e siècle* (Paris: Hachette, 1979), 108. The cattle plague is mentioned in Morton, "Conservative Revolution," 324; and "Fala do presidente Visconde de Camamu [1829]," Arquivo Nacional (hereinafter AN), cod. IJJ9, fol. 44–44v.

18. Morton, "Conservative Revolution," 324, 383–84; Schwartz, *Sugar Plantations*, 426–27.

19. AEBa, *Correspondência do presidente para o governo imperial* (hereinafter *Correspondência*), livro 681, fol. 41; on droughts and the food supply in Salvador see Mattoso, *Bahia*, 239ff., 243, 253–60.

20. AEBa, *Câmara de Cachoeira, 1824–1835*, maço 1269.

21. AEBa, *Tribunal da Relação*, maço 2188.

22. E. P. Thompson, "The Moral Economy of the English Crowd," *Past and Present* 50 (1971): 76–136.

23. President Pinheiro de Vasconcellos to Minister of the Empire, Salvador, 8 November 1833, AEBa, *Correspondência*, livro 681, fol. 35.

24. Ibid., livro 677, fols. 96, 130v.

25. AEBa, *Câmara de Cachoeira*, maço 1269; AN, cod. IJJ9, 336, II, fol. 147; AEBa, *Correspondência*, livro 681, fols. 11–11v, 23–23v; Morton, "Conservative Revolution," 327; "Commercial Report, 1836," Public Record Office, *Foreign Office* (hereinafter PRO/FO), 13, 139, fol. 46.

26. *O independente constitucional*, 107, AN, cod. IJJ9, 336, II, fol. 143; 337, fol. 8.

27. Kátia M. de Queirós Mattoso, "Sociedade e conjuntura na Bahia nos anos de luta pela independência," *Universitas* 15–16 (May–December 1973): 23.

28. AN, cod. IJJ9, 334, I, fols. 131ff., and II, fols. 42–43v; 337, fol. 4.

29. Ibid., 336, fols. 28ff.

30. Mattoso, *Bahia*, 225.

31. AEBa, *Correspondência*, livro 682, fols. 113–14, 167v; AEBa, *Oficios do Senado, 1828*, unpaginated.

Chapter 2   Revolts of the Free People

1. [The first monarch of independent Brazil was Emperor Dom Pedro I, son of Dom João VI of Portugal. Pedro remained in Brazil when his father and the court returned to Portugal, years after the routing of Napoleonic troops from that country.—trans.]

2. Quoted in Morton, "Conservative Revolution," 289.

3. Antônio d'Oliveira Pinto da França, ed., *Cartas baianas, 1821–1824* (São Paulo: Editora Nacional, 1980), 117, 122.

4. Provisional Government to the Minister of the Empire, Salvador, 15 and

20 December 1823, AEBa, *Correspondência*, livro 675, fols. 17, 18; Accioli, *Memórias históricas*, 4:101–11; Afonso Ruy, *História da Câmara Municipal de Salvador* (Salvador: Câmara Municipal de Salvador, 1953), 269ff.

5. AN, cod. IJJ9, 330, fols. 138–39.

6. Morton, "Conservative Revolution," 295.

7. Ibid., 305; Braz do Amaral, *História da Bahia do império à república* (Salvador: Imprensa Oficial do Estado, 1923), 99–100; Presidents Luís Paulo de A. Basto and João Gonçalves Cezimbra to Minister of the Empire, Salvador, 7 and 16 April 1831, AEBa, *Correspondência*, livro 679, fols. 167–167v, 171v–173; Accioli, *Memórias históricas*, 253ff.

8. Viridiana Barata to Dr. Alexandre José de Mello Moraes, Rio de Janeiro, 6 November 1868, Biblioteca Nacional, Rio de Janeiro (hereinafter BNRJ), cod. II, 33, 33, 3.

9. Consul João Pereira Leite to Portuguese Minister of Foreign Affairs, Salvador, 16 June 1831, Arquivo Nacional da Torre do Tombo, Lisbon (hereinafter ANTT); *Índice do Ministério dos Negócios Estrangeiros, Baía* (1831), caixa 1.

10. João Lourenço de Attaide Seixas, "Exposição dos acontecimentos da Villa de Santo Amaro da Purificação em abril de 1831," in AEBa, *Revolução Mata-Marotos (1831)*, maço 2852, fol. 5; Minute of the Cachoeira City Council, Cachoeira, 18 April 1831, AEBa, *Sedições, 1831–1833*, maço 2861-1.

11. Protest from the landowners in the Recôncavo, 18 May 1831, AEBa, *Levante de 1831. Abdicação do Imperador*, maço 2867. For a more thorough analysis of this important document see Reis, "A elite baiana," 365–68.

12. Consul Jacques Guinebaud to French Naval Minister, 27 October 1824, in Kátia M. de Queirós Mattoso, "O consulado francês na Bahia em 1824," *Anais do Arquivo do Estado da Bahia* 39 (1970): 201. For more information on the revolt see President Francisco Vicente Vianna to Minister of the Empire, 2 December 1824, AN, cod. IJJ9, 549, fols. 123ff.; Morton, "Conservative Revolution," 295–97; and Luís Henrique Dias Tavares, *O levante dos Periquitos* (Salvador: Universidade Federal da Bahia, Centro de Estudos Baianos, 1990).

13. Mattoso, "O consulado francês," 206.

14. Ibid., 213.

15. Morton, "Conservative Revolution," 297.

16. AN, cod. IJJ9, 331, fols. 75–76, 132–36, 165–67.

17. AEBa, *Conspiração contra a forma de governo*, maço 2855; Morton, "Conservative Revolution," 301, 304; Braz do Amaral, *História da Bahia*, 53. In support of Braz do Amaral's hypothesis, the French consul in Bahia described the assassination and offered the theories of the time (see Armand-Jean-Baptiste Marcescheau to French Ministry of Foreign Affairs, Salvador, 2 March 1830, Archives du Ministère des Relations Exterieures, Paris [hereinafter AMRE], *Correspondence Politique. Brésil* [hereinafter *CP/Brésil*], vol. 11, fols. 100–102). The British consul wrote that people in Bahia believed the assassination had nothing to do with politics (PRO/*FO*, 13, 7, fol. 216).

18. President Luís dos Santos Lima to Minister of Justice, 21 May 1831, AEBa, *Correspondência*, livro 679, fols. 179–80; Morton, "Conservative Revolution," 307.

19. Morton, "Conservative Revolution," 307–8.
20. AEBa, *Sedição militar. Processo crime, 1831,* maço 2857.
21. President Honorato J. Barros Paim to Minister of the Empire, Salvador, 16 November 1831, AEBa, *Correspondência,* livro 680, fols. 29v–30.
22. The entire text of this manifesto appears in Accioli, *Memórias históricas,* 4:354–56.
23. AN, cod. IJJ9, 336, II, fols. 12ff.
24. President Joaquim José Pinheiro de Vasconcellos to Minister of the Empire, Salvador, 19 January and 15 March 1833, AEBa, *Correspondência,* livro 680, fols. 138v–139, 162v–164.
25. AEBa, *Sublevação do Forte do Mar,* maço 2863. For information on the National Guard see Jeanne Berrance de Castro, *A milícia cidadã: a Guarda Nacional de 1831 a 1850* (São Paulo: Editora Nacional, 1977).
26. Mattoso maintains that the practice of *morgado* was uncommon in Bahia (Kátia M. de Queirós Mattoso, *Família e sociedade na Bahia do século 19* [Salvador: Corrupio, 1988], 50).
27. Paulo César Souza, *A Sabinada: a revolta separatista da Bahia (1837)* (São Paulo: Brasiliense, 1987), 146–50.
28. President Honorato José de Barros Paim to Minister of the Empire, Salvador, 28 February 1832, AEBa, *Correspondência,* livro 680, fol. 50v.
29. Morton, "Conservative Revolution," 306.
30. Seixas, "Exposição dos acontecimentos," fol. 5v.
31. Minute of the Cachoeira City Council, Cachoeira, 18 April 1831, AEBa, *Sedições, 1831–1833,* maço 2861-1; Cachoeira City Council to President of the Province, Cachoeira, 25 April 1831, AEBa, *Câmara de Cachoeira,* maço 1269.

Chapter 3   The Rebellious Tradition: Slave Revolts prior to 1835

1. Vilhena, *A Bahia no século 18,* 1:134.
2. Count of Ponte to Viscount de Anadia, Salvador, 7 April 1807, in *Anais da Biblioteca Nacional do Rio de Janeiro* 37 (1918): 450–51.
3. Ibid., 451.
4. Count of Ponte to Viscount de Anadia, Salvador, 16 June 1807, ibid., 461.
5. Howard M. Prince, "Slave Rebellion in Bahia, 1807–1835" (Ph.D. diss., Columbia University, 1972), 102–3; Joaquim Ignácio da Costa to Count of Ponte, Maragogipe, 31 January 1809, AEBa, *Cartas ao governo,* vol. 216; Count of Ponte to the Government, Bahia, 12 January 1809, AEBa, *Cartas do governo à Sua Magestade,* vol. 145, fols. 179–83; General superintendent in Feira de Santana to the Salvador City Council, Feira de Santana, 11 March 1809, AEBa, *Cartas do Senado,* maço 127; Luiz Roberto de Barros Mott, "Brancos, pardos, pretos e índios em Sergipe, 1825–1830," *Anais de história* 6 (1974): 175.
6. Concerning the *Ogboni* cult in Africa see Robert Smith, *Kingdoms of the Yoruba* (London: Methuen, 1969), 115–16; and esp. Peter Morton-William, "The Ogboni Cult in Oyo," *Africa* 30 (October 1966): 362–74. Concerning its role in the 1809 revolt see Raymundo Nina Rodrigues, *Os africanos no Brasil*

(São Paulo: Editora Nacional, 1932), 73. The Aja-Fon-Ewe groups of ancient Dahomey were called Jejes in Bahia. The Yorubas were called Nagôs. I shall use terms current in Bahia to designate African nations (see chapter 8).

7. Joaquim Ignácio da Costa to Count of Ponte, Maragogipe, 31 January 1809.

8. Accioli, *Memórias históricas*, 3:235−36 n. 34; Verger, *Flux et reflux*, 330−31. Concerning Arcos's era of progressiveness in Bahia see F. W. O. Morton, "The Governorship of the Count of Arcos in Bahia, 1810−1818: Enlightened Despotism in an Age of Revolution" (Paper presented at the conference on Late Colonial Brazil, University of Toronto, 1986).

9. For information on the 1814 rebellion see "Cópia do acordão proferido contra os Confederados Homens pretos naturais da Mina de Nação Aussá," BNRJ, cod. II, 33, 21, 72; Décio Freitas, *Insurreições escravas* (Porto Alegre: Editora Movimento, 1976), 40−41; Carlos Ott, *Formação étnica da cidade do Salvador*, 2 vols. (Salvador: Manu Editora, 1955), 2:103−8; and Prince, "Slave Rebellion," chap. 5. Concerning its repercussions in Alagoas see Abelardo Duarte, *Negros muçulmanos nas Alagoas (os Malês)* (Maceió: Edições Caeté, 1958), 58−59; Luiz Roberto de Barros Mott, "A escravatura: a propósito de uma representação a El Rei sobre a escravatura no Brasil," *Revista do Instituto de Estudos Brasileiros* 14 (1973): 127−36; and idem, "A revolução dos negros do Haiti e o Brasil," *História: questões e debates* 3, no. 4 (June 1982): 55−63.

10. For a description of the Bori (Hausa possession and trance cults) see A. J. N. Tremearne, *Hausa Superstitions and Customs* (London: J. Bale, Sons & Danielsson, 1913), 513−40; and Joseph Greenberg's ethnographic discussion, *The Influence of Islam on a Sudanese Religion* (Seattle: University of Washington Press, 1946). For more recent studies see Freemont E. Besmer, *Horses, Musicians, and Gods: The Hausa Cult of Possession Trance* (South Hadley, Mass.: Bergin & Garvey, 1983), 12−13; and Jacqueline Monfopuga-Nicolas, *Ambivalence et cult de possession: contribuition á l'étude du Bori haoussa* (Paris: Anthropos, 1972). One of Usuman Dan Fodio's objectives in his jihad in Hausaland was to purge Hausa Islam of local traditional beliefs (see Peter Clarke, *West Africa and Islam* [London: Edward Arnold, 1982], 113ff.). Concerning Muslim presence in the Our Lady of the Rosary Brotherhood, see Verger, *Flux et reflux*, 520.

11. For the remonstrance against Arcos see Maria Beatriz da Silva, *A primeira gazeta da Bahia: Idade d'Ouro do Brasil* (São Paulo: Cultrix and Ministério de Educação e Cultura, 1978), 101−3; and Ott, *Formacão étnica*, 2:103−8.

12. Antônio Augusto da Silva to Count of Arcos, Maragogipe, 20 March 1814, BNRJ, cod. II, 33, 24, 22. See Schwartz, *Sugar Plantations*, chap. 5, for information on the planting cycle; see p. 483 for more information on this uprising; and passim for much more on the Engenho da Ponta.

13. AEBa, *Cartas do governo a diversas autoridades*, vol. 168, fols. 360−61, 370. The count was zealous in attacking quilombos, according to several of his letters to local authorities.

14. Prince, "Slave Rebellion," chap. 5; Wanderley Pinho, *História de um engenho no Recôncavo* (São Paulo: Editora Nacional, 1982), 194−95; Henrique

Vilhena to Count of Arcos, Salvador, 6 April 1816, AEBa, *Cartas ao governo,* maço 245.

15. AEBa, *Cartas ao governo,* maço 232.

16. My remarks on the debates between Count of Arcos and the planters come from material published by Eduardo de Caldas Britto in "Levante de pretos na Bahia," *Revista do Instituto Geográfico e Histórico da Bahia* 10, no. 29 (1903): 88–94. For the reaction in Rio to Arcos see Marquis of Aguiar to Count of Arcos, Rio de Janeiro, 27 July 1816, BNRJ, cod. II, 33, 24, 35. See also Pandiá Calógeras, *O marquez de Barbacena* (São Paulo: Editora Nacional, 1936), 19–20.

17. Kátia M. de Queirós Mattoso, "Albert Roussin: testemunha das lutas pela independência da Bahia (1822)," *Anais do Arquivo do Estado da Bahia* 41 (1975): 128.

18. França, *Cartas baianas,* 60. Madeira de Mello's proclamation appears in AEBa, *Sublevações,* maço 2860. On Jamaica see Mary Reckord, "The Jamaican Slave Rebellion of 1831," in *Black Society in the New World,* ed. R. Frucht (New York: Random House, 1971), 50–66.

19. AEBa, *Insurreições escravas* (hereinafter *Insurreições*), maço 322.

20. Interim Government Council to Captain in charge *(capitão-mor)* of ordinance in Valença, Cachoeira, 19 November 1822, AEBa, *Independência,* maço 322.

21. Braz do Amaral, *História da Independência na Bahia,* 2d ed. (Salvador: Progresso Editora, 1957), 284–85. Morton informs that Labatut executed fifty-two slaves ("Conservative Rebellion," 280).

22. For information on the c. 1780 revolt on the Santana Plantation see Stuart B. Schwartz, "Resistance and Accommodation in Eighteenth-Century Brazil," *Hispanic American Historical Review* 57 (February 1977): 69–81; Schwartz first published the now famous list of demands ("peace treaty") of the Santana rebels. For the 1824 movement see João José Reis, "Resistência escrava em Ilhéus: um documento inédito," *Anais do Arquivo do Estado da Bahia* 44 (1979): 285–97. See also Ilhéus Circuit Judge *(Ouvidor da Comarca)* Miguel Joaquim da Costa Mascarenhas to the Lieutenant Colonel of the Valença Battalion, Ilhéus, 28 January 1824, AEBa, *Escravos (assuntos),* maço 2883. Mascarenhas asked for military help to combat the "revolutionary element among the slaves of this District." On the Cachoeira rebellion see Prince, "Slave Rebellion," 129–30; the anonymously written "Crônica dos acontecimentos da Bahia, 1809–1828," *Anais do Arquivo do Estado da Bahia* 26 (1938): 91; and Accioli, *Memórias históricas,* 4:346.

23. Wande Abimbola, *Ifá: An Exposition of Ifá Literary Corpus* (Ibadan: Oxford University Press, 1976), 210–11.

24. The documentation on the Urubu Quilombo can be found in AEBa, *Insurreições,* maço 2845. See also President Manoel Ignácio da Cunha to Minister of Justice, Salvador, 19 December 1826, AEBa, *Correspondência,* livro 676, fol. 192v; and Pierre Verger, *Notícias da Bahia—1850* (Salvador: Corrupio, 1981), 277. During the colonial period African religion was usually called *calundu* (see Laura de Mello e Souza, *O diabo e a Terra de Santa Cruz* [São

Paulo: Companhia das Letras, 1986], passim; and João José Reis, "Magia jeje na Bahia: a invasão do Calundu do Pasto da Cachoeira, 1785," *Revista brasileira de história* 8 [1988]: 58–82).

25. AEBa, *Escravos (assuntos)*, maço 2883.

26. Manoel da Cunha to Minister of Justice, Salvador, 19 December 1826, ibid.; Marquis of Nazaré to President of Bahia, Rio de Janeiro, 7 February 1827, AEBa, *Ofícios imperiais*, vol. 757, fol. 302. For the opinion of the French consul on the military situation in Bahia see AMRE, *CP/Brésil*, vol. 7, fol. 118v. In several reports from that time, the consul documented difficulties in Bahia caused by the war. He emphasized Bahians' antipathy for the conflict. For information on Felisberto Caldeira's performance in Uruguay see Calógeras, *O marquez de Barbacena*, chap. 5.

27. Prince, "Slave Rebellion," 139–40; Lt. Col. Anastácio F. de Menezes Dória to Commander in chief *(Comandante das Armas)*, Salvador, 20 April 1827, AEBa, *Quartel general do comando das armas*, maço 3367.

28. Cachoeira City Council to President of the Province of Bahia, Cachoeira, 24 March 1827, AEBa, *Câmara de Cachoeira*, maço 1269; Antônio Vaz Carvalho to President of the Province, 28 March 1827, AEBa, *Juízes. Cachoeira, 1823–31*, maço 2270. See also Isaias de Carvalho Santos Neto's architectural study of the remains of Engenho Vitória, "Oito histórias de um engenho da Bahia" (Asst. Prof. thesis, Universidade Federal da Bahia, 1974).

29. Consul Guinebaud to French Ministry of Foreign Affairs, Salvador, 9 May 1827, AMRE, *CP/Brésil*, vol. 5. fol. 170v. Concerning the mutiny aboard ship see AEBa, *Revoltas de 1822–23*, maço 2845. Olaudah Equiano tells, in the famous story of his life, how he was tormented by the idea he would be eaten by whites once he landed in the New World (See Olaudah Equiano, *Equiano's Travels*, ed. Paul Edwards [London: Heineman, 1967], 25–26, 31, 36).

30. Pedro Rodrigues Bandeira declared on his deathbed that he had always been a bachelor. His will also lists his plantations in Cachoeira (AEBa, *Inventários e testamentos*, maço 01/100/146/03, fol. 8). His sister Maria is listed in Antonio José da Palma, "Relação nominal das pessoas existentes nos engenhos Ponta, Buraco e Victoria [c. 1825]," APMC, uncatalogued.

31. See above, n. 26.

32. AEBa, *Insurreições*, maço 2845; Guinebaud to French Ministry of Foreign Affairs, Salvador, 9 May 1827. The consul, according to his own testimony, conservatively estimated the rebels' forces at one thousand but four days later reduced this number to six hundred. There were eighty deaths and thirty prisoners (Guinebaud to French Ministry of Foreign Affairs, Salvador, 12 and 16 March 1828, AMRE, *CP/Brésil*, vol. 7. fols. 118, 138).

33. Documentation for this revolt can be found in several collections of correspondence in the AEBa: *Juízes. Iguape*, maço 2394, and *Juízes. Cachoeira*, maço 2270. An 1835 census in Iguape registered 199 slaves on Colonel Rodrigo Falcão's Engenho Novo. Of those slaves, 108 were Africans and 91 native-born, counting 41 creole children under the age of twelve. On the four plantations involved in the uprising, the proportion of African adult slaves was 70 percent in 1835 (AEBa, *Polícia. Recenceamento*, maço 6175).

34. Dom Nuno Eugênio de Assis e Seilbiz to Commander of the Army,

Salvador, 18 April 1827, copy in AMRE, *Memoires et documents. Brésil,* vol. 5, fol. 159–159v.

35. Manoel M. Branco to Viscount of Camamu, Santo Amaro, 1 December 1828, AEBa, *Juízes. Cachoeira,* maço 2580.

36. Viscount of Camamu to Minister of the Empire, Salvador, 17 December 1828, AEBa, *Correspondência,* livro 678, fols. 32v–33. The plan appears word for word in AEBa, *Correspondência expedida,* vol. 6, fol. 164.

37. AEBa, *Correspondência expedida,* vol. 6, fol. 164.

38. Accioli, *Memórias históricas,* 4 : 346.

39. Viscount of Camamu to Minister of the Empire, Salvador, 17 December 1828.

40. Antônio Francisco de Barros to President of the Province, Itaparica, 1 January 1829, AEBa, *Juízes de Paz,* maço 2419; Viscount of Camamu to Minister of the Empire, Salvador, 5 November and 7 December 1829, AEBa, *Correspondência,* livro 678, fols. 14, 175.

41. Prince, "Slave Rebellion," 14–151; Marcescheau to French Minister of Foreign Affairs, Salvador, 20 January 1835, AMRE, *CP/Brésil,* vol. 16, fol. 15.

42. Luís Paulo de A. Bastos to Minister of Justice, 22 April 1830, AN, cod. IJJ1, 922. The slaveowners' protest was on 15 April 1830, or the date of dispatch by the president, AEBa, *Escravos (assuntos),* maço 2883.

43. Manoel Angelo Muniz Barreto to President of the Province, Pirajá, 7 September 1830 and 30 July 1831, AEBa, *Juízes,* maço 2681; Manoel Ferraz Pedreira to President of the Province, Iguape, 4 May 1831, AEBa, *Juízes. Iguape,* maço 2384.

44. Manoel Ferraz Pedreira to President of the Province, Iguape, 22 October 1831, AEBa, *Juízes. Iguape,* maço 2394.

45. Francisco Xavier de Barros to President of the Province, Itaparica, 1 December 1830, AEBa, *Juízes de Paz,* maço 2419.

46. Antônio Gomes de A. Guimarães to President of the Province, Salvador, 25 December 1830, Antônio Varella to President of the Province, Salvador, 29 December 1830, Pedro Manoel Barreto to President of the Province, Salvador, 29 December 1830, AEBa, *Juízes de Paz,* maço 2681; Consul Marescheau to French Ministry of Foreign Affairs, Salvador, 22 February 1831, AMRE, *CP/ Brésil,* vol. 12, fols. 206–7.

Chapter 4   The Battle for Bahia

1. Information on the events of the denunciation comes from "Devassa do levante de escravos ocorrido em Salvador em 1835," *Anais do Arquivo do Estado da Bahia* 38 (1968): 61–63; and "Peças processuais do levante dos malês," ibid. 40 (1971): 42–43. [These are key documents and will be referred to hereinafter as "Devassa" and "Peças processuais"—trans.]

2. Ibid.; President Francisco de Souza Martins to Minister of Justice, Salvador, 31 January 1835, AEBa, *Correspondência,* livro 681, fols. 195v–197v; Francisco Gonçalves Martins, "Relatório do chefe de polícia Francisco Gonçalves Martins," in Etienne Ignace Brazil, "Os Malês," *Revista do Instituto Histórico e Geográfico Brasileiro* 72 (1909): 116–17.

3. The story of the beginning of the rebellion is based mainly on testimony published in the "Peças processuais," 11ff., esp. 38ff.

4. The Trial of Pompeu, a Nagô, slave of José Pires de Carvalho e Albuquerque, AEBa, *Insurreições,* maço 2849, fols. 4v–5.

5. "Devassa," 65, 91; "Peças processuais," 43.

6. "Peças processuais," 43. For information on Sule's death in the first encounter see The Trial of Francisco, a Nagô, slave of the Sisters of the Mercês Convent, AEBa *Insurreições,* maço 2849, fol. 7; and "Devassa," 72 (testimony of Gaspar da Silva Cunha).

7. This testimony has been published in "Peças processuais," 40, 41, 43, 71–72.

8. President Martins to Minister of Justice, Salvador, 31 January 1835, fol. 196v.

9. "Devassa," 89.

10. Transcript of Trials at Conceição da Praia, AEBa, *Insurreições,* maço 2849, fol. 50v.

11. President Martins to Minister of Justice, Salvador, 31 January 1835, fol. 196v.

12. The Trial of Pompeu, fol. 4.

13. The Trial of Nécio, a Nagô, slave of Mellors Russell, AEBa, *Insurreições,* maço 2850, fols. 2v, 7v, 28–29, 44–48; Martins, "Relatório," 119.

14. The Trial of Nécio, fol. 44.

15. Ibid., fol. 28v; Consul John Parkinson to Duke of Wellington, Salvador, 29 January 1835, PRO/*FO,* 13, 21, fol. 39.

16. Martins, "Relatório," 120; "Devassa," 66, 86–91.

17. The Trial of Narciso, a Nagô, slave of José Maria de Souza Macieira, AEBa, *Insurreições,* maço 2846, fol. 10v.

18. This battle narrative is based on Martins, "Relatório," 117–18. Domingos's testimony can be found in the Transcripts of the Trials in Conceição da Praia, fol. 40v. The list of Africans caught fighting is found in The Trial of Lino, a Nagô, slave of José Soares de Castro, AEBa, *Insurreições,* maço 2846, fol. 4. In his letter to Wellington, Parkinson confirms the warship's participation (see above, n. 15).

19. Transcript of the Trials at Conceição da Praia, fol. 7. For information on Ratis's slaves see Martins, "Relatório," 118, as well as Magistrate Inocêncio Cardoso de Matos to President of the Province, Salvador, 25 and 27 January 1835, AEBa, *Juízes de Paz,* maço 2684.

20. Marcescheau to French Minister of Foreign Affairs, Salvador, 2 January 1835, AMRE, *CP/Brésil,* vol. 16, fol. 15. For the location of the plantations see Schwartz, *Sugar Plantations,* 311; and Pinho, *História de um engenho,* 171.

21. "Devassa," 130.

22. President Martins to Minister of Justice, 31 January 1835, fol. 197; Parkinson to Wellington, 29 January 1835; Marcescheau to French Minister of Foreign Affairs, Salvador, 26 and 29 January 1835.

23. André's quote comes from "Peças processuais," 49. For information on the gunsmith see "Devassa," 67. Two months after the uprising, two

bows and five arrows were found in the home of an English merchant named Abraham. These weapons seemed not to have been used. On the use of bows and arrows in Yorubaland, see J. F. A. Ajayi, "The Aftermath of the Fall of Oyo," in *History of West Africa*, 2 vols., ed. Ajayi and M. Crowder (London: Longman, 1974), 137; and Robin Law, *The Oyo Empire, c. 1600–c. 1836: A West African Imperialism in the Era of the Atlantic Slave Trade* (Oxford: Clarendon, 1977), 284.

24. The Trial of Higino, a Nagô, slave of José Maria Fonseca, AEBa, *Insurreições*, maço 2849, fol. 4; Trial of Nécio, fol. 34; Trial of Alexandre, a Jeje, slave of Domingos José Gonçalves Pena, ibid., maço 2848, fol. 9.

25. Marcescheau to French Minister of Foreign Affairs, 2 January 1835. Prince arrived at a similar estimate ("Slave Rebellion," 169). President Martins to Minister of Justice, 31 January 1835, fol. 197v. Brazil, "Os Malês," 92, estimated the number of conspirators to be fifteen hundred, but his counts are not based on any minimally reasonable evidence.

26. For Martins's estimates see his "Relatório," passim, and his "Supplemento à minha exposição dos acontecimentos do dia 7 de novembro," in *A revolução do dia 7 de novembro de 1837 (Sabinada)*, vol. 2 (Salvador: Arquivo do Estado da Bahia, 1938), 287–88; Parkinson to Wellington, 29 January 1835.

27. "Devassa," 68, 75. Transcript of the Trials at Conceição da Praia, fol. 3. The names of casualties were found in various places throughout the documentation pertaining to the rebellion and in Arquivo da Santa Casa de Misericórdia da Bahia (hereinafter ASCMB), *Livro do Bangüê, 1825–37*, vol. 1266, fols. 337v, 338, 338v. I have preserved the spelling of African or Islamic names found in Bahian documents.

28. This information has been culled from various parts of the documentation on the revolt. Only the families of Inocêncio José Cavalcante and Sergeant Tito Machado received indemnities, of 1,000 and 1,600 mil réis, respectively, from the government (Law 27, 23 June 1835). Cavalcante's widow died three years later, and his three daughters were remanded to an orphanage (Manoel José de F. Leite, the *provedor* of the Santa Casa to President of the Province, Salvador, 15 September 1868, AEBa, *Religião*, maço 5286). I am grateful to Sandra Lauderdale Graham and Richard Graham for this information.

Chapter 5 The Sons of Allah in Bahia

1. Martins, "Relatório," 122; President Martins to Minister of Justice, Salvador, 31 January 1835, *Correspondência*, livro 681, fol. 197.

2. M. G. Smith, "The Jihad of Shehu dan Fodio," in *Islam in Tropical Africa*, ed. I. M. Lewis (London: Oxford University Press, 1966), 296–315; J. S. Trimingham, *A History of Islam in West Africa* (London: Oxford University Press, 1970), 198ff.; H. A. S. Johnston, *The Fulani Empire of Sokoto* (Oxford: Oxford University Press, 1967), chaps. 4 and 5; Francis Castelnau, *Renseignments sur l'Afrique Centrale, etc.* (Paris: Bertrand, 1851), passim.

3. Ibid. See also Mahdi Adamu, "The Delivery of Slaves from the Central Sudan to the Bight of Benin," in *The Uncommon Market: Essays in the Economic*

History of the Atlantic Slave Trade, ed. H. A. Gemery and J. S. Hogendorn (New York: Academic Press, 1979), 176; and, in the same volume, Patrick Manning, "The Slave Trade in the Bight of Benin, 1640–1890," 127.

4. T. G. O. Gbadamosi, *The Growth of Islam among the Yoruba, 1841–1908* (Atlantic Highlands, N.J.: Humanities Press, 1978), 9.

5. Babatunde Agiri, "Slavery in Yoruba Society in the Nineteenth Century," in *The Ideology of Slavery in Africa,* ed. Paul E. Lovejoy (Beverly Hills: Sage, 1981), 136.

6. Allan G. B. Fisher and Humphrey J. Fisher, *Slavery and Muslim Society in Africa* (Garden City, N.Y.: Anchor, 1972), 36–37 and passim; Smith, *Kingdoms of the Yoruba,* chaps. 10 and 11; Law, *Oyo Empire,* pt. 3.

7. Agiri, "Slavery," 137.

8. Braz do Amaral's suggestion is quoted in Roger Bastide, *As religiões africanas do Brasil,* 2 vols. (São Paulo: Editora Pioneira and Editora da Universidade de São Paulo, 1971), 1:203 n. 3. See also Raymond K. Kent, "African Revolt in Bahia," *Journal of Social History* 3 (Summer 1970): 356; Rodrigues, *Os africanos,* 104; Verger, *Flux et reflux,* 352 n. 24; and Vincent Monteil, "Anályse de 25 documents árabes des Malés de Bahia (1835)," *Bulletin de l'Institut Fondamentale d'Afrique Noire,* ser. B, 29, nos. 1–2 (1967): 88. The best critical study is by Vivaldo da Costa Lima and is reproduced in Vânia M. C. de Alvim, "Movimentos proféticos, prepolíticos e contraculturais dos negros islamizados na Bahia do século 19" (Master's thesis, Universidade Federal da Bahia, 1975), 21–29. Lima discusses the term *muçurumim* or *musulmi.* The words come from Hausa and quite likely were used in Bahia during the early nineteenth century; however, they have not been documented in the written records of the period. Kathleen M. Stasik suggested the derivation of *imale* from *Mali* (see Stasik, "A Decisive Acquisition: The Development of Islam in Nineteenth-century Iwo, Southeast Oyo" [Master's thesis, University of Minnesota, 1975], 83). Bastide confused *Malê* with *Malinke* or *Mandingo* in Brazil, and Manoel Querino, *A raça africana e seus costumes* (Salvador: Editora Progresso, 1955), 113, also erroneously considered the Malês a specific ethnic group. On Labat's ethnic classification, see Manning, "Slave Trade in the Bight of Benin," 126–27.

9. Concerning black *irmandades* in Bahia see João José Reis, *A morte é uma festa: ritos fúnebres e revolta popular no Brasil do século XIX* (São Paulo: Companhia das Letras, 1991), chap. 2. For more information on traditional African religion, or Candomblé, in Bahia of the 1830s see João José Reis and Eduardo Silva, *Negociação e conflito* (São Paulo: Companhia das Letras, 1989), chap. 3. In Nagô candomblé, *bori* is the name of an initiation ritual (also known as "feeding the head") linked to religious initiation (see Querino, *A raça africana,* 60–63: and esp. Roger Bastide, *Le Candomblé de Bahia* [*rite nagô*] [Paris: Mouton, 1958], 25–28, and Pierre Verger, "Bori, primeira cerimônia de iniciação ao culto dos Orişá nagô na Bahia, Brasil," in *Olóórìṣà,* ed. C. E. M. de Moura [São Paulo: Ágora, 1981], 33–56).

10. Martins, "Relatório," 121.

11. "Devassa," 69–70.

12. The Trial of Antônio, a Hausa, slave of Bernardino José da Costa, AEBa, *Insurreições*, maço 2848, fol. 20.

13. The Trial of Gaspar, a Nagô, slave of Domingos Lopes Ribeiro, ibid., maço 2846, fol. 5; The Trial of Nécio, fol. 29; "Peças processuais," 72.

14. Bastide, *As religiões africanas*, 1:217, speaks of Malê passivity. J. S. Trimingham, *Islam in West Africa* (Oxford: Oxford University Press, 1959), chaps. 2 and 5, discusses the interaction between Islam and ethnic religions; he mentions the generalized use of Islamic amulets by non-Muslims (35). See Law, *Oyo Empire*, 257, concerning the faith Afonja had in these amulets. For the citation in the previous paragraph see John McLeod, *A Voyage to Africa with some Account of the Manners and Customs of the Dahomian People* (London: John Murray, 1820), 94–95. Stasik also discusses the tradition of attributing power to Muslim amulets ("Decisive Acquisition," 10, 54). The quote from Rodrigues comes from his *O animismo fetichista dos negros baianos* (Rio de Janeiro: Civilização Brasileira, 1935), 29. There were an impressive number of Malê "sorcerers" around the turn of the twentieth century in Rio de Janeiro (see João do Rio's *As religiões do Rio* [Rio de Janeiro: Editora Nova Aguilar, 1976], esp. chap. 1). These amulets were used throughout Brazil during the eighteenth century, especially in Bahia. They were called *bolsas de mandinga* ("Mandingo purses") even when their magical contents included strong folk Catholic prayers rather than Islamic writings. Possession of these "purses" was a crime punishable by the Inquisition (see Souza, *O diabo*, 210–26, esp. 219–21, where she discusses Bahia. For more information on the use of Malê talismans in Rio de Janeiro see Mary Karasch, *Slave Life in Rio de Janeiro, 1808–1850* [Princeton: Princeton University Press, 1987], 263).

15. The Trial of Lobão Maxado, Nagô-Ibo, ex-slave, AEBa, *Insurreições*, maço 2847, fol. 4.

16. Vincent Monteil, "Marabouts," in *Islam in Africa*, ed. J. Kritzeck and W. H. Lewis (New York: Van Nostrand–Reinhold, 1969), 95.

17. Vincent Monteil, "Anályse de 25 documents árabes," 88–89; Rolf Reichert, *Os documentos árabes do Arquivo do Estado da Bahia* (Salvador: Centro de Estudos Afro-Orientais, Universidade Federal da Bahia, 1979); idem, "L'insurrection d'esclaves de 1835 á la lumière des documents árabes des archives publique de l'Etat de Bahia (Brésil)," *Bulletin de l'Institut Fondamental d'Afrique Noire*, ser. B, 29, nos. 1–2 (1967): 99–104.

18. See Reichert, *Os documentos árabes*, nos. 29, 19, 21. The numbers in parentheses represent the lines in the original documents and are Reichert's.

19. The Trial of Silvestre José Antônio, a Hausa freedman, AEBa, *Insurreições*, maço 2849, fol. 6v; The Trial of José Gomes, a Hausa, and Pedro Pinto, Nagô, both freedmen, ibid., fol. 10.

20. For a good discussion on *isköki*, on their different types, nature, and power, as well as their relation to Islamic beliefs, see Greenberg, *Influence of Islam*, 27ff.; see also Trimingham, *Islam in West Africa*, 35–36, 54–55, 60, 63, 111, 155, and passim. For information on Yoruba counterparts of these spirits see Juana Elbein dos Santos, *Os nagô e a morte* (Petrópolis, Brazil: Vozes, 1976), 55ff. João do Rio identified the *aligenum* as "diabolical spirits to be

evoked for both good and evil [and found] in a book of magic (*livro de sortes*) which was marked here and there with red ink" (*As religiões do Rio*, 23). Concerning the belief that the wind brought illness, a common belief among slaves in southern Brazil, see Emília Viotti da Costa, *Da senzala à colônia* (São Paulo: Difusão Européia do Livro, 1966), 254. The "wind" was an important element in African divination practices throughout Brazil (see Souza, *O diabo*, 27, 266, 353). The quotes from Africans come from the Trial of Lobão Maxado, fol. 4; and The Trial of José, a Nagô-Ibo, slave of Gey de Carter, AEBa, *Insurreições*, maço 2847, fol. 9.

21. For more information on the amulet trade in Africa see Monteil, "Marabouts," 95; and Trimingham, *Islam in West Africa*, 81. The quotes in this paragraph come from The Trial of Antônio, AEBa, *Insurreições*, maço 2848, fol. 6v.

22. Marcescheau to French Minister of Foreign Affairs, Salvador, 26 January 1835, AMRE, *CP/Brésil*, vol. 16, fol. 16v.

23. "Devassa," 75. Samuel Johnson claims the *aqbada* was always made from colored cloth, whereas the *suliya* was made of white cloth (see *The History of the Yorubas* [London: Routledge & Kegan Paul, 1921], 111). However, the Yoruba pioneer historian seems to have been wrong: according to Stasik, "Decisive Acquisition," vi, an aqbada is a white Muslim garment.

24. The Trial of Higino; Transcript of the Trials at Conçeição da Praia, fol. 26v.

25. Johnson, *History of the Yorubas*, 194; The Trial of Cornélio, a Nagô, slave of João Firmiano Caldeira, AEBa, *Insurreições*, maço 2847, fol. 15; Transcript of the Trials at Conceição da Praia, fol. 66; Querino, *A raça africana*, 108. Costa maintains that during the 1870s silver rings were worn by members of black secret societies in southern Brazil (*Da senzala*, 279).

26. "Peças processuais," 108.

27. Ibid., 107. In 1835 Titara wrote, perhaps not merely coincidentally, his famous poem "Paraguaçu," praising Bahian independence. I thank Luciano Diniz and Paulo César Souza for this reminder.

28. Concerning these Malês' activities see "Peças processuais," 15–16; Transcript of the Trials at Conceição da Praia, fols. 28v ff.; The Trial of Nécio, fol. 15v; "Devassa," 7–9, 74ff.; Brazil, "Os Malês," 85 (for *machachalis*).

29. Quotes from the *Koran* come from N. J. Dawood's translation (Harmondsworth: Penguin, 1974).

30. Trimingham, *Islam in West Africa*, passim; Brazil, "Os Malês," 77–88. Concerning the black and red ink see Manoel Joaquim de Almeida to President of the Province, Salvador, 29 January 1835, AEBa, *Juízes de Paz*, maço 2684; see also Wetherell, *Stray Notes from Bahia*, 138.

31. Reichert, *Os documentos*, nos. 8 and 15 (Reichert's book has no page numbers).

32. The stages of initiation into Islam are discussed in Trimingham, *Islam in West Africa*, 34ff. Gaspar's citation comes from "Devassa," 35. See also Querino, *A raça africana*, 103; The Trial of José, slave of Gey de Carter, fol. 2; Transcript of the Trials at Conceição da Praia, fol. 14v. The scribe wrote: "a black rosary without a cross at the end and known as a pagan's rosary" (ibid., fol. 70).

33. Trimingham, *Islam in West Africa,* 73. Vincent Monteil (*L'Islam noir* [Paris: Seuil, 1971], 175–76) cites these suras from the *Koran,* but he argues that in black Africa Muslim women are independent and play important roles in some communities. Querino, *A raça africana,* 107. For information on Muslim women in Rio see Bastide, *As religiões africanas,* 1:210–11.

34. The Trial of Nécio, fols. 35v, 61; "Devassa," 8.

35. Trimingham, *Islam in West Africa,* 75, 80, 174; "Devassa," 131; Querino, *A raça africana,* 110–11.

36. For the conversion of dates from Muslim to Christian calendars, I have used G. S. P. Freeman-Greenville, *The Muslim and Christian Calendars* (London: Oxford University Press, 1963); The Trial of Nécio, fol. 18.

37. The Trial of Nécio, fols. 16, 44–45.

38. Ibid., fol. 20v; The Trial of Antônio, fol. 9v.

39. "Peças processuais," 33; "Devassa," 131; The Trial of Cornélio, fol. 15.

Chapter 6   A Bahian Caliphate? The Malês and Their Rebellion

1. "Devassa," 34.

2. Transcript of the Trials at Conceição da Praia, fol. 67.

3. Marcescheau to French Minister of Foreign Affairs, Salvador, 29 January 1835, AMRE, *CP/Brésil,* vol. 16, fol. 22–22v.

4. Trial of José, a Nagô-Jabu, a slave of José Maria da Silva, AEBa, *Insurreições,* maço 2846, fol. 6v; "Peças processuais," 8.

5. "Devassa," 73; The Trial of Nécio, fols. 18, 28v.

6. "Devassa," 130; "Peças processuais," 13.

7. "Devassa," 130; Rodrigues, *Os africanos,* 95.

8. Rodrigues, *Os africanos,* 86; "Devassa," 89–90; The Trial of Urbano, a Bornu, slave of Jacinta Joaquina da Silva e Sá, AEBa, *Insurreições,* maço 2850, fol. 5.

9. Freeman-Greenville, *Muslim and Christian Calendars.* Trimingham (*Islam in West Africa,* 78) translates *Qadr* as "power," whereas N. J. Dawood, the translator of the Penguin edition of the *Koran,* translates it as "glory."

10. Inves-Marie Bercé, *Fête et revolte* (Paris: Hachette, 1976), 50.

11. I. M. Lewis, "Introduction" to *Islam in Tropical Africa,* 70. See Trimingham, *Islam in West Africa,* 78, as well.

12. De la Rosière to French Minister of Foreign Affairs, Rio de Janeiro, 13 March 1835, AMRE, *CP/Brésil,* vol. 16, fols. 52v–53.

13. Monteil, "Anályse de 25 documents árabes," 94.

14. "Devassa," 62, 130.

15. There is considerable literature on slavery in Africa. Some important titles are: Paul E. Lovejoy, *Transformations in Slavery: A History of Slavery in Africa* (Cambridge: Cambridge University Press, 1983); Lovejoy, ed., *Ideology of Slavery in Africa;* Claude Meillassoux, ed., *L'esclavage en Afrique pre-coloniale* (Paris: Maspero, 1975); Suzanne Meier and Igor Kopytoff, eds., *Slavery in Africa* (Madison: University of Wisconsin Press, 1977); Fisher and Fisher, *Slavery and Muslim Society in Africa;* Claire C. Robertson and Martin A. Klein, eds., *Women and Slavery in Africa* (Madison: University of Wisconsin Press, 1983).

Concerning Mohammed see Castelnau, *Reseignments,* 39; concerning Solomon, Douglas Grant, *The Fortunate Slave* (London: Oxford University Press, 1968).

16. In a sample of 492 nineteenth-century ex-slaves leaving wills, nearly 63 percent owned slaves (see Maria Inês C. de Oliveira, *O liberto: seu mundo e os outros* [São Paulo: Corrupio, 1988], 41).

17. See The Trial of Nécio, fol. 28v; The Trial of José, fol. 3–3v; "Devassa," 36, 70, 73; and "Peças processuais," 27, 30.

18. Rodrigues, *Os africanos,* 66–67. See also Brazil, "Os Malês," 91; Arthur Ramos, *O negro na civilização brasileira* (Rio de Janeiro: Casa do Estudante, 1971), 52–53; Verger, *Flux et reflux,* 326–27; Bastide, *As religiões africanas,* 1:150–55; Jack Goody, "Writing, Religion, and Revolt in Bahia," *Visible Language* 20 (1986): 318–43.

19. [This is not the only linguistic coincidence between Bahian orisha cults and Islam. The name Oxalá is homophonous with Portuguese *oxalá* "may God will it," which comes from Arabic *wa sha illah,* both meaning "may God will it," an expression of Islamic origin and propagation in the Iberian Peninsula—trans.]

20. For the association of Muslims with white orishas see Stasik, "Decisive Acquisition," 96–97, 104–5. See also Bastide, *As religiões africanas,* 1:216–17. For Obatalá/Oxalá's relationship to whiteness and water see Santos, *Os nagô e a morte,* 58–59, 70, 75–79, et passim. On the alcohol taboo see E. Balaji Idowu, *Olódúmarè: God in Yoruba Belief* (London: Longmans, 1962), 151.

21. Stasik, "Decisive Acquisition," 106.

22. Bernard Maupoil, *La géomancie á l'ancienne Côte des Esclaves* (Paris: Institute d'Ethnologie, 1981), 537. According to Maupoil, *tula-meji* is the thirteenth *odu,* not the twelfth as Stasik maintains.

23. Cited in William Bascom, *Sixteen Cowries: Yoruba Divination from Africa to the New World* (Bloomington: Indiana University Press, 1980), 207.

24. Stasik, "Decisive Acquisition," 97.

25. Bastide, *As religiões africanas,* 1: chap. 7, esp. 214–16.

26. Arquivo Municipal de Salvador, *Atas da Câmara, 1833–35,* vol. 9.41, fols. 164v, 166v.

27. For more on the cult of Bonfim and for a hostile vision of *lavagem* see Carlos Alberto de Carvalho, *Tradições e milagres do Bonfim* (Salvador: Typographia Baiana, 1915). Manoel Querino is more sympathetic to lavagem and criticizes its prohibition at the end of the nineteenth century in *A Bahia de outrora* (Salvador: Livraria Econômica, 1922), 133–46.

28. Kent, "African Revolt in Bahia," 355. Dan Fodio repudiated pagan participation in the jihad, although many pagans fought on his side against King Yunfa (see Usuman Dan Fodio, *Bayān Wujūb al-Hijra 'Ala 'L-'Ibad,* ed. and trans. F. H. El Masri as *The Exposition of the Obligation of Emigration upon the Servants of God* [New York: Oxford University Press, 1978], chap. 20, 89 n. 1). This paragraph and the following one are based on João José Reis and P. F. de Moraes Farias, "Islam and Slave Resistance in Bahia, Brazil," *Islam et sociétés au sud du Sahara* 3 (1989): 56–58, and bibliography therein cited. For a detailed discussion of the historiography of the 1835 rebellion see also João José Reis,

"Um balanço dos estudos sobre as revoltas escravas baianas," in Reis, ed., *Escravidão e invenção da liberdade* (São Paulo: Brasiliense, 1988), 87–140.

Chapter 7 Malê Profiles

1. According to Islamic doctrine, "some types of basic products cannot be owned" (Maxime Rodison, *Islam and Capitalism*, trans. Brian Pearce [London: Allen Lane and Penguin, 1974], 15).
2. "Devassa," 36, 51, 73, 82.
3. Ibid., 62, 63, 73.
4. Ibid., 73.
5. Greenberg, *Influence of Islam*, 66.
6. Rodrigues, *Os africanos*, 88, 94.
7. "Devassa," 49, 90, 132–33, and passim.
8. For all of Francisco's declarations see ibid., 83–84.
9. Ibid., 89.
10. Ibid.
11. Ibid., 90.
12. For Licutan's interrogation see ibid., 48–49. For information on *muezzins* in West Africa see Trimingham, *Islam in West Africa*, 71.
13. "Devassa," 70, 71, 132.
14. Ibid., 73.
15. Ibid., 74, 122.
16. "Peças processuais," 41.
17. Transcript of the Trials at Conceição da Praia, fols. 29, 40v.
18. Ibid., fols. 29, 66v, 68.
19. The Trial of Nécio, fols. 18, 20v. This man is not Vitório Sule, Sabina's consort, the one killed on Ladeira da Praça. Freitas confuses them: *Insurreições escravas*, 77.
20. The Trial of Luís, a Nagô, slave of Domingos Pereira Monteiro, AEBa, *Insurreições*, maço 2847, fol. 20.
21. Trimingham, *Islam in West Africa*, 68.
22. See Prince, "Slave Rebellion," 201–6.
23. The Trial of José, a Nagô-Jabu, slave of José Maria da Silva, fol. 3–3v. The Trial of Luís, a Nagô, slave of Guilherme Benne, AEBa, *Insurreições*, maço 2847, fol. 4.

Chapter 8 Roots: Ethnic Motivation in 1835

1. Concerning Bahian slave trade see Luiz Vianna Filho, *O negro na Bahia* (Rio de Janeiro: José Olympio, 1946); and Verger, *Flux et reflux*. Concerning the African end of the slave trade see Manning, "Slave Trade in the Bight of Benin, 1640–1890," esp. 137.
2. Accioli, *Memórias históricas*, 3:288 n. 26.
3. E. Adeniyi Oroge, "The Institution of Slavery in Yorubaland with Particular Reference to the Nineteenth Century" (Ph.D. diss., University of Birmingham, England, 1971), 90–91; J. F. Ade Ajayi and Robert Smith, *Yoruba*

Warfare in the Nineteenth Century (Ibadan: Cambridge University Press and Institute of African Studies, University of Ibadan, 1971), esp. 13–15.

4. Of native-born slaves in Salvador between 1820 and 1835, 72 percent were blacks *(crioulos)*, 16.6 percent were mulattos, and 11.2 percent were "faded" blacks *(cabras)* (see Maria José da Silva Andrade, "A mão de obra escrava em Salvador de 1811 a 1860" [Master's thesis, Universidade Federal da Bahia, 1975], appendix table 4).

5. For more on this subject see Eugene D. Genovese, *From Rebellion to Revolution: Afro-American Slave Revolts in the Making of the New World* (New York: Vintage, 1979), 18–19 and passim. See also João José Reis, "'Poderemos folgar, brincar e cantar': o protesto escravo nas Américas," *Afro-Ásia* 14 (December 1983): 107–23.

6. Lígia Bellini, "Por amor e por interesse: a relação senhor-escravo em cartas de alforria," in Reis, *Escravidão e invenção,* 73–86; Kátia M. de Queirós Mattoso, "A propósito de cartas de alforria," *Anais de história* 4 (1972): 23–52; Stuart B. Schwartz, "The Manumission of Slaves in Colonial Brazil: Bahia, 1684–1745," *Hispanic American Historical Review* 57 (November 1974): 603–35.

7. Antônio Gomes de Abreu Guimarães to Viscount of Camamu, 28 August 1829, AEBa, *Juízes de paz,* maço 2688. The italics in the quote are mine. I have analyzed this document in more detail in Reis and Silva, *Negociação e conflito,* chap. 3.

8. Raymond Bauer and Alice Bauer, "Day-to-day Resistance to Slavery," in *American Slavery: The Question of Resistance,* ed. John H. Bracey (Belmont, Calif.: Wadsworth, 1971), 37–60; Maria Bárbara Pinto Garcez to Luiz Paulino de Oliveira Pinto da França, 2 March 1822, in França, *Cartas baianas,* 19; Henry Koster, *Travels in Brazil* (London: Longman, Hurst, Rees, Orme & Brown, 1816), 424, 434. George M. Frederickson and Christopher Lasch consider insubordination and boycotting forms of conformity in their article "Resistance to Slavery," in *American Negro Slavery: A Modern Reader,* ed. Allen Weinstein and Frank O. Gatell (New York: Oxford University Press, 1973), 118–33. I do not agree.

9. Rodrigues, *O animismo fetichista dos negros baianos,* 171.

10. Schwartz, "Resistance and Accommodation," 80.

11. See Reis and Silva, *Negociação e conflito,* chap. 5.

12. The Trial of Claudina Maria da Conceição, a Nupe, freedwoman, AEBa, *Insurreições,* maço 2849, fol. 14; The Trial of Pedro Pinto, a Nagô, freedman, ibid., fols. 20v–21; Transcript of the Trials at Conçeição da Praia, ibid., fol. 36v; The Trial of Antônio, a Hausa, freedman, ibid., fol. 3v; The Trial of Nécio, fol. 96v; The Trial of Manoel, a Nagô, slave of João Crisóstomo P. da Silva, ibid., maço 2850, fol. 9v; "Devassa," 35, 49, 89; Martins, "Relatório," 116; President Martins to Minister of Justice, 31 January 1835, AEBa, *Correspondência,* livro 681, fol. 197–197v. Parkinson to Wellington, 2 January 1835, PRO/*FO,* 13, 121, fol. 37; Marcescheau to French Ministry of Foreign Affairs, 29 January and 13 March 1835, AMRE, *CP/Brésil,* vol. 16, fols. 21v, 53.

13. The Trial of Manoel, a Nagô, slave of José Monteiro, AEBa, *Insurreições,* maço 2849, fol. 3v; The Trial of Pompeu, fol. 5.

14. Concerning the conflict between Dahomey and the Oyo empire see Law, *Oyo Empire*.

15. Authors who have accepted the theory that Angolas are peaceful and inferior include Johan B. Spix and Karl von Martius, *Viagem pelo Brasil*, 3 vols. (São Paulo: Melhoramentos, 1976), 2:141; Thomas Lindley, *Narrativa de uma viagem ao Brasil (1805)* (São Paulo: Editora Nacional, 1969), 176; Koster, *Travels in Brazil*, 421; Rodrigues, *Os africanos*, 57–58, 62, and passim; Ramos, *O negro na civilização brasileira*, 36–37; Vianna Filho, *O negro na Bahia*, esp. chap. 4; and Freitas, *Insurreições escravas*, 18–21.

16. Walter Rodney, "Upper Guinea and the Significance of the Origins of Africans Enslaved in the New World," *Journal of Negro History* 54 (Autumn 1969): 341ff.

17. Reis, "População e rebelião"; Maria José da Silva Andrade, *A mão de obra escrava em Salvador, 1811–1860* (São Paulo: Corrupio, 1988).

18. Concerning brotherhoods see Mattoso, *Etre esclave au Brésil*, 169–71; A. J. R. Russell-Wood, "Black and Mulatto Brotherhoods in Colonial Brazil: A Study in Collective Behavior," *Hispanic American Historical Review* 54 (November 1974): 567–602; Jefferson A. Bacelar and Maria da Conceição de Souza, "O Rosário dos Pretos do Pelourinho" (Salvador: Fundação do Patrimônio Artístico e Cultural da Bahia, 1974, mimeographed); Julita Scarano, *Devoção e escravidão* (São Paulo: Editora Nacional, 1975); and Patricia Mulvey, "The Black Lay Brotherhoods of Colonial Brazil" (Ph.D. diss., City University of New York, 1976). For descriptions of the coronation of a Congo "king" see Luiz da Câmara Cascudo, *Antologia do folclore brasileiro* (São Paulo: Martins, 1956), 67–69; and Rodrigues, *Os africanos*, 52–54. Cf. Joseph P. Reidy's analysis in his "Negro Election Day and Black Community Life in New England, 1750–1860," *Marxist Perspectives* 1, no. 3 (October 1978): 102–17.

19. Reis, *A morte é uma festa*, chap. 2.

20. See note 7.

21. Ibid.

22. George P. Murdock, *Africa: Its People and Their Cultural History* (New York: McGraw-Hill, 1959), 242–58, 290–302; Philip Curtin et al., *African History* (Boston: Little, Brown, 1978), 238–44, 261–68; Jan Vansina, *The Kingdoms of the Savanna* (Madison: University of Wisconsin Press, 1966).

23. Concerning processes in the creation of Afro-American cultures see Richard Price and Sidney Mintz, *An Anthropological Approach to the Afro-American Past: A Caribbean Perspective* (Philadelphia: Institute for the Study of Human Issues, 1976).

24. Both Antonio and José were slaves of Brigadier Manoel Gonçalves da Cunha (see The Trial of José, a Nagô, slave of José Maria da Silva, AEBa, *Insurreições*, maço 2846, fol. 3, and The Trial of José, a Nagô from Egba, slave of Gey de Carter, ibid., fol. 6v; and "Devassa," 6, 7, 63. See also Verger, *Flux et reflux*, 520). On the etymology of *nagô*, see Vivaldo de Costa Lima, "A família-de-santo nos candomblés jeje-nagôs da Bahia: um estudo de relações intra-grupais" (master's thesis, Universidad Federal da Bahia, 1977), 15–16.

25. Concerning Yoruba names see Johnson, *History of the Yorubas*, pt. 1,

chap. 5; Isaac O. Delano, *The Soul of Nigeria* (London: T. W. Laurie, 1937), chap. 12; and J. A. Ayorinde, "Oriki," in *Sources of Yoruba History,* ed. S. O. Biobaku (Oxford: Clarendon, 1973), 63–76.

26. "Devassa," 79, 80, 91, 93.

27. Ibid., 34; "Peças processuais," 37; The Trial of Gaspar, a Nagô, slave of Domingos Lopes Ribeiro, fol. 5v.

28. "Devassa," 140; Transcript of the Trials at Conceição da Praia, fol. 111v.

29. The quotes in this paragraph come from The Trial of Nécio, fol. 42; and "Devassa," 136.

Chapter 9   Workers, Slave and Freed:
Occupational Profile of the Accused

1. Kátia M. de Queirós Mattoso, "Os escravos na Bahia no alvorecer do século 19 (estudo de um grupo social)," *Revista de história* 97 (1974): 125–26; Andrade, "A mão de obra," 117. I alternately cite Andrade's masters thesis and her book of the same title because they provide different information.

2. Spix and Martius, *Viagem pelo Brasil,* 2:141; Andrade, "A mão de obra," 118, 120.

3. Vilhena, *A Bahia no século 18,* 1:93, 127, 129–30; Daniel P. Kidder, *Sketches of Residence and Travels in Brazil,* 2 vols. (London: Sorin & Ball and Wiley Putnam, 1845), 2:25.

4. Maria Graham, *Journal of a Voyage to Brazil and Residence There during Part of the Years 1821, 1822, 1823* (New York: Praeger, 1969), 133.

5. Kidder, *Sketches of Residence,* 2:20–21.

6. Randolph, *Life of General Sir Robert Wilson,* 1:344.

7. Wetherell, *Stray Notes from Bahia,* italics in the original.

8. J. da Silva Campos, "Ligeiras notas sobre a vida íntima, costumes, e religião dos africanos na Bahia," *Anais do Arquivo do Estado da Bahia* 29 (1943): 294.

9. E. P. Thompson, "Time, Work-Discipline, and Industrial Capitalism," *Past and Present* 38 (December 1967): 61.

10. Concerning the *parakoyi* see Gbadamosi, *Growth of Islam,* 2; and Smith, *Kingdoms of the Yoruba,* 116. Concerning the craft *bale,* see Peter Lloyd, "Craft Organization in Yoruba Towns," *Africa* 23 (January 1953): 34. "Querino, *A raça africana,* 88–89, describes the investiture of the African labor captain. See also Bastide, *As religiões africanas,* 1:76.

11. Johnson, *History of the Yorubas,* 119.

12. Alfred Ellis, *The Yoruba-speaking Peoples of the Slave Coast of West Africa* (Oosterhout, Netherlands: Anthropological Publications, 1966), 150.

13. "Devassa," 8, 69.

14. Andrade, *A mão de obra,* 139–43.

15. Transcript of the Trials at Conceição da Praia, fols. 44, 79; The Trial of Rufino João Portugal, a Hausa freedman, et al., AEBa, *Insurreições,* maço 2849, fol. 6–6v. The Islamic proverb comes from Rodison, *Islam and Capitalism,* 16.

16. Querino, *A raça africana*, 87; "Peças processuais," 53–54, 108.

17. Oliveira, *O liberto*, 18. See also Andrade, *A mão de obra*, 131–32.

18. "Devassa," 20–23, 28, 137; Transcript of the Trials at Conceição da Praia, fol. 23; The Trial of Antônio, a Hausa, slave of Bernardino José da Costa, fol. 6v; The Trial of Ivã, a Nagô, slave of Francisco Lacciaque, AEBa, *Insurreições*, maço 2846, fol. 1. Each Malê amulet cost 320 réis. See Marcescheau to French Ministry of Foreign Affairs, 2 January 1835, *CP/Brésil*, fol. 16v.

19. The Trial of Rufino Portugal et al., fols. 4–6v.

20. "Devassa," 136.

21. Oroge, "Institution of Slavery in Yorubaland," 197.

22. The Trial of Domingos, a Hausa, slave of João Pinto Coelho, AEBa, *Insurreições*, maço 2849.

23. The Trial of Higino; Transcript of the Trials at Conceição da Praia, fol. 209.

24. "Devassa," 85.

25. AEBa, *Legislativa. Abaixo-assinados, 1835–36*, maço 979.

26. "Peças processuais," 108.

27. The Trial of Pacífico Licutan, a Nagô, slave of Antônio Pinto de M. Varella, AEBa, *Insurreições*, maço 2846, fol. 5v.

Chapter 10   Making Do: Africans away from Work

1. See, e.g., Oliveira, *O liberto;* Mattoso, *Etre esclave au Brésil* and *Família e sociedade*, passim.

2. Between 1829–30 and 1835–36 there was a 26 percent increase in the number of letters of manumission registered with notary publics in Salvador (Mattoso, "A propósito de cartas de alforria," 41, table 4).

3. "Peças processuais," passim.

4. Oliveira, *O liberto*, 36, 37. Concerning the census results see Ana de Lourdes Costa, "*Ekabó!* Trabalho escravo e condições de moradia e reordenamento urbano em Salvador no século 19" (Master's thesis, Universidade Federal da Bahia, 1989), 204–5.

5. "Devassa," 35, 69–70; "Peças processuais," 19.

6. "Devassa," 7–10.

7. Transcript of the Trials at Conceição da Praia, fols. 18, 187–88.

8. The Trial of Luís Vieira, a Nagô freedman, AEBa, *Insurreições*, maço 2847; The Trial of Urbano, fol. 8.

9. Transcript of the Trials in Santana Parish, AEBa, *Insurreições*, maço 2846, passim; The Trial of Rufino Portugal, passim; "Devassa," 6 (freedman living with former master), 138 (Hausa peddlers); "Peças processuais," 35 (freedman living with former master), passim (Calafate's house).

10. "Devassa," 72–73, 135, 138–39.

11. Ibid., 20; Transcript of the Trials at Conceição da Praia, fol. 29 and passim.

12. Transcript of the Trials at Conceição da Praia, fol. 120v.

13. Luiz Roberto de Barros Mott, "Revendo a história da escravidão no Brasil," *Mensário do Arquivo Nacional* 127 (1980): 25.

14. Oliveira, *O liberto*, 110–12; Transcript of the Trials at Conceição da Praia, fol. 116.

15. For studies on homosexuality under slavery in colonial Brazil see Luiz Roberto de Barros Mott: "Escravidão e homossexualidade," in *História e sexualidade no Brasil*, ed. R. Vainfas (Rio de Janeiro: Graal, 1986), 19–40; *O sexo proibido* (Campinas, São Paulo: Papirus, 1988); and *Escravidão, homossexualidade e demonologia* (São Paulo: Icone, 1988).

16. Transcript of the Trials at Santana, fols. 4ff.; "Devassa," 63, 137.

17. Oliveira, *O liberto*, 62 and chap. 2; Murray Last, "Reform in West Africa: The Jihad Movements of the Nineteenth Century," in Ajayi and Crowder, *History of West Africa*, 1:24 (offspring of Fodio and Bello); "Devassa," 70–71.

18. "Devassa," 36, 83, 100. On the loyalty among *malungo* slaves see Koster, *Travels in Brazil*, 417.

19. Transcript of the Trials at Santana, fol. 67; "Devassa," 35, 137.

20. Transcript of the Trials at Santana, fol. 21; "Devassa," 62, 63, 136.

21. Ibid., 62.

22. Concerning kinship in West Africa see Murdock, *Africa*, 143, 246–48, 255–56. Concerning candomblé kinship in Salvador see Vivaldo da Costa Lima, "A família-de-santo nos candomblés jeje-nagôs da Bahia: um estudo de relações intra-grupais" (Master's thesis, Universidade Federal da Bahia, 1977).

23. Eric J. Hobsbawm, *Revolutionaries: Contemporary Essays* (New York: Pantheon, 1973), 223.

24. Herbert Gutman, *The Black Family in Slavery and Freedom* (New York: Pantheon, 1976), 223–24 and passim.

Chapter 11 The Repression after the Uprising

1. Braz Cordeiro to President of the Province, Salvador, 31 January 1835, and Custódio Ribeiro to President of the Province, Salvador, 2 February 1835, AEBa, *Juízes de paz*, maço 2684; João Nepomuceno Rocha to Justice of the Peace of the First District of Itaparica, 6 February 1835, ibid., maço 2419; Parkinson to Wellington, Salvador, 26 and 29 January, 2 February 1835, PRO/*FO*, 13, 121, fols. 37, 39, 40, 41; Marcescheau to French Ministry of Foreign Affairs, Salvador, 29 January 1835, fol. 37, AMRE, *CP/Brésil*, vol. 16, fol. 23; Consul Francisco António Filgueiras to Portuguese Ministry of Foreign Affairs, Salvador, 9 May 1835, ANTT, *Ministério dos Negócios Estrangeiros. Consulados de Portugal, Baía*, caixa 1.

2. Official correspondence of Justice of the Peace in the First District of São Pedro with Chief of Police, Salvador, 28 March 1835, AEBa, *Chefe de polícia*, maço 2949; Chief of Police Martins to President Martins, Salvador, 28 January 1835, ibid.

3. Marcescheau to French Ministry of Foreign Affairs, 29 January 1835, AMRE, *CP/Brésil*, vol. 16, fol. 22v.

4. H. S. Fox to Palmerston, Rio de Janeiro, 11 February 1835, PRO/*FO*, 13,

117, fol. 59; Robert Avé-Lallemant, *Viagens pelas províncias da Bahia, Pernambuco, Alagoas e Sergipe (1859)* (Belo Horizonte, Brazil: Itatiaia, 1980), 50.

5. Transcript of the Trials at Conceição da Praia, fols. 4, 109v, 129v, 209.

6. Arnold Wildberger, *Os presidentes da província da Bahia* (Salvador: Typographia Beneditina, 1949), 147ff.; *Colleção de leis e resoluções da Assembléia Legislativa da Bahia, 1835–1841,* 2 vols. (Salvador: Typographia de Antônio O. de França Guerra, 1862), 1:2.

7. Transcript of the Trials at Conceição da Praia, fol. 2v.

8. Wildberger, *Os presidentes,* 315ff.; Martins, "Supplemento à minha exposição dos acontecimentos," 267 n. 44.

9. The Trial of Nécio, fol. 6v; *Colleção de leis,* 1:2.

10. Thomas Flory, *Judge and Jury in Imperial Brazil, 1808–1871* (Austin: University of Texas Press, 1981), 74–75 and passim.

11. The Trial of Luís Vieira, fols. 2v–3; Transcript of the Trials at Conceição da Praia, fol. 3; Official correspondence of the Passo Justice of the Peace with Chief of Police, AEBa, *Chefe de polícia,* maço 2949.

12. Transcript of the Trials at Conceição da Praia, fol. 98.

13. Justice Caetano Galião to President of the Province, Salvador, 31 January 1835, AEBa, *Juízes de paz,* maço 2684; Marcescheau to Ministry of Foreign Affairs, Salvador, 26 and 29 January 1835, AMRE, *CP/Brésil,* vol. 16, fols. 16v–17, 21v; Foreign Office dispatch in Parkinson to Wellington, Salvador, 29 January 1835, PRO/FO, 13, 121, fol. 40; The Trial of Nécio, fol. 11.

14. The Trial of Torquato, a Nagô, slave of José Pinto de Novais, AEBa, *Insurreições,* maço 2846, fols. 4v–5, 13v.

15. Freitas to President of the Province, 18 March 1835, AEBa, *Polícia,* maço 3130.

16. The Trial of Luís Vieira, fols. 12v–13.

17. Chief of Police to Commandant of the Sea Fortress, 16 June 1835, AEBa, *Chefe de polícia,* maço 2949.

18. The public followed the trials in newspapers. Some examples are *Correio mercantil,* 12 March 1835, attached to Filgueiras's letter to the Portuguese Foreign Ministry, Salvador, 23 March 1835, ANTT, *Ministério dos Negócios Estrangeiros, Consulados. Baía,* caixa 1; and *Diário da Bahia,* 6 November 1836, in the periodical collection of the Public Library in Salvador. My description of this system of juries is based on Flory, *Judge and Jury,* esp. chap. 7, and on the trials of 1835. For more on the jury system see Patricia Aufderheide, "Order and Violence: Social Deviance and Social Control in Brazil, 1780–1840" (Ph.D. diss., University of Minnesota, 1977), chap. 8.

19. The Trial of Lino, a Nagô, slave of José Soares de Castro, AEBa, *Insurreições,* maço 2846, fols. 6v–7.

20. The Trial of Narciso, a Nagô, slave of José Maria de Souza Macieira, fol. 7; "Devassa," 83–84.

21. For examples of slaves who confessed see: Transcript of the Trials at Conceição da Praia, fols. 41, 46–47v, 48–48v, 50v. Other data in this paragraph come from The Trial of Manoel, a Nagô, slave of João Crisóstomo Pinto da Silva, fol. 26; "Devassa," 120.

22. The Trial of Domingos, a Hausa, slave of João Pinto Coelho, *Insurreições,* maço 2849, fols. 26–27; The Trial of Paulo Diogo Henriques, a Hausa freedman, AEBa, *Insurreições,* maço 2849, fol. 17–17v.

23. The Trial of Manoel, a Nagô, slave of João Crisóstomo Pinto da Silva, fols. 29–30; "Peças processuais," 91–92.

24. Eugene Genovese, *In Red and Black: Marxian Explorations in Southern and Afro-American History* (New York: Vintage Books, 1971), 75.

25. "Devassa," 114ff.; The Trial of Joaquim, a Nagô, slave of Antônio de Araújo, AEBa, *Insurreições,* maço 2850, fol. 4.

26. Transcript of the Trials at Conceição da Praia, fols. 111ff.; The Trial of José da Costa, a Jeje freedman, AEBa, *Processos Crimes,* maço 4296, doc. 12. José da Costa's petition appears to have been calculated to deceive. In his first interrogation he admitted that he had "some freed Nagô blacks come to his house to store their burdens [*guardar carregos*] and talk" (The Trial of José da Costa, fol. 4v).

27. Marcescheau to French Ministry of Foreign Affairs, Salvador, 19 February 1835, AMRE, *CP/Brésil,* vol. 16, fol. 43.

Chapter 12   The Punishment

1. Josino Nascimento Silva, *Código do império do Brasil* (Rio de Janeiro: Tipographia Eduardo Henrique Laemmert, 1859), 48–49. Concerning slaves punished by forced labor (*galés*) in Brazil see José Alípio Goulart, *Da palmatória ao patíbulo (castigos de escravos no Brasil)* (Rio de Janeiro: Conquista, 1971), 117–24.

2. AEBa, *Legislativa. Abaixo-assinados, 1835–1836,* maço 979.

3. President Martins to Minister of Justice, 14 February 1835, AEBa, *Correspondência,* livro 682, fol. 10.

4. Minister Manuel Alves Branco to President of the Province, Rio de Janeiro, 4 March 1835, AEBa, *Officios imperiais,* livro 890, fol. 55; *Colleção de leis,* 22. The French representative in Rio de Janeiro was mistaken when he claimed that the central government considered Bahia's plans for deportation unjust and that Bahians also intended to deport native-born freedmen (E. de la Rozière to French Ministry of Foreign Affairs, Rio de Janeiro, 13 April 1835, AMRE, *CP/Brésil,* vol. 16, fol. 72).

5. *Diário da Bahia,* 11 June 1836, 3. For Silvestre José's trial, including his interrogation, see AEBa, *Insurreições,* maço 2849.

6. Chief of Police Simões to President of the Province, AEBa, *Chefe de polícia,* maço 2949.

7. AEBa, *Insurreições,* maços 2845–50; José P. Requião to President of the Province, Salvador, 27 January 1835, AEBa, *Juízes,* maço 2684. Dundas's slave (Pedro) was sentenced to death based on a law passed after the Malê uprising, which is why the sentence was successfully challenged by the municipal judge (Caetano V. de Almeida to President of the Province, 14 March 1836, AEBa, *Escravos [assuntos],* maço 2896; AEBa, *Avisos imperiais,* vol. 890, fols. 226ff.).

8. See The Trial of Manoel, a Nagô, slave of João Crisóstomo da Silva;

"Peças processuais," 112; The Trial of Manoel, a Nagô, slave of José Monteiro, AEBa, *Insurreições,* maço 2849, fol. 20.

9. Transcript of the Trials at Conceição da Praia, fols. 206–210v; The Trial of Pompeu; The Trial of Higino.

10. The Trial of Nécio, fols. 70, 87, 88; The Trial of Cornélio, Carlos, and Tomás, Nagôs, slaves of José Soares and Frederick Robelliard, AEBa, *Insurreições,* maço 2850.

11. "Peças processuais," 27–30; President Martins to Minister of Justice, Salvador, 4 August 1835, AEBa, *Correspondência,* livro 683, fols. 18–18v, 74; *Officios imperiais,* livro 890, fols. 238–39.

12. Transcript of the Trials at Santana, fols. 4ff.

13. Ibid.; President Paraíso to Minister of Justice, Salvador, 23 March 1837, AEBa, *Correspondência,* livro 683, fols. 200, 294. The decree (16 June 1837) can be found in AEBa, *Officios imperiais,* livro 890, fols. 309–10.

14. "Rol dos Culpados [Roll of the Guilty]," in AEBa, *Insurreições,* maço 2849; Francisca da Silva to Provincial Assembly, Salvador, 14 March 1836, AEBa, *Legislativa. Petições (1836),* maço 1016. The records of Tomé and Domingos's trial cannot be found, but their names appear on the Roll of the Guilty (President Paraíso to Minister of Justice, Salvador, 20 April 1836, AEBa, *Correspondência,* livro 682, fol. 249; *Officios imperiais,* livro 890, fol. 203). I have published and discussed the Roll of the Guilty in Reis, "O 'Rol dos Culpados': notas sobre um documento da rebelião de 1835," *Anais do Arquivo do Estado da Bahia* 48 (1985): 243–61.

15. AEBa, *Correspondência,* livro 682, fol. 30v.

16. Decree of 28 March, registered in AEBa, *Officios imperiais,* livro 890, fols. 191–92.

17. "Devassa," 79, 91, 101, 102.

18. The Trial of Nécio, passim.

19. The Trial of Lino, a Nagô, slave of José Soares de Castro, fol. 4.

20. See "Rol dos Culpados"; President Martins to Minister of Justice, Salvador, 30 May 1835, AEBa, *Correspondência,* livro 682, fol. 96; and Rodrigues, *Os africanos,* 88. The interrogation of J. F. Gonçalves appears in "Devassa," 137.

21. This description of the executions is based on The Trial of Jorge da Cruz Barbosa, a Nagô freedman, AEBa, *Insurreições,* maço 2846, fol. 12–12v; and The Trial of Luiz, Nagô, slave of Guilherme Benne, ibid., maço 2847, unpaginated. For information concerning the attempts to locate an executioner see José Carlos Ferreira, "As insurreições dos africanos na Bahia," *Revista do Instituto Geográfico e Histórico da Bahia* 10, no. 29 (1903): 115–19. For more on the role of the Santa Casa see Caetano V. de Almeida, Jr., to the Santa Casa, Salvador, 12 May 1835, ASCMB, *Livro 4° de registros, 1832–43,* A-30°-88, fols. 66v–67. Concerning the political symbolism of public executions see Michel Foucault, *Discipline and Punish: The Birth of the Prison,* trans. Alan Sheridan (New York: Random House, 1979), esp. chap. 2.

22. Chief of Police Simões to President of the Province, AEBa, *Chefe de polícia,* maço 2949.

23. "Devassa," 53.

24. Ibid., 45−46; The Trial of Luiz, fol. 18; The Trial of Francisco and Agostinho, Nagôs, slaves of the Sisters of Mercy; The Trial of Sabino, a Nagô, slave of Bernardo José Ramos, AEBa, *Insurreições,* maço 2849, fol. 29.

25. The Trial of Luiz, fols. 19−22; Prince, "Slave Rebellion," 212.

26. The Trial of Luiz, fol. 22v; "Devassa," 124−28; "Peças processuais," 78ff., esp. 80. For more on the punishment of slaves with leg-irons and neck-irons see Goulart, *Da palmatória,* 135−39.

27. Rodrigues, *Os africanos,* 88; "Peças processuais," 78ff., esp. 80.

28. The Trial of Francisco, Carlos, and João, Nagôs, slaves of Clegg and Jones (Englishmen), AEBa, *Insurreições,* maço 2847, fols. 48−51. Aprígio Geraldo's petitions can be found in AEBa, *Escravos (assuntos),* maço 2885.

29. *Colleção de leis,* 23; Chief of Police Martins to President of the Province, Salvador, 11 June and 6 October 1835, AEBa, *Chefe de polícia,* maço 2949. See Captain Francisco da Cunha Bitancourt's petition of 10 October 1835, AEBa, *Escravos (assuntos),* maço 2883.

30. President Martins to Minister of Justice, 17 October 1835, AEBa, *Correspondência,* livro 682, fols. 153v−154.

31. Chief of Police Simões to President of the Province, Salvador, 24 April and 10 October 1835, AEBa, *Chefe de polícia,* maço 2949.

32. Chief of Police Simões to President of the Province, Salvador, 13 November 1835 and n.d., ibid.

33. Remonstrance of the Legislative Assembly to the Executive and Legislative Powers, Salvador, 11 May 1835, AEBa, *Legislativa. Representações e requerimentos, 1835−74,* uncatalogued, fol. 5v; President Martins to Minister of Justice, Salvador, 17 October 1835, fol. 154.

34. See the petition of João Duarte da Silva, Paulo da Silva, etc., AEBa, *Escravos (assuntos),* maço 2883; Chief of Police Simões to President of the Province, Salvador, 17 October 1835, and Chief of Police André Lima to President of the Province, Salvador, 7 July 1835, AEBa, *Chefe de polícia,* maço 2949; petition of Luís Xavier (1836), AEBa, *Legislativo. Abaixo-assinados, 1835−36,* maço 979.

35. Justice of the Peace Francisco Martins to President of the Province, 27 January 1835, AEBa, *Juízes de paz,* maço 2685; Joaquim Ignácio da Silva Pereira to Government Secretary, Salvador, 23 March and 8 April 1835, AEBa, *Legislativa. Ofícios recebidos, 1835,* uncatalogued. See also the many passport requests for slaves in AEBa, *Correspondência sobre escravos (1831−42),* maço 6306.

36. *Diário da Bahia,* 9 July 1836 (my italics); José Antônio de Araújo to President of the Province, Salvador, 17 February 1835, AEBa, *Juízes de paz,* maço 2684. Concerning tension and conflict created by the sale of slaves in Rio de Janeiro see Sidney Chalhoub, *Visões da liberdade: uma história das últimas décadas da escravidão na Corte* (São Paulo: Companhia das Letras, 1990), chap. 1 and passim.

37. This edict appears in Brazil, "Os Malês," 125−26.

38. See daily police reports in AEBa, *Polícia (assuntos),* maço 3112, and *Guarda Policial,* maços 3059−61; Ubaldino José da Cruz to President of the Province, 5 October 1835, AEBa, *Juízes de paz,* maço 2684.

39. Ignácio Joaquim Pitombo to President of the Province, Salvador, 11

August 1835, AEBa, *Juízes de paz,* maço 2684; Francisco E. N. dos Reis to President of the Province, Salvador, 21 October 1835, ibid., maço 2685; Manoel Alves de Sucupira to President of the Province, Salvador, 4 July 1835, ibid., maço 2686.

40. For in-depth work on anti-African laws after 1835 see also Manoela Carneiro da Cunha, *Negros, estrangeiros: os escravos libertos e a sua volta à África* (São Paulo: Brasiliense, 1985), 68ff.

41. *Colleção de leis,* 22–27.

42. AEBa, *Legislativa. Petições (1837),* uncatalogued.

43. AEBa, *Legislativa. Abaixo-assinados (1836),* uncatalogued.

44. Ibid.

45. *O censor: periódico mensal político, histórico e literário,* November 1837, 166–68.

46. *Colleção de leis,* 38–44.

47. *Diário da Bahia,* 5, 27 May and 4, 6 June 1836; João José Reis, "A greve negra de 1857," *Revista USP,* 18 (1993), 6-29.

48. Chief of Police Martins to President of the Province, Salvador, 27 November 1835, AEBa, *Chefe de polícia,* maço 2949. Other laws discriminating against blacks in the urban workplace between 1840 and 1860 are analyzed by Cunha in *Negros, estrangeiros,* 90–100.

49. The Trial of Paulo, a Nagô, slave of Rita da Paixão, AEBa, *Insurreições,* maço 2849, fol. 12.

50. Fox to Foreign Office, Rio de Janeiro, 13 March 1835, PRO/FO 13, 117, fols. 207–8; E. de la Rozière to French Minister of Foreign Affairs, Rio de Janeiro, 13 April 1835, AMRE, *CP/Brésil,* vol. 16, fols. 72v–73v. Concerning the imperial government's misgivings and its measures for controlling the population in Rio de Janeiro see AN, *Regência,* 334, fols. 9v, 11, 14, 15, 19. Concerning the law of 10 June 1835 and its application see esp. João Luiz D. Pinaud, "Senhor, escravo e direito: interpretação semântico-política," in *Insurreição negra e justiça,* ed. Pinaud et al. (Rio de Janeiro: Expressão e Cultura, 1987), 39–112; and Viotti da Costa, *Da senzala,* 287, 298. For more on crimes involving Bahian slaves and their reputation for unruliness see Chalhoub, *Visões da liberdade,* 32, 43, 54, 187–89; and Karasch, *Slave Life,* 26, 326.

Works Cited

Abimbola, Wande. *Ifá: An Exposition of Ifá Literary Corpus*. Ibadan: Oxford University Press, 1976.

Accioli, Ignácio. *Memórias históricas e políticas da Bahia*. Edited by Braz do Amaral. 6 vols. Salvador: Imprensa Oficial do Estado, 1931.

Adamu, Mahdi. "The Delivery of Slaves from the Central Sudan to the Bight of Benin." In Gemery and Hogendorn, 163–80.

Agiri, Babatunde. "Slavery in Yoruba Society in the Nineteenth Century." In Lovejoy, *The Ideology of Slavery in Africa*, 123–48.

Ajayi, J. F. Ade. "The Aftermath of the Fall of Oyo." In Ajayi and Crowder, 2:129–66.

Ajayi, J. F. Ade, and M. Crowder, eds. *History of West Africa*. 2 vols. London: Longman, 1974.

Ajayi, J. F. Ade, and Robert Smith. *Yoruba Warfare in the Nineteenth Century*. Ibadan: Cambridge University Press and Institute of African Studies, University of Ibadan, 1971.

Alden, D., and W. Dean, eds. *Essays Concerning the Socioeconomic History of Brazil and Portuguese India*. Gainesville: University of Florida Press, 1977.

Alvim, Vânia M. C. de. "Movimentos proféticos, prepolíticos e contraculturais dos negros islamizados na Bahia do século 19." Master's thesis, Universidade Federal da Bahia, 1975.

Amaral, Braz do. *História da Bahia do império à república*. Salvador: Imprensa Oficial do Estado, 1923.

———. *História da independência na Bahia*. 2d ed. Salvador: Progresso Editora, 1957.

Andrade, Maria José da Silva. "A mão de obra escrava em Salvador de 1811 a 1860." Master's thesis, Universidade Federal da Bahia, 1975.

———. *A mão de obra escrava em Salvador, 1811–1860*. São Paulo: Corrupio, 1988.

Aufderheide, Patricia. "Order and Violence: Social Deviance and Social Control in Brazil, 1780–1840." Ph.D. diss., University of Minnesota, 1977.

Avé-Lallemant, Robert. *Viagens pelas províncias da Bahia, Pernambuco, Alagoas e Sergipe (1859)*. Belo Horizonte, Brazil: Itatiaia, 1980.

Ayorinde, J. A. "Oriki." In Biobaku, 30–76.

Azevedo, Thales de. *O povoamento da cidade do Salvador.* Salvador: Editora Itapoã, 1969.

Bacelar, Jefferson A., and Maria Conceição de Souza. "O Rosário dos Pretos do Pelourinho." Salvador: Fundação do Patrimônio Artístico e Cultural da Bahia, 1974. Mimeographed.

Bascom, William. *Sixteen Cowries: Yoruba Divination from Africa to the New World.* Bloomington: Indiana University Press, 1980.

Bastide, Roger. *Le Candomblé de Bahia (rite nagô).* Paris: Mouton, 1958.

———. *As religiões africanas no Brasil.* 2 vols. São Paulo: Editora Pioneira and Editora da Universidade de São Paulo, 1971.

Bauer, Raymond, and Alice Bauer. "Day-to-Day Resistance to Slavery." In Bracey, 37–60.

Bellini, Lígia. "Por amor e por interesse: a relação senhor-escravo em cartas de alforria." In Reis, *Escravidão e invenção,* 73–86.

Bercé, Inves-Marie. *Fête et revolte.* Paris: Hachette, 1976.

Besmer, Freemont E. *Horses, Musicians, and Gods: The Hausa Cult of Possession Trance.* South Hadley, Mass.: Bergin & Garvey, 1983.

Bethell, Leslie. *The Abolition of the Brazilian Slave Trade: Brazil and the Slave Question, 1807–1867.* Cambridge: Cambridge University Press, 1970.

Biobaku, S. O., ed. *Sources of Yoruba History.* Oxford: Clarendon, 1973.

Bracey, John H., ed. *American Slavery: The Question of Resistance.* Belmont, Calif.: Wadsworth, 1971.

Brazil, Etienne Ignace. "Os Malês." *Revista do Instituto Histórico e Geográfico Brasileiro* 72 (1909): 69–126.

Britto, Eduardo de Caldas. "Levante de pretos na Bahia." *Revista do Instituto Geográfico e Histórico da Bahia* 10, no. 29 (1903): 69–94.

Calógeras, Pandiá. *O Marquez de Barbacena.* São Paulo: Editora Nacional, 1936.

Campos, J. da Silva. "Ligeiras notas sobre a vida íntima, costumes, e religião dos africanos na Bahia." *Anais do Arquivo do Estado da Bahia* 29 (1943): 289–309.

"Carta de José da Silva Lisboa a Domingos Vandelli, Bahia, 18 October 1781." *Anais da Biblioteca Nacional do Rio de Janeiro* 32 (1910): 494–506.

Carvalho, Carlos Alberto de. *Tradições e milagres do Bonfim.* Salvador: Typographia Baiana, 1915.

Cascudo, Luiz da Câmara. *Antologia do folclore brasileiro.* São Paulo: Martins, 1956.

Castelnau, Francis. *Renseignments sur l'Afrique Centrale, etc.* Paris: Bertrand, 1851.

Castro, Jeanne Berrance de. *A milícia cidadã: a Guarda Nacional de 1831 a 1850.* São Paulo: Editora Nacional, 1977.

Chalhoub, Sidney. *Visões da liberdade: uma história das últimas décadas da escravidão na Corte.* São Paulo: Companhia das Letras, 1990.

Clarke, Peter. *West Africa and Islam.* London: Edward Arnold, 1982.

Cohen, D. W., and Jack P. Greene, eds. *Neither Slave Nor Free: The Freedman of African Descent in the Slave Societies of the New World.* Baltimore: Johns Hopkins Press, 1972.

Colleção de leis e resoluções da Assembléia Legislativa da Bahia, 1835–1841. 2 vols. Salvador: Typographia de Antônio O. de França Guerra, 1862.

Costa, Ana de Lourdes. *"Ekabó!* Trabalho escravo, condições de moradia e reordenamento urbano em Salvador no século 19." Master's thesis, Universidade Federal da Bahia, 1989.

Costa, Emília Viotti da. *Da senzala à colônia.* São Paulo: Difusão Européia do Livro, 1966.

"Crônica dos acontecimentos da Bahia, 1809–1828." *Anais do Arquivo do Estado da Bahia* 26 (1938): 47–95.

Cunha, Manuela Carneiro da. *Negros, estrangeiros: os escravos libertos e a sua volta à África.* São Paulo: Brasiliense, 1985.

Curtin, Philip, S. Feierman, L. Thompson, and J. Vansina. *African History.* Boston: Little, Brown, 1978.

Dan Fodio, Usuman. *Bayān Wujūb al-Hijra 'Ala 'L-'Ibad.* Edited and translated by F. H. El Masri as *The Exposition of the Obligation of Emigration upon the Servants of God.* New York: Oxford University Press, 1978.

Delano, Isaac O. *The Soul of Nigeria.* London: T. W. Laurie, 1937.

"Devassa do levante de escravos ocorrido em Salvador em 1835." *Anais do Arquivo do Estado da Bahia* 38 (1968): 1–142.

"Discurso preliminar histórico e introductivo com natureza de descripção da Comarca da Bahia." *Anais da Biblioteca Nacional do Rio de Janeiro* 27 (1905): 281–349.

Duarte, Abelardo. *Negros muçulmanos nas Alagoas (os Malês).* Maceió: Edições Caeté, 1958.

Ellis, Alfred. *The Yoruba-speaking Peoples of the Slave Coast of West Africa.* Oosterhout, Netherlands: Anthropological Publications, 1966.

Eltis, David. "The Nineteenth-century Transatlantic Slave Trade: An Annual Time Series of Imports into the Americas Broken Down by Region." *Hispanic American Historical Review* 67 (February 1987): 109–38.

Equiano, Olaudah. *Equiano's Travels.* Edited by Paul Edwards. London: Heineman, 1967.

Ferreira, José Carlos. "As insurreições dos africanos na Bahia." *Revista do Instituto Geográfico e Histórico da Bahia* 10, no. 29 (1903): 103–19.

Fisher, Allan G. B., and Humphrey J. Fisher. *Slavery and Muslim Society in Africa.* Garden City, N.Y.: Anchor, 1972.

Flory, Thomas. *Judge and Jury in Imperial Brazil, 1808–1871.* Austin: University of Texas Press, 1981.

Foucault, Michel. *Discipline and Punish: The Birth of the Prison.* Translated by Alan Sheridan. New York: Random House, 1979.

França, Antônio d'Oliveira Pinto da, ed. *Cartas baianas, 1821–1824.* São Paulo: Editora Nacional, 1980.

Frederickson, George M., and Christopher Lasch. "Resistance to Slavery." In Weinstein and Gatell, 118–33.

Freeman-Greenville, G. S. P. *The Muslim and Christian Calendars.* London: Oxford University Press, 1963.

Freitas, Décio. *Insurreições escravas.* Porto Alegre: Editora Movimento, 1976.

Frucht, R., ed. *Black Society in the New World*. New York: Random House, 1971.

Gbadamosi, T. G. O. *The Growth of Islam among the Yoruba, 1841–1908*. Atlantic Highlands, N.J.: Humanities Press, 1978.

Gemery, H. A., and J. S. Hogendorn, eds. *The Uncommon Market: Essays in the Economic History of the Atlantic Slave Trade*. New York: Academic Press, 1979.

Genovese, Eugene D. *In Red and Black: Marxian Explorations in Southern and Afro-American History*. New York: Vintage, 1971.

———. *From Rebellion to Revolution: Afro-American Slave Revolts in the Making of the New World*. New York: Vintage, 1979.

Goody, Jack. "Writing, Religion, and Revolt in Bahia." *Visible Language* 20 (1986): 318–43.

Goulart, José Alípio. *Da palmatória ao patíbulo (castigos de escravos no Brasil)*. Rio de Janeiro: Conquista, 1971.

Graham, Maria. *Journal of a Voyage to Brazil and Residence There during Part of the Years 1821, 1822, 1823*. New York: Praeger, 1969.

Grant, Douglas. *The Fortunate Slave*. London: Oxford University Press, 1968.

Greenberg, Joseph. *The Influence of Islam on a Sudanese Religion*. Seattle: University of Washington Press, 1946.

Gutman, Herbert. *The Black Family in Slavery and Freedom*. New York: Pantheon, 1976.

Hobsbawm, Eric J. *Revolutionaries: Contemporary Essays*. New York: Pantheon, 1973.

Idowu, E. Balaji. *Olódúmarè: God in Yoruba Belief*. London: Longmans, 1962.

Johnson, Samuel. *The History of the Yorubas*. London: Routledge & Kegan Paul, 1921.

Johnston, H. A. S. *The Fulani Empire of Sokoto*. Oxford: Oxford University Press, 1967.

Karasch, Mary. *Slave Life in Rio de Janeiro, 1808–1850*. Princeton: Princeton University Press, 1987.

Kent, Raymond K. "African Revolt in Bahia." *Journal of Social History* 3 (Summer 1970): 334–56.

Kidder, Daniel P. *Sketches of Residence and Travels in Brazil*. 2 vols. London: Sorin & Ball and Wiley Putnam, 1845.

Klein, Herbert. "Nineteenth-Century Brazil." In Cohen and Greene, 309–34.

———. "A demografia do tráfico atlântico de escravos para o Brasil." *Estudos econômicos* 17 (May–August 1987): 129–49.

Koran. Translated by N. J. Dawood. Harmondsworth: Penguin, 1974.

Koster, Henry. *Travels in Brazil*. London: Longman, Hurst, Rees, Orme & Brown, 1816.

Kritzeck, J., and W. H. Lewis, eds. *Islam in Africa*. New York: Van Nostrand–Reinhold, 1969.

Last, Murray. "Reform in West Africa: The Jihad Movements of the Nineteenth Century." In Ajayi and Crowder, 1:1–29.

Law, Robin. *The Oyo Empire, c. 1600–c. 1836: A West African Imperialism in the Era of the Atlantic Slave Trade*. Oxford: Clarendon, 1977.

Lewis, I. M., ed. *Islam in Tropical Africa*. London: Oxford University Press, 1966.

Lima, Vivaldo da Costa. "A família-de-santo nos candomblés jeje-nagôs da Bahia: um estudo de relações intra-grupais." Master's thesis, Universidade Federal da Bahia, 1977.

Lindley, Thomas. *Narrativa de uma viagem ao Brasil*. São Paulo: Editora Nacional, 1969.

Lloyd, Peter. "Craft Organization in Yoruba Towns." *Africa* 23 (January 1953): 30–44.

Lovejoy, Paul E., ed. *The Ideology of Slavery in Africa*. Beverly Hills: Sage, 1981.

———. *Transformations in Slavery: A History of Slavery in Africa*. Cambridge: Cambridge University Press, 1983.

Lugar, Catherine. "The Portuguese Tobacco Trade and Tobacco Growers of Bahia in the Late Colonial Period." In Alden and Dean, 26–70.

McLeod, John. *A Voyage to Africa with Some Account of the Manners and Customs of the Dahomian People*. London: John Murray, 1820.

Manning, Patrick. "The Slave Trade in the Bight of Benin, 1640–1890." In Gemery and Hogendorn, 107–41.

Martins, Francisco Gonçalves. "Relatório do chefe de polícia Francisco Gonçalves Martins." In Brazil, 115–23.

———. "Supplemento à minha exposição dos acontecimentos do dia 7 de novembro." In *A revolução do dia 7 de novembro de 1837 (Sabinada)*, vol. 2, pp. 263–300. Salvador: Arquivo do Estado da Bahia, 1938.

Mattoso, Kátia M. de Queirós. "O consulado francês na Bahia em 1824." *Anais do Arquivo do Estado da Bahia* 39 (1970): 149–222.

———. "A propósito de cartas de alforria." *Anais de história* 4 (1972): 23–52.

———. "Sociedade e conjuntura na Bahia nos anos de luta pela independência." *Universitas* 15–16 (May–December 1973): 5–26.

———. "Os escravos na Bahia no alvorecer do século 19 (estudo de um grupo social)." *Revista de história* 97 (1974): 109–35.

———. "Albert Roussin: testemunha das lutas pela independência da Bahia (1822)." *Anais do Arquivo do Estado da Bahia* 41 (1975): 116–68.

———. "Um estudo quantitativo de história social, a Cidade do Salvador, Bahia de Todos os Santos, no século 19: primeiras abordagens, primeiros resultados." *Estudos históricos* 15 (1976): 7–28.

———. *Bahia: a Cidade de Salvador e seu mercado no século 19*. São Paulo: HUCITEC, 1978.

———. *Etre esclave au Brésil, 15e–19e siècle*. Paris: Hachette, 1979.

———. *Família e sociedade na Bahia do século 19*. Salvador: Corrupio, 1988.

Maupoil, Bernard. *La géomancie á l'ancienne Côte des Esclaves*. Paris: Institute d'Ethnologie, 1981.

Meier, Suzanne, and Igor Kopytoff, eds. *Slavery in Africa*. Madison: University of Wisconsin Press, 1977.

Meillassoux, Claude, ed. *L'esclavage en Afrique pre-coloniale*. Paris: Maspero, 1975.

Monfopuga-Nicolas, Jacqueline. *Ambivalence et cult de possession: contribution á l'étude du Bori haoussa*. Paris: Anthropos, 1972.

Monteil, Vincent. "Anályse de 25 documents árabes des Malés de Bahia (1835)." *Bulletin de l'Institut Fondamentale d'Afrique Noire,* ser. B, 29, nos. 1–2 (1967): 88–98.

———. "Marabouts." In Kritzeck and Lewis, 88–109.

———. *L'Islam noir.* Paris: Seuil, 1971.

Morton, F. W. O. "The Conservative Revolution of Independence." Ph.D. diss., Oxford University, 1974.

———. "The Governorship of the Count of Arcos in Bahia, 1810–1818: Enlightened Despotism in an Age of Revolution." Paper presented at the conference on Late Colonial Brazil, University of Toronto, 1986.

Morton-William, Peter. "The Ogboni Cult in Oyo." *Africa* 30 (October 1966): 362–74.

Mott, Luiz Roberto de Barros. "A escravatura: a propósito de uma representação a El Rei sobre a escravatura no Brasil." *Revista do Instituto de Estudos Brasileiros* 14 (1973): 127–36.

———. "Brancos, pardos, pretos e índios em Sergipe, 1825–1830." *Anais de história* 6 (1974): 139–84.

———. "Revendo a história da escravidão no Brasil." *Mensário do Arquivo Nacional* 127 (1980): 21–25.

———. "A revolução dos negros do Haiti e o Brasil." *História: questões e debates* 3, no. 4 (June 1982): 55–63.

———. "Escravidão e homossexualidade." In Vainfas, 19–40.

———. *Escravidão, homossexualidade e demonologia.* São Paulo: Icone, 1988.

———. *O sexo proibido.* Campinas, São Paulo: Papirus, 1988.

Moura, Clóvis. *Rebeliões da senzala.* São Paulo: Edições Zumbi, 1959.

Mulvey, Patricia. "The Black Lay Brotherhoods of Colonial Brazil." Ph.D. diss., City University of New York, 1976.

Murdock, George P. *Africa: Its People and Their Cultural History.* New York: McGraw-Hill, 1959.

"Offícios do Conde da Ponte para o Visconde de Anadia, 7 April 1807 and 16 April 1807." *Anais da Biblioteca Nacional do Rio de Janeiro* 37 (1918): 450–51, 460–61.

Oliveira, Maria Inês C. de. *O liberto: seu mundo e os outros.* São Paulo: Corrupio, 1988.

Oroge, E. Adeniyi. "The Institution of Slavery in Yorubaland with Particular Reference to the Nineteenth Century." Ph.D. diss., University of Birmingham, England, 1971.

Ott, Carlos. *Formação étnica da cidade do Salvador.* 2 vols. Salvador: Manu Editora, 1955.

"Peças processuais do levante dos malês." *Anais do Arquivo do Estado da Bahia* 40 (1971): 7–170.

Pinaud, João Luiz D. "Senhor, escravo e direito: interpretação semântico-política." In *Insurreição negra e justiça,* ed. Pinaud et al., 39–112. Rio de Janeiro: Expressão e Cultura, 1987.

Pinho, Wanderley. *História de um engenho no Recôncavo.* São Paulo: Editora Nacional, 1982.

Price, Richard, and Sidney Mintz. *An Anthropological Approach to the Afro-*

American Past: A Caribbean Perspective. Philadelphia: Institute for the Study of Human Issues, 1976.

Prince, Howard M. "Slave Rebellion in Bahia, 1807–1835." Ph.D. diss., Columbia University, 1972.

Querino, Manoel. *A Bahia de outrora*. Salvador: Livraria Econômica, 1922.

———. *A raça africana e seus costumes*. Salvador: Editora Progresso, 1955.

Ramos, Arthur. *O negro na civilização brasileira*. Rio de Janeiro: Casa do Estudante, 1971.

Randolph, Herbert. *Life of General Sir Robert Wilson*. 2 vols. London: John Murray, 1862.

Reckord, Mary. "The Jamaican Slave Rebellion of 1831." In Frucht, 50–66.

Reichert, Rolf. "L'insurrection d'esclaves de 1835 á la lumière des documents árabes des archives publiques de l'Etat de Bahia (Brésil)." *Bulletin de l'Institut Fondamental d'Afrique Noire*, ser. B, 29, nos. 1–2 (1967): 99–104.

———. *Os documentos árabes do Arquivo do Estado da Bahia*. Salvador: Centro de Estudos Afro-Orientais, Universidade Federal da Bahia, 1979.

Reidy, Joseph P. "Negro Election Day and Black Community Life in New England, 1750–1860." *Marxist Perspectives* 1, no. 3 (Fall 1978): 102–17.

Reis, João José. "A elite baiana face aos movimentos sociais: Bahia, 1824–1840." *Revista de história* 108 (1976): 341–84.

———. "Resistência escrava em Ilhéus: um documento inédito." *Anais do Arquivo do Estado da Bahia* 44 (1979): 285–97.

———. "População e rebelião: notas sobre a população escrava na Bahia na primeira metade do século 19." *Revista das ciências humanas* 1 (1980): 143–54.

———. "'Poderemos folgar, brincar e cantar': o protesto escravo nas Américas." *Afro-Ásia* 14 (December 1983): 107–23.

———. "O 'Rol dos Culpados': notas sobre um documento da rebelião de 1835," *Anais do Arquivo do Estado da Bahia* 48 (1985): 243–61.

———. "Magia jeje na Bahia: a invasão do Calundu do Pasto da Cachoeira, 1785." *Revista brasileira de história* 8 (1988): 58–82.

———. "Um balanço dos estudos sobre as revoltas escravas baianas." In Reis, *Escravidão e invenção*, 87–140.

———, ed. *Escravidão e invenção da liberdade*. São Paulo: Brasiliense, 1988.

———. *A morte é uma festa: ritos fúnebres e revolta popular no Brasil do século XIX*. São Paulo: Companhia das Letras, 1991.

———. "A greve negra de 1857." *Revista USP*, 18 (1993), 6-29.

Reis, João José, and P. F. de Moraes Farias. "Islam and Slave Resistance in Bahia, Brazil." *Islam et sociétés au sud du Sahara* 3 (1989): 41–66.

Reis, João José, and Eduardo Silva. *Negociação e conflito*. São Paulo: Companhia das Letras, 1989.

Rio, João do. *As religiões do Rio*. Rio de Janeiro: Editora Nova Aguilar, 1976.

Robertson, Claire C., and Martin A. Klein, eds. *Women and Slavery in Africa*. Madison: University of Wisconsin Press, 1983.

Rodison, Maxime. *Islam and Capitalism*. Translated by Brian Pearce. London: Allen Lane and Penguin, 1974.

Rodney, Walter. "Upper Guinea and the Significance of the Origins of Africans Enslaved in the New World." *Journal of Negro History* 54 (Autumn 1969): 327–45.

Rodrigues, Raymundo Nina. *Os africanos no Brasil*. São Paulo: Editora Nacional, 1932.

———. *O animismo fetichista dos negros baianos*. Rio de Janeiro: Civilização Brasileira, 1935.

Russell-Wood, A. J. R. "Colonial Brazil." In Cohen and Greene, 84–133.

———. "Black and Mulatto Brotherhoods in Colonial Brazil: A Study in Collective Behavior." *Hispanic American Historical Review* 54 (November 1974): 567–602.

Ruy, Afonso. *História da Câmara Municipal de Salvador*. Salvador: Câmara Municipal de Salvador, 1953.

Santos, Juana Elbein dos. *Os nagô e a morte*. Petrópolis, Brazil: Vozes, 1976.

Santos Neto, Isaias de Carvalho. "Oito histórias de um engenho da Bahia." Asst. Prof. thesis, Universidade Federal da Bahia, 1974.

Scarano, Julita. *Devoção e escravidão*. São Paulo: Editora Nacional, 1975.

Schwartz, Stuart B. "The Manumission of Slaves in Colonial Brazil: Bahia, 1684–1745." *Hispanic American Historical Review* 57 (November 1974): 603–35.

———. "Resistance and Accommodation in Eighteenth-Century Brazil." *Hispanic American Historical Review* 57 (February 1977): 69–81.

———. "Patterns of Slaveholding in the Americas." *American Historical Review* 87 (February 1982): 55–86.

———. *Sugar Plantations in the Formation of Brazilian Society: Bahia, 1550–1835*. Cambridge: Cambridge University Press, 1985.

Silva, Josino Nascimento. *Código criminal do império do Brasil*. Rio de Janeiro: Tipographia Eduardo Henrique Laemmert, 1859.

Silva, Maria Beatriz da. *A primeira gazeta da Bahia: Idade d'Ouro do Brasil*. São Paulo: Cultrix and Ministério de Educação e Cultura, 1978.

Smith, M. G. "The Jihad of Shehu dan Fodio." In Lewis, 296–315.

Smith, Robert. *Kingdoms of the Yoruba*. London: Methuen, 1969.

Souza, Laura de Mello e. *O diabo e a Terra de Santa Cruz*. São Paulo: Companhia das Letras, 1986.

Souza, Paulo César. *A Sabinada: a revolta separatista da Bahia (1837)*. São Paulo: Brasiliense, 1987.

Spix, Johan B., and Karl von Martius. *Viagem pelo Brasil*. 3 vols. São Paulo: Melhoramentos/IHGB/Ministério de Educação e Cultura, 1976.

Stasik, Kathleen M. "A Decisive Acquisition: The Development of Islam in Nineteenth-century Iwo, Southeast Oyo." Master's thesis, University of Minnesota, 1975.

Tavares, Luís Henrique Dias. *O levante dos Periquitos*. Salvador: Universidade Federal da Bahia, Centro de Estudos Baianos, 1990.

Thompson, E. P. "Time, Work-Discipline, and Industrial Capitalism." *Past and Present* 38 (December 1967): 56–97.

———. "The Moral Economy of the English Crowd." *Past and Present* 50 (1971): 76–136.

Tremearne, A. J. N. *Hausa Superstitions and Customs*. London: J. Bale, Sons & Danielsson, 1913.

Trimingham, J. S. *Islam in West Africa*. Oxford: Oxford University Press, 1959.

———. *A History of Islam in West Africa*. London: Oxford University Press, 1970.

Vainfas, R., ed. *História e sexualidade no Brasil*. Rio de Janeiro: Graal, 1986.

Vansina, Jan. *The Kingdoms of the Savanna*. Madison: University of Wisconsin Press, 1966.

Verger, Pierre. *O fumo da Bahia e o tráfico de escravos do Golfo de Benin*. Salvador: Universidade Federal da Bahia, 1966.

———. *Flux et reflux de la traite des nègres entre le golfe de Benin et Bahia de Todos os Santos*. Paris: Mouton, 1968.

———. "Bori, primeira cerimônia de iniciação ao culto dos Orişá nagô na Bahia, Brasil." In *Olóórìṣà*, edited by C. E. M. de Moura, 33–56. São Paulo: Ágora, 1981.

———. *Notícias da Bahia—1850*. Salvador: Editora Corrupio, 1981.

Vianna Filho, Luiz. *O negro na Bahia*. Rio de Janeiro: José Olympio, 1946.

Vilhena, Luís dos Santos. *A Bahia no século 18*. 2 vols. Salvador: Editora Itapoã, 1969.

Weinstein, Allen, and Frank O. Gatell, eds. *American Negro Slavery: A Modern Reader*. New York: Oxford University Press, 1973.

Wetherell, James. *Stray Notes from Bahia, Being an Extract from Letters during Residence of Fifteen Years*. Liverpool: Webb & Hunt, 1860.

Wildberger, Arnold. *Os presidentes da província da Bahia*. Salvador: Typographia Beneditina, 1949.

Index

Abadá, agbada, aqbada (garment), 103,
104, 107, 120, 124, 196, 203, 246 n.23
Abolition, 145
Abrantes, 29, 59
Adeluz, Mama (slave casualty), 92, 155
Afonja, 98, 104
Africans: acculturation of, 201, 202,
203, 204; adaptations of, to New
World, 153; animosity of, toward
native-born, 54; animosity between
West and South, 179; ceremonies,
164, 165, 171; Christian names, 155, 156,
157; coast, 66; deities, 41, 57, 58, 95,
124, 125, 144, 151, 152, 165; housemates,
179; labor ethos, 163, 164, 169, 170;
manumission, 142, 143; names, 63,
154, 155; native-born and, 5, 63, 142;
native cooperation, 57, 143; rebels, 63;
religious gathering (*candomblé*), 56,
57, 58; resistance, 164, 165, 174; respect
for age, 135; revolts, 69, 146–53; ritual
kinship, 185; royalty, 54, 55, 150; slaveowners, 95; taxes on, 225, 226, 227;
women, 180
Agiri, Babatunde, 95, 96
Agostinho (Nagô slave conspirator),
78, 83
Água de Meninos (cavalry barracks
and battle site), 35, 84, 85, 86, 87, 88,
89, 90, 91, 196, 198, 216, 218
Ahuna (rebel leader), 73, 98, 115, 129,
130, 134, 135; Pedro Lima (Mina freedman), 130
Aja-Fon, 121, 158; Aja-Fon-Ewe (= Jejes),
139
Alafin (king), 44, 94, 95
Alagoas, rebels in, 47

Albino (Hausa slave), 88
Albuquerque, Antônio Joaquim Pires
de (militia chief, Santo Amaro), 38
Albuquerque family, 29, 30, 31, 38, 39
Alcamin, José Pedro de Souza (slave-
owner), 62
Alexandre (Jeje slave), 90
Alfonja, 94–95
Aligenum, 245 n.20
Alim, 134
Allo (Hausa), 106
Almami, 117, 130
Almeida, Antônio Pereira de (jailer),
81, 131, 147
Almeida, Wenceslau Miguel de (slave
merchant), 66
Alqueires, 197
Alufás, 47, 96, 99, 102, 105, 108, 115, 117,
119, 125, 133, 134, 135, 207
Amaral, Braz do, 30, 54, 96
Amaral, Lázaro Vieira do (police lieu-
tenant), 77
Ambassador (rebel title), 43, 48, 68
Amulets, 42, 48, 98, 99, 102, 110, 120,
128, 171, 178, 194, 195, 200, 201,
245 n.14; manufacture, 102, 103; Mus-
lim, 93
André (rebel), 90
Angolas, 148, 150, 180, 182, 208, 220; af-
finity with native-born, 151; African
culture, 153
Anjonu, 102, 124
Anti-Africanism, 143, 152, 195, 196, 200,
201, 203, 205, 207, 208, 221, 222, 223–
24, 225, 229, 230; role of the press
and, 207
Anti-Portuguese: disturbances, 23–28;

Anti-Portuguese (*continued*)
sentiment and action, 14, 32, 34, 36,
38, 39, 114, 191, 192; soldiers in, 31. See
also *Mata-marotos*
Anti-slave sentiment, action, legislation, 38, 41, 44
Antônio: candomblé owner, 57, 58;
Hausa slave, amulet manufacturer,
102, 103
Antônio, Simpliciano, 84
Aprígio (rebel sedan chair porter,
bread seller), 75–76, 104, 105, 133, 135,
169, 173, 177; death sentence of, 209
Arabic, 95, 96, 154; Magrebian, 99;
teaching and learning, 109, 110, 133;
writing, 88, 89, 93, 97, 98, 99, 100,
104, 105, 117, 120, 121, 184, 192, 194,
195, 213, 214, 245n.14; writing and
reading, 199, 203, 207
Aragão e Vasconcelos, Antônio de
Brito, 58
Arcos, Count of (governor of Bahia,
1810–18), 44–52, 59, 113, 157; policies
of, 45, 48; slave revolts under (1814),
45, 46, 47
Are-ona-kakanfo, 94
Armazém, 178
Arsenals, 27; forced labor, 42
Artillery corps revolt, 31
Artisans, 8, 11, 12, 19, 20, 22, 36, 203;
products, 169; rebel, 166; slave, 169,
170
Authorities, pressure on, 16, 17, 18, 19,
20, 21, 22, 24, 25, 33, 38, 190

Babalawos, 124, 125
Bábbá malãmi (great malãm), 130
Baiana (frigate), 75, 85
Baixa dos Sapateiros, 84
Balaiada (rebellion), 21
Bandeira, Pedro Rodrigues, 59, 60, 61,
65
Bantu, 148–49, 154, 157; absence of, in
rebellion, 148; catechumens, 149
Banzé, 120
Baraka, 102, 131, 134
Barata, Cipriano José, 26, 36
Barata, Viridiana, 26, 39
Barbalho Meadow, 49
Barbosa, Jorge da Cruz (Ajahi), 215–16

Barreto, Colonel Jerônimo Fiúza, 50
Barris, 116, 171
Basto, Luís Paulo de Araújo (provin-
cial president), 26, 67
Batalhão dos Henriques, 30
Batanhos (slave casualty), 92
Batuques (drum dances), 48
Bay of All Saints, 3, 66
Benguela (Angola), 47
Benguelas, 148
Benin: Bight of, 94, 97, 139; Republic
of, 139
Bento (Nagô slave), 103, 104
Bento, Custódio, 35
Bilãl, 132
*Bismillah (Bi-si-mi-lai, Bismika Alla-
humma),* 108
Black market, 16, 37
Blacks, 4–6; occupations of, 160
Block inspectors, 75, 87, 91, 92, 191, 192,
194, 216
Boa Viagem (neighborhood), 184
Bofetão, 178
Bolsas de mandinga, 245n.14
Bomcaminho, Antônio Manoel do
(Nagô ex-slave, rebel), 90
Bonfim, Senhor do, 73, 75, 84, 85, 87;
Islamic syncretism, 126
Bori, 97; Hausa possession cult, 48
Bornus, 94, 95, 97, 171, 179, 180, 182,
208, 221
Brandão e Vasconcelos, José Ignácio
Acciavoli, 53
Brincadeira, 119–20
Brinquedo, 120
British consulate, 17
Brito, Commander Antero de, 31
Brotas (Parish), 157, 193, 224
Brotherhoods, black, Catholic lay, 48,
149, 150, 152, 153; Jejes and Nagôs in,
151

Cabinda, 158; ethnicity, 148
Caboqueiro, 167
Cabras, 5; skin color term, 121
Cabrito, 84, 89
Cabula (neighborhood), 50, 55, 171
Cachaça, 50
Cacheteira, 161
Cachoeira, 4, 15, 16, 27, 32, 35, 39, 49,

63, 87, 144, 189, 209, 212, 213; city council, 33; defenses, 62, 64; district, 55, 59; manifesto, 33, 34; rebellion, 62
Cajazeiras (Pirajá district), 55
Calabar, 179
Calafate, Manoel (rebel leader, Malê elder), 74, 75, 77, 105, 108, 116, 117, 129, 130, 133, 135, 141, 175, 177, 178, 179, 188, 198, 209, 214
Calçada (neighborhood), 85; Square, 164
Caldeira, General Felisberto Gomes, 29, 55, 59
Callado, João Crisóstomo, 26
Calmon Du Pin e Almeida, Antônio (planter), 65
Camamu, Gordilho de Barbuda, Commander José, viscount of, 20, 30, 31, 65, 67, 68
Cameroon, 209
Campo da Pólvora, 217, 218
Canalha, 22
Candomblé (religion and meeting place), 56, 97, 110, 125, 151, 152, 157, 165; African coast, 145, 154, 185; Angolan, 152; Gantois (native-born), 145; Santo Antônio, 145
Cantos, 104, 164, 169, 227, 228; captain, 164–65, 228; solidarity, 165
Capataz, 227, 228
Capatazias, 227, 228; inspectors, 227; taxes on, 228
Capitães do mato (slave hunters), 41
Capitão de entradas e assaltos, 222
Carambola, 161
Career officers, 28
Caribbean area, 141
Carioca, sailors' mutiny on, 31
Carvalhal, Francisco Teles (commandant), 85
Casa da Moeda (mint), 19
Casa de Correição, 219
Cash crops (sugar, tobacco, cotton), 14
Castelnau, Francis de (French consul), 94
Castro, Major José Antônio da Silva (commandant), 29
Castro Alves Square, 83
Catholic (religion and practitioners), 111, 184, 201, 202, 203, 213, 225, 226;

harassment of, 110; hierarchy, 8; official religion, 153; prayers, 245
Cavalry garrison, 219
Censor, O, 227
Censorship, 25, 34, 55
Central High School, 84
Cezimbra, João Alves (provincial president, merchant), 31
Chobi, Major João Francisco, 49
Cidade, Francisco, 47, 48
City hall, 81
City jail, 81, 82, 88
Civilian casualties, 92
Civil servants, 8
Clovis (rebel slave), 77
Coelho, José Mendes da Costa (justice of the peace), 74, 78
Coffee plantations, 145
Comadre, 74
Combé (slave casualty), 92
Commodities, 23
Commutations of sentences, 213, 216
Conceição da Praia (business district, Salvador), 73, 87, 133, 175, 190, 193, 194
Confederação do Equador, 21, 29
Congos, 147, 148, 208
Conspiração dos Alfaiates (Tailors' Conspiracy), 145
Constantino (Nagô slave), 91
Constitutional Assembly, 23, 25
Constitution of 1824, 32
Copper, 17
Coquilho, 169
Cornélio (Nagô slave), 90
Corpus Christi Rebellion, 43
Costa, Judge Joaquim Ignácio da, 44
Costa, Maciel da, 25
Cotegipe, 66
Counterfeit(ers), 30, 37; money, 16, 17, 34
Criminal code, 34, 205, 206, 207, 209
Crioulos (native-born blacks), 5, 10, 39, 54, 150, 151, 182, 200; absence of, in rebellion, 141–46; dissimulation by, 144; females, 142; relations of, with Africans, 145
Cruz, Sabina da (Nagô, ex-slave), 74, 75, 78, 130, 184, 185
Cunha, Belchior da Silva, 105, 111, 116, 117, 130, 132, 133, 135, 175, 177, 178, 180,

Cunha, Belchior da Silva (*continued*) 183, 184, 194, 207, 213, 216; death sentence of, 209
Cunha, Brigadier Manoel Gonçalves da, 179
Cunha, Fortunato José da (slaveowner), 74
Cunha, Gaspar da Silva (Nagô freedman), 103, 107, 117, 132, 133, 147, 155, 156, 175, 180, 182, 183, 184, 194, 207, 213, 216; death sentence of, 209; slaveowner, 122
Cunha, Major Joaquim Sátiro da, 30
Cunha, Manuel Ignácio da (marina owner), 45
Curandeira, 171
Curfews, 44, 223, 224
Customs House (rebel target), 43, 69

Dahomey, 94, 95, 98, 139, 146, 148, 151, 158, 221
Damiana, 220
Dances, African, 41, 42, 44, 48; paraphernalia, 57
Dandará (Elesbão do Carmo), 97, 105, 107, 113, 116, 129, 133, 134, 169, 180, 181, 207
Dan Fodio, Sheik Usuman, 94, 127, 183
Dassalu (slave casualty), 92, 129, 134
David, Duke of the Island, 47, 48
Decolonization, 20
Denunciation of Malê Rebellion, 73
Deportation, 207, 208, 209, 213, 220–23, 224, 225, 229, 230; leaders' attitudes toward, 221; slaves' attitudes toward, 223
Desembargadores (appellate judges), 37
Dessalines, 48
Desterro Convent, 110, 178
Diário da Bahia, 223, 228
Dias, Henrique, 30
Domingos (slave), 85
Dom Miguel, King (of Portugal), 191
Dom Pedro I (first emperor of Brazil), 20, 21, 23, 24, 25, 26, 29, 34, 52, 59, 65, 191, 193; abdication of, 27, 28
Dom Pedro II (second emperor of Brazil), 209, 213, 214, 215, 220
Doplê, Ajadi Luís, 183, 214; death sentence of, 209

Drought, 15
Duarte, Joaquim (freed Hausa, rebel), 58
Duque, 48
Dutch, the, 30

Edum (black woman), 74
Efô, 109
Egba, 154, 164
Elite, Bahian, 23, 28, 33, 45, 66; attitudes of, 203, 204
Emereciana (Dandará's companion), 107, 133, 179, 180, 181, 207
Engenhocas, 75
Engenhos, 14
English, the, in Salvador, 83, 84, 105, 109, 116, 134, 163, 175, 195, 208, 209, 213, 216, 219; slaves of, 92
Engomadeira, 62
Erie (American gunboat), 189
Estimates (rumors) of numbers of participants in rebellion, 91
Eşuşu (credit institution), 165–66
Ethnic animosity, 157
Ethnic identity, 154
Eugênio, Dom Nuno (interim president), 64
Eusébio (Nagô slave), 83
Executions, 217
Exile, 47
Export commerce, 14
Expulsion, 213

Falcão, Colonel Rodrigo Antônio Brandão, 35, 63, 64, 65, 68
Federalist Manifesto, 36; reforms in, 36, 37
Federalist rebellions, 31, 32–39; attitudes of, toward slavery, 37, 38, 39; slaves in, 39
Feira de Santana, 35, 44
Fernandes, Custódio José, 75
Floggings, 205, 206, 207, 209, 212, 213, 218, 223, 229
Florentino (slave), 64
Folguedo, 119
Fon, 154
Foodstuffs, 36–37, 40, 161, 197, 228, 229; speculation in, 15, 16, 18, 24
Forced labor, 42, 205, 206, 219

Fort Barbalho, 26, 27, 28, 220
Forte do Mar (Fort São Marcelo), 35,
    36, 196, 219
Fort São Pedro, 31, 83, 84, 88, 116;
    Água de Meninos, 194, 196
Fortunato, Domingos (freed slave), 73,
    121, 122
Francisco (slave, turncoat witness), 131
Freedmen: contact of, with slaves, 173,
    174; homeowners, 177, 178; mobility,
    177; occupations, 174; rebels, Brazil-
    ian attitudes toward, 173; rights, 192;
    role of, in rebellion, 206, 207
Freitas, Lieutenant Daniel Gomes de,
    35
French consul, 39, 121. *See also* Guine-
    baud, Jacques; Marcescheau
French naval attaché, 53
Fulanis, 94, 95, 121, 127, 152
Funfus, 124

Galião, Caetano Vicente de Almeida
    (justice of the peace), 77, 78, 117, 193
Ganho system, 161, 164, 165, 172–73,
    179; *ganhadeiras,* 161; *ganhadores,* 161,
    170
Gargalheira, 219
Gaveré (kafir, kafirai), 110
Germany, 66
Gold Coast, 96
Gomes, Antônio (magistrate), 157
Gonçalo, Saint, 126
Gouveia Osório (Portuguese military
    officer), 53
Graça: Meadow, 49; Road, 116
Gravatá, 77; New Gravatá Road, 133
Guadalupe (neighborhood), 75, 78, 79,
    130, 133; Square, 183
Guinebaud, Jacques (French consul),
    24, 29, 30, 61, 64, 162
Gurma, 180
Gustard (slave casualty), 92, 134

Haiti, 39, 48, 53, 66
"Harmonizing Army, The," 35
Hausas, 43, 44, 48, 49, 58, 82, 93, 97,
    102, 113, 121, 127, 130, 133, 139, 147, 148,
    151, 153, 158, 159, 171, 179, 180, 182, 207,
    208, 217; African culture, 152; lan-
    guage, 47, 96, 106, 132; Muslim, 47;

pagan, 48; slaves, 94; trades and
    professions, 94, 169, 170, 172
Henrique (slave), 91
Herculano, Francisco Lourenço, 62
Higino (Nagô, ex-slave), 90, 103, 104,
    212, 213
Hipólito (Nagô slave), 91
Homosexuality, 182–83
Hospital da Misericórdia (charity hos-
    pital), 91
House searches, 43
Huguby (Gaspar), 98

Ifá (African deity), 57
Ignácio (Nagô slave), 75, 105
Iguape, 144; rebellion, 49; Recôncavo,
    63
Ijebu Nagô-Jabu, 154
Ilhéus, 51, 55
Ilorin, 94, 95, 96, 103
Imales, 96, 124, 146
Imperial government, 8, 58
Income, 8
Independence, 14, 21
Infant mortality, 7
Inflation, 12, 17, 18, 23, 37
Irmandades (Catholic lay brother-
    hoods), 48
Isköki, 102
Islam, 43, 93–111, 114, 135; ambiguity,
    95; and Christianity, 102; democratic
    tendencies, 134; dietary practices, 108;
    expansion, 112–13; festive aspect, 120;
    slavery, 121; syncretism, 48; unifying
    force, 113; urban environment, 104;
    women (Rio de Janeiro), 107
Itapagipe, 75, 84, 87, 89, 102, 171
Itaparica Island, 47, 53, 66, 179, 189
Itapuã, 62, 64

Jaguaripe, 226
Jama'a, 95
Jamaica, 53; slaveowners, 229
Janeiristas, 24
Jejes (Aja-Fon), 44, 90, 108, 139, 143,
    148, 150, 151, 157, 158, 167, 171, 180, 181,
    208, 221, 225, 226; culture, 141
Jihads, 94, 95, 122, 123, 126–27, 128, 174
Jinns, 102, 119, 124
Joanes River, 46

João: *Malomi,* 47; Nagô freedman, 104
Joaquim (Hausa slave), 82
José (Congo slave), 103
José (Nagô slave), 102
José (slave), 64
Juiz de direito, 192
Julião (neighborhood), 87
Juntas de alforria. *See* Manumission
Júri de Acusação, 197
Júri de Sentença, 197, 199, 207
Jury system, 197
Justices of the peace, 37, 74, 75, 77, 78, 79, 91, 109, 116, 117, 131, 143, 144, 191, 192, 193, 194, 195, 196, 197, 198, 199, 212, 213, 224, 225, 227, 228

Kafirai, 110, 123
Kent, R. K., 96
Ketu kingdom, 151
Koran, 93, 98, 99, 100, 105, 106, 107, 108, 110, 119; Exordium, 106

Labatut, General Pedro (foreign general), 54
Ladeira da Palma (residence), 194, 214
Ladeira da Praça (Calafate's loge), 77, 78, 88
Ladino, 62
Lagos, 221; = Eko, Onim, 94
Lailat al-Miraj, 109, 110, 134, 157, 213; importance of, in revolt, 115
Lailat al-Qadr (Night of Glory), 119
Landowners, 52
Lapa Square (Largo da Lapa), 84; barracks, 88
Largo do Teatro (Castro Alves Square), 30, 83
Lavagem (temple washing), 126
Lessa, Severino da Silva (slave hunter), 42
Liberia, 221
Licutan, Pacífico (Malê elder), 81, 105, 108, 119, 129, 130, 131, 134, 135, 147, 173, 175, 179, 198, 207; imprisonment of, 115, 130–32
Life expectancy, 7
Lighter (*saveiro*), 77
Lima, Judge Manuel Ignácio de (planter), 64
Lima, Luís dos Santos, 21

Limeira, Ignácio (Nagô freedman), 77
Lisboa, José da Silva, 7
Lisboa, José Ignácio da Silva (rebel slave), 12, 39
Literacy, importance of, 127
Loges, 75, 77, 177, 178, 185, 192, 194, 196, 214, 225
Loyalist troops, 35
Loyal slaves, 78

Macedo, Luís Tavares (witness), 79
Machado, Justice Francisco José da Silva, 109
Machado, Sergeant Tito Joaquim da Silva, 83
Maciel de Baixo (neighborhood), 217
McLeod, John, 98
Madureira, Maria Bárbara Garcez Pinto de, 24, 53, 144
Magic, 99, 106. *See also* Sorcery
Magistrate, attitudes of, 65
Maioral (straw boss), 129–30
Makwas (African ethnic group), 61
Malāms, 47, 96, 115, 121
Malê (sect and rebellion), 88, 97, 103, 106, 115, 116, 117, 118, 119, 159, 166, 174 passim; attitudes, 110, 111, 112, 122; calendar, 108, 109, 119; composition, 97; dietary practices, 124; dress, 79, 194, 199, 200, 201; elder, 97, 106; expansion, 115, 116; freedmen's role, 116; gatherings, 108; goals, 45, 47, 121, 122, 123, 127, 132, 158, 199; identity, 110; leader, 134; names, 132; non-Muslim participation, 123; origin of name, 96; prestige, 103–4, 114, 123; priestly class, 146, 160; proselytizing, 98, 135; resistance, 132, 133, 216; rings, 107, 184, 199, 200, 201, 207; strategy, 114, 133; syncretism, 127; teachers, 132, 195; testimony, 117; weapons, 134, 194, 209, 214; women, 10
Malheiros, Francisco Antônio, 74
Malinkes (*mandingos*), 93
Mallais (Hausa slave traders), 97
Malomi, 47
Malungos, 184
Mandingos, 93, 121
Mangueira canto, 169
Manifesto (liberal-federalist), 33

Manumission, 131, 132; African slaves, 146, 148; crioulos, 42; *juntas de alforria*, 165, 169, 170; mestiços, 142; prejudice, 165; purchase, 130, 149, 165, 171, 176, 181, 183
Mao Tse-tung, 108
Maragogipe, 49; anti-Slave precautions, 44
Marcelina (slave), 97
Marcescheau (French consul), 68–69, 87, 88, 89, 90, 91, 103, 114, 147, 189, 190, 195, 203
Marinas, 40, 45, 62
Marital status: Africans and Brazilians, 181, 182; endogamy, 182; freedmen, 181, 182; slaves, 181
Maroon communities. See *Quilombos*
Marques, Antônio (block inspector), 84, 109, 115, 135, 195
Marriage: Africans with Africans, 182, 184, 185; Brazilians with Africans, 226
Martins, Francisco de Souza (provincial president), 6, 75, 81, 83, 90, 91, 93, 152, 190, 191, 192, 207, 215, 217, 221
Martins, Francisco Gonçalves (police chief), 75, 85, 87, 91, 92, 93, 97, 147, 189, 190, 191, 192, 193, 196, 216, 217, 223, 226, 228
Mata Escura, 54
Mata-marotos, 22, 26, 27, 32. *See also* Anti-Portuguese
Matos, Joaquim de (Nagô freedman), 77
Maxado, Lobão, 102
Melo, Brigadier Ignácio Madeira de, 53
Menezes, Manoel Ignácio da Cunha (provincial president), 58, 62, 64
Mercês, Geraldo das, 84
Mercês Convent, 78, 83, 84
Merchants, 8, 9, 11, 16, 17, 23, 34, 36, 48, 53, 59, 79, 87; African, 106; African Muslim, 96; English, 14; Muslim, 102; Portuguese, 14; role of, in Islam, 169; urban, 3; Yoruba, 95
Mestres, 96
Middle class, 28, 31
Militarism, West African, 152–53
Military: Minas Gerais Battalion, 26, 28, 30, 64; officers, 8; revolts, 59; unpreparedness, 59; unrest, 28

Minas (African ethnic group), 145, 148, 179, 221
Mineiro, Bernardo Miguel Guanaes (militia captain), 32, 35
Ministry of justice, 65
Misericórdia, Santa Casa de, 92, 196, 217, 218
Mohammed (prophet), 132
Monarchists, 32
Moquecada, 161
Morgado (primogeniture), 37
Moscoso, Luís da França d'Athaide (slaveowner), 88
Mosques, 105, 115, 135
Mozambique, 61
Mu'allim, 47, 96
Mubakar, Mala (iman), 117, 130
Muezzin, 132
Mulattos, 4, 5, 6, 10, 54, 55, 57, 68, 75, 79 passim; antagonism of, toward slaves, 63; anti-African, 191; as victims, 84; attitudes of, 142; enslavement of, 121; manumission of, 142
Mundubis, 167, 208, 221
Municipal Guard, 31, 32, 75, 85, 190, 191, 194, 217
Muslims: apparel, 104, 124, 132; calendar, 77, 109; in revolt, 146; names, 108, 155; pagan syncretism, 124, 125; prayers, 93, 97; preachers, 4, 7; sacristan, 166; slaves, 83. *See also* Islam
Mutiny, slave, 61

Nagôs (Yoruba), 44, 47, 57, 58, 69, 74, 75, 77, 78, 90, 91, 109, 110, 123, 125, 126, 129, 131, 133, 146, 147, 148, 151, 153, 154, 157, 159, 171, 172, 177, 179, 180, 182, 183, 184, 195, 202, 208, 212, 213, 214, 216, 219, 221, 222; animosity toward, 158; culture, 141, 152; in revolt, 124
National debt, 34
National Guard, 36, 77, 78, 83, 87, 91, 143, 191, 194, 224
Native-born blacks, 22 passim; antagonism with Africans, 64, 145; professions, 149; slaves, 38
Naval Arsenal, 18, 20, 203, 219
Nazaré (neighborhood), 43
Nazaré das Farinhas (1809 Rebellion), 43, 44

Nicobé: rebel leader, 129, 134; slave casualty, 92
Nigeria, 94, 139, 221
Night patrols, 75
Ninety-Second Militia Battalion, 226
Nobility, 8, 9
Noé (Nagô slave), 91
Noite das Garrafadas, 26
North American slaveowners, 229
Noviciado Highway, 85
Nupes (Tapas), 94, 95, 97, 132, 139, 221; kingdom, 94

Oba, 95
Odu, 124
Oeiras, 191
Ogboni, 44
Ojo-Obatalá, 125–26
Ologuns, oloroguns, 141
Olorum (Olorumuluá), 125
Onofre, Lieutenant Luís, 35
Oriṣalá, 124
Orisatalabi, 124
Orishas, 171; cults, 124, 125, 155; worship, 184
Oshossi (African deity), 57
Otua meji, 124
Ouidah (Benin), 220
Ouricori, 169
Our Lady of Guidance (rebellion on saint's day), 73, 127
Our Lady of the Rosary (Angolan Catholic lay brotherhood), 48, 150–51
Overseers, 53, 59, 61, 63, 64; capataz (urban), 227, 228; people of color as, 143
Ovimbundos, 148
Oxalá, 124, 126
Oyo, 95, 103, 127, 146, 152, 154, 158; militarism, 141; Yoruba kingdom (empire), 44, 55, 139

Paim, Barros (president), 32
Paixão, Felicidade Maria da, 183, 214
Palace Guard, 82
Palace Square (Praça Municipal), 78, 79, 81, 82, 83, 133, 175
Palmares (maroon community), 149
Pano da costa (West African cloth), 103, 143, 166
Paraguaçu River, 32, 59

Parakoyi, 164
Pardos, 5
Parentes, 185
Parkinson, John (British consul), 84, 89, 91, 147, 189, 195
Parliament, 25, 26
Parnaíba, Viscount of, 191
Parnaíbas (knives), 66
Passo (Parish), 193
Patacas, 102, 171, 178
Paternalism, 16, 61, 143, 144
Patrício, 185
Pedreiras (neighborhood), 165
Pedro (Nagô slave), 84
Pelourinho Square (and area), 66, 84, 150
Penha (Parish), 224
Pereira, Felizardo (rebel bandit leader), 68
Periquitos Rebellion, 30
Pernambuco, 29, 144; Rebellion, 52
Piaui, 75, 91; Batallion, 31
Pilar (Parish), 175, 193
Pina e Mello, Colonel José Maria de (planter), 66
Pinto, Maria Clara da Costa, 104
Pirajá, 62, 67, 68; militia regiment, 58; viscount of, 212. See also Albuquerque family; Santo Amaro
Plague (cattle), 15
Plantations: Acutinga, 63; Água Boa, 59; Aramaré, 24; Boa Sorte, 59; Boa Vista, 53; Buraco, 59; Caju, 59; Campina, 63; Canabrava, 59; Cassarangongo, 49; Cruz, 63; Engenho da Conceição, 59, 87; Engenho da Ponta, 68; Engenho da Praia, 64; Engenho Desterro, 68; Engenho do Tanque, 64; Engenho Novo, 63, 68; Engenho Velho, 157; Felipe, 59; Jacu, 59; Moinho, 59; Nazare, 35; Paciência, 59; Pandalunga, 59; Papagaio, 192; Pimentel, 59; Ponta, 49, 51; Quibaca, 49, 50; Retiro, 59; Rosário, 83; Santa Ana, 65; Santana (Ilhéus), 51, 55, 62, 145
Planters, 8, 11, 12, 15, 23, 26, 27, 28, 29, 35, 49, 59, 149, 153, 189 passim; attitudes of, 51, 52, 64, 65, 148, 225; Bahian elite, 31; sugar barons, 14
Plebe, 22

Police force, 58, 59
Political prisoners, 31, 34, 35
Political rivalry, 21
Political spectacle, 34
Pompeu (Nagô rebel slave from Santo
   Amaro, major witness), 77, 83, 88, 116,
   147, 194, 212, 213
Ponte, Saldanha da Gama, count of,
   41–42, 43, 44, 50, 51, 113, 141, 152, 157,
   203
Pontes, Brigadier Felisberto Caldeira
   Brant, 51–52
Populaça, 22
Population: divisions, 5; growth, 6;
   male and female slaves, 7; Recôn-
   cavo, 4
Portão de São Bento, 164
Portugal, 26
Portuguese, 5, 10, 17, 33, 54; consul, 27,
   39; forces, 14; officials in Brazilian
   government, 23; Overseas Council, 42
Poverty, 10–12
Prayers, 42, 102, 103, 105, 106, 107, 110
Preguiça (neighborhood), 83
Preguiça shipyards, 82
Presinganga, 34, 196
Primeiro Batalhão de Milícias, 30
Primeiro Conselho dos Jurados, 197
Prison, abuse in, 47
Provincial Council, 18
Provisional government, 17
Punishment, 43, 49, 51, 58, 61, 62, 64,
   66, 67, 68, 78, 107, 109, 110, 135, 190,
   191, 194, 195, 201, 203, 228, 229

Quilombos, 40, 41, 42, 43, 45, 47, 50, 52,
   53, 55, 59, 62, 149, 153, 222; near Salvador, 42
Quimbundos, 149
Quitandas, 161

Racism, 24, 30, 37
Ramadan, 108, 109, 124, 131, 132; impor-
   tance of, in rebellion, 119
Ratis, João Franciso (slaveowner), 87,
   89, 135
Reading, 106
Rebellions, Confederação do Equador,
   Balaiada, Cabanagem, Farrapos, 21
Rebels: Africans, 141, 142; ages, 172,
   173; city dwellers, 16; clothing 103,

104; European nomenclature, 47–48;
   familiarity of, with Salvador, 177;
   freedmen, 199; goals, 145, 177; leaders,
   68, 87, 117, 205, 206, 209; legal defense, 58, 133; residences, 175–80, 194;
   resistance, 172, 174, 198; strategy, 89,
   90; weapons, 43, 208; women, 167,
   168
Recôncavo, 2, 3, 13, 17, 27, 29, 32, 35, 39,
   40, 43, 44, 49, 50, 51, 75, 87, 89, 115,
   134, 139, 144, 166, 169, 171, 174, 177,
   178, 189, 208, 226; defense, 65, 66, 68;
   drought, 15; population, 4; pressure
   from, 65; Santo Amaro, 129
Red, importance of, 57
Red flag (Shango), 55
Relação Jail, 218, 219
Religion: celebrations, 51, 73, 190;
   Muslim ceremony, 107; official, 113;
   rivalry in Bahia, 97; role of, in rebel-
   lion, 51, 73, 93, 113
Republicans, 32
Revolts: free people, 22; Kiriri Indians,
   22; liberal/federalist, 22; middle class
   in, 23; military, 21, 22, 28–32
Rio de Janeiro, 17, 20, 23, 25, 26, 33, 48,
   51, 52, 99, 107, 190, 191, 192, 202, 209,
   229, 230, 245n.14
Rio Vermelho, 189, 190
Ritual kinship, 184
Roll of the Guilty, 197, 206, 208, 217
Rosário brotherhood, 151
Rua Direita de São Pedro (house), 194
Rumor of slave revolt, 66, 68, 73, 189,
   190, 224, 232
Rural slaves, 43

Sá, Domingos Marinho de (mulatto,
   ex-slave), 75, 79, 141, 177, 219
Sabinada (federalist revolt), 32, 38, 219
Saboeiro, 54
Sacramento, Father Bernardino de
   Sena do (witness), 79
Saint Domingue, 48
Salah (prayer session), 105
Salvador, 53, 54, 55, 56, 57, 59, 66, 76, 80
   passim; defenses, 64, 67; economic
   classes, 8, 24; outskirts, 56, 63; popu-
   lation growth, 5; *quilombos*, 41; slave
   population, male and female, 7, 8;
   slave rebellions, 41, 67; vicinity, 62

Sande, Colonel Manuel Coelho de Almeida (Municipal Guard), 75

Sanim, Luís (Malê elder), 105, 117, 129, 132, 133, 134, 175, 202, 209, 216, 219

Santa Bárbara, 179

Santa Bárbara Market, 133, 134, 169

Santana (Parish), 193

Santana, Joaquina Rosa de, 177

Santana, Pedro José de (block inspector), 78

Santana, Rosa de (mulatto, ex-slave), 75

Santana do Catu (Parish), 16

Santo Amaro, 4, 38, 39, 50, 77, 83, 116, 129, 130, 133, 135, 192, 209, 212; defenses, 64, 65; rebellion, 49; rebel slaves, 74; town council, 27

Santo Amaro de Ipitanga, 46

Santo Antônio, 176, 193

Santos, Father Francisco Borja (cane grower, slaveowner), 63, 64

São Bento: barracks, 88; Convent, 83

São Félix (rebellion), 32, 33, 34, 35

São Francisco, 50

São Francisco do Conde, 51, 52, 59, 87; 1816 Rebellion, 49

São Joaquim Orphanage, 10–11

São Mateus, 53–54

São Pedro, 31; Parish, 197; revolt, 32

São Pedro Velho, 193

São Tiago (Parish), 68

São Tiago de Iguape (Parish), 234

Sarkin Bori (Malê leader, Hausa possession cult), 48

Sé (Parish), 74, 75, 175, 193

Sedan chairs, 12, 162 passim; porters, 166, 169–72

Seixas (council secretary), 39

Seixas, João Lourenço de Attaide, 27

Sentences, 205, 209; appeals, 209, 212; death, 30, 47, 208, 209, 213–16, 230; deportation, 214, 215; forced labor, 212, 213; role of masters, 216

Sergipe (rebels), 44

Sertão (backland), 44

Shango, 55, 57, 95

Silva, Pompeu da (witness), 79

Silveira, André Pinto da, 74

Silvestre, 66

Skin color differences, 5, 10

Slaveowners, 12, 13, 42, 48; attitudes, 67, 190, 202, 213; investments and returns, 161; livelihood, 12; small-time, 12

Slaves: abuse, 63; attitudes and behavior, 144; banquets, 50; casualties, 91, 92; celebrations, 157; children, 183; families, 142; female, 161; financial strategies, 132, 133, 165; flight, 15, 144; freed, 10; freedmen and, 104; gatherings, 49, 54; hunters, 55; of Englishmen, 88; labor scarcity and, 15; leaders, 57; legal defense, 61, 199; loyal (to masters), 65, 73, 74; male, 162; marital status (defined), 180; names, 215; population, 7; price, 12, 15; punishment, 54; rebellions (independent Bahia), 55; reputation, 67, 149; residence, 181; resistance, 56, 144, 181, 232; suicide, 47; trade, 14, 15, 220; uprisings, 15; urban, 41, 47; urban and rural, 186; wages, 133, 171, 179; weapons, 47, 54, 56, 57, 66, 68, 69, 75, 77, 79, 83, 85, 87, 90, 92; women's roles and occupations, 55, 56, 57, 169

Sobrados, 67

Social class, 9–10, 11; flexibility, 10; hierarchies, 3; lower, 22; mixing, 73; mobility, 10; racism, 10

Sociedade dos Artífices (Craftsmen's Society), 19

Sokoto, 127, 146, 152; caliphate, 94

Soldiers, 8, 30; blacks, 29; in rebellions, 39; living conditions, 28–31; loyalist blacks, 30; rebelliousness, 190

"Song of Songs," 103

Sorcery, 61, 99, 100, 102, 119, 170, 171, 199, 201, 245n.14

Souza, Guilhermina Rosa de (freed slave, loyal to whites), 73, 74, 75, 121, 122, 129, 184

Souza, Sergeant José Joaquim de, 58

Spirits, 102

Straw boss (maioral), 129–30

Streets: Ajuda, 79, 83, 84; Barroquinha, 84; Capitães, 79; Guadalupe, 74; Julião, 164; Ladeira da Palma, 183, 206; Ladeira da Praça, 74, 75, 79, 90, 105, 133, 141, 175, 177, 183, 196; Ladeira de Guadalupe, 83; Ladeira de Santa Teresa, 171; Ladeira do Taboão, 66, 84; Laranjeiras, 179, 180; Mangueira,

104, 164; Oração, 105, 155, 175, 180, 216; Pão de Ló, 79, 132; Piedade, 84, 85, 164; Rua Direita de São Pedro, 179; São Raimundo, 84; Tijolo, 58, 79; Verônicas, 77
Street vendors, 8
Sucupira, Alexandre Ferreira (fictive royalty), 48
Sudanese (West Africans), 148, 151, 154
Sugar: business, 28; cash crop, 15; competition and prices, 14; engenhos, 3; mills, 17; plantation (price), 12; plantations, 14; plantations (Iguape, largest), 49; ruling class, 3
Sugar barons: Itapororocas, 65; Jaguaripe, 65; Rio de Contas, 65
Sule, Nicobé, 134
Sule, Vitório, 74, 78, 92, 130, 135, 184, 185
Supreme Court, 209

Tapas, 147, 148, 180, 182, 208; = Nupes, 139. See also Nupes
Tax reform, 37
Teixeira, João José (witness), 79
Teófilo (slave), 62
Termo de busca e apreensão, 195
Terreiro de Jesus, 83, 84, 105
Terreiros, 143
Tessubá (Malê rosary), 107
Third Battalion, 29
Third Militia Regiment, 226
Titara, Ladislau dos Santos, 105
Torture, 199, 212, 218
Town Council, 25; Cachoeira, 27
Tribunal da Relação, 16, 209
Tribunal de Júri Universal, 137

Umbundos, 148
Unemployment, 18, 19, 20, 31, 37
United States of America, 221
University of Coimbra, 58, 191, 192
Upper Guinea, 149
Urubu (vulture), 55, 56, 57
Uruguay, 64; annexation, 59

Vagabonds, 8, 9
Varella, Dr. Antônio Pinto de Mesquita (master of Licutan), 130

Vasconcelos, President Joaquim José Pinheiro de, 36
Velho, Souza (slaveowner), 74
Vianna, President Francisco Vicente, 25, 30, 65
Vigilantes, 50
Vilhena, Judge Henrique Luis dos Santos, 4, 8, 18, 19, 41, 161, 162
Villas Boas, Lieutenant Gaspar Luís Lopes, 30
Violence, 24
Viscount of Pirajá, 31, 35. See also Albuquerque family; Pirajá
Vitória (neighborhood and Parish), 83, 84, 88, 90, 105, 109, 115, 121, 134, 147, 157, 189, 193, 198, 199, 212, 213, 224; foreigners in, 166, 175; Road, 108, 109

Wages, 18
Wala, patako, 106
War of Independence, 14; slaves in, 53–54
Wealth, 11, 12
West Africa, 93; slavery, 121; warfare, 94
Wetherell, James, 12
White (symbolic color), 124
Wilson, Sir Robert, 3
Wind and magic, 102, 245n.20
Writing, 102, 106; Arabic and Latin, 103, 106; slates and paper, 106, 107

Xixi Fountain, 87

Yansan (African deity), 57
Yorubas, 55, 57, 58, 90, 95, 96, 121, 124, 147, 148, 154, 164, 165; language, 47, 96, 102, 106, 132, 154, 157; = Nagô, 93, 139, 146; names, 155; religion, 125; week, 126; Yoruba-Ijebu slave, 110; Yorubaland, 95, 127, (Nagôland), 171. See also Nagôs
Yunfa, King (of Gobir), 94

Zeferina (rebel slave), 57, 58

Related Titles in the Series

William Roseberry, Lowell Gudmundson, and Mario Samper Kutschbach, eds., *Coffee, Society, and Power in Latin America* (1995)

Peter Wade, *Blackness and Race Mixture: The Dynamics of Racial Identity in Colombia* (1993)

Neville A. T. Hall, *Slave Society in the Danish West Indies: St. Thomas, St. John, and St. Croix,* edited by B. W. Higman (1992)

Philip Poulin Boucher, *Cannibal Encounters: Europeans and Island Caribs, 1492–1763* (1992)

Thomas C. Holt, *The Problem of Freedom: Race, Labor, and Politics in Jamaica and Britain, 1832–1938* (1992)

Dale W. Tomich, *Slavery in the Circuit of Sugar: Martinique and the World Economy, 1830–1848* (1990)

Richard Price, *Alabi's World* (1990)

Richard M. Morse, *New World Soundings: Culture and Ideology in the Americas* (1989)

Philippe I. Bourgois, *Ethnicity at Work: Divided Labor on a Central American Banana Plantation* (1989)

Michel-Rolph Trouillot, *Peasants and Capital: Dominica in the World Economy* (1988)

David Barry Gaspar, *Bondmen and Rebels: A Study of Master-Slave Relations in Antigua, with Implications for Colonial British America* (1985)